Soviet Education in the 1980s

Edited by J.J. TOMIAK

CROOM HELM
London & Canberra
ST. MARTIN'S PRESS
New York

©1983 J.J. Tomiak
Croom Helm Ltd, Provident House, Burrell Row,
Beckenham, Kent BR3 1AT
Croom Helm Australia, PO Box 391, Manuka,
ACT 2603, Australia

British Library Cataloguing in Publication Data

Soviet education in the 1980's.
    1. Education--Soviet Union
    I. Tomiak, J.J.
    370'.947   LA832
    ISBN 0-7099-2429-1

Library of Congress Cataloging in Publication Data
Main entry under title:

Soviet education in the 1980's.

    Includes index.
    Contents: Long term trends in Soviet education/
Mervyn Matthews--Linguistic and ethnic minorities in
the USSR/Nigel Grant--Now they are six/John
Dunstan--[etc.]
    1. Education--Soviet Union--Congresses.
I. Tomiak, J.J.
LA832.S735 1983   370'.947   83-13845
ISBN 0-312-74777-2 (St. Martin's Press)

Printed and bound in Great Britain

CONTENTS

TABLES AND FIGURES

Tables

TABLES AND FIGURES

INTRODUCTION

Janusz Tomiak

The Soviet system of education is, in its entirety,
one of the most crucial and potent influences shaping
the lives of millions of Soviet citizens and
fundamentally conditioning the whole future of
Soviet society and the Soviet state. Today, some
100 million Soviet people - well over a third of the
entire population of the USSR - attend one form of
educational establishment or another. The real
impact of what is being done there and of how it is
being done, should not be underestimated by anyone.
Centrally directed and controlled, oriented towards
clearly identifiable objectives and goals, the diverse
constituent parts of the Soviet system of education
have to respond to both ideological exhortations
embodied in governmental directives and Party
resolutions as well as social and economic pressures.
The two elements are in practice intertwined and
frequently intimately fused together and result in
administratively and organisationally integrated
measures, designed to reach the particular targets
and objectives. Yet, in their substance, they
constitute two different dimensions which are rooted
in two kinds of Soviet reality: on the one hand,
the constant preoccupation with building the new
communist society and creating the new Soviet man
and, on the other, the mounting pressures arising
out of urbanisation, modernisation, industrialisation
as well as the mechanisation, automation and the
growth of technical sophistication of the process of
production.
     The all-embracing and all-pervading nature of
Soviet education and 'the enlightenment process'
should be seen in its wider ramifications as a
closely integrated network of schools, vocational
and technical training establishments, higher
education institutions, research training facilities,

opportunities for the improvement of professional qualifications, as well as a vast and diversified range of courses, meetings and contacts, designed to foster wider cultural interests or to intensify political commitment - the Party's own educational system involves no less than 23 million people in some form of experience of political education.

The distinctive features of the so-called democratic centralism should not be obscured. In his report to the XXVIth Congress of the CPSU in February 1981 Leonid Brezhnev thought it important to stress the fact that in the five year period between the XXVth and the XXVIth Congress there were eleven meetings of the Central Committee, but 236 regular meetings of the Politbureau. Nothing could give a more correct indication of where the crucial and most consequential decisions are being taken; nothing more is needed to indicate the structure of power relations and the character of the decision taking mechanism in the Soviet Union.

But beyond this lie the hard facts and features of social and economic reality with which the educational system has to interact. To mention just a few of those from Leonid Brezhnev's own speech: the impact upon the economy and upon the population structure of the decline in the number of live births in the USSR in the 1960s (5,341,000 in 1960; 4,253,000 in 1965; 4,088,000 in 1968); the lagging of some sectors of the national economy behind the system as a whole; the natural inclination of the people to move from north to south and from east to west, rather than in the opposite directions, as the needs of economy require; perpetual difficulties with securing an adequate level of production in agriculture; slow progress in tapping the enormous natural wealth in the vast territories of Central and Eastern Siberia; egoism, philistinism and persisting indifference towards the concerns and affairs of the people among some Soviet citizens.

From the longer perspective of time, it is however necessary that at this stage - sixty-five years after the October Revolution and sixty years after the establishments of the Soviet Union - an attempt be made to see where the Soviet educational system as a whole has got itself to, what are its still unresolved problems and what are its prospective lines of further development in the 1980s, and, indeed, for the rest of this century.

Examining this is an interesting, if at the same time a difficult, kind of exercise. No very penetrating comments came from the Soviet educationalists themselves, when they attempted to answer this question in recent times. And yet, it seems, this is the stage which is of crucial significance. This is the stage in which expansion in quantitative terms ceases to be an appropriate criterion for comparative assessment and when change of qualitative character becomes of paramount significance. This is the time when measuring improvement gets divorced from merely counting the numbers of individuals involved in the educational process; the time when the qualitative take-off must take place or else continued stagnation sets in to become a permanent feature of the system. This is the time when one must cease talking about the wonders that are to come and critically examine what precisely has been attained. The system's viability must be ascertained on the basis of the quality of life that has been attained and not on the basis of what may come, for come it may not. And what is, reflects not so much the existing natural potential, but rather the existing features of organisation in the use of the resources available, the way in which human effort and human talent has been successfully mobilised, synchronised and utilised. No amount of rhetoric must be allowed to obscure the picture, or to take the place of the identification of tangible results in terms of positive contributions of the educational system to the quality of life as it is actually lived now, to the socio-cultural and economic and political realities of daily life in the country. As this is highly diversified and complex, it is more appropriate to combine the efforts of several individuals working in the field to examine the different aspects of Soviet education in so far as they have come to affect up to now, and in so far as they are bound to affect in the years ahead the cultural, social, political and economic development of the USSR.

The papers included in this volume are those presented in a series of ten seminar meetings devoted to Soviet education in the 1980s in the University of London School of Slavonic and East European Studies in the autumn term of the academic year 1981/2. The meetings took place largely thanks to the support which came from the Ford Foundation and the British Universities' Association of Slavists in the shape of a grant which made the running of the seminar possible.

The contributors to this volume have come from a variety of backgrounds. They look at the different aspects of Soviet education of their own

choice according to the evidence they have found
available and - as they work in an open society -
they interpret what they have found according to
how they conceive educational advancement and social
and economic change.   There is enough room in this
for a variety of outlooks, interests and approaches,
even though one must accept that ten papers cannot
possibly exhaust the comments on this subject.
What unites the contributors, however, is a genuine
respect for ordinary people - millions of men,
women and especially children and young people -
who live, learn and study in the vast area
stretching between the Baltic and the Black Seas in
the west and the Sea of Okhotsk and the Bering
Straits in the east, and between the mountain ranges
extending from the Caspian Sea to the Sea of Japan
in the south and the frozen shores of the Arctic
Ocean, in the north.

Chapter 1

LONG TERM TRENDS IN SOVIET EDUCATION

Mervyn Matthews

The Soviet educational system is at present one of
the largest in the world. According to Soviet data,
it is providing instruction in a variety of schools
and colleges for some 50 million people. Nearly as
many more are said to be improving their still levels
on the job. Clearly, the long term development of
this colossus is of very considerable interest.
     In the papers which follow a number of specialist
observers discuss, in some detail, different parts of
the edifice, and the educational problems which each
of them poses in the eighties. Here I shall limit
myself to a review of some of the more salient trends
over the period since the death of Stalin in March,
1953. Those I have chosen are: the pattern of
coverage and educational opportunity; the ideological
content of what is taught; the vocational character
of Soviet education; and the joint matters of
standardisation and free choice.1

Coverage and Educational Opportunity

A ten-year general education for all children - that
is a leaving age of 17 plus - was set as a central
aim of government policy in the third 5-year plan
(1938-42). This plan was, of course, disrupted by
the Second World War, but by the late forties enrolments in full-time general school as a whole stood at
something over a half of all young people in the
relevant age groups. Stalin, Khrushchev and Brezhnev
all pursued policies aimed at increasing coverage
which was naturally done from the lower classes upwards. The process was simplified by the massive
fall in births registered during the war. This
'dent', as I like to call it, began to affect the
lowest general school age-groups about 1949, and is
clearly shown in Figure 1.

1

Primary education for all children aged 7-11 seems to have been re-established fairly soon after the war. Achievement of the incomplete secondary education was somewhat complicated by its extension, after 1958, to cover the 12-15, rather than 12-14 year olds. Something approaching full coverage here (in other words, a school-leaving age of 15) arrived in the mid-1970s. This was fair progress, but represented a level which the USA had reached about two decades earlier.

The provision of schooling for young people aged fifteen and over, presented more complex problems (we use the term 'schooling' to exclude, for the moment, the VUZ, that is the higher education sector) because at this point arrangements must be made for vocational specialisation. The curriculum of the senior classes of the general school, developed during the thirties, was highly standardised and not suitable for all young people. Furthermore, some provision had to be made for those who had to leave early for family reasons. These classes were therefore supplemented by three other channels: a) vocational schools, some of which did not have a 'general' element in their curriculum, b) secondary specialised educational institutions which did, and c) general education schools operating on a part-time basis for persons in full-time employment. What in quantitative terms happened to each of these sectors?

As for the senior classes of the general school, Khrushchev, as we know, seriously considered lessening their coverage, and he did his utmost to get some diminution written into the reform law of December, 1958. The administrative and social pressures against it were, however, too great, and the 8-10th classes continued to be considered as the principal, and most desirable channel for secondary education. It seems that by the late seventies throughout the country perhaps sixty per cent of the 15-17 plus age group were acquiring a full general education by this means.

The number of pupils in the senior classes in fact reached a peak (6.3 million) in 1976-7, but since then has fallen back. Given the impressive expansion of the general school which preceded it, this trend is rather strange. I would suggest two possible explanations. First, it was probably encouraged by the expansion of the other educational channels open to the relevant age groups, to be discussed below. Secondly, the population estimates available show that the number of 16 year olds (to take a single year) falls from a peak of 5.3 million

in 1977 to a trough of about 4 million in 1986.
The most 'dented' age group is now about 12 years
old. As this works its way up it will cause the
numbers in subsequent classes to fall, and this will
facilitate the solution of coverage problems. The
eighties in this sense will be a propitious period
for general education, though falling numbers bring,
of course, problems of their own.
In any case the general school as a whole seems
to have reached a point of maximum expansion,
numerically. To judge from present policies, its
further development will involve:

    a) Induction of children at six, instead of
seven, bringing the Soviet school more into line
with practice abroad.
    b) Consequent rearrangement of the teaching
material.
    c) The expansion of 'lengthened school day'
arrangements, to assist working parents (in 1976
over seven million children were covered by them).
    d) Enlargement of school units, and improvement
of facilites, particularly in rural areas.
    e) More aid for poor children.

It is noteworthy that the drive to get all children
of school age into the classrooms has been backed by
improvements in school assistance funds, the
provision of free textbooks, free travel and (more
recently) family allowances. But the government has
generally been slow to promote such measures, and
their furtherance depends much on economic factors.
So much for the general school. The <u>vocational
schools</u>, which did not originally offer a school-
leaving certificate, have a rather uneven history of
development. Vocational training in itself has been
the focus of a long-standing debate triggered by its
relationship to the general school on the one hand,
and to productive work on the other. Stalin, it
will be remembered, solved the first problem simply
by separation: he virtually excluded such training
from the general school curriculum and set up, in
1940, an entirely distinct vocational system called
the State Labour Reserves. The SLR offered very
short manual courses and were closely linked to
productive enterprises. Stalin anticipated that
they would eventually become the main form of
vocational training. In fact the SLR schools never
flourished, and the great majority of new workers
continued to get their instruction, such as it was,
directly on the job. (The relative neglect of

3

production training by historians of Soviet education
is an irony which I hope will one day be corrected.)
     Anyway, a revival of formal vocational schooling
was very much part and parcel of Khrushchev's 1958
reform: and thereafter the vocational schools,
(renamed PTU's) went from strength to strength
(Figure 2).
     Graduations rose from about a third of a million
in 1953 to 2.3 million in 1979.   But here again a
plateau seems to be in sight, because the average
output for each of the five years 1981-5 has been set
at only 2.6 million.   The lack of flow data once
more makes it difficult to estimate what proportion
of new labour this was, but the cohort of 17-year
olds in 1980 was around 5 million.
     No less noteworthy a development is the grafting
of a general education component on to the PTU
curriculum.   Experiments of this kind had been made
with the SLR in the early fifties;   after 1959,
however, the movement proceeded apace, and in 1979
half a million PTU leavers completed their courses
with a certificate of general education.   The
figure is to be raised to about 1.3 million by 1985.[2]
Graduations from the full-time general school in 1979
were, by way of comparison 2.8 million.
     The further implicasion of this trend are of
particular interest, social as well as educational.
The PTU vary in the length of their courses;   their
'fit' with the general school;   and their attractiveness to the public.   It is possible that the
expanding 'general PTU' sector will replace the more
polytechnised variants of the general school proper.
The better technical provision of the PTU, and their
closer association with productive enterprises give
them obvious vocational advantages.   They will
probably appeal to less privileged children.   Moreover, if the PTU contingents are <u>fixed</u> and <u>large</u>,
while the cohorts of young people are falling, then
there will be even fewer of the latter going into
the senior classes of the general school.   This
again will enhance the selectivity of these classes,
and help them reacquire their earlier role as a
haven of the more favoured, or able, children.
     The <u>secondary specialised educational
institutions</u> were fairly close to Khrushchev's
educational ideals.   They all offered a middle-grade
specialist skill, and were organised so as to take
either 8 or 10-year school-leavers, the former being
provided with a full general education in addition
to the specialisation.   In institutional terms the
SSEI changed little, but the contingents of pupils

grew very quickly during Khrushchev's years of
office (Figure 3). After 1965, however, this growth
was restricted, and the ninth five-year plan (1971-5)
targets required no further expansion. The 1980
intake, on a full and part-time basis, was about
1.5 million, of whom nearly a million had a school-
leaving certificate already.

The part-time general school was expanded to
serve about 5 million pupils under Khrushchev, and
has been maintained at about that level since
(Figure 1). It has, however, changed its clientele
very considerably. Originally it was for older
people who had missed schooling in the past. But by
the seventies the great majority of pupils were in
the last three, rather than in the lower, classes,
and drawn from young people in their early twenties.
The old correspondence courses were largely phased
out, and after the December (1958) reform the
institutions were renamed Evening (Shift) Schools.
To judge from official pronouncements, this channel
is not only to be retained, but developed. This
means, to look at the problem from another angle,
that the authorities regard the implementation of
full-time general education for everybody, either in
the general school, or in PTUs, as impracticable;
that considerable numbers will continue to leave the
general school after 8 classes; and that on-the-job
training will continue to be important for the
economy.

Speaking at the 18th Congress of the Komsomol
in April, 1978, M. A. Prokof'ev, Minister of
Education for the USSR, declared that 96 per cent of
all young people were getting a general education by
one means or another. Therefore in its present,
mature form, the educational system for under 18's
must cater for a very differentiated demand, and a
complex society. There is nothing surprising in
that; but it does place a question mark over the
official concept of increasing social homogeneity.
By and large, the senior classes of the full-time
general school, in any given locality, offer better
educational service and potential prospects than the
'general' PTUs or specialised secondary educational
institutions; all these types give a better deal
than on-the-job training. Of course, within each
system there are hierarchies of quality and
desirability. The degree to which this differentiation may be compared with that of bourgeois
educational systems is a matter of considerable
interest.

Whereas it is usual to talk of the 'coverage' of

5

general schools, or others like them, higher
education is best discussed in terms of 'access',
since such education, by definition, can be
usefully offered only to the more intellectually
able members of society.   What pattern have we here?
The provision of higher education, both in its full
and part-time variants, had been improving steadily
through the late forties and early fifties.   When
Khrushchev came to power total VUZ enrolments were
about one and a half million.   The years 1954-7 saw
a significant fall-back in intakes (the best measure
of government policy) to 438,000;   when this was
overcome, they were allowed to expand until about
1966, when they stood at 897,000.   At this point
another change of policy took place, and intakes fell
again by 1 per cent or so in 1967 and 1968.   This
was followed by much more cautious growth, averaging
1.5 per cent a year through the seventies.   Nearly
all of this was, in fact, in the evening and
correspondence sector.   These variations are
reflected, albeit indirectly, in the graph for total
enrolments (Figure 4).

The first question which arises is where this
expansion leaves the Soviet Union in terms of higher
educational opportunity.   If we compare the full and
part-time intakes of successive years with the
available estimates of the 18-year age groups (this
being a reasonable one to take for the purpose), we
find firstly that in 1980 the equivalent of about one
person in eight went into a full-time VUZ, while a
fifth gained full or part-time entry.[3]   Secondly,
the level of higher educational opportunity has
remained incredibly static since the cut-back of
the mid-sixties.   In fact, if we generalise on the
basis of the most likely annual cohorts, such
opportunity has tended to fall.

Behind this trend, obviously, must lie careful
calculation.   I do not think this is necessarily a
question of the proportion of young people who, in
the opinion of the planners, could benefit from
higher education.   Financial considerations, and
the perceived need for specialists, are probably
preponderant.   Higher education is not only
expensive, but much more sensitive to the cost of
technological advance than less advanced types of
schooling, particularly as the Soviet SSEI and VUZ
systems are so technically orientated.   In this
five-year period, clearly, the government does not
desire, or cannot afford, further expansion.

LONG TERM TRENDS IN SOVIET EDUCATION

The Ideological Slant

This topic is familiar to most students of Soviet
education, so the background needs little
elaboration. Here I wish to comment only on the
most palpable changes to be observed during the
period under review. A more detailed consideration
would occupy far too much space.

All Soviet educational theory, and indeed,
practice, is said to be based on Marxist-Leninist
premises. If I dare reduce the creed to a few
sentences, it involves a materialistic explanation
of reality and historical change; a 'class' analysis
of any given society, with, in the pre-socialist
stages, inevitable exploitation and polarisation; a
revolutionary outcome, leading to a new, egalitarian,
utopia. Lenin tried to apply this theory to Russia,
though the fit was exceptionally poor. The
Bolsheviks were particularly concerned to use certain
Marxist ideas to secure and justify their own power;
to maintain negative and hostile attitudes towards
capitalism, both in Russia and abroad; to emphasise,
in true Slavophile tradition, Russia's unique mission
of leadership; and to promise an ideal society in
the future, one based on the true exploitation-free
cohesion of all the Soviet peoples. In sociological
terms, official theory may be categorised as an
amalgam of crude Marxism with an exceptionally bland
functionalism.

Ideology comes into the general school
curriculum mainly through the medium of the so-called
social studies (obshchestvovedenie), history
anthologies, literary texts and economic geography.
Various ministerial instructions, however, leave no
doubt that all subjects should whenever possible be
related to ideological precepts.[4] At higher levels
the teaching takes more specific forms, and I will
come to these in a moment.

We can state in general terms that the core of
Marxist-Leninist theory has retained a granite-like
solidity since the Revolution. This is not
surprising when one thinks how unchanging Russian
attitudes have been since the time of Ivan the
Terrible. The teaching materials, of course,
reflect this rigidity. A perusal of the social
studies course for 1978-9, for example, reveals no
real departure from any long-standing tenets.
Moreover, neither of the two kinds of change which I
have been able to discern are particularly striking.
Firstly, important new pronouncements and state
legislation are systematically included in what is
taught. Good examples are the 1977 Constitution,

selected elements of the last CPSU Programme, current
five-year plan indicators, and certain decisions of
the post-Khrushchev CPSU Congresses. Elaborate
arrangements have been made for parts of Leonid
Brezhnev's award-winning literary trilogy, Malaya
Zemlya, Vozrozhdenie and Tselina, to be read in
classes.5

Secondly, lesser shifts in the interpretation
of Soviet social and political development, economic
and foreign policy, etc., may be discerned. The
USSR, for example, has now ceased to be a dictator-
ship of the proletariat, and is becoming a state of
the 'whole people', led by the CPSU; Soviet youth
is being urged more strongly 'to protect the
conquests of socialism'; inward-looking nationalism
seems to have increased; and children are exhorted
to 'struggle against the influence of outside customs
and traditions.'6

Apart from such expected changes of content,
there seems, in comparison to the Khrushchev years,
to be a greater emphasis on the ideological component
in education, rather akin to that observable under
Stalin. At the general school level, it is true,
the number of hours devoted to the arts has fallen
since the mid-fifties. But the social studies
course has been maintained (since 1959) at 70 hours;
a thirty-three hour course of Soviet law has gone
into the curriculum of the eighth class; there
are arrangements for the new 'optional' hours to be
used for a course on Leninism. In addition there
have been clear efforts to increase Komsomol
activities. The pupil and student membership of
this remarkable organisation rose from about 11-16
million between 1966 and 1978. Such rough
calculation as I have been able to make shows a rise
in the participation rate of from about 45 to 57 per
cent.

Intensificiation is very evident at the VUZ
level, too. Obligatory courses in ideological
subjects have long taken up, in most cases, 8-12 per
cent of the teaching time, depending on subject, and
formed part of the final, state examinations. In
1956 three separate subjects, Dialectical and
Historial Materialism, Political Economy and the
History of the CPSU were stipulated for all
institutes and universities (formerly the institutes
had only two).7 1963 saw the appearance of a new
course called 'Scientific Communism', designed, as
far as I understand it, to coordinate and summarise
the materials given in the other ideological classes.
A decree of June 1974 redistributed the teaching of

the ideological subjects over all years of the VUZ
course, whereas it had previously been restricted to
the first three.   At the same time Scientific
Communism was made examinable in the final year.
Here, too, there is evidence of increased back-up
activity by the Komsomol, with the establishment of
courses on public speaking, political agitation, and
of political essay competitions.
     Two other points may be mentioned in this
context.   Atheism has always, of course, been part
and parcel of the Marxist-Leninist package.   In
1964 'Scientific Atheism' was introduced as a new
course at the VUZ level, in some cases optional, in
others obligatory, and this has, I believe, been
retained up to the present.   Soviet patriotism
receives separate expression in the form of
obligatory military training.   Up until 1962, at
the general school, boys had one or two hours of such
training a week, from the eighth class onwards,
together with 17 days' camp in the summer holidays of
the ninth year.   In February of that year such
training was abolished.   But the break with Russia's
martial past was evidently unacceptable to the
Brezhnev leadership, and in 1968 military training
was re-established as part of the school curriculum.
It also finds a place in the vocational and
secondary specialised schools.   In the VUZy
military training for all full-time male, and some
female students, has been maintained throughout.
Information is not easy to come by, but time inputs
seem to run at 4-6 hours a week on the senior
courses, with two military camps in the vacations.
There is a final state exam in military matters,
and graduates are commissioned as officers.   The
cost of such training - as indeed of all ideology
teaching - must be considerable.
     The indications we have are that ideological
topics are popularly regarded as boring and super-
fluous.   Their overall effectiveness must be a
matter of conjecture.   The benefits which the
authorities derive may be great, in that crude though
it is, Soviet Marxism-Leninism satisfies many less
critical souls;   provides a kind of justification for
Soviet policies;   and fills what could only otherwise
be an information vacuum, given the enthusiastic
activities of the state censorship.   Yet the barrage
of Marxism-Leninism by no means excludes critical
discussion outside the classroom.   Recent Western
estimates of Soviet radio audiences suggest that
despite jamming, upwards of nine million adults   8
regularly listen to the BBC (among other stations).

This figure is by no means firm, but anything of that order indicates widespread distrust of the Soviet media. The ideological teaching may, on the other hand, inculcate an unorthodox, yet Marxist interpretation of any facts subsequently acquired, or excite curiosity unwelcome to officialdom.

Vocationalism

The Soviet educational system has always been profoundly vocational in its orientation. The concept of schooling as something intended merely to broaden the mind, or satisfy the individual's personal needs, is deeply foreign to Soviet practice. The problems of adapting school to the economic requirements of society appeared immediately after the Revolution. The Soviet school, it will be remembered, was then 'polytechnised', which meant that a) the relevance of school subjects to workaday activities was stressed, b) pupils were taught about production processes, c) instruction was made as practical as possible and d) the pupils were involved in physical labour. Such experimentation more or less came to an end with the onset of enforced industrialisation, in the early thirties; the senior school, which was naturally most affected, then assumed less practical, VUZ-orientated characteristics, and it still had them when Khrushchev came to power. By the early fifties these classes were regarded purely as a path to a VUZ, and the practical element in their curriculum comprised, according to my calculation, only about 8 per cent. The majority of children were still leaving the general school after seven classes anyway. In terms of labour supply this arrangement was quite satisfactory: but socially it was inequitable, since failure to obtain a general school certificate precluded pupils from admission to higher education establishments. The growth in the coverage of the senior school meant that its role could no longer be limited to that of a supplier of VUZ entrants. Moreover, the widespread training of young workers and peasants 'on production', was becoming less tolerable.

Khrushchev was anxious to ease the discrepancy and encourage more equality of opportunity. His response was reflected in a great deal of legislation, but most forthrightly in the oft-commented reform law of December, 1958. This involved four major changes, which may be categorised as follows:

In the general school sector:
1) The reintroduction of a massive polytechnical component into the curriculum, with practical orientation of subject matter, the teaching of manual skills, involvement of pupils in the production processes and manual jobs, and the creation of direct school-enterprise links. To accommodate the extra activities Khrushchev planned to lengthen the full general school course by a year, increasing it from about ten to thirteen thousand hours, and adding work activities in the school holidays. The weight of the practical cycle was to rise to about 28 per cent.
2) Most children would, he hoped, leave school at 15, after the 8th class, thereby limiting the cost of the operation. There would be improved provision for general school-leavers who worked full-time, so that they could complete their course on a part-time basis.

In the other sectors:
3) The old State Labour Reserve Schools were to be refurbished and upgraded, with the long-term object of having them replace on-the-job training. The secondary specialised institutions were left more or less unaltered.
4) Most kinds of VUZ courses were to be revamped to include part-time or 'sandwich' arrangements.[9]

The official pressures for polytechnisation reached a peak around 1959, and then, in most cases, began to recede. On the whole, the drive failed, the most likely explanations being opposition by educationalists, enterprise managers and parents; lack of interest among school-children; inadequate financing and equipping; and the numerous administrative impracticabilities. Khrushchev had, in a word, attempted to marry the whole educational system with productive enterprises in far too direct and thoughtless a manner. As far as the general school was concerned, the proposed 11-year curricula were never properly implemented, and were abandoned in 1966. After the initial drive, to quote Soviet observers, 'teaching workshops were closed down in the majority of schools'.[10] It was common, even where manual skills were taught, for only 10 or 15 per cent of the recipients to use them when they started work.
November, 1966 saw the publication of a new, 'Brezhnev' law on the general school which, though carefully upholding the principle of vocationalism,

11

gave it much less prominence. The new school
curricula which were then brought out reduced the
practical component to about 17 per cent of class
hours. A few years of relative quiescence followed.
The general school, however, was now so broad
in its coverage that its potential as a supplier of
manual skills could not be ignored. In the early
seventies there were signs of a new emphasis on
polytechnisation, albeit of a more subtle character.
True, the time allotted to practical classes,
excursions and production practice remained unchanged,
but arrangements were made to send pupils to a
relatively new kind of institution 'production
training centres', or 'combines', which were supposed
to be properly equipped and staffed. By 1981 the
number of these had grown to 2,000, and there were
plans for them to accept, for example, up to 85 per
cent of senior urban pupils in the RSFSR.[11] At the
same time particular efforts were made to train
young peasants in mechanising procedures. The
trend was reinforced by the December 1977 decree on
the general school, which strongly emphasised the
need for the 'link with life', and envisaged the use
of the new optional classes for such instruction.
According to a new set of tables in the 1979 Narodnoe
khozyaistvo statistical yearbook (the publication of
such tables in itself being rather novel) by 1979-80
no less than 88 per cent of the full-time general
schools had arranged 'deepened labour instruction'
for their pupils, and no less than 4.6 million pupils
(or some 80 per cent of those in the ninth, tenth and
eleventh classes) were involved in it. We may
therefore be witnessing something approaching a
solution to the problem of vocationalism in the
general school sector.
It is apposite to mention two other developments
at this point. The first is the growth, particularly
after 1966, of a system of planned youth employment.
Labour planning is, of course, a cherished Soviet
principle, and has long antecedents in Russia. This
particular variant has involved 'Youth Employment
Commissions', attached to local soviets, which
operate on the basis of 'youth quotas' in enterprise
labour plans. The second development was the
establishment, on a countrywide scale, of vocational
guidance or counselling. Immense efforts have been
put into persuading young people in each and every
school to fill vacancies in the locality where they
live. The operation has generated a flood of
counselling literature.
The absence of data on vacancies, hirings, and

unemployment makes it difficult to estimate how well
all these measures - polytechnisation, placement and
counselling - have worked.   In the RSFSR, for
example, in 1981 it was said that over half of the
urban 10-year school leavers took skill qualification
tests, of whom 61 per cent (i.e. about a third of the
total number of leavers) 'stayed to work in production,
or entered special educational institutions in
accordance with their speciality'.[12]   These are two
very diverse paths, so the statement leaves us
absolutely in the dark about how many youngsters
willingly took jobs in the skills they had learnt at
school.   The most important determining factor is
what young people want to do.   A series of social
surveys conducted between the mid-sixties and early
seventies (the sociologist Yu. M. Kozyrev, for
instance, listed 25) showed that in all cases about
80-90 per cent of the older school-children wanted
to go on to higher education.   More recent surveys
show a fall in the proportion to about half.   This,
of course, would still leave a great imbalance between
the careers young people want, and the jobs to be
filled.[13]
     The authorities' most successful effort in
vocational training in recent years has undoubtedly
been in the PTU sector.   The history of the State
Labour Reserves contained many dismal pages;   for
years the system required involuntary recruitment,
contained a large proportion of poor, underprivileged
children, and had the reputation of fostering
delinquency.   The reorganisation following the
December, 1958 decree was intended to popularise the
vocational schools and bring them up to a state
which would eventually allow them to supercede
initial training on the job.   Since 1959 they have,
as we noted, shown a remarkably steady rate of growth,
and achieved an output of 2.3 million young people in
1979.   The growth and transformation of the PTU
network means a better deal for some of the less
privileged children in society, since they can aspire
to a general education while they are trained
manually.   Beyond this we must not, however, forget
that masses of young people still get their training
on the job.   The official figure for the acquisition
of new skills in state enterprise and collective
farms in 1979 was no less than 6.3 million, the
number of new entrants to the labour force being
contained within it.   The secrecy surrounding this
particular issue is of many decades' standing, and
may well conceal negative social connotations.
     The difficulties encountered in polytechnisation

of the general school in the early sixties prompted
the authorities to look again at the matter of
on-the-lob training. In May, 1963 detailed new
training statutes were issued, the first comprehensive
set, it appears, since 1922.[14] Subsequently the
problem continued to receive greater attention, at
least in productive enterprises, and efforts were
made to improve conditions for learners, and better
the payment of the workers who had to teach them.

Higher education in the USSR is exclusively
vocational, so there are fewer fluctuations to
report. Khrushchev attempted to bring the VUZy
'closer to life', by introducing sandwich courses,
as already mentioned, by admitting more students of
non-white collar background, and by increasing the
role of the part-time sector. He also wished to
erase the distinction between students' production
'practice' and 'work'. These policies were
expressed in many decrees, apart from the reform law
of December, 1958.

The VUZy, however, proved very resilient to
change. After the failure of the reform, the
multiple provisions for sandwich courses were quietly
dropped; the proportion of students of worker and
peasant origin which had, indeed, risen somewhat,
fell back; and the size of the part-time contingents
was significantly reduced. The Brezhnev leadership
did, however, renew efforts to improve the selection
chances of workers and peasants (albeit in the less
attractive VUZy); and to judge from some data
available, the policy enjoyed some success. Under
popular pressures part-time facilities were increased
from the mid-1970s. Something was done to raise the
effectiveness of the students' production practice,
which under Khrushchev had all too frequently
degenerated into unstructured manual labour.

To conclude, the vocational character of Soviet
education has in general become more marked over the
last three decades, as the system has expanded. But
vocationalism has been promoted with greater
sensitivity, more administrative expertise and
material back-up, than hitherto. This beneficial
development may be attributed to thoughtfulness on
the part of educational planners, and to an easement
of the pressures for rapid growth which dominated the
educational scene earlier.

Standardisation and Free Choice
Some degree of standardisation is a hallmark of most,
if not all, 'advanced' education systems, but Soviet
education is rather unique in the extent to which this

14

is taken. All administrative staffing and school procedures are set out in ministerial regulations, and are strikingly uniform throughout the land. Virtually all named courses offered at any institution require ministerial approval and their actual content is determined in detail through centrally approved textbooks, subject to one of the strictest systems of censorship in the modern world. Examinations are to a large extent textually uniform. The fact that there is no recognised independent sector (apart from a few religious institutions and some private coaching) scarcely needs mention. Beyond this standardisation there lies a marked reluctance to allow pupils or students much freedom of choice at points where choice is normal in more liberal systems. I would now like to look at efforts which have been made to reduce rigidity in this matter.

The General School. With the partial exception of 'special' and 'national minority' schools, Soviet parents have to send their offspring to the single establishment in whose catchment area they live. There has been no significant relaxation of this usage over the years. The children, when they get to school, study a basic, common curriculum of up to 36 hours, all of which has to be followed in its entirety. Examinations are obligatory in all subjects. A few dozen minor variants are allowed, principally for a) children who normally speak local languages and have to be introduced to Russian gradually b) children in the various kinds of special school (language, sport, artistic, mathematical, etc.) c) young people in part-time schools and d) children with various kinds of mental or physical handicap. Furthermore, the configuration of the curriculum has remained remarkably firm for decades. Of the 20 obligatory subjects listed for teaching in the senior classes of the RSFSR schools in 1978, no less than 17 corresponded to entries in the 1947 version.[15] An analysis of O and CSE examinations in 1973 by the British Schools Council required, may I add, 51 headings to cover all subjects offered, and some of these headings were themselves generalised to cover several (rare) examinations. Under the circumstances, the subject matter in Soviet schools has to be updated by ministerial order, of which there have necessarily been many. Piecemeal innovations were made under Khrushchev, while a comprehensive revision of RSFSR textbooks took place between 1966 and 1976. Within this rather unpromising framework, what kinds of choice is the Soviet school-child offered,

and how have these changed over time? Polytechnisation, and the introduction of manual skills
meant, of course, variations in the practical cycle
as between schools, and sometimes a choice of skill
within them. To facilitate this was, indeed, one
of the objects of the teaching 'combines' introduced
in the seventies. I have seen no coherent
statistics on this kind of diversification (apart
from the break-down of training by branch of
industry given in Narodnoe khozyaistvo). However,
we know that some five thousand individual skills
are officially recognised in the USSR, so there is
scope for variety. Choice of this kind does not,
of course, mean escape from ministerial control,
because all topics have to be authorised, and handbooks have been issued for teaching many of them.

A second change was the introduction, in the
standard RSFSR curriculum of 1966, of optional or
facultative classes designed to help senior pupils
study recognised school subjects in more detail.
The classes were only allotted 638 hours - a mere
6 per cent of the time - but were such a clear
departure from the practice of decades that they
attracted considerable attention. Was this a way,
at last, of easing the leathery rigidity of the core
curriculum? Alas, it seems not. The right to
authorise new courses was soon firmly deposited with
local educational offices; by 1978 the number of
hours available had been reduced to 461; and some
schools were directed to use some of these for manual
and ideological topics currently in vogue, or (in
non-Russian schools) supplementary Russian. Development here, then, has been rather disappointing.

The wave of interest in the so-called 'special'
schools for talented children may be regarded as
another facet of the same problem. In the early
fifties the most common types were the language and
sports schools; but there were also a few
establishments for children gifted in music, ballet
and art. (Of course, many ordinary schools ran
extracurricular classes, particularly for children
interested in music and the arts, mostly, it seems,
on a self-financing basis.) The 'special' sector,
in the early fifties, probably contained a few
hundred establishments. Despite his egalitarian
leanings, Khrushchev was anxious to protect, and
even develop them. He encouraged their growth, and
seems to have insulated them from the more artisan
aspects of polytechnisation. The attitude of the
Brezhnev leadership has also been profoundly
positive. The November, 1966 law allowed certain

schools to offer, in the senior classes, a 'profound'
study of certain sciences, and coordinate their
teaching with that of local VUZy. By the mid-
seventies these schools numbered about 250, out of
a total of 150,000 throughout the country.[16]   In
addition, the network of older schools with extra
classes continued to expand. By 1975, for example,
over a million pupils were doing additional music or
art, and 1.6 million had extra sport. It is
difficult to estimate the availability of the various
kinds of special courses, because many types are not
included in the systematic statistics. I believe
that the expansion of the 'special' sector is a
necessary concession to diversity and even elitism,
so that the system may better develop the nation's
talent. There are intriguing questions to be
answered on its efficiency and its role in social
mobility. I suspect this is the reason for official
reticence about its functioning.

To turn to the matter of the internal
organisation of the general school, many features of
it are determined by the age-capabilities of the
pupils, and the character of the knowledge to be
imparted. A perusal of the various sets of
regulations which came out under Khrushchev and
Brezhnev nevertheless shows a remarkable degree of
conservatism. I have in mind here: the didactic
form of the lesson, involving the predominance of
the teacher; rote-learning; adherence to standard
texts; heavy courses; home-work, rising to five
hours a day in the tenth class; a system of tests
and examinations, which, though subject to some
relaxation in 1956, is still regarded as the key-
stone of the system; and the fact that the general
school is still not able to issue anything less than
a full leaving certificate. Pupils' conduct
continues to be regulated by sets of rules which
have not been greatly modified since the thirties,
and standard uniforms are still obligatory. It is
not, I believe, possible to discern any change in the
work of the Pioneers and Komsomol organisations,
except in terms of strengthening.

As for the role of the school directors and
staff, the pedagogical and parents' committees,
I would argue that no significant shifts have been
reflected in the legislation introduced since the
forties. It may be that subtle changes have taken
place in the running of schools which are not
reflected in documentation or press reports. Perhaps,
in practice, teaching methods have become more progressive, the pupils more active, and the rules less

meticulously observed.   The growth in the number of
pupils, and the switch to larger schools, may have
brought their own changes.   If so, concrete
evidence of them is still lacking.

Higher Education.   The Soviet school leaver has
always, of course, had a relatively open choice of
higher educational establishment.   I say
'relatively', because behind the 'open' principle
one can trace various restrictions - administrative,
political and even social.   The administrative and
political restrictions concern quotas, official and
unofficial, for certain minorities, or for the sexes;
and the need for Party, military or other recommendations to get into special or prestigious institutes.
Unfortunately, it is well-nigh impossible to trace
changes in so ephemeral a sphere.

The individual's choice at this point is
governed ultimately by his ability, for the Soviet
authorities, after some post-revolutionary
hesitations, firmly embraced the bourgeois principle
of selection by academic prowess.   At the same time,
the problem of social influence on VUZ intakes has
remained a matter of intense concern.   In general
terms, the children from white-collared and better-
off families have for the usual reasons always had
better higher educational potential than have those
of worker or peasant background.   Both the
Khrushchev and Brezhnev leaderships made considerable efforts to even things out - but in rather
differing ways.   By and large Khrushchev tried to
improve the chances of workers and peasants entering
most kinds of VUZ (a few 'closed' ones being the
main exceptions).   The Brezhnev leadership has
tried to ease their admission into VUZy which teach
less attractive and prestigious subjects.   On the
whole, therefore, the more privileged children still
tend to predominate in the better VUZy.   Clearly,
egalitarisnism is not something which the
authorities wish to press too far in this particular
sphere.

The range of subjects from which the would-be
applicant may choose has naturally broadened with
the advance of knowledge.   All VUZ materials are
encased in a comprehensive set of specialisations,
numbered and approved by the ministry;   there are
also sub-specialisations which depend on the
specialisation, but may vary from one VUZ to another.
If we compare the 1954 list of 274 full specialisations with the 449 existent a quarter of a century
later, we find that:

a) a few older specialisations (like steam locomotive engineering) no longer appear as full specialisations;

b) most of the new ones are in energy technologies, automation, electronics, applied technology, etc.;

c) some new courses in management, administration and economics have come in;

d) a great number of Asian and African languages (which are of interest to the government for its international strategies) are now taught in their own right;

e) there is no doubt that many new specialisations of a military character have also become available.[17]

At the same time, the expected ideological lacunae remain. Among the most interesting, in my view, is that of sociology, which seemed to impinge on historical materialism, and showed itself capable of raising too many awkward questions about Soviet reality. Despite a huge expansion of the discipline in the mid-sixties, its adherents had not by the late seventies managed to get it recognised as a separate degree.

In the matter of course administration older practices were faithfully maintained. Thus similar specialisations are still standardised as much as possible right across the country. Soviet VUZ students, having chosen their courses, have very little choice during their four or more years of study. The principal ones are the sub-specialisations (which take up only 1 or 2 per cent of the time), extra-curricular electives, and the topic for their final-year dissertations. This pattern has remained unchanged since the thirties. The same could, indeed, be said of VUZ organisation in general.

The Soviet authorities have not found it necessary to introduce any new types of qualification, so there are still only the certificates of complete secondary, and secondary specialised education; the VUZ diploma; and the research degrees of Candidate and Doctor of Sciences. Maybe there was indeed an advantage in avoiding the plethora of 'Masters' degrees and 'Diplomas' which have swamped other systems.

Most Soviet graduates, it will be recalled, do not need to worry about finding a job when they finish their studies; obligatory employment for three years, established as long ago as 1928, releases most of them from the agonies of choice.

Usually such a choice is offered only when things go wrong, and a graduate cannot be placed in an organised manner. No body in authority, it seems, has ever considered it possible to relax (let alone abolish) this system, despite its gross inefficiency and its unpopularity among (for example) Muscovites directed to beauty spots in Siberia. On the contrary, in 1963, Khrushchev made it stricter: under new regulations graduates were to receive their diplomas only after they had been at their appointed post for a year. In November, 1964, the rules were changed again so as to deprive them of this valued document if they deserted. But this rigour could not have been very successful either, because it was abandoned in September, 1966. Under the terms of a recent major law on higher education (that of the 29th June, 1979) the authorities are proposing to increase the lead-time for issuing distribution orders from a few months to one to three years before graduation, and ultimately put it on a five-year basis. So a solution to these long-standing difficulties is again being sought in centralised, longer-term planning. The exclusion of free choice and refusal to allow any play of market forces in the matter of salaries leaves the authorities with no choice but manipulation of the planning and placement procedures.

May I conclude with a few broad generalisations on the themes I have chosen. The attainment of a 'mature' educational system with near-complete coverage up to the secondary level, and few possibilities of numerical expansion, means that the Soviet authorities can now devote more attention to improving quality and internal organisation. The indications of change are not, however, too favourable. The Soviet educational system undoubtedly performs many admirable functions, but it does less than its organisers hoped. Its growth has, for example, been matched by a long-term _fall_, and not rise, in the country's rate of economic growth. A host of serious social problems - caused by the young products of the Soviet school - continues to darken the picture of Soviet reality. Although to some extent accommodating to changing needs, the education system has remained exceptionally centralised and rigid. When change has come, it has generally taken the form of a reversion to earlier Soviet practices. I distinguish no signs of effective cures for the most obvious shortcomings in the near future. But Russia can always surprise us.

NOTES

1. Some of the propositions mentioned here
are discussed more fully in my book Education in the
Soviet Union, Policies and Institutions since Stalin
(Allen and Unwin, London, 1982).
The data for enrolments, etc., used in the text and
figures may be easily located in the relevant numbers
of Narodnoe khozyaistvo SSSR, and Narodnoe obrazovanie,
nauka i kultura v SSSR (Moscow, 1977). I have
endeavoured not to burden the text with all the
specific references for data and legislation which
may be found in Education ... The background
figures for age cohorts have been taken from a set
of estimates made by Dr M. Feshbach under the
auspices of the US Bureau of the Census.
2. Izvestiya, December 2, 1980.
3. The methodological shortcomings of this
comparison are obvious, but it gives, I think, a
fair idea of the situation overall.
4. Narodnoe obrazovanie, no. 6, 1981, p. 105.
5. Ibid, no. 9, 1980, p. 102.
6. Obshchestvovedenie, Programma dlya srednei
obshcheobrazovatel'noi shkoly i srednikh spetsialnykh
uchebnykh zavedenii, Moscow, 1978.
7. The legislation mentioned here and below
may be found in the legal collections Vysshaya shkola,
osnovnye postanovleniya, prikazy i instruktsii (Eds.
L.I. Karpov and V.A. Severtsev) Moscow, 1957; and
Vysshaya shkola, sbornik osnovnykh postanovlenii,
prikazov i instruktsii, (Ed. E.I. Voilenko) 2 vols.,
Moscow, 1978.
8. RFE-RL, Soviet Area Audience and Opinion
Research, Trend Report, AR 9-81.
9. Ob ukreplenii svyazi shkoly s zhiznyu i o
dalneishem razvitii sistemy narodnogo obrazovaniya v
SSSR, (Ed. F.I. Kalinychev) Moscow, 1961, p. 18.
10. Kommunist, no. 14, 1974, p. 37.
11. Narodnoe obrazovanie, no. 6, 1981, p. 6;
no. 8, 1981, p. 109.
12. Ibid, no. 8, 1981, p. 109.
13. See for example, Yu. N. Kozyrev, Vysshee
obrazovanie v zhiznennykh planakh molodezhi, Moscow,
1975; Sotsiologicheskie issledovaniya, no. 2, 1977,
p. 48.
14. Kommentarii k zakonodatelstvu o trude,
(Eds., A.N. Mishutkin, and others) Moscow, 1965,
p. 430.
15. Entries from the ministerial order on the
school curriculum for 1978, and E.N. Medynskii,
Narodnoe obrazovanie v SSSR, Moscow, 1947, p. 76.

16. Fillipov, F.P. Vseobshchee srednee
obrazovanie, Moscow, 1976, p. 59.
17. Vysshaya shkola (1957) p. 55, Byulleten'
Ministerstva vysshego i srednego spetsial'nogo
obrazovaniya, no. 12, 1975, p. 2.

BIBLIOGRAPHY

Byulleten' Ministerstva vysshego i srednego
    spetsial'nogo obrazovaniya, no. 12, 1975
F.P. Filippov, Vseobshchee srednee obrazovanie
    (Moscow, 1976)
Izvestiya, December 2, 1980
Kalinychev, F.I., Ob ukreplenii svyazi shkoly s
    zhiznyu i o dalneishem razvitii sistemy
    narodnogo obrazovaniya v SSSR (Moscow, 1961)
Karpov, L.I. and Severtsev, V.A. (eds.), Vysshaya
    shkola, osnovnye postanovleniya, prikazy i
    instruktsii (Moscow, 1957)
Kommunist, no. 14 (1974)
Kozyrev, Yu. N., Vysshee obrazovanie v zhiznennykh
    planakh molodezhi (Moscow, 1975)
Matthews, M., Education in the Soviet Union, Policies
    and Institutions since Stalin (Allen and Unwin,
    London, 1982)
Medynskii, E.N., Narodnoe obrazovanie v SSSR (Moscow,
    1947)
Mishutkin, A.N. and others, Kommentarii k zakono-
    datelstvu o trude (Moscow, 1965)
Narodnoe khozyaistvo SSSR v 1977 godu, (Moscow, 1978)
Narodnoe khozyaistvo SSSR v 1979 godu, (Moscow, 1980)
Narodnoe obrazovanie, no. 6 (1981)
Narodnoe obrazovanie, nauka i kultura v SSSR
    (Moscow, 1977)
Obshchestvovedenie. Programma dlya srednei
    obshcheobrazovatel'noi shkoly i srednikh
    spetsial'nykh uchebnykh zavedenii, (Moscow,
    1978)
RFE-RL, Soviet Area Audience and Opinion Research,
    Trend Report (1981)
Sotsiologicheskie issledovaniya, no. 2 (1977)
Voilenko, E.I. (ed.), Vysshaya shkola, sbornik
    osnovnykh postanovlenii, prikazov i instruktsii,
    2 vols. (Moscow, 1978)

TOTAL ENROLMENTS – MILLIONS

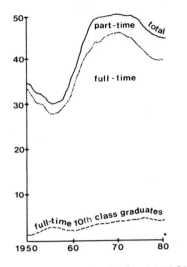

Figure 1 **GENERAL SCHOOL**

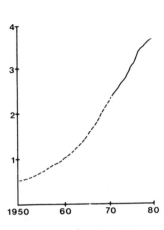

Figure 2 **SLR–PTU**

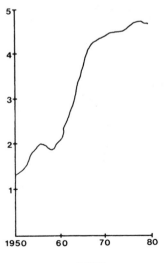

Figure 3 **SSEI**

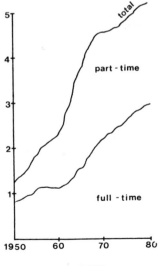

Figure 4 **VUZy**

23

Chapter 2

LINGUISTIC AND ETHNIC MINORITIES IN THE USSR -
EDUCATIONAL POLICIES AND DEVELOPMENTS

Nigel Grant

The Linguistic and Demographic Background
Although the terms 'Russian' and 'Soviet' are
commonly used as though they were synonymous - not
altogether surprisingly in view of the USSR's development from the Russian Empire - the Soviet Union is
legally as well as demographically a multilingual
and multinational state. The latest Census (1979)[1]
lists 103 nationalities, ranging in size from 137
million Russians down to tiny groups, numbered in
hundreds, mostly in the Far North, the Far East and
the Caucasus.[2] Many of the peoples are quite
numerous by any international standards. There are
22 nationalities with over a million members. The
Ukrainians, with over 42 million, come nearly into
the same league as the French; there are roughly
as many Uzbeks (over 12 million) as Czechs; the
Belorussians, with over nine million, compare with
the Swedes and clearly outnumber the Bulgarians and
Greeks; and there are more Kazakhs, Tatars and
Azerbaidzhanis than there are Scots or Danes. The
smaller nationalities, then, may be tiny by
comparison with the Russians, but they are by no
means negligible entities.
    There is also a great variety of language
types, which may be of educational significance. It
is possible that there are few learning difficulties
facing a speaker of Ukrainian or Belorussian in
acquiring competence in Russian - these are all
closely related Slavonic languages, and the Slavs
have a clear majority of the population. On the
other hand, such closeness may make penetration by
the majority language easier. Linguistic distance,
by contrast, may in some circumstances protect a
minority tongue, while adding to the difficulties of
learning the majority one. Either way, a large
minority of the population (and an overwhelming

24

majority of the nationalities) belong to language-
groups whose affinity with Russian is slight or non-
existent. Many do belong to the same Indo-European
family - the Lithuanians and Latvians (Baltic); the
Moldavians (Romance - their language is virtually
identical to the Romanian spoken over the border,
but is written in the Cyrillic script); the Yiddish-
speaking Jews (Teutonic); the Tadzhiks and
Ossetians (Iranian); and the Armenians, whose
language forms a distinct branch of Indo-European.
But this is equally true of practically all the
European languages (except for Finnish, Lappish,
Hungarian, Basque, Turkish and Maltese), which does
not ease the task of the learner beyond the
perception of some structural similarities and some
cognate vocabulary. In any case, most of the other
Soviet peoples belong to quite unrelated language
families, principally Turkic (the Uzbeks, Kazakhs,
Kirgiz and Turkmens of Central Asia and the
Azerbaidzhanis of Transcaucasia), Finno-Ugric
(Estonians, Karelians and many smaller groups),
Buryat-Mongol, Caucasian (Georgian and a few much
smaller groups, such as Lesgin and Avar), and the
small isolated minorities of the Far North and the
Far East. There are even populations of Chinese
and Koreans. For sheer variety, the USSR can
almost rival India as a tower of Babel (see Table 1).
     But linguistic differences pose problems for
education that go beyond philology. There is, for
instance, the question of how far a particular
language is suitable for the needs of formal schooling. All languages evolve to meet the social and
environmental needs of the peoples using them at
any given time, whether they be concerned with food-
gathering and spirit-worship, nomadism and
shamanistic religion, or literacy and the type of
developed society we are pleased to term civilisation.
In the case of Georgian and Armenian, with their
long-standing indigenous and literate cultures,[3] and
to a lesser extent the Baltic peoples and the
Moldavians, there was no great problem; but many of
the others, especially in Central Asia and the Far
North, were faced with difficulties of adaptation.
     This is not to accept the widespread super-
stition that some languages are inherently too
'primitive' to cope with the exigencies of modern
society; generalisations of this kind are usually
based on little more than the prejudices of nineteenth
century colonial administrators, whether Russian,
French or British (who were also most likely to meet
indigenous languages in a Creolised form anyway).

25

But they may, at any particular time, lack the
specific vocabulary, and probably the written form,
to cope with hitherto unfamiliar needs. The lack
of writing is not, in itself, an unsurmountable
obstacle; if necessary, it can be created and
supplied (as indeed the Academy of Sciences of the
USSR has done in many cases,[4] just as the Catholic
and Orthodox missionaries made Europe literate during
the middle ages, or the Arabs spread their script to
Turkish, Persian, Swahili and Malay).[5] Writing is
only the dress of a language, and can be acquired
when needed.

Vocabulary may be another matter. Few
languages develop words they do not need (though
they may retain some), and at the time of the
Revolution many of the nationalities lacked the
verbal equipment to deal with the realities of any
twentieth-century industrial state. Again, there
is nothing new about this; languages can and do
form new lexical material to meet new needs. They
can do this either by building up from native roots
- the method favoured by Arabic, Chinese, German and
to an extent the Slavonic languages - or by borrowing
and adapting from somewhere else. This is a
perfectly normal process; English drew so heavily
on French, Latin and Greek, Romanian on Slavonic,
and Persian and Swahili on Arabic, that they all now
have hybrid vocabularies. In the same way, the
Soviet Turkic and Northern languages have borrowed
extensively from Russian. This can create some
problems; if the cultural levels of the two
language-communities are too far apart, the
borrowing language can be inundated with
unassimilated loan material to the extent of
disrupting communication amongst its speakers.
English came close to this at one time, and had in
turn had similar effects on languages as diverse as
Hindi and Gaelic. But the problem need not be
permanent - English did survive, after all - although
until the borrowed material is assimilated, entry to
formal schooling can induce culture-shock and the
danger of alienation from the rest of the speaker's
group.

Although not strictly linguistic, there are
other problems that are likely to raise complications
- some geographical and economic, some cultural in
the broad sense. It is admitted, for example, that
there are still serious inequalities between the
urban and rural populations of the Soviet Union, not
only in educational achievement but in aspiration as
well.[6] This affects many Russians, of course; but

where minority populations are disproportionately
rural - as in Moldavia, for instance - this can
exacerbate and confuse the whole spectrum of
educational problems. So can religion. Zvi Halevy and Eva Etsioni-
Halevy[7] have examined the levels of scholastic
attainment among certain Soviet nationalities,
classifying them by their traditional religious
background, in order to test Nicholas Hans' hypothesis
that formal educational attainment is connected with
religious affiliation (actual or traditional) in
descending order from Jewish at the top, through
Protestant, Catholic and Orthodox, to Muslim at the
bottom. Their findings generally support Hans' proposition, at any rate until the Central Asian
peoples began to close the gap during the 1970s.
It is possible to object that the original
disparities reflected the levels of social advancement of the various groups, and that they have been
diminishing as living standards have improved, rather
than postulate a connection with religious belief or
background. Nevertheless, the correlations up to
the recent past do raise some questions, though how
far they can be explained by actual religious
adherence is more doubtful. After all, religion,
like language, can serve as the most conspicuous
badge of identity for a group, a convenient short-
hand for a whole cluster of customs and values that
may have little to do with actual doctrine. Northern
Ireland probably offers the most obvious (and
baleful) example of this: 'Catholic' and 'Protestant'
serve as much to label rival factions by summarising
their historical and political identity as to
describe their theological beliefs (which are often
hazy in the extreme). Less divisively, Yugoslav
Bosnians tend to describe themselves as Muslims to
distinguish themselves from the Serbs, whose language
they share.[8] In most Muslim countries, 'traditional'
attitudes towards women are strong, though not all go
as far as Saudi Arabia and forbid women to work
alongside men or drive cars. It has been questioned
how far these practices, along with others like the
veil and infibulation, have any warrant in the Qur'an
at all; but they have become associated with Islam
culturally, and can thus survive even the decline of
belief. Even now, one still hears of cases in
Soviet Central Asia of girls being taken away from
school at the age of thirteen for arranged marriages
(both illegal), of the exaction of bride-price (which
seems to rise in inverse proportion to the girl's
educational qualifications, presumably because

27

ignorance is bliss from the dominant male point of
view).[9]   It can so happen, then, that when the
authorities are dealing with a linguistic minority,
they find themselves coming up against cultural
differences that go much deeper than questions about
the language of instruction in the schools.
     To these background factors we must add current
trends likely to affect educational policy. Governmental action apart, there appears to be a continual
tension between cultural assimilation and self-
assertion, which works differently with different
groups. The legal position of the Ukrainian and
Armenian languages, for example, is nearly identical,[10]
and both are in conspicuous use, at least for official
purposes; yet one rarely hears Ukrainian spoken in
the streets of Kiev, or Russian in Erevan.[11]   About
80 per cent of the schools in the Ukraine as a whole
use Ukrainian as the medium of instruction, and
teach Russian as a second language; but in Kiev
itself the position is almost exactly reversed. In
Armenia, however, only about three per cent of the
schools teach in Russian, though all children study
it;   and the normal language of communication is, at
all levels, Armenian.   (It may be relevant that only
73.6 per cent of the population of the Ukrainian SSR
are Ukrainian by nationality, and 21.1 per cent are
Russians.   In the Armenian SSR, 89.7 per cent are
Armenians, only 2.3 per cent Russians.   Further,
of those describing themselves as Ukrainians, only
82.8 per cent claim Ukrainian as their first
language;   the equivalent figure for Armenians'
attachment to the language of their nationality is
90.7 per cent.)   (See Table 2.)[12]
     The reasons for such differences may be partly
political. Ukrainian nationalists would certainly
argue this, pointing out that the Ukraine is a
large area, geopolitically sensitive, and therefore
subject to Russifying pressures; Armenia, on the
other hand, is too small and peripheral to be of any
danger, particularly in view of the experiences of
Armenian minorities in other countries.   (Some
Russians might even agree with this, pointing to the
map and to the incidence of collaboration with the
Nazis in the Ukraine during the War.)   This could
well be so;   it fits the world of Realpolitik, if
not the Constitution.   There are many parallels
elsewhere, such as the plantation of Ulster with
Scottish and English Protestants by James VI and I,
in order to drive a wedge between his troublesome
Gaelic subjects in Ireland and Scotland.   At least
James was frank about what he was doing;   modern

governments have been less forthcoming. The
political explanation may have some force, then, but
can hardly be the only factor. The Tsars tried
hard enough to Russify Poland, Franco tried to
extirpate Catalan and Basque, and they failed. Even
if we do care to assume ulterior political motives,
therefore, we have to find other mechanisms as well.
    This could be a case where linguistic affinity
plays some part in the process. Ukrainian is close
enough to Russian to be replaced by it under certain
circumstances, by a process akin to standardisation
within a speech-community. Again, there are
parallels, in the Soviet Union and elsewhere.[13] In
Central Asia, what are now the standard forms of
Kazakh, Uzbek, Kirgiz, and Turkmen were developed
from a patchwork of over twenty Turkic dialects. In
Western Europe, there is the case of Norwegian, long
dominated by Danish as a result of close linguistic
affinity and centuries of political control. (One
form of modern Norwegian, Nynorsk, is largely an
artificial creation, developed after independence to
be as unlike Danish as possible.) Similarly, Scots
began to lose its status as a literary and court
language with the publication of the King James
Bible, close enough to be understood yet different
enough to establish an external standard form.
Political unification and cultural penetration
continued the process, reducing Scots to a series of
local dialects (and some literary forms). Indeed,
there are some tempting parallels between Scotland
and the Ukraine in this regard at least. Most
people in Kiev speak Russian with a Ukrainian accent,
while the rural population speaks Ukrainian. Most
people in Edinburgh speak English with a Scottish
accent, while much of the surrounding area speaks
some form of Lowland Scots. The most obvious
difference (apart from the scale) is that Ukrainian
is standardised and used officially and educationally;
none of this applies to Scots.
    The position of Armenian, in practice, is quite
different. It is distinctive, being no closer to
Russian than to Persian or Greek (or English); it
has had its own script and literary culture since
the fifth century AD, much longer than Russian. The
population is small (just over four millions) but
fairly compact,[14] and is thus culturally self-
sustaining. The common expectation that larger
groups will inevitably absorb smaller ones is thus
much too simple. Pressures to assimilate, official
or otherwise, do exist, but so do the reactions that
produce minority self-assertion. Both of these

tendencies are commonplace, and are bound to affect
the USSR as much as any multi-national society.
Most significantly of all, the balance of the
population is changing, since fertility rates differ
strikingly from one group to another. Between 1959
and 1970, the population of the USSR increased by
15.8 per cent. The increase in the Russian
population was lower (13.1 per cent), as was that of
the Belorussians (14.4), Ukrainians (9.4), Lithuanians
(14.6), Latvians (12.1), and Estonians (1.8). The
rate was much higher in the Caucasus (Armenians 27.7,
Georgians 20.5), but the really spectacular increases
were among the Azerbaidzhanis (49.0) and the Central
Asian peoples (Kirgiz 49.8, Kazakhs 46.3, Uzbeks,
Tadzhiks and Turkmens all over 50 per cent). By
the next Census in 1979, there had been a general
slowing down in the rate of growth - 8.4 per cent for
the country as a whole; Russians 6.5, Belorussians
4.5, Ukrainians 3.9, Armenians 16.6, Georgians 10.0,
Azerbaidzhanis 25.0, Kazakhs 23.7, and Uzbeks, Kirgiz,
Tadzhiks and Turkmens all over 30 per cent. (See
Table 2 for details, and Table 2a for percentage
annual growth rates.) Clearly, what emerges from
the morass of figures is not only that the Central
Asian and Caucasian peoples are maintaining a high
increase rate (however expressed), but that the
Russians themselves are well on the way to becoming
an overall minority. In 1959, they were 54.6 per
cent of the total; in 1970 this was down to 53.4,
and by 1979 to 52.4 per cent.
This is not supposed to matter, in theory, in a
multi-national state of 'brother-peoples', but it
would be astonishing if the Russians were not
anxious about the erosion of their own position,
especially when the biggest increases are amongst
the Turkic and Iranian peoples of Central Asia, with
the spectre of Islamic revivalism across the frontier.
Responses are far less easy to guess, though some
will advance this as an argument for Russification
as a security measure (this kind of thing has been
done before, in Lithuania as well as in Northern
Ireland), while others will look to the development
of pluralism (based on bilingualism in Russian) as
a viable alternative. Which view will prevail is
uncertain, but either way political considerations
are bound to affect educational policy, overtly or
otherwise. We shall be returning to this point
later.

The Legal Position - Theory and Practice

Legally, the position of the nationalities is quite
clear: all citizens of the USSR may choose to use
their mother tongue, or any other Soviet language,
for all purposes, including their children's
schooling.[15]   In practice, it is not as simple as
that, nor could it be. There are many small
nationalities in the Far North, the Caucasus and
Central Asia who lack a written language of their
own. Many of these use Russian as their written
language; most of the Northern peoples do, as do
the Aisor in the Caucasus. But other languages may
be used for this purpose. In the Far North, the
Barabas use Tatar, the Bolgans Yakut, and the Kerek
Chukchi; in the Caucasus, many small groups use
Azerbaidzhani, others use Georgian or the related
Avar or Lesghin. Most of the small Central Asian
groups use Tadzhik, a form of which used to serve as
a lingua franca for much of the area, but Turkmen
and Kazakh are preferred by some. Many of these
groups have Russian as a second written language,
but not all. Although the language of choice
usually does mean the mother tongue, therefore, it
is hardly practicable for schooling when it does not
exist in written form. (For details, see Table
3.)[16]
   Russian, however, does enjoy a special position.
It is taught in all the non-Russian schools, and may
be chosen as the language of instruction; this is
particularly common in Kazakhstan and Latvia, and in
the urban Ukraine. How effective this is as a means
towards national cohesion is uncertain. It is the
normal medium of all-Union communication, and has
even been described as the eventual 'second native
language' for the minorities. As yet, however, it
is far from that; according to the 1970 Census,
only among urban Tatars, Belorussians, Moldavians,
Lithuanians, Latvians and Kazakhs did more than 50
per cent among the major nationalities claim fluent
knowledge of Russian as a second language, and even
amongst these the proportion of the rural population
making a similar claim was much lower. By the time
of the 1979 Census, considerable advances had been
made: the total percentages claiming fluency had
risen above the half-way mark for the Belorussians,
Kazakhs, Lithuanians, Latvians, Tatars, Chuvash,
Bashkirs, Mordvins and the peoples of Dagestan, and
very close to it for the Ukrainians, Uzbeks and
Moldavians. Some of the advances, like the Uzbek
jump from 14.5 to 49.3 per cent in nine years are so
great as to strain credulity,[17] but generally it

would seem that considerable efforts have gone into
promoting effective bilingualism. These continue:
in 1980, plans for teacher training envisaged special
attention to the supply and quality of teachers of
Russian in non-Russian schools, and there are constant
efforts to propagandise on behalf of Russian, such as
the 1980 conference in Tashkent on the theme of 'The
Russian language - the link of friendship between
the peoples of the USSR'.[18] This is not the same
thing, however, as linguistic Russification; there
is some of that - at any rate, the proportion of the
major nationalities claiming the language of their
group as their first language declined in virtually
every case between 1970 and 1979, usually in favour
of Russian - but the percentage is extremely small
in most cases; the growth of second-language fluency
in Russian is of quite a different order. (See
Table 4.) Generally, however, it is only amongst
the old and the very young that many can be found
with no Russian at all. Fluency, however defined,
requires a high standard, and is still claimed by
only 23 per cent of the non-Russian population.
(See Table 5.) Moderate competence, however, is
much more widespread.
  But practical constraints go beyond questions
of literacy and knowledge of Russian. Literacy,
as already remarked, can be supplied, and has been
with all the major groups and many of the minor ones
as well. In modern times, written forms were
already available for Ukrainian, Belorussian,
Armenian, Georgian and the languages of the Baltic
Republics, but the Central Asian languages were
another matter. Most of them were not written at
all before the Revolution, though something
approaching the literary forms of Turkish and
Persian were widely used. They used the Arabic
script, but this adapts ill to non-Semitic
languages - especially Turkish, which makes extensive
use of vowel-harmony, rather awkward in a script
consisting essentially of consonants. The
introduction of the Latin instead of the Arabic
alphabet has sometimes been seen as a form of
cultural imperialism,[19] but it is worth remembering
that Kemal Atatürk did exactly the same thing in
Turkey itself, and for the same reasons. Latin
was later replaced by Cyrillic, additional letters
being added when needed - a far less fundamental
step, as the two alphabets (both adaptations of the
Greek) are of essentially the same type. Not all
the gaps have been filled; as we have seen, some
of the smaller nationalities still lack a written

version of their own language, and others, though supplied with one, never took to it. (Written Karelian, for example, never caught on because the closely-related Finnish was already available.)[20] For the major groups, however, the absence of a standard written language (and thus one that could be used for formal schooling) proved only a temporary handicap.

Numbers, however, can impose severe limitations. It is quite feasible to provide the whole range of instruction from pre-school to higher education (and to develop the textbooks and teaching materials) in Uzbek or Ukrainian or Georgian, but not in the languages of the tiny groups in the Far North or Central Asia, some of whom number only a few hundreds. In practice, therefore, the viability of vernacular schooling depends to a large extent on the size of the potential school population. Broadly, the full range of schooling is available in the languages of the Union Republics and Tatar, though generally only in their own areas. Only Russian-medium instruction is ubiquitous, a sore point with many Ukrainians, of whom five million live outside the Ukraine. The extent to which native-language instruction is actually taken up varies. In Kazakhstan, for instance (where only 36 per cent of the population are Kazakhs anyway, and 40.8 per cent are Russians) a high proportion of the Kazakhs have their children taught in Russian. This, however, is quite untypical of Central Asia (see Table 6), where the vernacular is much stronger, especially in Uzbekistan. But at least such provision is possible in these cases. Elsewhere, it is not so easy, and the normal solution is a compromise, depending mainly on numbers. With groups of over 100,000 speakers it is usually possible to offer the first eight years (age 7-15) in the vernacular, while smaller ones (roughly 10,000 to 100,000) may have only the first three years, using Russian or another vernacular thereafter. For the very small groups, Russian or another language may have to be used throughout, though there is provision for special training of teachers to cope with the transition period, using the first language orally until the children have sufficient command of Russian (or whatever) to proceed. (The Northern Department in the Herzen Pedagogic Institute in Leningrad, which trains members of northern minority groups for this purpose, is a case in point.)[21]

It has to be stressed, however, that in so far as a policy of pluralism is being followed, it is strictly linguistic. It may extend to some cultural idioms as well, but not to political matters and emphatically not to social mores when they conflict with the official ones. Young Azerbaidzhanis, Uzbeks and Tadzhiks may be taught in their own languages, but not about such stalwarts of nineteenth-century resistance to Russian imperial expansion as Shamyl or Yakub Beg.[22] Nor is there any allowance (not officially, at any rate) for 'traditional' attitudes towards (for example) the role of women.[23] The object is to develop a culture 'national in form but socialist in content' - Stalin's phrase, though the source is seldom acknowledged nowadays, except perhaps in Georgia. (As one Georgian put it: 'We don't really like Stalin - we just pretend, to annoy the Russians.') The medium of teaching, then, may be a matter for local variation; but the general policy of the system, the content of the curriculum and, most important of all, the values taught, remain substantially uniform throughout the Soviet Union.

Recent Development and Implications for Policy

How, then, do the various groups perform? If we examine the comparative rates of educational attainment, we do find inequalities, but not always the ones we might expect from a simple model of Russian dominance. The Russians do come out relatively well, but they are not at the top of the league-table. If we use the proportions with higher education as a measure (a rough one, admittedly), eight of the major nationalities come above the average for the USSR as a whole. Jews (who count as a nationality in the Soviet Union) have a surprising 39.9 per cent; Georgians, 10.5; Armenians, 7.5; Tatars (in Uzbekistan), 6.8; and Estonians, 6.0 per cent, with the Azerbaidzhanis (5.3), Yakuts (4.6) and Lithuanians and Ukrainians (both 4.5) following after. The Turkic peoples of Central Asia tend to score much lower (Chuvash 2.4, Bashkirs 2.2), but so do the Moldavians (also 2.2). The pattern for proportions with complete secondary education is not identical but it is similar; this time, Jews, Georgians and Armenians still top the list, followed by Uzbeks, Tatars, Russians and Lithuanians. Just below the average come the Latvians, Estonians and Azerbaidzhanis. (See Table 7.)[24]

Nathan Kravetz[25] has suggested that the particularly high performance of Jews could be attributed to well-known cultural traits, and that

of the Georgians to Stalin's special favour. The
first suggestion is convincing enough, the second
less so. It is doubtful that Stalin was, latterly,
particularly conscious of being a Georgian;
certainly, many of his actions suggest that he
thought of himself as a Russian, and the heir of the
Tsars for good measure. In any case, he has been
dead for a long time, and his successors can hardly
have had any special interest in defending his
memory by continuing to show preference to his
compatriots (if that is how he saw them). More
generally, Kravetz seeks to relate the different
levels of performance to two factors: the level of
urbanisation, and the proportion claiming fluency in
Russian as a second language. (He calls the latter
the 'Index of linguistic Russification', which is
rather misleading; to be bilingual is not
necessarily to be assimilated. That term should
be more properly applied to the proportion claiming
Russian as a **first** language, which as we have seen
presents a different and much smaller picture.) But
up to a point the connection holds. Jews in the
USSR are 95 per cent urban, over 75 per cent have
Russian as their **first** language, and are clearly
(though diminishingly) the most successful group.
Russians are highly urbanised (68 per cent),
obviously speak Russian, and come fairly high in
the rank order of achievement. But other high-
scoring groups do not fit so well. Tatars are high
on Russian fluency, but low on urbanisation (55 per
cent). With the Armenians it is the other way
round - high urban proportion (64.8 per cent),
relatively low Russian fluency (38.6 per cent).
Georgians score low on both counts, yet come second
in formal educational attainment. At the other end
of the scale, the Moldavians score high on fluent
Russian (47.4 per cent), but very low on urbanisation.
Among the lower scorers, most of the Central Asian
nationalities, the correlations are similarly
inconclusive. (The Bashkirs and Chuvash have,
along with the Tatars, Mordvins and the peoples of
Dagestan, some of the highest levels of second-
language Russian fluencey in the country - all over
60 per cent, which is higher even than the Belorussians and the Baltic peoples; yet they come far
down the league, despite recent advances.)26
It would seem, then, that the level of
urbanisation is a factor in some cases, but by no
means all; and fluency in Russian is an even less
reliable guide for the most part. At a guess, it
is possible that access to Russian is an advantage

where the indigenous cultures are relatively weak
(as in Kazakhstan, for example), but of little
relevance where they are strong (as in Georgia and
Armenia). But before this possibility is further
explored, we need to know more about the relative
strengths of the minority cultures, and have some
means of quantifying them, at least roughly, instead
of having to rely quite so much on subjective
impression (or subjective report). In the meantime,
we have to accept that there are other factors at
work, whose strength we can only guess.
    One such factor may be government policy. Not
that governments are omnipotent, even in the USSR;
but they can affect the fortunes of nationalities to
some extent - indirectly by the diversion of
resources, directly by (say) a quota system for
admission to higher education. The 1979 Census data
on the educational attainments of the various nationalities should be illuminating. Unfortunately,
satisfactory figures are not yet available at the
time of writing (the 1980 brochure, summarising the
results, is usefully detailed on some matters, and
infuriatingly uninformative on others, for which the
raw data must have been assembled), and we will have
to make do with some older figures and assume the
continuation of certain trends. Kravetz has
usefully compared the 1970 Census figures with
others for 1976-7, still a time of expansion in the
system, and demonstrates that in entry to higher
education, for example, the gaps between the more
and less successful nationalities have been closing,
and their relative positions changing. Most groups
show a net advance, most noticeably among the Central
Asians. If the later figures are expressed as a
proportion of the earlier (i.e. 1976-7/1970), the
Chuvash, Bashkirs, Tartars, Tadzhiks, Kazakhs and
Kirgiz all exceed 120; and the Belorussians,
Lithuanians, Latvians, Uzbeks, Turkmens and the
peoples of Degestan are all above the national
average of 108. The Estonians come just on the
average, the Moldavians, Ukrainians and Russians
just under it, and the Armenians well below with 101.
By contrast, the Georgians show a small net drop and
the Jews a dramatic one (down by nearly 40 per cent).
    Kravetz argues that these developments are
consistent enough to indicate a deliberate policy of
discrimination, positive towards the Central Asians
and negative towards the Georgians and Jews, through
the manipulation of the admission quotas to higher
education. He is in all probability right, though
this does not tell the whole story either. (Some of

the fall in Jewish enrolment is bound to reflect the decline of the Jewish population generally, through the double pressures of assimilation and emigration.) Enrolment in higher education gives, at best, an approximate measure of a group's educational advancement; but it is at this point in the system that control can be most readily exercised. Yet it is easier to contract than expand. The drastic reduction of Jewish (and, to a lesser extent, Georgian) entrants <u>could</u> be achieved by a quota system, and the contrast with their previous situation suggests that this has in fact happened. But it is far less easy to discriminate <u>positively</u> by this means. Simply opening up higher institutions to more Tadzhiks and Kirgiz does little to improve their position, unless the supporting school structure is there to prepare them to take advantage of it; and in any case, it has to be remembered that entry to higher education is only an indicator of educational advancement, not its sum total. As overall improvements can hardly be achieved overnight, the betterment of the position of the Central Asian and other peoples suggests not only that a quota system is in operation, but that there has been a much longer-term policy of positive intervention, including a major diversion of resources. The possibility of Islamic revival in these areas may be one reason behind this - the Soviet government has never hesitated to use education as a social and political tool. As for negative discrimination, most of the attention in the West has so far been focussed on the position of the Jews. This is hardly surprising in the light of their former preeminence in the educational system, the deterioration of their place in Soviet society, their marked numerical decline (against the trend), and of course the allegations of anti-Zionism (acknowledged by the authorities) and anti-Semitism (denied). But this is not an isolated issue; the Jews are considered to be a nationality (though not, in most cases, a linguistic one),[27] and their changing position, whatever else it might betoken, is also part of a wider policy towards nationalities in education - the use of a quota, and the redistribution of resources, to reduce inequalities, not only by favouring the disadvantaged groups but also holding back the hitherto more fortunate.

Accusations of Russification are frequent, and just as frequently denied. But there is one school of thought that talks, somewhat vaguely, of 'convergence', the eventual fusion of the Soviet

peoples into one language community. Isayev,[28] one
of those taking this position, makes much of the fact
that large numbers of members of various nationalities
have left their original areas to live in other parts
of the USSR, though he tactfully omits to mention
that in many cases the move was not by choice.
Mobility does encourage linguistic convergence.
This has been the general experience elsewhere,
usually in the form of eventual assimilation, and
as we have seen from the Census figures there has
been a continuing, if very slight, trend in this
direction among most of the nationalities. He also
mentions, in some detail, influences of Russian on
the minority languages and (to a much lesser extent)
the other way round. But the examples he gives are
mostly of word-borrowing, a normal enough procedure;
languages can and do take on large amounts of
foreign material without affecting their basic
structure in the slightest. Most of the minority
languages in the Soviet Union are quite different
from Russian in basic grammatical structure as well
as vocabulary; it is hard to see how the process
described by Isayev could lead to linguistic
'convergence', unless this does mean eventual
assimilation to Russian. 'Convergence' may seem a
more respectable aim than assimilation, but it
could be a highly dangerous policy, since there is
enough prejudice under the surface to be triggered
off by confusion between the two concepts - and
enough resentment to be brought to the surface as a
reaction, especially with the balance of the
population shifting in favour of the non-Russians
anyway. Nor is it everywhere true that the
Republics are becoming more mixed. True, there are
now very slightly fewer Russians, proportionally,
in the RSFSR itself, and more in the Baltic
Republics, Belorussia, the Ukraine and Moldavia;
but elsewhere, the proportion of Russians, whether
high as in the Central Asian Republics or low as in
the Caucasus, has been declining, and the proportion
of the titular nationality growing. Mixing and
'convergence' are by no means guaranteed in these
areas. Attempts to improve Russian teaching and
encourage bilingualism continue, but assimilation
seems hardly realistic, even if it were desirable.
    Alternatively, linguistic pluralism could be
strengthened and developed (and in principle this
is quite compatible with bilingualism in Russian).
That there are problems is obvious enough, but there
are minorities with long-standing and lively cultures,
and others which have developed since the Revolution.

Without underestimating the difficulties of fostering genuine pluralism, it would seem that the alternative, Russification by stealth or openly, would be a recipe for conflict rather than security. Linguistic pluralism at least, with all its complexities, is a relatively straightforward matter compared with pluralism of content, a possibility which has been less frequently considered, apart from artistic idioms. But it may well arise in the future, for minority cultures do not consist only of languages. This is a question, of course, not for the Soviet Union alone;[29] the problem of reconciling diversity with unity is exercising many states, and is taking on even greater importance with the growth of supranational groupings like the EEC, the Nordic Council, or for that matter Comecon. Finding ways not only of reconciling unity and diversity but having them reinforce each other is bound to be an increasing preoccupation in education and society into the next millennium. The experiences of the USSR - the faults and difficulties as well as the achievements - must be of growing interest to the rest of the world, faced with tasks and challenges which, under the surface, are essentially similar.

Table 1: Major Nationalities of the USSR (over
1 million) by Number (1979), Language Family and
Script

Nationality	No. (millions)	Language Family	Script
Russians	137.4	Slavonic (IE)	Cyrillic
Ukrainians	42.3	Slavonic (IE)	Cyrillic
Uzbeks	12.5	Turkic	Cyrillic
Belorussians	9.5	Slavonic (IE)	Cyrillic
Kazakhs	6.6	Turkic	Cyrillic
Tatars	6.3	Turkic	Cyrillic
Azerbaidzhanis	5.5	Turkic	Cyrillic
Armenians	4.2	Armenian (IE)	Armenian
Georgians	3.6	Caucasian	Georgian
Moldavians	3.0	Romance (IE)	Cyrillic
Tadzhiks	2.9	Iranian (IE)	Cyrillic
Lithuanians	2.9	Baltic (IE)	Latin
Germans	1.9	Teutonic (IE)	Latin
Kirgiz	1.9	Turkic	Cyrillic
Jews	1.8	Teutonic (IE)	Hebrew*
Chuvash	1.8	Turkic	Cyrillic
Latvians	1.4	Baltic	Latin
Bashkirs	1.4	Turkic	Cyrillic
Mordvins	1.2	Finno-Ugric	Cyrillic
Poles	1.1	Slavonic (IE)	Latin
Estonians	1.0	Finno-Ugric	Latin

Note: *This applies to Yiddish; the great majority
of Soviet Jews, however, are Russian-speaking and
have no Yiddish.
(IE = Indo-European)

LINGUISTIC AND ETHNIC MINORITIES IN THE USSR

Table 2: Nationalities over 1 million - Numbers and
Percentage Increase, 1970 and 1979

	No. in thousands		% increase since previous Census	
	1970	1979	1970	1979
Total USSR of whom:	241,720	262,085	15.8	8.5
Russians	129,015	137,397	13.1	6.5
Ukrainians	40,753	42,347	9.4	3.9
Uzbeks	9,195	12,456	52.9	35.5
Belorussians	9,052	9,463	14.4	4.5
Kazakhs	5,299	6,556	46.3	23.7
Tatars	5,931	6,317	19.4	6.5
Azerbaidzhanis	4,380	5,477	49.0	25.0
Armenians	3,559	4,151	27.7	16.6
Georgians	3,245	3,571	20.5	10.0
Moldavians	2,698	2,968	21.9	10.0
Tadzhiks	2,898	2,851	52.9	35.7
Lithuanians	2,665	2,851	14.6	7.0
Turkmens	1,525	2,028	52.2	33.0
Germans	1,846	1,936	14.0	4.9
Kirgiz	1,452	1,906	49.8	31.3
Jews	2,151	1,811	-5.2	-15.8
Chuvash	1,694	1,751	15.2	3.4
Dagestan peoples	1,365	1,657	44.6	21.4
Latvians	1,430	1,439	2.1	0.6
Bashkirs	1,240	1,371	25.4	10.6
Mordvins	1,263	1,192	-1.7	-5.6
Poles	1,167	1,151	-15.4	-1.4
Estonians	1,007	1,020	1.8	1.3

Note: Nationalities in 1979 rank order.

Table 2a: U.S.S.R.: Union-Republic Nationalities -
% of total, 1959-1979, and Annual Growth Rate

	% total population			Annual growth rate	
	1959	1970	1979	1959-70	1970-79
Russians	54.6	53.4	52.4	1.3	0.9
Ukrainians	17.8	16.9	16.2	1.1	0.7
Belorussians	3.8	3.7	3.6	1.2	0.5
Slav group:	76.2	74.0	72.2		
Uzbeks	2.88	3.80	4.75	4.0	3.4
Kazakhs	1.73	2.19	2.50	3.5	2.4
Tadzhiks	0.67	0.88	1.11	4.0	3.5
Turkmens	0.48	0.63	0.77	3.9	3.2
Kirgiz	0.46	0.60	0.73	3.8	3.1
Central Asia:	6.22	8.10	9.86		
Azerbaidzhanis	1.41	1.81	2.09	3.7	2.5
Armenians	1.33	1.47	1.58	2.3	1.7
Georgians	1.29	1.34	1.36	1.7	1.1
Caucasian:	4.03	4.62	5.03		
Lithuanians	1.11	1.10	1.09	1.2	0.8
Latvians	0.67	0.59	0.55	0.2	0.07
Estonians	0.47	0.42	0.39	0.2	0.1
Baltic:	2.25	2.11	2.03		
Moldavians	1.06	1.12	1.13	1.8	1.1

Note: Nationalities are grouped geographically,
not linguistically (except for the Slavs, where
the criteria coincide nearly enough).   Thus:
Central Asian group are all Turkic, except
Tadzhiks (Iranian);   Baltic group includes (here)
the Finnic Estonians;   and all three Caucasian
nationalities are disparate.

Table 3: Languages normally used by Small Ethnic Groups as Written Medium

Written Languages	Peoples
1. Far North and Siberia	
Russian	Aleuts, Alyutor, Itelmen, Kats, Nganasans, Nagidal, Orok, Orochi, Saame, Tofalar, Udege, Chulym, Enets, Yukagir
Tartar and Russian	Barabas, Kamasin
Yakut and Russian	Dolgan
Chukchi and Russian	Kerek
Russian and Khakas	Shor
2. Caucasus	
Avar and Russian	Audi, Archi, Adkvakh, Bavglat, Bezhita, Botlikhe, Ginukhe, Gunzil, Godoberi, Dido, Karati, Kisti, Tat (Dagestan), Tindi, Khvarshi, Chemali
Lesghin and Russian	Agul
Georgian	Bat, Svan
Georgian and Azerbaidzhani	Udi
Azerbaidzhani	Budukhe, Kryz, Khinalug
Azerbaidzhani and Russian	Rutul, Talysh, Tat (Azerbaidzhan)
Azerbaidzhani and Lesghin	Taakhur
Russian	Aisor
3. Central Asia	
Tadzhik	Oroshor, Yagnobe, Yangulam
Tadzhik and Russian	Bartan, Wakhi, Ishkashim, Rushan, Shugne
Turkmen and Russian	Baluchi
Kazakh and Russian	Dungan
4. Others	
Russian	Vepsians, Izhorians
Russian and Lithuanian	Livonians
Ukrainian and Lithuanian	Karaimes

Table 4: Percentage of Major Nationalities claiming Fluency in Russian as a Second Language, and Proportion giving Language of Nationality as First Language, 1970 and 1979

	% claiming fluent Russian as second language		% giving language nationality as first language	
	1970	1979	1970	1979
Russians	O.1	O.1	99.8	99.9
Ukrainians	36.3	49.8	85.7	82.8
Belorussians	49.0	57.0	80.6	74.2
Uzbeks	14.5	49.3	98.6	98.5
Kazakhs	41.8	52.3	98.0	97.5
Tadzhiks	15.4	29.6	98.5	97.8
Turkmens	15.4	25.4	98.9	98.7
Kirgiz	19.1	29.4	98.8	97.9
Azerbaidzhanis	16.6	29.5	98.2	97.9
Armenians	30.1	38.6	91.4	90.7
Georgians	21.3	26.7	98.4	98.3
Lithuanians	35.9	52.1	97.9	97.9
Latvians	45.2	56.7	95.2	95.0
Estonians	29.0	24.2	95.5	95.3
Moldavians	36.1	47.4	95.0	93.2
Tatars	62.5	68.9	89.2	85.9
Chuvash	58.4	64.8	86.9	81.7
Dagestan peoples	41.7	60.3	96.5	95.9
Bashkirs	53.3	64.9	66.2	67.2
Mordvins	65.7	65.5	77.8	78.6

Table 5: Percentage of Nationalities claiming
Fluency in a second Soviet language, Russian or
Other (1979 census)

	% claiming second language fluency in	
	Russian	Other Language
Russians	0.1	3.5
Ukrainians	49.8	7.1
Uzbeks	49.3	2.8
Belorussians	57.0	11.7
Kazakhs	52.3	2.1
Tatars	68.9	4.9
Azerbaidzhanis	29.5	2.0
Armenians	38.6	5.7
Georgians	26.7	0.9
Moldavians	47.4	3.9
Tadzhiks	29.6	10.6
Lithuanians	52.1	1.5
Turkmens	25.4	1.6
Germans	51.7	1.1
Kirgiz	29.4	4.1
Jews	13.7	27.6[*]
Chuvash	64.8	5.5
Dagestan peoples	60.3	8.3
Latvians	56.7	2.2
Bashkirs	64.9	2.8
Mordvins	65.5	7.7
Poles	44.7	13.1
Estonians	24.2	1.9
U.S.S.R.	23.4	4.7

Note: *Most Soviet Jews give Russian as their
first language.

LINGUISTIC AND ETHNIC MINORITIES IN THE USSR

Table 6: Members of Titular Nationality and
Russians as Percentage of Populations of Union
Republics, 1970 and 1979

	1970		1979	
	Tit. Nat.	Russians	Tit. Nat.	Russians
R.S.F.S.R.	82.8	82.8	82.6	82.6
Ukraine	74.9	19.4	73.6	21.1
Belorussia	81.0	10.4	79.4	11.9
Uzbekistan	65.5	12.5	68.7	10.8
Kazakhstan	32.6	42.4	36.0	40.8
Tadzhikistan	56.2	11.9	58.8	10.4
Turkmenia	65.6	14.5	68.4	12.6
Kirgizia	43.8	29.2	47.9	25.9
Azerbaidzhan	73.8	10.0	78.1	7.0
Armenia	88.6	2.7	89.7	2.3
Georgia	66.8	8.5	68.8	7.4
Lithuania	80.1	8.6	53.7	32.8
Estonia	68.2	24.7	64.7	27.9
Moldavia	64.6	11.6	63.9	12.8

Note: Numbers do not add up to 100 per cent, since
other nationalities are not counted. Clearly, in
the 'European' areas the proportion of Russians has
been rising, that of the titular nationalities
falling, in Caucasia and Central Asia, the trend is
the reverse.

NOTES

1. Naselenie SSSR po dannym perepisi naseleniya 1979 goda. (Moskva, Politizdat, 1980).
2. The Census summary (v.s.) lists only 103 nationalities by name, but other small groups, entered under 'other nationalities', would bring the total to about 130. Isayev (v.i.) gives the figure of 133.
3. Georgian and Armenian both have their own scripts, literatures (and autocephalous churches) dating from around the fifth century, which gives their written languages far greater antiquity than the Russian, a point which they are seldom slow to make.
4. K.M. Musaev, Alfavity yazykov narodov SSSR (Moskva, Nauka, 1965).
5. All but Persian (of those listed) have now changed to the Latin alphabet.
6. E.g., 'Sotsial'no-ekonomicheskie problemy narodnogo obrazovaniya (Obzor materialov Vsesoyuznoi nauchnoprakticheskoi konferentsii).' Sovetskaya pedagogika, 1980, no. 3, pp. 15-34.
7. Zvi Halevy and Eva Etsioni-Halevy, 'The "Religious Factor" and Achievement in Education,' Comparative Education, vol. 10, no. 3, 1974, pp. 193-200.
8. 'Muslims' in Yugoslav Census returns usually means Bosnians. The Albanians of Kosovo and Macedonia, and the smaller populations of Turks in Macedonia and Serbia, most of whom are Muslims, record themselves as Albanians and Turks respectively.
9. Uchitel'skaya gazeta, 27 January 1973; Kommunist Tadzhikistana, 8 June, 1973; Turkmenskaya iskra, 2 February 1972.
10. The position is not quite identical: Armenian, like Georgian is defined as the State language by the Constitution of the Republic.
11. Personal observations, Kiev and Erevan, February 1976.
12. Unless otherwise stated, all figures are drawn from Naselenie SSSR with some more detailed analyses in some cases from The All-Union Census of 1979 in the USSR (Radio Liberty Research Bulletin, Munich, September 1980).
13. For an examination of parallels in the West, see E. Haugen, J.D. McLure, D.S. Thomson (eds.), Minority Languages Today (Edinburgh University Press, 1981).

47

14. It is becoming more compact, as are the indigenous populations elsewhere in the Caucasus and in Central Asia. See Table 6.
15. Constitution of the USSR, Article 121.
16. M.I. Isayev, National Languages in the USSR: Problems and Solutions (Moscow, Progress Publishers, 1977) (Adapted).
17. The First Secretary of the Communist Party in Uzbekistan, Rashidov, is known to be strongly committed to the fostering of second-language fluency in Russian; this may have produced the results, or at least influenced the returns.
18. V.K. Rozov, 'Sotsial'no-ekonomicheskie problemy pedagogicheskogo obrazovaniya i povysheniya effektivnosti ispol'zovaniya pedegogicheskikh kadrov', Sovetskaya pedagogika, 1980, no. 2, pp. 97-102.
19. John Gunther, Inside Russia (Penguin, 1965), suggested that the change from Arabic to Latin and then Cyrillic script deprived the Central Asian peoples of their Islamic heritage. The fact remains that the Arabic alphabet presents non-Semitic languages with several problems. It is essentially a consonantal alphabet (as is the Hebrew), and suits quite well the peculiarities of Semitic languages; but, as a rule, on long vowels can be indicated in the body of the written word, and then only vaguely. Short vowels can be shown by 'pointing' the use of diacritics above or below the consonant, though these are not usually necessary in Arabic. But they may be in non-Semitic languages, where the vowels are both more important and exhibit a greater phonetically significant variety than even 'pointed' Arabic can cope with effectively (classical Arabic being poor in vowel-sounds). This is quite apart from the consideration that the Arabic script has developed as a cursive and joined form of writing, calligraphically beautiful but (since the letters are not easy to violate) not easily adapted to printing and quite difficult to read. This, at least, was the view taken by the Turkish leader Kemal Atatürk in 1924, when he had written Turkish changed from Arabic to Latin. More recently, Bahasa Malaysia (Malay) has shifted from the use of the Jawi ('Eastern') form of the Arabic alphabet to the Latin. Finally, it needs to be stressed that Latin and Cyrillic, like their Greek common parent, differ little by comparison; their distinguishing characteristic is that isolable signs or letters give equal weight to consonants and vowels, and are thus more flexible than the consonantal Semitic type (Arabic, Hebrew, Syriac) or the Indian Devanagari

script and its modern variants, essentially modified syllabaries.
20. Isayev, National Languages in the USSR.
21. Personal communications, Herzen Pedagogic Institute, Leningrad.
22. Shamyl in the Caucasus and Yakub Beg in Central Asia led the resistance to Russian expansion in the 19th century. Their place in national history and legend could be compared with that of William Wallace in Scotland, Wilhelm Tell in Switzerland, Skanderbeg in Albania or Hereward the Wake in England.
23. See W.K. Medlin, W.M. Cave, F. Carpenter, Education and Development in Central Asia: A Case Study on Social Change in Uzbekistan (Leiden, E.J. Brill, 1971).
24. Narodnoe khozyaistvo SSSR v 1976 g.: Statisticheskii ezhegodnik (Moscow, Statistika, 1977).
25. Nathan Kravetz, 'Education of Ethnic and National Minorities in the USSR: A Report on Current Developments', Comparative Education, vol. 16, no. 1, March 1980, pp. 13-24.
26. The urbanisation figures are from the 1970 Census; Naselenie SSSR gives urban-rural figures for republics, but not by nationalities.
27. Only 14.2% of Jews gave the language of their own nationality as their native language in the 1979 Census (down from 17.1% in 1970 and 21.5% in 1959). This usually means Yiddish, though in 1959 the figure included 36,000 Georgian Jews who considered Georgian as their first language, 21,000 in Central Asia who gave Tadzhik and 25,000 in the Caucasus who gave Tatar as their native language. Of the rest (82.3%), the great majority consider Russian as their first language; 167,000 claimed a good knowledge of their nationality language (usually Yiddish) as a second language.
28. Isayev, National Languages in the USSR.
29. For a further discussion, see N. Grant, 'European unity and national systems', in B. Simon and W. Taylor (eds.), Education in the Eighties: The Central Issues (Batsford, 1981), ch. 5, pp. 92-107.

Chapter 3

NOW THEY ARE SIX: SOVIET PRIMARY EDUCATION IN
TRANSITION

John Dunstan

A Promise of Change

The most interesting educational task to appear in
the 'Guidelines' for the XI Soviet Five-Year Plan
(1981-5) issued in December 1980 was to work towards
the lowering of the age of starting school. It had
been debated for some years, it had been the subject
of experiment and innovation, but this was the first
time that it had received such prominence in a major
national policy document. The goal was 'to create
the preconditions for the gradual transition to
teaching children from the age of six in preparatory
classes at general-education schools'.[1] Though
cautiously worded, this betokened a new official
commitment. It may serve as the pivot for a
discussion of change in Soviet primary education.
     Two points must be stressed at the outset.
First, the term 'primary education' is used
advisedly. In September 1970 there were 15.1 million
Soviet pupils of primary age, following the three-year
course (recently reduced from four years) begun at
seven; but only 2.3 million of them were at primary
schools. Five years later, with a total of 12.7
million primary pupils, reflecting the decline in
the birthrate over the 1960s, only 1 million were at
primary schools. By 1980 the total had risen again
to 13.8 million, whereas children at primary schools
had decreased to 0.6 million.[2] The rest were at
schools designated 'incomplete secondary' (eight-
year) or 'secondary' (ten-year; eleven-year in
certain republics), with a few at special schools
for the handicapped. Those of us who are familiar
with a state education system in which the primary
stage is much more institutionally self-contained
have to remember that in Soviet schooling a linear
curriculum from the first school year has been
official policy since November 1966. Thus, to move

to the second point, the Soviet school has to a considerable degree extricated itself from the problems of primary/secondary continuity which exercise some western educationists; but links with the pre-school stage have been either non-existent or tenuous. Continuity of the latter kind has elicited much attention and indeed contention with proposals to change the school starting age, for one man's promise may be another man's threat. Any consideration of Soviet primary education nowadays therefore involves sooner or later the nursery school as well.

Primary Education in Context
In view of the earlier contributions to this collective enterprise, we may keep general background considerations to the minimum. There is the long-standing problem of the cultural lag of country localities, an important reason for the migration of the population to the cities, for the difficulty of attracting specialists to work in such places, and for the greater one of persuading them to stay. The elimination of the urban-rural gap is a well-known ideological imperative. In a general situation of very high employment, the fall in the birth-rate during the 1960s, halted only in 1970, has led to an increasingly worrying shortage of young workers, those with technical skills being especially in demand; but affluence is also rising, and with it consumerist attitudes and even a certain privatisation of life-style. Thus the inculcation of communist values - or, to quote Mr Brezhnev at the XXV Party Congress in February 1976, 'an active stance for living and a conscious attitude to public duty, when the unity of word and deed becomes an everyday norm of behaviour' - remains enormously important. The scientific and technical revolution and the information avalanche make it more and more necessary for Soviet citizens to be able to orientate themselves, distinguish between the significant and the trivial, and penetrate to the concepts underlying the facts. In a world of international competition for power and prestige this is of obvious importance for the training of leading specialists, but its implications are far wider than that and extend to the citizenry at large.

Against this backcloth, the education system has the twin tasks of training recruits for the workforce and forming the New Soviet Person, who combines the civic virtues with as high as possible a level of intellectual development, aesthetic

awareness and physical fitness. Thus the
Legislative Principles of the USSR and the Union
Republics on Public Education (1973), in enumerating
the objectives of the secondary general school,
begins with a call for education appropriate to the
current requirements of the social and scientific
and technological progress, and with stress on the
cognitive ('to equip pupils with a deep and firm
knowledge of the principles of academic subjects');
but it immediately goes on to link the cognitive
with the affective ('to inculcate a desire for the
constant improvement of their knowledge and an
ability independently to widen and apply it' and
'to form a Marxist-Leninist world-view'), and
proceeds from there to patriotism, high moral
qualities, harmonious all-round development, and
preparation for 'active labour and public work and
the conscious choice of an occupation'.[3] It should
be noted that no objectives are set out specific to
the primary school. Ten years of general education
for all (in a continuous period) has been a recent
rallying cry and a goal now mainly, if diversely,
achieved. Now let us consider how the Soviet
school, or more precisely its primary stage, copes
with its tasks in relation to particular aspects of
its setting.
     To consider rural education first of all, this
is where small schools are naturally commonest; they
are likely to be short of equipment and facilities,
and even if they are lucky enough to secure a
dedicated teacher who is competent into the bargain,
the problems of efficient teaching are of course
compounded if she is faced with a number of age-
groups simultaneously. Primary schools are
predominantly rural (94.6 per cent in 1970, 95.5 per
cent in 1975), and the average roll of rural primary
schools was 27.3 in 1970 and 19.2 in 1975.[4] The
chances of such small schools achieving their goals
are generally agreed to be much less than those of
larger ones and urban ones, and they are
disproportionately expensive.
     It is therefore not only ideologically desirable
but good economic sense to amalgamate small schools
and centralise them, increasing the number of
complete secondary schools, which should be more
efficient and incidentally retain the older children
of specialists who might otherwise move away. In
some areas this follows a common pattern of
consolidation of smaller agricultural units,
amalgamation of settlements and centralisation of
services. Thus in rural areas the total number of

primary schools decreased from 70,463 in 1970/71 to
45,710 in 1975, while secondary schools rose from
24,919 to 29,488.[5] The fall in average rural
primary school enrolments is likely to be mainly due
to the fact that the remoter they are, the more
difficult it is to organise suitable alternatives
for younger children; residential and transport
facilities are being gradually expanded, but are not
necessarily acceptable for pupils of primary age;
so the proportion of very small remote schools may
well have increased.

The swing of emphasis to the vocational aspect
of education has been increasingly manifest in the
1970s, at first in the injection of senior-level
general education into vocational-technical schools
- which is only superficially paradoxical because
this was not just a means to help to achieve the
ten-years-for-all goal but also an attempt to make
the typically unglamorous vocational sector more
attractive - next in the development of careers
guidance and vocationally-oriented options in the
general school, and recently of 'advanced labour
training' at the senior stage of virtually every such
school. But, in contrast to the Khrushchev era, when
even for 7-year-olds manual work was upgraded from
one to two periods a week, this seems to have had no
impact on primary education; nor should it have been
expected, given the more pragmatic and age-
specifically selective approach to the vocational
aspect in the 1970s.

The reverse is true of the concomitant trend to
stress the affective or 'upbringing' side of Soviet
education. It has never been unimportant, but from
about the mid-1960s to the early 1970s it was somewhat overshadowed by other imperatives, as will be
seen presently. Already in 1968, however,
I.S. Mar'enko of the Academy of Pedagogical Sciences
(in Russian APN) had issued his Primernaya programma
vospitaniya uchashchikhsya vos'miletnei i srednei
shkoly (Model Syllabus for the Upbringing of Eight-
Year and Secondary School Pupils), including of
course the primary stage, and this was followed by
others during the 1970s; among these we may single
out the Azbuka nravstvennogo vospitaniya (ABC of
Moral Education) edited by I.A. Kairov and
O.S. Bogdanova, (1971-2 and 1975), which is a
combined syllabus, methodological handbook and
anthology of stories, etc. for the primary teacher,
the editors' wish being to integrate moral education
systematically into the lesson.[6] There is,
apparently, a tendency for 'upbringing work' to be

carried out haphazardly and regarded as something separate from normal classroom teaching. It is not very sensible to draw a rigid distinction between the affective and the cognitive in any school system, let alone in the USSR's where ideology explicitly requires them to interact and combine. A.M. Pyshkalo, who is responsible for research on primary education at the Institute of Curriculum and Method of the APN, identifies two trends whereby the upbringing function of this stage of education is enhanced. One is the improvement of the content and method of teaching in all subjects with upbringing in view; the other is the introduction of special subjects for upbringing purposes. Pyshkalo and colleagues have been experimenting with a subject entitled 'Man in Nature and Society', taught to six-year-olds for four periods a week and covering three years in all. Its purpose is to help to instil norms of behaviour and its content relates to physical and labour education and to aesthetic, moral and socio-political education.[7] How it does so may be gleaned from the following summary of the syllabus for the first two years:

> Rules of behaviour, road safety rules, pupil's hygiene, civil defence. Our house, street and town. Local animals and plants. Protection of nature. Labour and leisure: meetings with famous people. Artistic and technical modelling. Action games, chess and draughts. Pioneers and Octobrists. Current events (local, national and foreign).[8]

Thus upbringing is brought squarely into the time-table, and such a synthetic subject is claimed to acquire more importance in young children's eyes than would its conventional breakdown into separate and infrequent components. Its creators are at pains to point out, lest pedagogical bells be rung, that it has nothing in common with the outlawed complex method of the 1920s, since it does not interfere with basic subjects.[9]

Mention of basic subjects brings us to the concluding part of this section and to the cognitive concerns of the Soviet school. Although the four-year period of compulsory primary education had an obligatory three-year middle stage attached to it over the period 1949-51 - Khrushchev was to add an eighth year in 1959-61 - the curricula of the two stages remained self-contained. By the end of the 1950s this divided structure and the overloaded, lagging syllabuses with their fact-laden content were felt to be more and more inappropriate to the requirements laid upon the USSR's economy and its citizens by the scientific and technical revolution.[10] The schools would have to produce people who were much more able to observe and to appraise, to solve unfamiliar problems and to adapt to unfamiliar situations; in short - and despite the Soviet view that the highest level of autonomy is relative - to think for themselves.

By the same date, research was under way on the mental development of primary-age children and its implications for teaching them that was to have important consequences for the curriculum reform of the mid-1960s. The salient names were L.V. Zankov and D.B. El'konin. From 1952 Zankov and his colleagues had worked on the hypothesis that the primary school could increase its effectiveness by a new basis of teaching oriented on the development of general mental abilities; first tested in a Moscow school in 1957, over the next decade the research was extended to well over a thousand experimental classes. Zankov based his 'New Didactic System' on Vygotsky's view that teaching must outpace development, but went beyond him: the teacher must not only help with leading questions but also by organising the material so as to promote the most effective development of each individual as he or she is left to get on with it.[11] Zankov was critical of the traditional content-oriented or knowledge-oriented approach with its stress on systematicity; tendency to uniformity and conviction that development would automatically follow teaching. In fact, it depended on the nature of the teaching and the school environment: general abilities (analytical observation, abstract thinking and solving practical tasks) were best developed by a high level of difficulty, a rapid pace of learning, and high cognitive value as the criterion for selection of knowledge to be mediated, all set in a friendly community of teachers and pupils where thinking and discovering would be its own joyful reward.[12]

El'konin considered that Zankov had departed too far from the notion of the leading role of the teacher in favour of the independent activity of the pupil. He accepted Zankov's trinity of difficulty, pace and cognitive value, but unlike him attached less importance to the teaching/learning process than to content and in particular to concepts and their systematic formation. El'konin's

contribution to Soviet educational theory, tested
experimentally from 1959, is that 'each science
(academic subject) possesses a 'logical structure'
which must be matched in the school syllabus,
necessitating linear progression, and the mastery of
this logic promotes mental development.[13] We are
continually reminded of the educational debates in
the West at about the same time, themselves prompted
in no small measure by the scientific and technical
revolution, not to mention the three 'sputniks'
(October 1957-May 1958); in the USA, the Woods Hole
Conference on primary and secondary science education
(September 1959) resulted in Bruner's The Process of
Education (1960), the first translation of which was
into Russian.[14]

Back in the USSR, despite enormous criticism of
Zankov from 1962 onwards, mainly because of his
alleged neglect of content, his research and that of
El'konin furnished the theoretical framework for the
reform of the primary school (and to some extent for
that of the secondary) following the deliberations
of the Curriculum Commission of 1964-6. This was
accompanied by nationwide discussion and terminated
in the decree of 10 November 1966, whereby, among
much else, the primary stage was to be compacted
from four years into three, with new textbooks and
syllabuses in accordance with the new ten-year
linear pattern; this was implemented by 1971. The
new syllabuses were intended to stress the development of thinking by including material calculated to
raise the level of understanding and generalisation,
bringing together separate problems with common
factors for purposes of comparison, reducing factual
material, and encouraging the formation of
independent work habits.[15]

Almost immediately, however, the reform
resulted in criticism: overloading remained a
problem. Younger pupils were increasingly fatigued,
weaker ones were over-extended,[16] and in a sort of
last testament maintaining his position a few months
before his death Zankov himself mentioned that this
had led to instances of primary children being
deemed incapable of studying in ordinary schools and
removed to special ones. He attributed the problem
to a discrepancy between the new curriculum and the
old methods.[17] This is frequently mentioned and
bears credibility, in that the discovery methods
associated with the new curriculum, the group
teaching that might be recommended, and the freer
interpersonal relationships that these things often
imply can scarcely have been adopted rapturously by

the rank and file of teachers with a longer or
shorter life of talk, chalk, rote-learning and formal
discipline behind them nor, one suspects, by a lot
of teacher-trainers. Even for the enthusiastic and
the enterprising, they make heavy demands of time and
effort. Whether as a consequence of employing the
new methods or disregarding them, many teachers of
the first two years had to give extra lessons to
enable pupils to keep up, thereby extending the
vicious circle of fatigue to themselves. The new
textbooks also attracted much complaint, on grounds
of both content and method, and although the latter
deficiency is an explanation more easily accepted as
well as given, there is still evidence that the
conceptual level was pitched too high.[18]
  On the other hand, much effort has gone into
improving the new textbooks and teaching aids, and
it has been said that the bulk of the criticism and
concern applied to the post-primary stages, where
the input of preparatory research had been much less.
In 1973 the APN Institute of Curriculum and Method
conducted an investigation on pupil performance in
the basic skills. The attainment of some 6000
ten-year-olds in a variety of schools and locations
was evaluated in reading, writing and arithmetic.
The majority, it was said, coped with the demands of
the new syllabuses; but much remained to be done in
the sphere of personality development and upbringing
work.[19]
  An up-to-date assessment of the situation from
the pen of M. Zvereva, Zankov's colleague and
successor as head of the Laboratory on the Teaching
and Development of Schoolchildren, suggests that the
problem is not only one of persuading teachers to use
modern methods, but which modern methods; primary
school methodologists have themselves not yet given
due attention to the experimental methodology with
its hallmarks of flexibility, variety and enthusiasm.
The root of the problem lies in the contradictory
demands made on primary education: its methods are
supposed to solve developmental tasks, but the
efficiency of the ordinary school is assessed on
performance criteria alone, which involves drills,
repetition and tests, which in turn preoccupy at
least some methodologists. Meanwhile the Laboratory
is applying itself in particular to the learning
environment, widely defined; it seeks enjoyment in
the pupils at its experimental schools, high morale
(nravstvennoe samochuvstvie) in the teachers, and
satisfaction in the parents, which, since there are
no complains about overloading yet syllabuses are

covered, it reckons it has achieved.[20]

And yet, even if the problems engendered by the urban-rural gap were to be overcome, even if teachers were to inculcate the desired virtues much more effectively, and even if, one fine day, the progressive methods favoured by Zankov and other reformers were to be realised in practice as well as honoured in theory: would not severe limitations on the school's effectiveness remain? For at a joint session of the APN and the Academy of Medical Sciences in 1971, the hypothesis was advanced that about 80 per cent of the development of mental abilities had taken place by the age of eight.[21] If this is true, the school as the traditional agency of purposeful intellectual development, which itself may be regarded as a sector of upbringing which interacts and combines with other sectors to form the New Soviet Person, must a priori be in a relatively weak position to achieve it. Questions then arise about the extension of the school's influence and about its relationship to other institutions such as the family and the nursery school; and it is to the latter which we now turn.

Pre-school Education and Primary Schooling

The aims of pre-school education, according to the 1919 Party Programme, were to improve social upbringing and to further the amancipation of women. According to the 1973 Legislative Principles on Public Education, its aims are to create the most favourable conditions for the upbringing of children of that age and to give the necessary assistance to the family.[22] We note the shift of emphasis, which dates from the 1930s, to the family as a necessary partner in the enterprise of education, but also one which requires help. There is a hint of inadequacy here, supported by ample evidence of households which do not train up children in the way they should go; but to a considerable extent the inadequacy is created by a labour situation in which, in 1970, 86 per cent of all women aged 20 to 29 and 93 per cent of those aged 30 to 39 were employed[23] and some ten years later 85 per cent of all women of working age (16 to 55) had jobs. It is moreover upbolstered by psychological constraints on women about not going out to work, by a level of consumer services which produces much stress, and not infrequently by uncooperative husbands.

The objectives of pre-school education, as spelled out in the Legislative Principles, are as follows:

Children's pre-school institutions, in close
cooperation with the family, effect the
harmonious all-round development and upbringing
of the children; protect and strengthen their
health; instil in them elementary practical
habits and a love of physical work; see to
their aesthetic education; prepare the children
for their studies in school; and bring them up
in a spirit of respect for their elders and
love for the socialist Motherland and their
native region.[24]

The emphasis on childrearing, very broadly interpreted,
is reflected in the fact that the staff of nursery
schools are known as 'upbringers' (vospitateli), not
teachers.

Crèches (day nurseries or nurseries with overnight facilites) are intended for children aged six
months to three years, and nursery schools for those
from three to six years; increasingly the two types
of institutions are combined, and statistics often
do not distinguish between them. In March 1979, an
eminent educationist informed me that one-third of
the relevant age-groups were in pre-school education.
(This must mean permanent establishments, for at the
end of the X Five-Year Plan (1980) 50.2 per cent were
in permanent and seasonal ones.) Pre-school places
had increased from 11.5 million in 1975 to 14.5
million in 1980.[25]

These global figures, however, conceal much
variation among age-groups and republics and between
town and country. The older the child, the more
likely he or she is to have a place, especially in
the top year ('preparatory groups'). If in 1980
the USSR average provision was still about 33 per
cent, at the start of the year it was far higher in
Estonia at 58 per cent (cf. 42 per cent in 1970),[26]
near the nationwide average in Kazakhstan at 35 per
cent (cf. 32 per cent in 1976),[27] and at the end of
the year only 13-15 per cent in Tadzhikstan and
Azerbaidzhan.[28] The town and country differences
overall have decreased slightly since 1969, when it
was reckoned that about 45 per cent of eligible
urban children but only 10 per cent of rural ones
could be accommodated;[29] in 1979, 53 per cent of
urban children and 21 per cent of rural youngsters
were in pre-school institutions.[30] In large cities,
however, the demand is considered to have been
satisfied, although in Leningrad at least there may
be a waiting list if one lives on the periphery.
Rural provision also varies, from about 10 per cent

in Central Asia (Tadzhikstan, Turkmenia) through
33 per cent in the Ukraine to some 80 per cent in
Moscow Region.[31]
    It is clear, therefore, that with certain
geographical exceptions a major shortcoming of the
pre-school system is its availability. To be sure,
this defect is mitigated by an important fact: in
1979/80 an average of about 56 per cent of first-year
pupils[32] (and 85 to 95 per cent of such in big
industrial cities in 1980/81[33]) had come from nursery
schools, that is had spent at least a year in them.
Nevertheless, a lot of children have escaped the
pre-school net, or, to put it more accurately, have
frequented pools where the fishing has been patchy
or non-existent; if, of the 4.5 million admitted
to the first year in 1981,[34] 44 per cent or 1.98
million were not ex-nursery school,[35] and if we
deduct the 700,000-plus who had been attending
preparatory classes at general schools[36] (of which
more later), we are still left with about one and a
quarter million straight from home. The shortfall
in pre-school places is due not to lack of funds but
to low priorities on the part of local agencies and
branch ministries,[37] meaning that scarce resources
of manpower and materials are applied elsewhere.
    Distribution deficiencies in the pre-school
network, which may incur criticism from primary
school educationists,[38] are by no means the only
problem affecting this sector or the only fault laid
at its door. Dissident writers complain of a high
rate of morbidity and poor standards of child care,[39]
which have also been cited, though understandably in
more moderate terms, by a deputy education minister.[40]
This seems to be primarily due to the supply and
quality of the staff or 'upbringers'; apparently
demand for personnel is only 40-45 per cent
satisfied.[41]   Apart from the general labour shortage,
the sector lacks prestige and offers low salaries.
Too often, it seems, the women who fill the posts
are no more than child minders; 'it would be
wonderful if the word "upbringer" were to regain its
original meaning', sighs one writer to the press.[42]
Thus not only are the caring and the childrearing
frequently defective, but the preparation for
formal schooling is so too, witness the RSFSR
Ministry of Education circular of 1970 which
complained that upbringers were insufficiently versed
in methods of teaching reading and writing.[43]   In
effect, as will be seen, the teaching of these skills
was intended to have been discontinued, except
experimentally.

Professor I. Bestuzhev-Lada, head of the
Department of Social Prognostics at the Institute
of Sociological Research of the USSR Academy of
Sciences, feels that the only answer is to change
the popular perception of the nursery school as a
public utility institution and for people to go in
and help the upbringers.   Some nursery schools

send out 7-year-olds more like 3-year-olds in
their mental level.   If, on top of that,
their parents have not given them sufficient
attention, such first-formers are clearly in
a very difficult situation in their school
desks, surrounded by coevals who in all
points surpass them by far.[44]

Such coevals must have either attended good nursery
schools or preparatory classes, or been brought up
at home;   the implication is that in some cases
family upbringing is actually superior to pre-school
education in its present form.
   Before continuing our discussion, it is high
time to interject a comment.   This view of Soviet
nursery schooling, based on Soviet data, may
surprise people who have visited kindergartens in
the large cities or who have read enthusiastic
reports by western visitors.   A complementary, if
hardly complimentary, picture is nevertheless
necessary, not only to begin to understand the scope
of current problems but also to appreciate the
progress so far achieved despite great difficulties.
And it would be foolish to throw out the baby - or
the pre-school child - with the bathwater.   So let
it be emphasised forthwith that there are some
nursery schools which are excellent.   It may well
be, as a Moscow education officer has said, that
the general level of development of children entering
school from nursery school has become noticeably
higher;   she cites their good speech development,
their ability to cope with fairly complicated mental
tasks and with material from the first-form syllabus,
and their liveliness and sociability.[45]   But Moscow
is seldom typical of the country as a whole, and
even in Moscow, as she herself shows, there are not
a few exceptions.
   Bestuzhev-Lada, in his article cited above,
touches upon the complex problem of continuity
between pre-school and primary education.   Although
the Legislative Principles of 1973 do no more than
mention 'preparing the children for their studies in
school' among other objectives of nursery education,

it is understandable that the performance-oriented general schools regard it as the paramount one, and it is clear that in their view the goal is being insufficiently achieved. All sorts of variables may have combined to complicate the tasks of the primary stage: the extent of pre-school provision and its calibre; the degree of active parental support for it and the quality of that support; the presence of children who have not been to nursery school and the level of their family upbringing. The problem can be seen essentially as one of inequality in start positions, which has been said to create not only teaching difficulties but also excessive ambitions in some pupils and a sense of inferiority in others.[46] The seriousness with which this is regarded, and the lack of coordination that may prevail, can be seen in the RSFSR Ministry of Education's rather dramatic action of 1970 when in effect it banned the APN Institute of Pre-School Education's scheme for six-year-olds at nursery school to cover part of the first-year primary syllabus.[47] A glance at the Ministry circular, where the existing and amended pre-school programmes are juxtaposed, suggests that the one for elementary mathematical concepts was greatly simplified and that for reading and writing deleted altogether.[48]

The general schools and their spokesmen feel that the nursery schools lack their efficiency and systematicity, at least where six-year-olds are (or would be) concerned,[49] whereas the nursery schools and their defenders believe that they are better able to foster the general development and meet the physical and upbringing needs of the age-groups in question.[50] Others, as we have just discerned, have advocated that they take over part of the primary course.[51] The converse plan to lower the general-school starting age may be construed as an attack on the pre-school sector, and we shall turn to that presently; but by no means all the discussion has been conducted in such polarised terms.

In the realm of educational theory and its practical applications, and in line with innovation further up the educational ladder, not only with regard to curriculum change in general but also because of the reduction of the primary course to three years, much has been made of the necessity for the nursery school to enhance the cognitive side of its activities; it should be less preoccupied with mediating basic literacy and numeracy skills, and more concerned with developing the child's intellect.

This involves developing the ability to analyse,
compare, synthesise, generalise and draw
conclusions - given the right conditions, even
youngsters of four or five are capable of this at
a simple level, as research at the Institute of
Pre-School Education has shown - and also moral and
volitional qualities.[52] Because of the cardinal
importance of the character of the child's age-
related activity, the emphasis of the nursery school's
cognitive role does not mean that he or she should be
taught in the form of the traditional lesson; wide
use should be made of teaching games, imitation and
practical work.[53] But the mention of moral and
volitional qualities is not accidental; it is a
carefully controlled freedom that educationists have
in mind, and the transfer from nursery school to the
first-year primary class, with the concomitant change
from predominantly play activity to much more formal
learning activity, is a good deal less traumatic if
the children not only know how to get on with their
peers and the teachers but have acquired habits of
concentration, persistence, carefulness and
precision in the performance of their assigned
tasks.[54]
     All this is a counsel of perfection, not easy
to realise, but on the instructions of the USSR
Ministry of Education the Institute of Pre-School
Education has recently pointed the way by preparing
a draft standard syllabus for the six-year-old group,
together with methodological guidance, based on the
above principles;[55] the Minister has spoken
approvingly of it.[56] On an organisational level
the transition can be made considerably smoother by
cooperative arrangements between the pre-school and
primary sectors. They are often described and
sometimes discussed in the educational press.
Liaison seems usually to be an initiative of the
general school, as should be expected of the body
possessing the more relevant expertise; there is
certainly more about it in the primary education
journal than the pre-school one. The teacher's
newspaper achieves more balance: of 34 new pupils
in class 1B at Secondary School no. 78, Riga, 29 are
from preparatory groups at neighbouring Nursery
School no. 44. Their upbringers accompanied them to
the annual opening ceremony (the 'First Bell'); they
know them well and have taught them well. But how
often, remarks the commentator, this wealth of
experience remains within the walls of the nursery
school, and class 1 teachers have a form like a
terra incognita! The older nursery school children

are invited to the First Bell ceremony; the
Pioneers and Octobrists visit their school to help
the upbringers, and the teachers join in activities
including staff and parents' meetings there.[57]
Similar links exist between schools and
kindergartens in Moscow, and are applauded, but
there is some difference of opinion about the wisdom
of filling school classes from specific nursery
school groups en bloc; sometimes the classes are
very organised and well-disciplined, sometimes quite
the reverse and only the children brought up at
home are beyond reproach.[58] A whole year may be
needed to transmute such a base collective into one
of gold, while an inexperienced teacher had better
be assigned to an 'arbitrarily-formed' class.[59]
Anyone who has been privileged to attend a First Bell
ceremony and moreover visited a more typical new
first-year class of awe-struck seven-year-olds, even
now clay awaiting the hands of the pedagogical potter,
will appreciate this advice. But if the schools find
the performance of the kindergartens unsatisfactory in
their major role as upbringing institutions as well as
in their increasingly important subsidiary one of
developing intellectual abilities, and also if their
forces are clearly insufficient to cover their
territory and likely long to remain so, a gradual
takeover of the most strategically significant part
of that territory is scarcely to be wondered at.

Lowering the School Starting Age
Such, then, is the background to the general school's
annexation of the education of an increasing number
of six-year-olds in order to prepare them for school
by furthering (and perhaps levelling up) their
all-round mental and social development. Of late,
this increase has gained momentum. In 1970 the
school was instructed merely to provide ten-day
summer courses.[60] By 1975, 0.23m or about 5.4 per
cent of six-year-olds were enrolled in so-called
'zero classes' or preparatory classes[61] (these
entities, referring to general schools, are not to
be confused with the preparatory groups comprising
the parallel year at nursery schools). In 1977
the total was 0.24m[62] or some 5.5 per cent. By
1979, however, more than 0.5m[63] or over 11.4 per
cent of the age-group were attending preparatory
classes. At the end of the X Five-Year Plan (1976-
80) numbers had risen to over 0.7m[64] or an estimated
15.4 per cent, just a little short of the plan target
which had been set at 0.75m;[65] the combined total in
preparatory classes and groups amounted to about

70 per cent,[66] so the share of the former was
already more than significant. On 1 September 1981
more than 0.8m six-year-olds or over 17.3 per cent
of the age-group were at their desks in general
schools.[67]
Reactions to this trend, though in general it
commands support, have not invariably been of
unalloyed enthusiasm. As has already been mentioned,
the pre-school sector feels itself to be the
repository of expertise vis-à-vis the age-group
concerned; and it has accused those in favour of
reducing the school starting age of wanting to
shorten childhood. It is no impugnment of the
pre-school champions' integrity to say that they also
fear a cut in their budget.[68] They have allies in
the medical profession who consider that the nursery
school routine (full meals, afternoon sleep) is
better for six-year-olds, 20 per cent of whom are
allegedly not physically ready for school, so it is
in the nursery school that they should be educated.[69]
Others too feel that they should have another year to
run around, for their health's sake,[70] and the Soviet
Minister of Education himself - in a very balanced
statement, be it said - cites the view that one must
not overtax the child's developing brain.[71] Many
parents are not against the principle of the earlier
start, but their experience of the extended school
day gives rise to fears that their children will not
be properly looked after;[72] thus they in effect
share the medical position. The financial
authorities are also rumoured to have opposed a
development which would involve much teacher training
and retraining and at least raise the possibility of
an additional school year.
The implications of the lowering of the starting
age for the length of the school course seem to have
been largely disregarded in recent writing, but there
was certainly much interest in the matter on the
occasion of my visit to the Soviet Union in 1979,
and supporters of the change were divided about it.
Sociologists writing in 1977 had assumed that
schooling would also finish a year earlier than at
present,[73] and it was suggested to me that those
concerned about the acute manpower shortage would
welcome recruits to the workforce a year younger.
Educationists and scientists, on the other hand,
typically favour the idea of an extra year at
school; they are mostly agreed that six-year-olds
are intellectually capable of making more profitable
use of their time. Then, however, their ways part,
for the educationists see the additional year as the

solution to the hoary old problem of the overloading
of the school curriculum, whereas the scientists,
who frequently complain about the standards achieved
at school by many candidates for higher education
courses, regard it as a golden opportunity for them
to be taught more material. Some educationists
clearly feel that the scientific lobby called the
tune in the mid-1960s debate, with similar priorities,
and that this is why, far from eliminating overloading, the reformed curriculum perpetuated it.
They do not want a repeat performance in the latest
reform.

Against the doctors and parents who have mis-
givings about their children's health and well-being,
there are others who say 'We'll be only too happy to
send our six-year-old to school, he's already fed up
with nothing to do',[74] and physiologists who, after
a seven-year longitudinal study of the health and
labour efficiency of pupils who began a particular
school at six, found no deviations from normal
growth and development which might be connected with
the earlier start.[75] Two educationists committed
to schooling from the age of six have said that if
it means keeping the same routine timetable, curriculum and methods, they agree that it is too early;
but if it means teaching six-year-olds in full
accordance with their age-specific characteristics,
then they agree that the change is overdue.[76]

Specific variants of a new timetable and
curriculum will be considered presently, but of
course these are not all that is required: a new
or renewed generation of teachers equipped with
materials embodying the new methods is also
indispensable. Providing the additional staff at
all, let alone appropriately qualified ones, must
be a major problem at a time of critical shortage
of teachers, and an important reason why the
transition is to be gradual. Early in 1981, however, it was reported that the USSR Ministry of
Education and the APN had prepared a 'Methodological
Timetable and Syllabus of Courses for the Training
and Re-training of Teachers and Upbringers for Work
in the Preparatory Classes of General Education
Schools', apparently intended for the so-called
Institutes for the Improvement of Teachers (instituty
usovershenstvovaniya uchitelei, IUU) which provide
in-service training,[77] and with existing primary
teachers mainly in view;[78] the reference to
upbringers most likely embraces extended-day schools
and possibly boarding schools, although the question
of retraining a number of nursery teachers will

presumably arise sooner or later in the relatively
few places where there are enough of them. As for
initial training, recommendations on the training of
future teachers of six-year-olds had been issued for
the education faculties of pedagogical institutes
and training schools (uchilishcha). The experience
of organising preparatory classes was currently
being studied and generalised in all the republics.
Attractive teaching aids, workbooks and other
materials were ready for publication or already
available in seven of them.

Pre-school educationists' stress on the need for
methods used with six-year-olds to be qualitatively
different from those applied to their slightly older
siblings and to be based on play has been accepted by
their colleagues as being equally relevant to the
preparatory classes at schools. In the words of
the report:

> Teaching methods are based on the specific
> features of the types of activity and forms
> of thinking chracteristic of young children.
> The main form of their activity is play;
> thus, during the period when children are
> prepared for school, teachers must strive
> to find the optimum correlation between
> play and learning.[79]

Or, in slightly blunter terms, 'elements of play must
be brought into the assimilation of the material'.[80]
Put this way, the task perhaps sounds less problematic
for the primary teacher; but given the well-
authenticated formal structure and serious atmosphere
of the Soviet classroom and lesson, she is unlikely
to find it easy to adapt.

The traditional ambience is not at all typical
of experimental schools, which report splendid results
and great popularity; but then such schools enjoy a
special sort of kudos in the USSR and can draw on
special resources. If their practices can be
successfully implemented in ordinary schools, this
will do much to assuage lingering parental doubts
and fears; but it will not be an easy undertaking.
These experimental schools are nevertheless described
sometimes as schools of the future. Let us take a
closer look at the activities of some of them. One
is School no. 170 in Moscow; I have more data on the
progress of the experiment there than on its beginning.
Another school is situated at Pushchino-na-Oke, a
little town in Moscow Region, reasonably accessible
from the metropolis but not within commuting distance

(one reason why it was chosen, I was told; otherwise
parents would have put the school under siege). Even
the press were kept away for eight years since the
experiment began in September 1971.[81]
Four experimental classes were set up, with
120 six-year-olds. At the same time, 118 seven-
year-olds were admitted to four ordinary classes at
the same school as a control group. At Pushchino
all the children attend nursery schools; the
subjects of the experiment were mainly taken from
two of them, leaving six-year-olds in other nursery
schools for comparative purposes. Of the 120
pupils, 105 completed the first year; twelve were
withdrawn for medical reasons and three on the
request of their parents. Thirteen were children
of research workers, 41 of white-collar workers, and
51 of manual (mainly construction) workers. Special
preparation at home for the classes did not arise,
since the decision to open them was not announced
until the end of August.[82] Since we have already
discussed at some length the theoretical considerations underpinning primary-school reform, we may
concentrate now upon organisational questions,
making reference also to experimentation in other
parts of the USSR.
At the Moscow school at least, it was felt
advisable to limit the class size to 25-30 pupils,
so that the teacher might more effectively influence
the development of their 'habits of behaviour and
conscientious independent work'.[83] (The maximum
number of pupils for classes 1 to 8 laid down by the
School Statute of 1970 is 40.[84]) The lessons,
normally 45 minutes long in Soviet schools, were
first divided at Pushchino into two with a five-
minute break for physical exercises. This had
little effect, so the onset of loss of interest was
monitored and found to occur predominantly in the
thirty-fifth to thirty-eighth minute. On this
evidence the standard lesson length became
35 minutes, retaining the break.[85] The 35-minute
period seems to have also been used in Georgia and
Kazakhstan, where there is wide-scale teaching of
six-year-olds, but because a confusing dual system
of bells was necessary, the Moscow school opted for
two 20-minute periods (with a break) for the first
two school years, thus fitting neatly into the
existing timetable.[86] In Latvia and the Ukraine,
educationists and pupils are apparently made of
sterner stuff, and a continuous period of 30 minutes
is recommended.[87]
The normal working week for Soviet seven-year-

olds consists of six days with four periods a day,
plus extracurricular activities and up to an hour's
homework on five days. Homework is said to be the
weakest point of conventional arrangements, because
parents represent an arbitrary factor: an APN study
of the homework performance of pupils of this age
found that the parents of about 20 per cent of the
children exerted no supervision, those of others (up
to 50 per cent) were excessively demanding, while
those of the remainder supervised the work by doing
most of it themselves.[88] At the Moscow school there
were six 20-minute periods for the preparatory
classes, increasing to seven later in the year,
Thursdays were reserved for music, games and
excursions, and there was no homework (except
reading, drawing, etc.), but instead private study
supervised by the teacher.[89] Similar arrangements
for 'independent work' applied at Pushchino; these
were timetabled in mid-afternoon after the children
had had a 90-minute rest, and were followed by
organised activities.[90] These are, of course,
common practices in well-organised extended-day
schools. In the Latvian experiment, the children
had to work a notably longer day of seven 30-minute
periods, with the most demanding subjects in the
first three. Their afternoons were on much the
same lines as at Pushchino, but they had Saturdays
completely free, which was very popular with
parents.[91]
     The question of the five-day school week,
incidentally, has been much discussed during the
1970s, largely at the instigation of the newspaper
Literaturnaya gazeta. A small-scale experiment on
this has been in progress for over a decade at
Lipetsk in the RSFSR; at Tallinn and Piarnu in
Estonia a further experiment has been related
specifically to six-year-olds. The main arguments
in favour of the free Saturday were that it would
increase children's opportunities for healthful
recreation and leisure; it would consequently
improve their academic performance; it would
provide an opportunity for remedial work with the
backward (some saw an inconsistency here); it would
lighten teachers' workload; it would facilitate
contact within the family, and this would be
particularly useful in helping younger children to
adjust to school; and it would be in line with
social trends, since more and more parents were
working a five-day week.
     Those who opposed the idea denied the first two
points, one of them citing research in Latvia

indicating diminished efficiency. The notion of
making the backward attend lessons on Saturdays
would have socially divisive results within the
school community. Extra work on the other days
would nullify the effects of the free day, and
teachers would gain nothing because they would be
expected to spend their Saturdays teaching the
backward or organising activities for those pupils
whose parents were not free. Overall, however, the
proposal enjoyed support.[92] Literaturnaya gazeta
finally polled its readers: 2,600 replied, of whom
85.5 per cent were overwhelmingly in favour and
another 6 per cent in favour or moderately so.[93]
The newspaper was accordingly disgusted at the RSFSR
Ministry of Education's subsequent decision merely to
continue the Lipetsk experiment.[94] A recent statement on the subject by the Soviet Education Minister
again links the question of the five-day school week
to the teaching of six-year-olds; a new experiment
is to be mounted, but there are no plans for
expansion.[95]
     To conclude our survey of experimental work,
let us now move briefly from organisational matters
to subject teaching. The integrated subject
intended to serve primarily affective goals, 'Man in
Nature and Society', figured much earlier in this
chapter; to that we might add the Latvians'
'Introduction to Environmental Studies', taught to
preparatory groups for five periods a week, but
perhaps rather more concerned than the former with
cognitive development.[96] The traditional 'hard'
subjects are tending to lose something of their
dominant position. In the ordinary schools of the
RSFSR, Russian language with twelve weekly periods
comprises 50 per cent and mathematics (six periods)
25 per cent of the first-year course for seven-year-
olds. At School no. 170, Moscow, Russian accounts
for about 35 per cent and mathematics 20 per cent of
the preparatory course for six-year-olds, out of a
smaller total of lessons.[97] The Russian syllabus
has abandoned the traditional synchronous teaching
of reading and writing, and of the cursive script,
for both physiological and psychological reasons
(e.g. lack of congruence between different
manifestations of the same sound causes confusion,
and stress on writing is considered to lower interest
in language). The children learn to speak correctly
and to read, with the use of simplified printed
letters, before learning to write in them by the
end of the second year.[98]
     One particularly interesting experiment has been

the teaching of English to six-year-olds at
Pushchino and three other RSFSR schools. The aim
was to investigate the effectiveness of early
foreign-language (FL) learning at school; if this
were successful, the FL syllabus could be lightened
later as a contribution to solving the problem of
overloading.[99] Soviet and foreign psychologists
had confirmed that the age 4 to 8 was especially
favourable for colloquial FL learning because of
'imprinting', the facility in children of that age
for rapidly recalling whole sentences in
conversation[100] as with their native language, and
because of their imitative ability. Oral methods
were employed exclusively until towards the end of
the second year. After initial problems when
reading was introduced, a mixture of the Doman and
Decroly methods was devised, focussing on the form
of complete words and on sentences. On the whole,
the results achieved over the primary stage were
better than in the middle years of the ordinary
school. Teaching was certainly easier, and with
this early start the amount of FL at the middle
stage could certainly be reduced.[101] A major
problem, however, would be the training of primary
teachers in FL teaching competence.
     When, after waiting nearly eight years,
Literaturnaya gazeta was finally permitted to
despatch a reporter to the Pushchino school, they
sent a woman whose writing combines sharpness of
eye with trenchancy of comment. She visited several
classes and was at pains to point out that the
children were not really different from those at
ordinary schools - she was perhaps thinking of the
pupils at special schools for high-ability children
who are sometimes said to be smug and arrogant -
except that the older ones were still keen to learn.
In a memorable phrase, she referred to the 'cult of
goodwill' prevailing in the school and the attention
paid to every child. The new methods and the
shortened lesson were for her part of that warmth,
and this was her message for the ordinary school
if it was to take over the education of six-year-
olds: they must enjoy going to school. Because
of this they were indeed far ahead of their coevals
at nursery school, as researchers had concluded.[102]
The lady did not end by quoting A.A. Milne, who has
been translated into Russian; but the children
might have done so, not from arrogance but with
six-year-old candour and the confidence that the
school had given them: 'Now we are six, we're as
clever as clever'. In fact, being collectively-

71

minded, they would thus have blended two quotations;
but as good little Soviet citizens, committed to
realising their potential, I doubt that they would
have continued 'So we think we'll be six now for
ever and ever'.

Retrospect and Prospect
Early in 1981 the XXVI Party Congress confirmed the
directives for the new Five-Year Plan. The
lowering of the school starting age to six years at
last became official policy, but the goal was
expressed in cautious and gradual terms which
reflected the scope of the undertaking and the
problems related to it. It can be seen as an
outcome of curricular concerns dating back to the
1950s - the scientific and technical revolution and
its implications for the schooling and upbringing of
Soviet youth - concerns translated into action in the
mid-1960s as regards formal curriculum content, and
increasingly evident in the 1970s as to teaching
methods and moral education. But there were two
conspicuously weak links in the system: country
schools, frequently small, expensive and inefficient,
particularly primary ones which in 1975 despite
seventeen years of closures constituted 39 per cent
of all rural schools but accommodated only 4.3 per
cent of rural pupils;[103] and pre-school institutions
which overall could take only a third of the
relevant age-groups, tended to be underdeveloped in
rural areas, and were more concerned with child-care
than education. At the same time it was coming to
be felt more and more that greater cognizance should
be taken of the importance of the pre-school years
for general mental development.
    The nursery schools expanded their preparatory
groups for six-year-olds, covering more than half of
them by the end of the 1970s; but they had problems
of staffing, and doubts were voiced as to whether
their 'upbringers' were able to cope with the
cognitive tasks that were now being stressed. In
any case a lot of children were left unprovided for
by the state, and family upbringing was unpredictable
and therefore suspect. So during the 1970s a
further form of educational provision for six-year-
olds developed, preparatory classes at general
schools; by 1981 they were accommodating an
estimated 17.3 per cent or more of the age-group.
On a visit to three Soviet cities in 1979 I was told
that the lowering of the school starting-age was
likely to become law with the introduction of the
next Five-Year Plan, but that the whole matter was

controversial; it indeed seemed to be more a
matter for conversation than for press discussion.
In the event, the pre-school, medical and financial
objectors were defeated by the powerful though
variously motivated alliance of planners, scientists
and educationists; parents tended to agree in theory
with the idea but to express worries in practice.
Now that the Party Congress has set its seal on the
change, debate on the principle will cede to
discussion on the best ways to achieve the aim.

The lowering of the school starting age has
been taken as our pivotal theme partly because of
its dominant topicality, partly because the education
of six-year-olds provokes interesting questions about
the curriculum content and the methods of teaching
and bringing up primary pupils in the school of the
future, and partly because an organisational change
of this kind, whether accompanied by qualitative
change or not, is bound to affect the whole course of
secondary schooling and what lies beyond. Unless it
is eventually decided to extend primary education by
one year, children will be reaching the beginning of
the middle stage of school at the age of nine-plus
and will complete this stage at about fourteen,
instead of a year later in both cases as hitherto.
Secondary vocational, medium-level technical, or
senior-stage general education will presumably begin
a year earlier. What will happen thereafter is not
yet apparent; a possible scenario is that
economists and planners will joyfully welcome
recruits to the skilled workforce a year earlier
than at present, while scientists and educationists
will press for an extra (third) year at the senior
stage. (Early in 1982, however, it was being
suggested that the primary course would revert to
four years.)

Opposition from economic quarters but support
from Academe would raise the very interesting
possibility of a three-year senior course limited
to the general school. At Pushchino-na-Oke a
three-year course for senior pupils is currently
being tried out; it envisages a considerable
lightening of the heavy senior syllabus and
extensive use of optional subjects.[104] This provokes
further questions: whether options will again acquire
their pristine importance[105] (one has the impression
that in the late 1970s they have been in the doldrums);
whether the content of the senior-stage curriculum
will provide another juicy bone for scientists to
pick with educationists; and whether the senior
general course, given the continuation of current

attempts to reduce intakes to it in favour of the
secondary vocational sector, will become more and
more restricted and regain the paramount function of
preparing for higher education which in recent years
with the spread of compulsory ten-year schooling it
has had increasingly to share with other functions.
Intensified differentiation of this kind would have
far-reaching social implications.

The introduction of the earlier start to school
will make itself felt downwards as well as upwards.
The pre-school sector has shown anxiety lest it
should be bereft of its six-year-olds, and in some
places this has presumably already happened, but,
for the time being at least, the teaching of these
children is envisaged, apparently on common lines,
in both general and nursery schools.[106]   This is
dictated by necessity; but if a general long-term
policy on the relative roles of the two institutions
in the matter has indeed been formulated, its nature
is not explicit, and the Soviet Minister of Education
has so far refrained from publicly taking sides.
Once the entire age-group has been accommodated in
one institution or the other, an appraisal and a
decision is more likely to be forthcoming.   Recent
discussion and developments would lead one to
expect an extension of the sway of the general
school.   A countervailing factor, however, is that
some authorities uphold the nursery school, for
example Belorussia, committed to educating all
six-year-olds by 1984, considers it 'the best form
of preparing children for school', but sees
preparatory classes as inevitably filling the gap
in rural areas.[107]

Since appraisals must needs have regard to
qualitative change, let us conclude with the
prospects for this.   As nursery schools and primary
education are both to be responsible for the
preparation of six-year-olds, there is no doubt that
reading and writing, outlawed from nursery education
during the 1970s, have been rehabilitated.[108]   For
the nursery school with its staffing problems, much
will depend on how it rises to this challenge, and
also how in future it copes with heightened
expectations as to the cognitive development of
younger children.   But our main spotlight is
focussed on the primary stage.   We have looked in
some detail at experimental schools because these
are said to be the blueprints for the school of
the future.   They may be epitomised in terms such
as: high level of mental development, challenge,
all-round upbringing; but also, encouragement of

desire to learn, individualisation of teaching/
learning process, teacher as discreet organiser of
child's activity, discovery methods, creativity,
assessment on less subject-oriented criteria; and
above all, enjoyment and the 'cult of goodwill'.
If we can imagine not only their aims but also their
success applied to the ordinary school, the millennial
year rushes on to our view.   It would be a
magnificent achievement in any society.   In the
Soviet Union it will entail a massive renewal and
replenishment of human and material resources,
particularly the former, the teachers;   and, as if
that were not enough, a new mental outlook in the
taught.   The fundamental question is, of course,
whether the social context will permit it.   But
speculation must stop.   Now they are six;   let us
first wait and see what they will be like at
sixteen or seventeen.

NOTES

1. Pravda, 2 Dec. 1980.   Such classes had
been briefly mentioned in the Legislative Principles
on Public Education of 1973, and their expansion
had been included among a host of provisions in the
1977 decree on general education (Pravda, 29 Dec.
1977), but without specific universal implications.
    2. Narodnoe obrazovanie, nauka i kul'tura v
SSSR (Statistika, Moscow, 1977), pp. 26-7, 90-1;
Narodnoe khozyaistvo SSSR v 1980 godu (Finansy i
statistika, Moscow, 1981), p. 456.
    3. N.G. Salishcheva, E.M. Koveshnikov and
L.A. Steshenko, O narodnom obrazovanii (Yuridicheskaya
literatura, Moscow, 1974), pp. 106-7.
    4. Narodnoe obrazovanie, nauka, pp. 26, 30-31
(derived).   Similar statistics are not to hand for
1980.
    5. Ibid., p. 30.
    6. J. Dunstan, 'Soviet Moral Education in
Theory and Practice', Journal of Moral Education,
vol. 10, no. 3 (1981), pp. 197-8.
    7. A.M. Pyshkalo, 'Problema dal'neishego
sovershenstvovaniya uchebnogo plana i soderzhaniya
obucheniya mladshikh shkol'nikov' in Struktura i
soderzhanie nachal'nogo obucheniya v shkole budushchego
(NII obshchei pedagogiki APN SSSR, Moscow, 1977),
pp. 5-6.
    8. K.I. Neshkov, A.M. Pyshkalo and O.N.
Sorotskaya, 'Chelovek v prirode i obshchestve' in
Uchebnyi plan i organizatsiya obucheniya i vospitaniya
v shkole s nachalom obucheniya s 6 let (NII SiMO APN

SSSR, Moscow, 1976), p. 29.
    9. Ibid., pp. 32-3.
    10. J. Dunstan, 'Curriculum Change and the
Soviet School', Journal of Curriculum Studies, vol. 9,
no. 2 (1977), p. 113.
    11. The most useful treatment of Zankov known
to me is that of B. Schiff, Die Reform der
Grundschule in der Sowjetunion (Quelle and Meyer,
Heidelberg, for Osteuropa-Institut, [West] Berlin,
1972), here pp. 8, 12-16, 22. Part of Zankov's
major work is available in English: L.V. Zankov,
Teaching and Development: A Soviet Investigation,
B.B. Szekely (ed.) (M.E. Sharpe, White Plains, New
York, 1977).
    12. Schiff, Die Reform, pp. 17-21, 23, 29,
44-5.
    13. Ibid., pp. 47-50; El'konin's work as of
1961 is described in B. Simon, Intelligence,
Psychology and Education: A Marxist Critique
(Lawrence and Wishart, London, 1971), pp. 144-6.
The idea of logical structure had been disputed on
the grounds that subject-matter has to be adapted so
as to accord with age-related potential and to serve
upbringing goals.
    14. J.S. Bruner, The Process of Education,
2nd edn. (Harvard University Press, Cambridge, Mass.
and London, 1977), introduction, p. x.
    15. A.M. Pyshkalo, 'Nachal'naya shkola
razvitogo sotsialisticheskogo obshchestva' in
Organizatsiya obucheniya i vospitaniya v sovremennoi
nachal'noi shkole (NII obshchei pedagogiki APN SSSR,
Moscow, 1977), p. 17.
    16. Schiff, Die Reform, p. 55.
    17. Pravda, 20 Aug. 1977.
    18. Dunstan, 'Curriculum Change', p. 118.
    19. M.P. Kashin, 'Ob itogakh perekhoda sovetskoi
shkoly na novoe soderzhanie obshchego obrazovaniya',
Sovetskaya pedagogika, no. 3 (1976), p. 25. No
further details of the study are given in this
source.
    20. Uchitel'skaya gazeta, 11 July 1981.
    21. A.G. Kharchev and V.G. Alekseeva, Obraz
zhizni, moral', vospitanie (Politizdat, Moscow, 1977),
p. 71.
    22. Salishcheva et al., O narodnom obrazovanii,
p. 104.
    23. M.P. Sacks, 'Women in the Industrial Labor
Force' in D. Atkinson, A. Dallin and G.W. Lapidus
(eds.), Women in Russia (The Harvester Press,
Hassocks, 1978), p. 199.
    24. Salishcheva et al., O narodnom obrazovanii,
p. 104.

25. V. Usanov, 'Vstupaya v odinnadtsatuyu
pyatiletku', Narodnoe obrazovanie, no. 2 (1981), p. 27.
26. F. Eisen, 'Estonskaya SSR', Narodnoe
obrazovanie, no. 4 (1980), p. 38.
27. O. Volodin, 'Sovershenstvovat'
obshchestvennoe doshkol'noe vospitanie', Narodnoe
obrazovanie, no. 10 (1980), p. 34 (comment by
K.B. Balakhmetov).
28. Usanov, 'Vstupaya', p. 27.
29. Schiff, Die Reform, p. 59.
30. Uchitel'skaya gazeta, 26 June 1979.
Volodin ('Sovershenstvovat'', p. 31) gives 50% and
25% respectively for 1980; the plan targets had been
some 55% and 28% (M.A. Prokof'ev, 'Problemy shkoly v
desyatoi pyatiletke v svete reshenii XXV s''ezda
KPSS', Sovetskaya pedagogika, no. 7 (1976), p. 9).
31. Uchitel'skaya gazeta, 26 June 1979.
32. M. Prokof'ev, 'Osushchestvlyaem zavety
Lenina', Narodnoe obrazovanie, no. 4 (1980), p. 6.
This appears to be the sense of an awkwardly-phrased
comment.
33. 'V Ministerstve prosveshcheniya SSSR',
Sovetskaya pedagogika, no. 1, (1981), p. 146.
34. Uchitel'skaya gazeta, 1 Sept. 1981.
35. This may be slightly in excess as the
percentage for 1979/80 has had to be applied;
however, although provision has increased since then,
so has the number of children needing it.
36. Usanov, 'Vstupaya', p. 29.
37. Ibid., p. 27; such comments are legion.
38. K.I. Neshkov and A.M. Pyshkalo, 'Uchebnyi
plan i organizatsiya obucheniya' in Uchebnyi plan,
p. 9.
39. Women and Russia (Sheba Feminist
Publishers, London, 1980), pp. 39, 54-5.
40. Uchitel'skaya gazeta, 25 Dec. 1976.
41. G. Makushkin, 'V Ministerstve
prosveshcheniya SSSR', Sovetskaya pedagogika, no. 1
(1981), p. 146. See also Prokof'ev,
'Osushchestvlyaem', p. 8.
42. Literaturnaya gazeta, 8 Aug. 1979.
43. 'Ob uporyadochenii podgotovki k shkole
detei shestiletnego vozrasta', Sbornik prikazov
i instruktsii Ministerstva prosveshcheniya RSFSR,
no. 18 (1970), p. 2.
44. Komsomol'skaya pravda, 3 Feb. 1981.
45. A. Shishova, 'O zadachakh doshkol'nykh
uchrezhdenii po dal'neishemu sovershenstvovaniyu
obucheniya i vospitaniya detei i dostoinoi vstreche
XXVI s''ezda KPSS', Doshkol'noe vospitanie, no. 11
(1980), p. 6. Dissemination of the experience of

good schools is perhaps the most important function
of this attractive journal.
46.   Kharchev and Alekseeva, Obraz zhizni, p. 72.
47.   Neshkov and Pyshkalo, 'Uchebnyi plan',
p. 12.
48.   'Ob uporyadochenii', pp. 6-10.
49.   Neshkov and Pyshkalo, 'Uchebnyi plan',
pp. 8, 14.
50.   Literaturnaya gazeta, 8 Aug. 1979;
Makushkin, 'V Ministerstve', p. 148.
51.   Schiff, Die Reform, pp. 66-7.   Or indeed
all of it - see Literaturnaya gazeta, 8 Aug. 1979.
52.   Schiff, Die Reform, pp. 64-5, 68;   A.
Zaporozhets, 'Intellektual'naya podgotovka detei k
shkole (soderzhanie, formy i metody)', Doshkol'noe
vospitanie, no. 8 (1977), pp. 30-1.   Zaporozhets was
head of the APN Institute of Pre-School Education
until his death in 1981.
53.   Ibid., pp. 31-3.   For a survey of Soviet
research on pre-school education see N. Grant,
'USSR' in M. Chazan (ed.), International Research in
Early Childhood Education (NFER Publishing Company,
Windsor, 1978), pp. 203-8.
54.   L. Kamalina, 'Kak podgotovit' detei k
obucheniyu v shkole', Doshkol'noe vospitanie, no. 12
(1980), pp. 70-1.
55.   Uchitel'skaya gazeta, 30 June 1981.
56.   Uchitel'skaya gazeta, 26 May 1981.
57.   Uchitel'skaya gazeta, 3 Sept. 1981.
58.   Compare I.M. Povarova, 'Shkoly - k s''ezdu:
shkola no. 134 Moskvy', Nachal'naya shkola, no. 12
(1980), p. 15, with N.I. Kopyrina, 'Plyusy i minusy
klassa-gruppy', Nachal'naya shkola, no. 8 (1980),
p. 43.
59.   Ibid., p. 44.
60.   'Ob uporyadochenii', pp. 3-4.
61.   K. Nozhko, 'Glavnoe - kachestvo i
effektivnost'', Narodnoe obrazovanie, no. 5 (1977),
p. 13.   This and the following percentages, derived
from birth statistics kindly supplied by my
colleague Dr Ann Helgeson, are approximate.
62.   Uchitel'skaya gazeta, 7 Feb. 1981.
63.   Uchitel'skaya gazeta, 14 Feb. 1980.
64.   Uchitel'skaya gazeta, 7 Feb. 1981.
65.   Nozhko, 'Glavnoe', p. 13.
66.   Usanov, 'Vstupaya', p. 29.
67.   Uchitel'skaya gazeta, 1 Sept. 1981.
68.   These points were put to me during a visit
to the USSR in 1979.
69.   Literaturnaya gazeta, 8 Aug. 1979.
70.   Neshkov and Pyshkalo, 'Uchebnyi plan',

p. 5; Literaturnaya gazeta, 30 May 1979.
71.   Prokof'ev, 'Osushchestvlyaem', p. 8.
72.   Literaturnaya gazeta, 8 Aug. 1979.
73.   Kharchev and Alekseeva, Obraz zhizni,
p. 72.
74.   Literaturnaya gazeta, 8 Aug. 1979.
75.   M.V. Antropova, 'Izmenenie rabotosposobnosti
i sostoyaniya zdorov'ya detei 6-14 let pod vliyaniem
bolee rannego nachala sistematicheskogo obucheniya
v shkole' in Itogi obucheniya detei s shesti let v
vos'miletnei shkole (NII SiMO APN SSSR, Moscow,
1979), p. 21.
76.   Neshkov and Pyshkalo, 'Uchebnyi plan', p. 5.
77.   Uchitel'skaya gazeta, 7 Feb. 1981.
78.   Uchitel'skaya gazeta, 17 Feb. 1981.
79.   Uchitel'skaya gazeta, 7 Feb. 1981.   The
Ministry has involved pre-school and primary
specialists in collaborative work on the new
syllabuses and methods, along with hygienists,
physiologists and doctors.
80.   Uchitel'skaya gazeta, 26 Mar. 1981.
81.   Literaturnaya gazeta, 8 May 1979.
82.   T.P. Slavgorodskaya, 'Uchebnyi rezhim v I-kh
klassakh shestiletok' in Shestiletki-pervoklassniki.
Materialy nauchno-prakticheskoi konferentsii po
itogam obucheniya shestiletok v shkole g. Pushchino-
na-Oke (1971-1972 uchebnyi god) (NII SiMO APN SSSR,
Moscow, 1972), pp. 10-11.
83.   Neshkov and Pyshkalo, 'Uchebnyi plan',
pp. 16-17.
84.   Narodnoe obrazovanie v SSSR.   Obshcheobrazovatel'naya shkola.   Shornik dokumentov 1917-
1973 gg. (Pedagogika, Moscow, 1974), p. 229.
85.   Slavgorodskaya, 'Uchebnyi rezhim', p. 12.
86.   Neshkov and Pyshkalo, 'Uchebnyi plan',
p. 18.
87.   A. Ya. Karule and D. Ya. Al'brekhta,
'Aktual'nye voprosy obucheniya shestiletnikh detei
v shkolakh Latviiskoi SSR' in Problemy didaktiki
(obucheniya) v nachal'noi shkole (NII SiMO APN SSSR,
Moscow, 1977), p. 46; Uchitel'skaya gazeta,
26 Mar. 1981.
88.   I.A. Mel'kova, 'O domashnikh zadaniyakh v
1 klasse shkoly' in Problemy didaktiki, pp. 29-30.
89.   Ibid., p. 32; Neshkov and Pyshkalo,
'Uchebnyi plan', pp. 20-3, 25-7.   The private study
began halfway through the year.
90.   A.M. Pyshkalo, 'Eksperimental'noe obuchenie
shestiletnikh detei', in Shestiletki-pervoklassniki,
p. 5; Slavgorodskaya, 'Uchebnyi rezhim', p. 12.
91.   Karule and Al'brekhta, 'Aktual'nye voprosy',
pp. 46-8.

92. <u>Literaturnaya gazeta</u>, 4 Oct. 1978,
13 Dec. 1978, 21 Feb. 1979, 16 May 1979 and
29 Aug. 1979; <u>Izvestiya</u>, 11 Oct. 1977 and 18 Nov.
1977.
93. <u>Literaturnaya gazeta</u>, 16 May 1979.
94. The research provoked unusually scathing
official criticism; see <u>Uchitel'skaya gazeta</u>,
21 July 1979.
95. <u>Uchitel'skaya gazeta</u>, 17 Feb. 1981;
N. Yur'ev, 'Namechaya novye zadachi', <u>Narodnoe</u>
<u>obrazovanie</u>, no. 5 (1981), p. 8.
96. Karule and Al'brekhta, 'Aktual'nye voprosy',
pp. 49-51.
97. Derived from Neshkov and Pyshkalo,
'Uchebnyi plan', p. 27.
98. K.I. Neshkov, A.M. Pyshkalo and A.N.
Matveeva, 'Osobennosti obucheniya shestiletnikh
detei russkomu yazyku' in <u>Uchebnyi plan</u>, pp. 34-9.
99. A.D. Klimentenko, 'Eksperimental'noe
obuchenie angliiskomu yazyku detei s shesti let v
shkole', <u>Inostrannye yazyki v shkole</u>, no. 2 (1978),
p. 37.
100. A.D. Klimentenko, 'Nado li obuchat'
inostrannomu yazyku s shesti let?' in <u>Uchebnyi plan</u>,
p. 40.
101. <u>Ibid.</u>, p. 41; Klimentenko,
'Eksperimental'noe obuchenie', pp. 38-9, 46.
102. <u>Literaturnaya gazeta</u>, 30 May 1979.
103. <u>Narodnoe obrazovanie, nauka</u>, pp. 30-1
(derived).
104. <u>Literaturnaya gazeta</u>, 30 May 1979.
105. The fullest discussion of options is in
J. Dunstan, <u>Paths to Excellence and the Soviet</u>
<u>School</u> (NFER Publishing Company, Windsor, 1978),
pp. 177-96.
106. Yur'ev, 'Namechaya', p. 8; 'Istoricheskie
resheniya XXVI s''ezda KPSS - v zhizn'', <u>Sovetskaya</u>
<u>pedagogika</u>, no. 4 (1981), p. 7.
107. Makushkin, 'V Ministerstve', p. 148; on
1984 see <u>Uchitel'skaya gazeta</u>, 7 Feb. 1981.
108. Kamalina, 'Kak podgotovit'', p. 71;
M. Karklin', 'Rastit' detei zdorovymi, garmonicheski
razvytimi', <u>Narodnoe obrazovanie</u>, no. 2 (1981),
p. 36; <u>Uchitel'skaya gazeta</u>, 30 June 1981. The
outlawing and rehabilitation apply to the RSFSR.

SOVIET PRIMARY EDUCATION IN TRANSITION

BIBLIOGRAPHY

Antropova, M.V. 'Izmenenie rabotosposobnosti i
    sostoyaniya zdorov'ya detei 6-14 let pod
    vliyaniem bolee rannego nachala sistematicheskogo
    obucheniya v shkole' in Itogi obucheniya detei
    s shesti let v vos'miletnei shkole (NII SiMO APN
    SSSR, Moscow, 1979), pp. 11-21
Bruner, J.S. The Process of Education, 2nd edn.
    Harvard University Press, Cambridge, Mass. and
    London, 1977)
Dunstan, J. 'Curriculum Change and the Soviet School',
    Journal of Curriculum Studies, vol. 9, no. 2
    (1977), pp. 111-23
-----Paths to Excellence and the Soviet School
    (NFER Publishing Company, Windsor, 1978)
-----'Soviet Moral Education in Theory and Practice',
    Journal of Moral Education, vol. 10, no. 3
    (1981), pp. 192-202
Eisen, F. 'Estonskaya SSR', Narodnoe obrazovanie,
    no. 4 (1980), p. 38
Grant, N. 'USSR' in M. Chazan (ed.), International
    Research in Early Childhood Education (NFER
    Publishing Company, Windsor, 1978), pp. 197-210
'Istoricheskie resheniya XXVI s''ezda KPSS - v zhizn'',
    Sovetskaya pedagogika, no. 4 (1981), pp. 3-8
Kairov, I.A. and Bogdanova, O.S. (eds.) Azbuka
    nravstvennogo vospitaniya (Prosveshchenie,
    Moscow, 1975)
Kamalina, L. 'Kak podgotovit' detei k obucheniyu v
    shkole', Doshkol'noe vospitanie, no. 12 (1980),
    pp. 70-1
Karklin', M. 'Rastit' detei zdorovymi, garmonicheski
    razvytimi', Narodnoe obrazovanie, no. 2 (1981),
    pp. 34-7
Karule, A.Ya. and Al'brekhta, D.Ya. 'Aktual'nye
    voprosy obucheniya shestiletnikh detei v
    shkolakh Latviiskoi SSR' in Problemy didaktiki
    (obucheniya) v nachal'noi shkole (NII SiMO APN
    SSSR, Moscow, 1977), pp. 44-51
Kashin, M.P. 'Ob itogakh perekhoda sovetskoi shkoly
    na novoe soderzhanie obshchego obrazovaniya',
    Sovetskaya pedagogika, no. 3 (1976), pp. 24-32
Kharchev, A.G. and Alekseeva, V.G. Obraz zhizni,
    moral', vospitanie (Politizdat, Moscow, 1977)
Klimentenko, A.D. 'Nado li obuchat' inostrannomu
    yazyku s shesti let?' in Uchebnyi plan i
    organizatsiya obucheniya i vospitaniya v shkole
    s nachalom obucheniya s 6 let (NII SiMO APN
    SSSR, Moscow, 1976), pp. 40-1
-----'Eksperimental'noe obuchenie angliiskomy yazyku

detei s shesti let v shkole', Inostrannye
yazyki v shkole, no. 2 (1978), pp. 37-47
Kopyrina, N.I. 'Plyusy i minusy klassa-gruppy',
Nachal'naya shkola, no. 8 (1981), pp. 43-4
Makushkin, G. 'V Ministerstve prosveshcheniya SSSR',
Sovetskaya pedagogika, no. 1 (1981), pp. 146-8
Mar'enko, I.S. (ed.) Primernaya programma vospitaniya
uchashchikhsya vos'miletnei i srednei shkoly
(publisher not stated, Moscow, 1968)
Mel'kova, I.A. 'O domashnikh zadaniyakh v 1 klasse
shkoly' in Problemy didaktiki (obucheniya) v
nachal'noi shkole (NII SiMO APN SSSR, Moscow,
1977), pp. 28-32
Narodnoe obrazovanie, nauka i kul'tura v SSSR
(Statistika, Moscow, 1977)
Narodnoe obrazovanie v SSSR. Obshcheobrazovatel'naya
shkola. Sbornik dokumentov 1917-1973 gg.
(Pedagogika, Moscow, 1974)
Neshkov, K.I. and Pyshkalo, A.M. 'Uchebnyi plan i
organizatsiya obucheniya' in Uchebnyi plan i
organizatsiya obucheniya i vospitaniya v
shkole s nachalom obucheniya s 6 let (NII SiMO
APN SSSR, Moscow, 1976), pp. 5-27
-----Pyshkalo, A.M. and Matveeva, A.N. 'Osobennosti
obucheniya shestiletnikh detei russkomu yazyku'
in Uchebnyi plan i organizatsiya obucheniya i
vospitaniya v shkole s nachalom obucheniya s
6 let (NII SiMO APN SSSR, Moscow, 1976),
pp. 34-9
-----Pyshkalo, A.M. and Sorotskaya, O.N. 'Chelovek
v prirode i obshchestve' in Uchebnyi plan i
organizatsiya obucheniya i vospitaniya v
shkole s nachalom obucheniya s 6 let (NII SiMO
APN SSSR, Moscow, 1976), pp. 28-33
Nozhko, K. 'Glavnoe - kachestvo i effektivnost'',
Narodnoe obrazovanie, no. 5 (1977), pp. 11-16
'Ob uporyadochenii podgotovki k shkole detei
shestiletnego vozrasta', Sbornik prikazov i
instruktsii Ministerstva prosveshcheniya RSFSR,
no. 18 (1970), pp. 2-31
Povarova, I.M. 'Shkoly - k s''ezdu: shkola no. 134
Moskvy', Nachal'naya shkola, no. 12 (1980),
pp. 13-16
Prokof'ev, M.A. 'Problemy shkoly v desyatoi pyatiletke
v svete reshenii XXV s''ezda KPSS', Sovetskaya
pedagogika, no. 7 (1976), pp. 3-13
-----'Osushchestvlyaem zavety Lenina', Narodnoe
obrazovanie, no. 4 (1980), pp. 2-8
Pyshkalo, A.M. 'Eksperimental'noe obuchenie
shestiletnikh detei' in Shestiletki-
pervoklassniki. Materialy nauchno-prakticheskoi

konferentsii po itogam obucheniya shestiletok v
shkole g. Pushchino-na-Oke (1971-1972 uchebnyi
god (NII SiMO APN SSSR, Moscow, 1972), pp. 5-9
Pyshkalo, A.M. 'Nachal'naya shkola razvitogo
sotsialisticheskogo obshchestva' in
Organizatsiya obucheniya i vospitaniya v
sovremennoi nachal'noi shkole (NII obshchei
pedagogiki APN SSSR, Moscow, 1977), pp. 3-26
-----'Problema dal'neishego sovershenstvovaniya
uchebnogo plana i soderzhaniya obucheniya
mladshikh shkol'nikov' in Struktura i soderzhanie
nachal'nogo obucheniya v shkole budushchego (NII
obshchei pedagogiki APN SSSR, Moscow, 1977),
pp. 3-8
Sacks, M.P. 'Women in the Industrial Labor Force'
in D. Atkinson, A. Dallin and G.W. Lapidus
(eds.), Women in Russia (The Harvester Press,
Hassocks, 1978), pp. 189-204
Salishcheva, N.G., Koveshnikov, E.M. and Steshenko,
L.A. O narodnom obrazovanii (Yuridicheskaya
literatura, Moscow, 1974)
Schiff, B. Die Reform der Grundschule in der
Sowjetunion (Quelle and Meyer, Heidelberg, for
Osteuropa-Institut, [West] Berlin, 1972)
Shishova, A. 'O zadachakh doshkol'nykh uchrezhdenii
po dal'neishemu sovershenstvovaniyu obucheniya
i vospitaniya detei i dostoinoi vstreche XXVI
s"ezda KPSS', Doshkol'noe vospitanie, no. 11
(1980), pp. 4-7
Simon, B. Intelligence, Psychology and Education:
A Marxist Critique (Lawrence and Wishart,
London, 1971)
Slavgorodskaya, T.P. 'Uchebnyi rezhim v I-kh
klassakh shestiletok' in Shestiletki-
pervoklassniki. Materialy nauchno-prakticheskoi
konferentsii po itogam obucheniya shestiletok v
shkole g. Pushchino-na-Oke (1971-1972 uchebnyi
god) (NII SiMO APN SSSR, Moscow, 1972),
pp. 10-13
Usanov, V. 'Vstupaya v odinnadtsatuyu pyatiletku',
Narodnoe obrazovanie, no. 2 (1981), pp. 27-30
'V Ministerstve prosveshcheniya SSSR', Sovetskaya
pedagogika, no. 1 (1981), p. 146
Volodin, O. 'Sovershenstvovat' obshchestvennoe
doshkol'noe vospitanie', Narodnoe obrazovanie,
no. 10 (1980), pp. 31-5
Women and Russia (Sheba Feminist Publishers, London,
1980)
Yur'ev, N. 'Namechaya novye zadachi, Narodnoe
obrazovanie, no. 5 (1981), pp. 7-9

Zankov, L.V. Teaching and Development: A Soviet
    Investigation, B.B. Szekely (ed.) (M.E. Sharpe,
    White Plains, New York, 1977)
Zaporozhets, A. 'Intellektual'naya podgotovska detei
    k shkole (soderzhanie, formy i metody)',
    Doshkol'noe vospitanie, no. 8 (1977), pp. 30-4

Chapter 4

ENVIRONMENTAL EDUCATION IN THE USSR

Elisabeth Koutaissoff

Environmental education is a new and as yet a
rather ill-defined subject which is being introduced
only gradually into Soviet schools and universities.
However, it is bound to grow in importance for two
obvious reasons and a third more controversial one.
The first reason is that it comes in response to the
present ecological crisis which is threatening
mankind and from which the Soviet Union is not
immune.   The second reason is its intrinsically
educational value due to the interdisciplinary
approach with which it can imbue many subjects and
thus counter the fragmentation of knowledge by
excessive specialisation.   The third, more
controversial reason will be discussed later.

The Challenge of the Ecological Crisis
The realisation that humanity is threatened by an
ecological crisis came to be widely discussed in the
1960s and early 1970s.   It had by then become
evident that the technico-scientific revolution
entailed excessive exploitation of non-renewable
natural resources and an over-use of the renewable
ones by an exponentially increasing population
possessed by the idea that economic growth was
essential to human welfare.   Moreover, it resulted
in an often irreversible pollution of air, water and
land by solid wastes, noxious gases and dangerous
radiation.
        In 1968 UNESCO convened its first conference on
'Man and the Biosphere'.   This was followed by the
Stockholm Conference on the Human Environment.
This conference set up the United Nations
Environmental Programme (UNEP) and put forward in
its recommendation no. 96 the need for environmental
education.   In preparation for the Stockholm
Conference an unofficial report, based on papers by

numerous experts, was compiled by Barbara Ward and René Dubos under the title Only one Earth; the Care and Maintenance of a small Planet.[1]
        Meanwhile in April 1968, on the initiative of the Italian industrialist Aurelio Peccei an international group of scientists, economists and businessmen had laid the foundations of the Club of Rome and commissioned a research team at the Massachussetts Institute of Technology to produce a report on what the Club termed 'the Predicament of Mankind'.   In 1972 the team published its findings under the title The Limits to Growth.[2]   The book met with much criticism but triggered off a vast 'survival' literature.
        The Soviet Union did not attend the Stockholm Conference in protest at the GDR not having been invited, but it joined UNEP.   It also took part in founding the International Institute for Applied Systems Analysis (IIASA) at Laxenburg, Austria, where research was initially concerned with various resources estimates.
        In the Soviet Union, The Limits to Growth and other books advocating zero growths were fiercely criticised, partly because their authors implicitly assumed that the world would continue to develop on capitalist lines, but also, and perhaps even more so, because the Soviet leadership is totally committed to economic growth.   Its entire policy is to expand productive forces and build a wealth-creating material and technical basis capable of sustaining a Communist way of life, that is one making a reality of the slogan 'from everyone according to his abilities, to everyone according to his needs'.   As to the deleterious effects of the technico-scientific revolution, they were imputable to the capitalist mode of production and were not an inevitable result of scientific progress.   The assertion that overpopulation was the root cause of the ecological crisis cut little ice with people whose country suffered tremendous loss of life during World War II (twenty million according to official data and probably more in actual fact) and where the falling birth rate was going to cause labour shortages in the near future.   Nor could the depletion of resources loom ominously while geologists were discovering rich deposits of oil and minerals in the frozen wastelands of Siberia.
        On the other hand, increasing pollution could not be denied.   It came to a head when two giant pulp-and-paper mills were established on Lake Baikal, the deepest in the world, said to contain one fifth

of the Earth's fresh water - unsurpassed for its purity - as well as renowned for its unique flora and fauna such as freshwater seals and marine species of fish. Elsewhere the discharge of domestic and industrial wastes into the slow-flowing Russian rivers was making their water undrinkable while pesticides, washed off the fields into streams, rivers and lakes were endangering fish stocks. The state of the Volga was particularly disturbing because of the many industrial towns along its course and the intense river traffic it carries to and from the Caspian Sea. The latter was itself increasingly polluted by the oil industry, particularly by off-shore drilling. Nor was the Baltic in a much better state, though the Marine Protection Agreement signed by the Soviet Union and other states bordering on the Baltic in 1976 may still save life in this ecologically moribund sea.

Other side-effects of man's activity were also becoming apparent. Fishing in the Azov Sea had declined both because of over-fishing and also because of its growing salinity due to the lack of fresh water from the Don and smaller in-flowing rivers as a result of their water having been diverted upstream to vast irrigation schemes. In the North, the oil industry with its drilling, pipe-laying and heavy transport vehicles was destroying the sparse and fragile tundra vegetation, while the old evil of deforestation had an adverse effect on the run-off of rivers, on the accelerating disappearance of wildlife (including valuable fur animals) and possibly even on the albedo of the earth. There were other side-effects too. In Central Asia irrigation without adequate drainage brought out the salinity of the subsoil; in western Belorussia the draining of marshes had caused the drying up of wells in neighbouring villages. The use of ill-chosen fertilisers benefited weeds more than crops. The siting of atomic power-stations close to large industrial towns was worrying the scientific community.[3]

Some legislation to combat air pollution by factories, to regulate land and water use and to protect Lake Baikal had been passed by the Soviet government over the years. In 1972, the Supreme Soviet of the USSR devoted an entire session and enacted its first comprehensive law for the protection of natural resources and their better utilisation. It was designed to conciliate the fundamentally conflicting aims of further industrial development and environmental conservation. One of its provisions required the spreading of information on the protection of nature among the population and to explain the importance of a more rational use of its riches. Recent years have seen further legislation making it mandatory for the polluter to bear the costs of pollution control and to protect wildlife.[4]

In a centrally planned economy responsibility for the building of polluting factories, mines, power-stations, etc., rests with the planners and their scientific advisers. So, in the wake of the 1972 legislation, a special department dealing with environmental problems was set up within the State Planning Commission (Gosplan), while an inter-departmental scientific and technical council to coordinate research into the complex problems of the environment was added to the State Committee for Science and Technology. A network of observation posts to monitor air and water pollution has been established by the State Committee for Hydro-meteorology and Control of the Natural Environment. Indeed, responsibility towards future generations is embodied in Article 18 of the Soviet Constitution.

In the Draft Guidelines for the eleventh five-year plan, section II 'The basic tasks of the country's economic and social development in 1981-5 and up to 1990', Article 5 reads 'To step up the protection of nature, agricultural land, the air, water, and the plant and animal world; to ensure the rational utilisation and reproduction of natural resources', while under section III 'The development of science and the acceleration of technical progress', there is a clause setting the goals of 'increasing the effectiveness of measures in the field of environmental protection and the rational utilisation of the resources of the biosphere, the world's oceans and sea shelves, and the improvement of forecasting the weather and other natural phenomena'.[5]

In presenting the Draft Guidelines to the 26th Congress of the CPSU, L.I. Brezhnev explained the slower and more costly growth of the economy in the foreseeable future by the fact that development would take place in the harsh regions of the north-east of the country and also because of the costliness of environmental protection measures.[6]

The new approach to the environment will be not only costly, it will require a new understanding of the broader and eventually global issues of 'man-society-nature', interconnected as they are by a web of multiple and intricate relations, many of which are still unknown or misunderstood. So,

further research into natural phenomena is a pre-
condition for any meaningful and successful
environmental education. Another essential pre-
condition is to reverse our present 'consumer'
mentality which views the bounties of nature as
objects to be exploited here, now and as fast as
possible for the benefit of today's generation. So
knowledge - both theoretical and practical - and the
will to protect the environment are equally important.
Developers must learn to foresee the possible dire
consequences of their projects and, what's more, to
modify and even abstain from their implementation
however tempting the return on investment.
Environmental education implies a fundamental change
in the traditional belief in the inexhaustibility of
resourses and the ability of nature for self-
rehabilitation. It also undermines the
anthropocentric outlook - long cherished in the
USSR - that man can and must transform and improve
nature. It also undermines the Marxist view that
human development owes more to social than to natural
factors such as climate and geographical conditions;
this rejection of geographical determinism is based
on the argument that changes in civilisation from the
stone age to our technological societies took place
in the same geographical areas. Concern with man-
induced degradation of nature does not justify mere
'conservation' but heralds a new stage of human
history characterised by mankind's wise management
of nature. This is reflected in the now fashionable
Russian word prirodopol'zovanie.

The Response - Environmental Education

As already mentioned, the idea of environmental
education was first broached at the 1972 UNESCO
Conference in Stockholm. This was followed by an
International Environmental Workshop which met in
Belgrade in 1975 (13-20 October). The outcome was
a Charter outlining the goals and objectives of
environmental education. This stressed the need
to arouse the awareness of people to ecological
problems, expand their knowledge of and alter their
attitude to the environment and encourage the
participation of schools at primary, secondary and
tertiary levels in environmental education as well
as that of the public at large.[7]
     In 1977 (14-26 October), UNESCO and UNEP
sponsored an Intergovernmental Conference which was
held in Tbilisi, Caucasus. While reiterating the
aspirations expressed in Belgrade, it discussed ways
to help learners to discover the symptoms and real

causes of environmental problems, emphasising their complexity and, therefore, the need to develop critical thinking and problem-solving skills; it also indicated the need to utilise diverse learning environments and a broad array of educational approaches to teaching/learning about and from the environment with due stress on practical activities and first-hand experience.[8]

Following upon these conferences several countries undertook pilot projects on the feasibility and organisation of environmental studies. In the Ukraine, the Faculties of Natural Science and Geography of the Kiev Pedagogical Institute in collaboration with the Central Young Naturalists' Association and the Scientific Research Pedagogical Institute of the Ukrainian SSR inaugurated a project on 'The methodology and interdisciplinary research concerning the integration of school and society in the field of environmental education.' The study included: 1) obtaining data on the perception, attitudes and behaviour of 12-16 year-old teenagers vis-à-vis their natural and social environment; 2) making them identify environmental problems in their study of the proper use and protection of their environment; 3) testing those involved in the project and the control group; 4) evaluating the methods used to expand the pupils' knowledge and improve their behaviour towards nature, and 5) selecting the best methods and materials to be used within the Soviet Union and possibly beyond. Apart from schools, several communities with different physical, ecological, social and economic characters took part in the project.[9]

The novelty and impending importance of the subject for Soviet society as a whole led to the calling of an All-Union Conference in Minsk in 1979 (3-6 July). The outcome was a number of recommendations directed to the Ministry of Education of the USSR and those of the Union Republics, the Central Committee of the Komsomol, the State Committee for Technical and Vocational Training, the Ministry of Higher and Secondary Specialised Education of the USSR and those of the Union Republics, the State Committee for Publishing and Book Trade, the State Committee for Cinematography and the councils of the Societies for the Protection of Nature, which were all called upon to contribute in their respective fields formal and informal education and disseminate ecological information.[10]

Steps to promote research and teaching in this new field had already been taken by several

institutions of higher education and will be
described further. As to the Academy of Educational
Sciences of the USSR, it had set up (within its
Research Institute of Content and Methods of
Teaching) a Laboratory of Ecological Education with
a staff of ten research workers. During the 1976-80
five year period its research centred on estimating
the interdisciplinary nature of environmental
education. In the course of the present (1981-85)
period the main emphasis is on how to develop in
pupils a sense of responsibility towards their
environment, including also moral and legal issues.[11]

Extensive urbanisation often results in children
growing up in an urban, so-called 'grey environment'
and they may never develop any knowledge of or
feeling for the 'green environment', that is the
countryside. They may visit it occasionally on a
day's outing as indifferent, ignorant and possibly
destructive tourists or else, later, as insensitive
developers whose perception of the landscape will be
limited to evaluating whether the site is appropriate
for building a factory or power-station.
Environmental education is called upon to alter this
approach whilst also arousing among rural youth a
love of nature that will encourage them to stay on
the land.

Surveys of juveniles' attitudes and understanding
of ecological problems have been carried out not only
in the Ukrainian project mentioned above. In 1978
and 1979, pupils in the Tartar and Mordovian ASSR
were asked to answer the following questions: 1) what
causes have made it necessary to protect nature?
2) how can it be done? 3) why is it necessary to
conserve a great variety of species? 4) what forms
of pollution do you know? 5) what is the meaning of
the term 'anthropogenous factor'? and 6) what forms of
nature utilisation can be called rational? Some
4,500 essay-type answers were analysed as well as
oral answers recorded during 62 lessons and those
of participants in two school olympiads in the
Tartar ASSR (232 in 1978 and 241 in 1979). Children
aged 11-12 perceived the protection of nature in
personal terms such as not throwing cans, bottles
and rubbish into rivers and lakes, lighting bonfires
in woods, breaking or chopping down trees, raiding
birds' nests, etc. Older teenagers stressed the
importance of natural parks and hunting restrictions;
the majority knew of the existence of the 'red book'
of protected species but were uncertain about the
species listed. Those aged 16-17 were aware of the
adverse effect of polluted air and water on human

health and tended to single out industrial chemicals as the main polluters. Even among senior form pupils, aged 17 plus, the idea of a rational utilisation of nature was understood as limiting forest felling, excessive hunting and over-fishing. Few were those who knew of the wider issues such as the rising level of CO_2 in the atmosphere, desertification or the side-effects of modern agricultural methods. Earlier sample surveys carried out in 1973-4 and 1976 by the Laboratory of Ecological Education of the Academy of Educational Sciences of the USSR had revealed a similarly patchy and often out-of-date understanding of modern problems.[12]

Hitherto environmental education was carried out mainly in pioneer and Komsomol summer camps, in young naturalists' circles and in the course of other out-of-school activities. Now, it is being introduced into science and literature lessons and lessons in productive labour. The latter take up two to four weekly hours of the school timetable and also a continuous period of about four weeks of the last summer vacation between grades IX and X. There are moreover voluntary summer 'rest and work camps' as well as juvenile forestries and agricultural communities where youngsters spend part of their summer vacation.

An All-Union Conference on the Problems of Ecological Education in the Secondary School was held in 1980 in Tallin, Estonia. Of its four sections one dealt with papers on environmental education as a part of Communist education, stressing its ideological, moral, aesthetic and international aspects and also its interdisciplinary value. Another section was devoted to the role of environmental education in the teaching of school subjects, especially geography, the biological sciences, literature and productive labour. Since the study of the environment has its roots in out-of-school activities, possibly the most imaginative papers were presented in the relevant third section, while the fourth turned its attention to new approaches in teacher training and refresher courses designed to bring older teachers up-to-date on problems of environmental education.

There was a general consensus that environmental education should not be yet another school subject, but that it should introduce a new understanding of the actual and impending man-made changes in nature and instil in the young the principles of a rational and caring management of the biosphere and the noosphere. So far, hardly any textbooks have been written or teachers trained in didactic methods to explain to the young the links of causality, conscious endeavour and historical processes which bind nature and society. Starting from V.I. Vernadskii's view that humanity has now become an ecological force,[13] the teacher has to translate this broad concept into the day-to-day contents of his lessons. This is bound to affect the syllabus of several school subjects, for instance that of biology, where the tendency has been hitherto to study first the cell, then the organism and the species, while postponing to much later the notions of biocenosis and biosphere. Similarly, in geography, the emphasis has been on regional and economic factors and little was said about ecosystems. But it is perhaps in the teaching of the social sciences that most changes will have to be made because environmental education involves many ideological, moral, aesthetic and legal implications. While a good deal of discussion is going on about these theoretical aspects, there is an equal preoccupation with practical methods and experimentation in the field of environmental education.

Since such experiments are of general interest even in capitalist societies, a few examples of practical environmental education are worth reporting before going on to more controversial issues. For example, in the town of Piarnu, Estonia, pupils decided to transform some waste land in the old and derelict part of the city into a small park, doing all the spade work and planting trees themselves. Later, when the town decided to lay out a forty-eight hectare park, pupils were called upon to help; now the tradition is for every senior form to plant one oak tree to commemorate graduation; so the number of trees grows annually, maintaining a link between former pupils and their school.[14]

In many parts of the USSR there are school forestries, some of which are quite famous like the Berendei in Karelia and others in the Urals, the Bryansk province and in Transcarpathia. In the RSFSR in 1979, they numbered nearly seven thousand, covering an area of two and a half million hectares and attracting over 300,000 teenagers.[15] Belorussia boasts even a Junior Forest Academy; it is run on the lines of extension courses and has two faculties 'Sylviculture' and 'Forest Conservation'. Introductory lectures are given by members of the Belorussian Technological Institute and subjects set for essays; the Ministry of Forests has organised 'consultation points' in the twelve forestry enterprises of the republic; in the following July teenagers do some practical work in the morphology and systematics of plants. At the end of this part-time three-year course, youngsters get a certificate which will facilitate their entry to higher technical institutes with a forestry bias.[16]

In less ambitious school forestries pupils help transplant saplings in spring, prepare artificial nests, establish ant-heaps, repair mangers in which fodder is left in winter for wild animals and birds; they map out and make tourist paths in the woods, placing notices to mark places of interest such as springs, or the habitat of rare plants, or simply to identify tree species; at marshy points they place planks or stones; in autumn they gather seeds and plant them in the forestry's nursery; in general, they are discouraged from picking flowers merely for herbaria.

At Aktyubinsk in Kazakhstan, older pupils with the help of the local Society for the Preservation of Nature act as tourist guides showing people through the countryside and impressing on them the need to protect the environment. In the Urals, some schools organise 'complex' expeditions to study types of soil, plants that grow on them, their distribution and association with other plants, kinds of ants and other insects to be found in the given ecosystem. Later in the school year they hold a conference at which speakers from among the participants describe their observations and contribute to the school museum of natural history.[17]

Many schools send out 'green patrols' to keep out poachers and vandals. There are also 'blue patrols' keeping an eye on lakes and rivers to protect spawning areas or discover possible sources of pollution, and observing the results such as the proliferation of algae; they take samples of water to be analysed during chemistry classes.

On a more modest scale, much useful work can be done and much natural history learnt within school grounds by sowing and tending plants or placing nest boxes for tomtits in public parks.

All these activities, apart from any practical usefulness, have important educational value since they train youngsters in the art of observation and teach them to understand the links between cause and effect in natural phenomena. The requirement to either fill in a questionnaire or write a report of their findings, often illustrated with maps and drawings, teaches them to be articulate and precise;

hopefully it prepares them for independent research.

In the senior forms, a broader aspect of environmental education is introduced especially into the social science course by bringing in the notion of 'nature-society'. Any purposeful management of the biosphere requires a thorough investigation into a great variety of factors and verges on systems analysis. Once a socially important goal is decided upon, the first step is to gather information about the present state of the system to be modified, then to foresee the possible effects of alternative methods to be used and evaluate the economic and technical costs of the project. For instance, to secure an adequate supply of electricity for the Baikal-Amur railway line now under construction, it was necessary to build a dam on the Angara river. Pupils were informed about the magnitude of the project and the geographical setting. They were given maps and data of the natural resources of the area to be flooded, account being taken of the interests of the agriculture, timber, fishing and mining industries as well as human settlements. A discussion followed regarding the two most suitable sites 'A' and 'B' as well as the possibilities of building not a hydropower station but a coal fuelled, or an atomic one. The teacher provided rough estimates of alternative costs. Eventually, under his guidance, they came to the same conclusion as the actual state planners who having first considered siting the hydropower station at point 'A', transferred their choice to 'B'.[18]

The element of novelty that environmental education is bringing into teaching is causing problems for teachers. Thus the biology teacher may be a middle-aged woman reluctant to lead a group of boisterous kids and share the primitive living conditions during an adventurous foray into some more or less uncharted wilderness; or she may excel in describing the morphology of familiar plants, but be less expert at observing their behaviour when growing on different soils and in different associations.

A teacher trained on the mainland may be bewildered by the ecosystems of the volcanic Kamchatka peninsula.[19] Among the Komsomol leaders in charge of pioneer camps - where up to ten million school children spend about four weeks of their summer vacation - many have a scant knowledge of botany and little understanding of the complexity of ecosystems. Indeed, many may be students from faculties of history or modern languages of some urban pedagogical institute doing their spell of practical training. They are themselves in need of environmental education. This is increasingly provided by the mass media and, in the case of teachers, by new courses in pedagogical institutes as well as refresher courses for older ones, particularly in the techniques of preparing and organising field work.[20] A considerable number of pamphlets are now being published on ways to protect the environment, on its effect on health and on the enforcement of the relevant legislation. The first advanced standard textbook on ecology has been published by the Moscow University press to supersede the hitherto much used Russian translation of E.P. Odum's Fundamentals of Ecology.[21]

Forest conservation is a recurrent theme partly because about one third of the USSR is still forested and partly because forests have suffered badly from excessive felling to meet construction and fuel needs and, in the western parts of the country, from the ravages of war. Apart from their economic value, forests reduce the adverse effects of pollution on human health and provide recreation grounds for the growing urban population. In fact, much of the reafforestation carried out after World War II has taken place in the industrialised European parts of the Soviet Union, and studies are now afoot to estimate which species of trees survive best and act most efficiently as natural filters.[22]

This brings us to the topic of research into anti-pollution technology and the wider aspects of environmental studies in establishments of higher education (VUZ). A set of rather general instructions was issued by the Ministry of Higher and Secondary Specialised Education of the USSR in April 1979 shortly before the Minsk Conference.[23] Faculties of social science were to introduce courses in the methodological, philosophical and economic aspects of the protection and rational utilisation of natural resources and train specialists to act as inspectors in this new field. More specialised courses in dust and smoke abatement, air and water purification systems are to be taught in higher technical and secondary specialised schools preparing engineers and technicians for industries liable to cause emission of pollutants. Diploma projects as well as more advanced research in environmental protection methods and devices are to be encouraged, ranging from new types of coagulating and absorbing agents or catalysts to the designing of closed cycle production processes when

wastes of the initial production can be used as raw
materials for the next or, at least, when water from
cooling towers can be re-used again and again.
There should be more research into the recultivation
of slag heaps, the opportunities of fish farming and
into mutagenous agents. Considering the inextricable
complexity of most environmental research projects it
is advisable that several - often highly specialised
VUZy - should combine into multidisciplinary centres.
     One such federation of VUZy exists already,
namely the North Caucasian Regional Scientific Centre
which encompasses several VUZy in the towns of Rostov,
Novocherkassk, Krasnodar, Stavropol' and those of
Daghestan. This centre has established close
relations with major industrial enterprises such as
Atom-mash, Rostsel'mash, Azot and the oil industries
of the Grozny region. As a result, gas in these oil
fields is no longer flared off but captured and put
to use.[24]
     Among other leading institutions in the field
of environmental education is the Belorussian
Technological Institute, where a Chair of Nature
Protection has been established. It draws up
programmes for other VUZy in the republic. As
mentioned earlier, it sponsors the Junior Forestry
Academy. The Ministry of Higher Education of Belorussia has twice organised seminars for lecturers in
this new field but so far the relevant courses are
still optional.[25]
     At the University of the Urals in Sverdlovsk
there is also a Chair of Biocenosis (ecosystems) and
Nature Protection. It provides courses which are
a regular part of the syllabus for biology and
chemistry students as well as optional courses for
students of other faculties. There also are more
specialised courses in the ecology of plants, of
animals and soils as well as one on the theory of
the biosphere based on the works of V.I. Vernadskii.
In 1959, research was started on the recultivation
of slag heaps resulting from coal-mining and the
mining of iron and non-ferrous ores. In 1961, a
Laboratory of Industrial Botany was set up within
the faculty of Biological Sciences and experiments
are now conducted by staff and students on areas
totalling five thousand hectares. The Laboratory
has been involved in joint projects with other
institutions such as the University of Perm', the
Research Institute of Soil Science and Agrochemistry
of the Siberian section of the Academy of Sciences
of the USSR, the Central Laboratory of Nature
Protection of the Ministry of Agriculture of the

USSR, etc. Results of this work are published in
its own periodical Rasteniya i promyshlennaya sreda
(Plants and Industrial Environment) or in other
scientific journals. The need for recultivation is
urgent, especially because of damage done by open-
cast mining in Siberia. The aim is to find plants that
will grow on rubble poor in nutrients and often
contaminated by salts of heavy metals. With the
addition of top soil saved (the layers of which are
thin in cold climates) and adequate fertilisers some
plants will grow but they are usually too contaminated
to be used as fodder, though the recultivated areas
can be made into parkland for recreational purposes and
eventually contribute to soil formation.[26]

In many VUZy, students take part in ecological
research, for instance in the 1979/80 All-Union
student science and technology competition, there
were 102 entries on environmental education out of a
total of 15,282; this compares unfavourably with the
809 on machine-building, but favourably with the 43
on astronautics.[27]

These are just examples and it is too early to
assess the results of measures taken by other
institutions to fulfil the injunctions of the
ministerial order of April 1979. In any case, it is
quite beyond the competence of the present writer to
give even an outline of the technico-scientific
research that would achieve the ultimate goal of
non-polluting production.

However, apart from courses in highly
specialised technology, there are others designed
to become constituent parts of those in philosophy,
political economy and scientific communism. One
such outline has been proposed by Prof. Morachevskii
of the Leningrad Hydrometeorological Institute. It
would deal with: (1), General problems, namely
a) the energy balance 'sun-atmosphere-surface of the
Earth' and forms of human intervention; b) ecological
effects of such intervention; c) optimal utilisation
of nature as reflected in Soviet legislation on the
environment. (2), Associated problems, namely
a) methods of pollution control appropriate to
various industries; b) indirect anthropogenous
actions on the biosphere and their possible results.
(3), Social problems, including a Marxist criticism
of Western conceptions of 'human development and the
environment'.[28] Essentially this would mean
criticising scientific determinism which fails to
take into account the possibilities of social change.

Environmental Education as a Component of Communist Upbringing

The value and effect of such courses as a part of Communist upbringing designed to culminate in the emergence of the New Man are bound to be controversial. Firstly, because it is not certain to what an extent ecology fits into the Marxist-Leninist ideology or whether it may underpin other ideologies even better. Secondly, because the very term prirodopol'zovanie is ambiguous, for it implies two different concepts – one is a knowledge and understanding of ecological systems and processes, while the other envisages a conscious endeavour to use this knowledge in order to manipulate and manage natural resources and phenomena for the benefit of human societies; such manipulation includes changing living species by selection and genetic engineering and eventually transforming climates. Hitherto our knowledge of ecology may have been inadequate or even erroneous, but the laws of nature as such apply equally in capitalist and socialist societies and – at least in the case of physical laws – apparently throughout the Universe. On the other hand, the actual ways in which man exploits and alters nature depend on deliberate choices. The ways chosen can and often have been destructive; hitherto – mainly through ignorance but, with greater knowledge, mankind may become even more destructive either through sheer malice or as a result of an international scramble for resources which would lead to nuclear, chemical or biological war and the extinction of life on Earth. Yet greater knowledge may be creative too, and – since the chain of cause and effect knows no political boundaries – such creativity may promote collaboration and not war. To put it differently, science is neutral but its application depends on choice.

Although Marxism postulates that there are objective laws of economic and social development, it also forecasts that when mankind will have overcome natural constraints it will pass from the realm of necessity to that of freedom; in other words the time will come when subjective choices between various options will become possible. We seem to be approaching that crucial moment for, given the will to do so, mankind has now the knowledge and capacity to overcome poverty, hunger and disease in the world, if only it would give up wasteful consumerism and the lunacy of the arms race.

A good management of the Planet implies the rational organisation of people as well as things. Hence the present Soviet concern with a rational

management of society, <u>nauchnoe upravlenie</u>
<u>obshchestvom</u>.   Such an organisation would free men
from the irrational forces of both Nature and the
Market.   On the other hand it would limit their
freedom of action <u>vis-à-vis</u> other individuals and
also to treat nature as they please - all too often
to the detriment of other people and nature as well.
So the choices become political and even moral.
Some problems are fundamental.   For instance, what
right has man to use and own what he has not created?
Can the Planet belong to individuals or even to
nations or is it the property of Humanity as a
whole?   The question is not purely academic - it has
arisen in respect of oceans and outer space - and the
United Nations have proclaimed both to be the
property of Humanity as a whole.   If Humanity is to
become an ecological force can it go on being split
into tribes, nations or military alliances?   Writers
- at least Soviet optimists - can imagine Humanity
only as united.   Some have even written books or
articles entitled <u>Humanity - what art thou?</u>[29] or
<u>Mankind - what is it for?</u>[30]   Some foresee a cosmic
role for mankind in the future, others of a more
practical bend propose to move house from an
unbearably polluted Earth into space, possibly on
some O'Neill type of platforms.   Probing further
into the Cosmos some have wondered whether Marxist
laws of development applied to extra-terrestial
civilisations or even if life in these far away
conscious beings was based on protein compounds.[31]
     But to return to Earth.   Quotations can be
found in the works of Marx and Engels to the effect
that Nature can take revenge if pressed too hard, or
that the wastes of one industry can become the raw
materials for another.   Lenin did initiate
environmental protection laws prompted by the sight
of some men sawing down trees for firewood in the
Sokolniki park.[32]   So there is a slot in Marxist-
Leninism to accommodate environmental education.   An
aesthetic appreciation of nature arouses love for
the countryside - the grace of the slender silver
birches in the heartland of Muscovy among the
Russians, or the grandiose mountain scenery of the
Caucasus among Georgians;   the very harshness and
silence of the long winters may evoke patriotic
feelings among the inhabitants of Siberia just as
much as lush orchards may among those of Moldavia.
Patriotism is regarded as a virtue in the Soviet
Union but what about nationalism - the love of one's
own little corner at the expense of a wider world
that may be shunned and its fellow men perceived as

aliens and possibly enemies?   After all,
environmental education does teach to preserve the
beauty of one's environment and keep out the
predators, the developers and, inevitably, the
representatives of the far away, central planning
authorities.   So could environmental education
breed militant local nationalism?

It might bring out even deeper emotions - an
unscientific quasi-superstitious attachment to
Mother Earth, mat' syra zemlya, a nostalgia for a
more primitive, pagan, pre-industrial way of life
which has inspired the writings of the Russian
derevenshchiki and probably even more so the
literature of ethnic minorities.   A kind of Antheus
complex.   Then the smoky chimneys, the dangerous
power stations, the spraying of crops is not merely
pollution but the rape and poisoning of Mother Earth
- matricide.   Whatever you may be told about the
wonders of mature socialism, you may turn away from
it to seek elsewhere a new heaven and a new earth.
So environmental education may sow the seeds of
doubt, doubt in a materialistic civilisation as the
ultimate goal of mankind.

Apart from seeking an ideological ally in
environmental education many hope to find in it an
ally in the moral upbringing of the young.   Much is
written about Communist morality.   In many ways it
is reminiscent of the Christian 'love thy neighbour',
that is of the horizontal relationship to the
creation;   but any vertical relationship, that is
any search for the Creator is denied, derided and
outlawed.   Like all forms of secular morality,
Communist morality is an acceptance of and
compliance with the ideas and attitudes conditioned
by contemporary human environment.   It is a set of
conditioned reflexes and internalised conventions.
Nature does not conform to human conventions of
right and wrong or good and evil.   There have been
over the centuries many discussions about 'natural
law' and a variety of utilitarian theories of
morality.   However, the observable evidence tends
to show that the overriding law of nature is the
survival of the fittest in the struggle for survival.
Unfortunately, this is often also the case in human
societies and the Soviet Union is no exception.
Unfortunately too, in human societies the word
'fittest' has many connotations such as the most
ambitious, resourceful, cunning, devious, ruthless,
etc.   This is sometimes known as social Darwinism.
Yet, despite the obvious fact that it is all too
often more advantageous to be selfish than altruistic,

man has always sought for something higher than himself, has always had a strange longing for unprofitable virtues and has been ready to sacrifice his life for an idea or an ideal. Communist morality also preaches selflessness and sacrifice for an ideology. Ecology does not seem to corroborate that this is a natural law. The New Man is not the natural man, for he, too, is expected to be something far superior to the average Soviet citizen. The New Man, like his predecessor, the eighteenth century Good Savage, can be found only in literary fiction.

However, if environmental education has little to contribute to Communist morality, it brings out the interdependence of ecosystems and in an indirect way the interdependence of human societies. Global problems have come to the fore. Their importance has been recognised in the Soviet Union and they are being studied at the All-Union Scientific-Research Institute of Systems Analysis attached to the State Committee for Science and Technology of the USSR.

Education is a two-way affair. Not everything that a teacher teaches sinks into the mind of the pupil. His mind is, naturally, selective. So what is the response of pupils to the new subject? It seems to go down well with the younger ones, possibly because much of it is taught away from the classroom, more by doing than listening and in an atmosphere of self-government. However, by the age of 15-17 years, the fun of taking part in green and blue patrols and planting trees has worn thin while problems of global ecology are beyond the horizon of the average teenager whose time and mind are involved in personal affairs. It is too early to forecast how the children of today will act when they become the planners and builders of tomorrow except that they will have a better grasp of ecological problems than their predecessors.

Conclusions

1. In the USSR, as elsewhere, the natural environment is at risk.
2. The Soviet leadership has reluctantly recognised the fact and seeks to reconcile development and the protection of nature.
3. Environmental education makes people aware of the problems; in small ways, but on a large scale, schools are helping to protect nature.
4. When present-day teenagers become the planners and engineers of the future, they will be

more sensitive to nature unless greed, fear of a
capitalist encirclement or plain miscalculations
prevail over good intentions.

    5.   Environmental education may be usefully
integrated into courses of Marxism-Leninism, but it
could also strengthen the appeal of nationalism and
sow doubt on the value of a materialistic civilisation
whether run on socialist or capitalist lines.

    6.   Lastly, it could lead a growing number of
people to face up to problems of global ecology and
the need for very large-scale, in fact, global
cooperation.

NOTES

    1.   Barbara Ward and René Dubos, Only One
Earth; the Care and Maintenance of a Small Planet
(André Deutsch, London, 1972).

    2.   D.H. Meadows et al., The Limits to Growth,
a Report to the Club of Rome, (Earth Island, London,
1972).

    3.   On dangers from atomic power stations,
N. Dollezhal' and Yu. Koryakin, 'Yadernaya
elektroenergetika: dostizheniya i problemy',
Kommunist, no. 14 (1979), pp. 19-28; Report of a
conference on the philosophical problems of global
ecology organised by the Pushchino Centre for
Biological Research and the Institute of Philosophy
of the AN USSR, Voprosy filosofii, no. 1 (1981),
pp. 163-168. See also Zh.A. Medvedev, Nuclear
Disaster in the Urals (Angus and Robertson, London,
1979).

    4.   Recent enactments of the Supreme Soviet
of the USSR on the environment: O merakh po
dal'neishemu uluchsheniyu okhrany prirody i
ratsional'nomu ispol'zovaniyu prirodnykh resursov,
20 Sept., 1972; Ob okhrane atmosfernogo vozdukha
and Ob okhrane i ispol'zovaniyu zhivotnogo mira,
25 June 1980: decrees by the CC of the CPSU and the
Council of Ministers of the USSR, Ob usilenii okhrany
prirody i uluchsheniyu ispol'zovaniya prirodnykh
resursov, 29 Dec., 1972 and O dopolnotel'nykh merakh
po usileniyu okhrany prirody i ratsional'nomu
ispol'zovaniyu prirodnykh resursov, 1 Dec., 1978.

    5.   Pravda, 2 Dec., 1980.

    6.   Pravda, 24 Feb., 1981.

    7.   Connect, vol. I, no. 1 (1976), pp. 1-9.

    8.   Idem., vol. II, no. 2 (1977), pp. 1-4 and
vol. III, no. 1 (1978), pp. 1-8.

    9.   Idem., vol. III, no. 2 (1978), pp. 5-6
and vol. VI, no. 2 (1981), p. 2.

10. Connect, vol. V, no. 2 (1980), pp. 3-4; Byulleten' Ministerstva vysshego i srednego obrazovaniya SSSR, no. 9, (1979), pp. 27-36.
11. Personal interview with I.D. Zverev, Director of the Laboratory.
12. I.D. Zverev and F.M. Eisen (eds.), Problemy ekologicheskogo obrazovaniya i vospitaniya v srednei shkole: tezisy dokladov Vsesoyuznoi konferentsii (Tallin, 1980), part I, pp. 78-82; A.N. Zakhlebnyi, Shkola i problemy okhrany prirody (Pedagogika, Moscow, 1981), pp. 27-28.
13. I.V. Kuznetsov, 'Estestvoznanie, filosofiya i stanovlenie noosfery: o rabote V.I. Vernadskogo Nauchnaya mysl', kak planetarnoe yavlenie', Voprosy filosofii, no. 12 (1974), p. 131; English translation entitled 'Vernadsky's Theory of the Noosphere', Social Sciences, no. 4 (1975), p. 40.
14. Zverev and Eisen, Problemy..., part II, pp. 5-8.
15. Zakhlebnyi, Shkola i problemy... p. 29; B.G. Ioganzen and N.A. Gorodetskaya, Sel'skaya shkola i okhrana prirody, (Prosveshchenie, Moscow, 1976), pp. 62-78.
16. Zverev and Eisen, Problemy..., part II, pp. 30-32.
17. Idem., part II, pp. 17-22.
18. Zakhlebnyi, Shkola i problemy..., p. 124.
19. Zverev and Eisen, Problemy..., part II, pp. 29-30.
20. Idem., part II, pp. 124-125.
21. V.D. Fedorov and T.G. Gil'manov, Ekologiya, vol. I (MGU Press, Moscow, 1980).
22. Yu. Z. Kulagin and E.M. Yafaev, 'K probleme ozdorovleniya promyshlennoi sredy', Rasteniya i promyshlennaya sreda (vol. 5, Sverdlovsk, 1978), pp. 136-142.
23. Byulleten' Ministerstva vysshego..., no. 6 (1979), pp. 13-15.
24. Yu. Zhdanov, 'Vuzovskii regional'nyi tsentr nauki', Kommunist, no. 14 (1979), pp. 29-38; V.G. Nemzer, 'Ekologicheskoe vospitanie budushchikh pokolenii', Vestnik vysshei shkoly, no. 8 (1980), pp. 25-26.
25. S.E. Savitskii and S.G. Kovchur 'Sdelat' kurs obyazatel'nym', idem., no. 11 (1980), pp. 34-35.
26. G.M. Pikalova, 'Itogi 15-letnikh nauchno-issledovatel'skikh rabot laboratorii promyshlennoi rekul'tivatsii zemel', narushennykh promyshlennost'yu', Rasteniya..., vol. 5 (1978), pp. 5-13.
27. Byulleten' Ministerstva vysshego... no. 12

(1980), pp. 12-13; idem., no. 3 (1981), pp. 31-32 and p. 37.

28. V.G. Morachevskii, 'Za shirotu ekologicheskikh znanii', Vestnik vysshei..., no. 11 (1980), pp. 33-34.

29. V. Davidovich and R. Abolina, Kto ty chelovechestvo ? teoreticheskii portret, (Molodaya gvardiya, Moscow, 1975).

30. I.V. Zabelin, 'Chelovechestvo - dlya chego ono?', Moskva, no. 8 (1966), pp. 172-186 and no. 5 (1968), pp. 147-161.

31. V. Abarstumyan and V. Kasyutinskii, 'Astronomiya i problemy mirovozzreniya', Obshchestvennye nauki, no. 3 (1977), pp. 119-122.

32. S.K. Gil', Shest'let s V.I. Leninym, (Moscow, 1957) quoted in G.T. Suvorova, Les v zhizni cheloveka (Arkhangel'sk, 1980), pp. 56-57.

Chapter 5

VOCATIONAL EDUCATION IN THE USSR

Felicity O'Dell

Vocational education in a broad sense is the theme
of this chapter. All the main aspects of Soviet
education that are directly aimed at teaching
people to work will be examined. Labour training
for school-leavers is one important area but it
does not stand alone in that education for work is
fundamental to the whole of the Soviet education
system from crèche onwards.

The topic falls into three areas each of
which will be examined in turn: (1), The place and
purpose of Soviet vocational education. (2), Labour
training at the different stages of the contemporary
education process. (3), Problems and trends in the
vocational schools and colleges. Concern throughout is with the contemporary situation and the ways
in which it is likely to develop in the eighties.

The Place and Purpose of Soviet Vocational Education

Soviet education is explicitly vocational. It
declares its main purpose to be the development of
people capable of being the 'Builders of Communism'.
What does this lofty title mean in practice? It
refers to a range of moral values and practical
skills which will enable Soviet citizens to bring
their country to the desired level. Many of these
values and skills are closely associated with labour
training in that communism is seen as being attain-
able only through the establishment of a strong
industrial state.

The reasons for the significance of
vocational education in the USSR are both ideological
and economic. Love of work occupies an important
position in the Soviet moral code. It is through
his attitude towards work that a man can ultimately
be judged.[1] The good citizen loves his own work
and aspires always to do it to the best of his

106

ability; he also respects the labour of others. The extent to which a person possesses these qualities is the yardstick whereby we can measure his worth. It is also through work that the individual is expected to find his purpose in living and his happiness. Because of this fundamental position of the virtue of love of work Marcuse has termed Soviet morality a <u>work-morale</u>.[2] From another point of view too, love of work is ideologically important; it is a quality which is both desired by the Soviet authorities and easily legitimated by reference to Marx and Lenin. It is much less easy to justify the other basic Soviet virtue of patriotism through quotations from the Marxist classics.[3]

Economically, the need for vocational education is clear. After taking power the Bolshevik Party were faced with an economy in ruins and a depleted and largely unskilled work force. To achieve their aim of rapid industrial growth they had to train people in the skills necessary to develop the economy and to instil in them the commitment to the cause that would make them willing to labour unstintingly in the name of communism.

The ideological and economic imperatives for the development of vocational education are no less significant now than they were in the twenties. In addition, there are certain aspects of the contemporary Soviet economic position which are causing concern and are affecting the current nature of labour training. There is still as strong a need as ever to develop disciplined, committed workers who are prepared to do humble jobs and to devote them-selves to the building of communism. Other factors, however, are new.

Certain of these are due to the nature of the technological revolution. This is leading in many cases to quick changes in the precise character of the jobs which many workers are required to carry out.[4] In other words, the economy now needs workers who are flexible enough to be able to change their specialisms as changing circumstances necessitate. Their initial labour training needs to give them the basic technical knowledge and skills which will stand them in good stead however technology develops. In addition, workers at all levels need to be creative if the economy is to benefit from the technological revolution to the full. Lack of an innovative, imaginative approach to work is one weak area of Soviet workers' attitudes which is causing planners concern and which they are currently trying to remedy through an improved labour training programme.

Another fundamental problem of the contemporary situation is the fact that labour is now quite a scarce resource. There are more jobs available than there are people. As a result labour turnover is high as people move from factory to factory trying to find the position which suits them best. Among a certain group of workers there is little fear of being punished for infringement of labour discipline - they know that if they lose their job they will find another without any difficulty. Excessive labour turnover is felt to be harmful to the economy and legislation has been introduced restricting the right to change jobs to twice in any one year without reduction of certain pension rights. Vocational training is also expected to play its part in reducing turnover by improving vocational guidance and by strengthening moral education to increase young people's feelings, of responsibility and discipline towards their work.[5]

The fact that labour is no longer plentiful means that productivity can be increased only through a better work discipline and a higher standard of working.[6] Recent Party pronouncements on work tend to emphasise quality and efficiency. A greater concern with these virtues is seen as essential for the improvement of the Soviet economy if it is to be able to satisfy its own requirements and to compete in world markets. The Soviet agencies of labour training are accordingly increasingly concerned with developing efficient work habits and attitudes of always striving to do one's best.

Two areas of activity have particularly suffered from their low prestige in the Soviet Union and attempts are currently being made to improve their position. These areas are the service sphere and agriculture. Young people have shown a reluctance to go into these fields and so there has been a heightened concern, on the one hand, with raising their status and, on the other, to promote more effectively the tenet fundamental to Marxist morality that all work is valuable no matter how humble it may seem.

The above problems relating to the technological revolution, scarce labour resources, quality of work and a low level of attractiveness for certain jobs are those which are currently giving rise to most debates among those involved in vocational education in the USSR and in looking at the contemporary labour training process it will be seen how attempts are being made to solve these problems.

Vocational education in the Soviet Union is seen as having three basic facets. At different levels of the education process these facets have differing degrees of importance. They are:

1. Moral education in the desired attitudes towards work.
2. Training in practical work skills and habits.
3. Vocational guidance.

The moral education element means giving young people certain attitudes towards work. They are to be trained to see in it their main path to individual fulfilment. They are to see it as a way of contributing to their motherland, which should be for them both a duty and a joy. They are to respect all kinds of work regardless of the level of qualification necessary to carry out the job in question. On the other hand, they must also be encouraged to study to the full extent of their abilities so that they can give 'more' to the motherland. The paradoxes inherent in some of these elements of the Soviet work ethic have been discussed elsewhere.[7] The moral education facet of the labour training process is important at all stages of the education system.

Training in practical skills also begins with the youngest pupils but becomes more precise as the children grow older, achieving its greatest significance perhaps in the post-school stages of vocational education. This facet of labour training does not consist merely of teaching youngsters how to use their hands and how to manage different tools and materials. It is also a matter of training people in certain work habits basic to the whole organisation of Soviet society in general and that of work-places in particular. This means learning to work as part of a collective, subordinating oneself to the requirements of the leaders of the collective and acting first and foremost in accordance with the needs of the group. Discipline is another work habit important to the Soviet structure of work. It is necessary to discipline oneself in order to fit in with the demands of the collective and of the plan. The plan is a feature of Soviet life dominating work in all spheres. From the earliest age, schoolchildren have to learn to regulate their activity according to a plan imposed from above. Socialist competition is another

characteristic of the structure of work in the
Soviet Union and this also is a feature of labour
training at all levels.   Many of these work habits
are learnt simply through the overall structure of
the activities of the school or college in that
these, with their pupil and staff soviets, their
plans and competitions and their collective
discipline, are but a parallel of Soviet work life
in general.

Vocational guidance is the third facet of labour
training and this is mainly limited to work in the
later years of the secondary school.   It is an area
to which greater attention is recently being paid.[8]
The aim is to guide pupils into those occupations
where the economy has a need of workers.

How are these three aspects of labour training
put into practice at the different stages of the
education process?

Labour Training at the Different Stages of the Contemporary Education Process

At present the Soviet child has a compulsory ten
years of education.   After eight years, at 15, he
can choose whether to stay at secondary school or to
enter a vocational school and combine the last years
of general schooling with a trade training.

Soviet educationalists divide their education
system into six areas - pre-school upbringing,
secondary schools, out-of-school education, technical
trade schools, secondary specialised colleges and
higher education - and the nature of vocational
education in each of these six areas is considered
below.   The vocational element is clearly most
significant in the technical trade schools and
secondary specialised colleges which have training
for work as their primary function but even pre-
school upbringing is expected to make its contribution
towards the training of the future Soviet work force.

Pre-school Upbringing.   Pre-school upbringing covers
training both at home and in an institution.   It is
naturally harder for the state to control the
upbringing of children at home.   Nevertheless, with
work training as with other aspects of moral upbringing, the state does try to guide parents to teach
children the values with which they would be
inculcated at pre-school institutions.   To do this
the help of all the media is enlisted.   Television
programmes for parents suggest the need for and ways
of teaching youngsters a love of work and children's
programmes demonstrate, for example, modelling skills

or show adults doing different jobs stressing the social significance of even the most humble work. Books and magazines for parents and pre-school children carry the same message. Some work-places run courses for parents of young children and labour training is an inevitable component of such a course. It is easier to organise systematic labour training if the pre-school child is at a kindergarten. There the child will spend a lot of his day playing, walking in the fresh air and resting but from the youngest group upwards there are expected to be some daily periods of learning activity. For the youngest pupils there will be one such session of 15-20 minutes in the morning and one in the afternoon. The frequency and duration of such activities increase as the children get older. Many of the learning sessions have a direct work training focus, for example, simple handicrafts and work on the kindergarten's plot of land. Children are also taught in such sessions about the jobs of adults, particularly about those doing work characteristic of the local area. Play too is expected to be directed to train, where possible, in basic labour skills and attitudes. All pre-school institutions possess a range of construction toys, model tractors and toy washing-machines.[9]

Such toys would be found in most Western kindergartens but a more Soviet flavour becomes evident when one looks at recommendations to Soviet upbringers on how to guide play and learning activities. These guidelines were prepared by an educationalists' conference on the work instruction of children in pre-school institutions.[10] The conference was held in 1978 and its proposals indicate areas where results have not been satisfactory up to now and to which especial attention must be paid in the eighties. Above all they stress that work activities are to be used to develop feelings of responsibility, duty and love for work. Work attitudes are, thus, given more prominence than actual practical skills. From the earliest age a greater independence is to be promoted. Children are to be helped to reason for themselves how best to do something rather than simply to be shown what to do. They must be trained always to do a task to the best of their ability, to distribute among themselves responsibilities for the work of the collective and to act in a cooperative way, planning their work as a team and giving help to each other where needed. The aim of what is being done is always to be made clear to the children and in such

a way that they are inspired to achieve the aim.
From the earliest opportunity the Soviet authorities
are trying to prepare the well-organised, perfect-
ionist, independently creative and work-loving adults
they would like to see in their factories and farms
but who, all too frequently, are lacking at present.

Secondary Schools. The training begun in the
kindergarten is continued and developed in the
secondary school. An important aspect of vocational
education here is that many schools have as their
patron one local factory or farm. As a result,
much of the labour training given at the school is
linked to the work of the patron enterprise.

The standard curriculum gives Soviet pupils
two lessons in labour training per week for the
first eight years of their course followed by four
hours in the ninth and tenth years. In addition
they have five full days of practice in the fifth,
sixth and seventh years and a month in the ninth
year. Children at schools where the language of
instruction is not Russian have an extra burden in
having to study their native language and literature
as well as Russian and a Western foreign language and
most such schools help to make time for this by
reducing labour training lessons from two periods to
one in the first seven years. Apart from the amount
of time allowed for options other subjects are not
affected. Labour training is possibly permitted to
be cut in this way because the work done in its
sessions is parallelled in so many extra-curricular
activities and the work attitudes taught are not
the exclusive concern of the labour training classes
but are reinforced in all other class subjects.[11]

In the secondary school attention is paid to
all three basic aims of vocational education. The
first two are an extension of those of the kindergarten - to socialise in attitudes of enthusiasm and
responsibility towards work and to teach practical
skills. The third aim, that of vocational guidance,
has been increasing in importance over the last
decade and is likely to continue doing so in the
eighties. It is hoped both to guide pupils into
jobs where there are acute labour shortages and to
avoid later labour turnover by a more thoughtful
and thorough system of careers guidance. A
pedagogics textbook for training teachers finds four
basic tasks for vocational education in the school,
though the first two just emphasise slightly
different aspects of the fundamental socialisation
goal.[12] Firstly, it points to the need to educate

an interest in and love for different kinds of work
and to foster a desire to work.   Secondly, there is
the nurturing of a communist attitude towards work.
Thirdly comes the equipping of pupils with labour
knowledge, skills and habits and, fourthly,
providing pupils with an interest in different kinds
of jobs, helping them to choose a profession for
themselves and to find suitable employment.
      What exactly are schoolchildren taught in their
labour lessons?   In the three primary years, they cut
paper, make plasticine, clay and papier-mâché models,
look after plants, arrange and tidy the classroom and
do other light school maintenance tasks.   Pupils
from the fourth to the eighth classes usually spend
their labour training lessons in the school workshops.
Objects are made from metal, cloth, wood and other
materials and pupils learn to handle simple tools and
machines.   During this period boys and girls often,
though not always, are separated for their labour
lessons with the traditional guiding of boys into
metalwork and girls into sewing.   It is at this age
also that serious vocational guidance work begins.
Work instructors and class teachers provide
information about the nature of specific jobs.
Where possible, outside speakers are brought in to
talk to the children about their work and workers
from the patron enterprise;   parents and instructors
from local vocational schools are made especial use
of here.[13]
      Thus pupils learn most about the kind of work
available in their local area.   The emphasis in
Soviet vocational guidance is much more on
encouraging people into specialisms for which there
is a local or general need rather than on analysing
the aptitudes of the individual and fitting these to
a profession regardless of whether or not there is
work available or social requirement for people with
that profession.
      After the eighth class an increasing number of
pupils leave to enter a vocational school.   Those
who remain at secondary general school have an even
greater element of vocational guidance in labour
lessons.   Excursions to local work-places are
organised and discussions with workers arranged.
At this age also pupils often do some of their
practical work in the ninth grade, in real factory
conditions, both helping the enterprise to fulfil
its plan and themselves to learn about the use of
real machines and materials.   They are also paid
for such labour.   The press prints glowing reports
of pupils who use their wages to buy their schools

equipment or to arrange excursions for groups of pupils. It was estimated in 1978/9 that of all senior pupils doing practical work in real working conditions 25 per cent were involved in work in industry, 39 per cent in agriculture, 17 per cent in transport and communications, 4 per cent in catering and trade and 2 per cent in construction.[14]

Apart from work actually in the factory, the building site or the fields or in the school workshops, there has been a growing tendency in the late seventies for pupils to receive much of their labour training in inter-school production combines. These started in Moscow but now exist in many other places.[15] They are frequently housed in schools that are no longer used and they consist of a range of workshops, laboratories, vocational guidance centres and labour museums. Local enterprises each have departments in the combine and send workers to act as instructors there, so that pupils are trained by specialists and in realistic conditions. Pupils from different schools attend the combine and have the advantage of being able to sample a variety of jobs while under one roof. It is likely that the provision of such combines will continue increasing and there will be attempts to improve their facilities. At present, pupils are often felt to spend too short a time per week there and the range of jobs in which the combines offer training is not always wide enough.[16]

As well as the timetabled labour lessons, other school classes have a direct vocational element. Once a week the class teacher has a period with her class and this is supposed to be used regularly to reinforce socialisation in work values. Optional subjects, for which two hours are now allowed in the seventh year, three in the eighth and four in the ninth and tenth, are frequently work-related. Car mechanics and typewriting, for instance, are subjects offered in many schools. Technical drawing is also studied once a week by all pupils in the seventh and eighth classes. All in all, the Soviet secondary school justifies, in the prominence it gives to a range of technical subjects, the description of polytechnical which it frequently applies to itself.

Even in less obviously relevant subjects a work training element is often present both in teaching about practical skills and in socialising the desired work attitudes. This is noticed, for example, even on the very first page of a primary class reading book. This addresses itself to Octobrists, the youth movement for the youngest pupils and it says

> Octobrists are the Pioneers of the future.
> Octobrists are industrious children who love
> their school and respect their school. They
> respect older people.
> Only those who love to work can be called
> Octobrists.[17]

Geography courses emphasise the economic geography
of the countries studied and point out the
differences in working conditions under capitalism
and socialism.   Practical work is also an
important part of geography classes with much field
work involving use of map, compass and so on.[18]   In
the teaching of all science subjects the applied
possibilities of any topic are always stressed.
History lessons look particularly at workers' movements over the years in different parts of the world.
Soviet history for fourth formers focusses on such
work-related topics as 'the labour victories of
Soviet people after the Great Patriotic War...
electrification...the construction of new plants and
factories...on the collective farm...shock-workers of
Communist labour'.[19]
   Few English eleven-year olds would have their
history lessons give such attention to British
labour achievements or parallel aspects of working
life here.
   Foreign language classes read texts
emphasising the heroic nature of Soviet work,
contrasting it with alienated labour in the West.
English textbooks particularly stress how Lenin
studied and loved English.   A typical poem about
Lenin follows.   This encourages children to work
and study and be inspired by Lenin and it is
intended for use as choral recitation practice by
fourteen-year old learners.   The verses go well
to the tune of 'Thy hand, O Lord, has guided Thy
flock from age to age' and the words have a not
dissimilar religious feel.

> We stand before a portrait
> Upon the schoolroom wall
> We see the face of Lenin
> So known and loved by all.
>
> We often bring him flowers
> And twine them round the frame
> We children honour deeply
> His ever cherished name.

> We promise 'we shall study
> To master all you taught'
> And say 'we're always ready
> In lessons, work and sport'.[20]

The social studies course for final year pupils
has a section devoted exclusively to labour which,
it says, will be the main purpose of the private life
of each person under communism.   The communist man
will not only have a deep need for work, he will also
need to work according to his full abilities.[21]
In different ways, therefore, all subjects in
the Soviet school curriculum now play some part in
vocational education.   How is the role of the
secondary school in labour training likely to develop
in the eighties?   There are not infrequent press
reports of dissatisfaction with what is done at the
moment.   The odd paradox has been noted, for example,
that children spend more time writing in labour
lessons than in Russian language classes.[22]   Fewer
than a quarter of school-leavers and young workers
in one survey said that a school teacher or even a
parent had been the deciding factor in their choice
of future job.[23]   There is criticism that labour
lessons are dull, irrelevant and waste useful
resources.[24]   That the socialisation work carried
out by the school as a whole is not fully
satisfactory is evident from the reiterated demands
to improve in this area.
Already new syllabuses for labour training
courses have been drawn up and have started being
implemented in 1981/2.   The overriding aim here
seems to be to give pupils skills which will be
directly useful to society.   Some pupils in the
fourth to sixth classes are now following courses
dealing with service labour - they learn, among
other things, how to prepare sandwiches and coffee,
how to use and repair a sewing machine and how to do
simple household electrical work.[25]   There is a
growing tendency to give schoolchildren labour tasks
to perform which are in themselves beneficial to the
economy.   Some educationalists feel that children
would be better encouraged to work as postmen or in
the service sphere rather than to do unproductive
exercises in school workshops.[26]   An extremely
effective agricultural brigade of schoolchildren in
the Altai region is commended.   This brigade has
organised a highly mechanised plot of land whose
revenue has risen from 16,000 roubles in 1970 to
52,000 in 1973.[27]   Both the moral benefits for the
schoolchildren involved and the economic benefits for

society are to be admired.   Greater creativity and
independent thought are to be promoted.   Praise is
given to schools in Azerbaidzhan where pupils are
involved in all sides of agricultural work on the
schools' plots of land - planning, book-keeping and
evaluation of results as well as practical work on
the land.[28]   Attention is also drawn to the practice
of schools in Buryatia where labour training
frequently takes the form of problem-solving
activities.   Children are sent out to do research
into the working habits and histories of people in
their area.[29]   Other groups of children in Dagestan,
are studying the effects of pests in forest areas
and are trying to find ways of combating them.[30]
To sum up, vocational education in the secondary
school in the eighties is likely to develop along the
following lines suggested above:

1.   The tendency to increased vocational
guidance will continue and attempts will be made to
improve as well as to increase provisions for
fulfilling this aim.
2.   There will also be an increase in both
the quality and the quantity of inter-school
production combines.
3.   There will be more emphasis in labour
training syllabuses and classes on skills that are
most urgently needed by contemporary society.
4.   Schoolchildren will be increasingly used
to carry out productive tasks useful to the economy.
5.   Ways will be investigated of encouraging
pupils to think in an independent and creative manner.
6.   The struggle will continue to try to
educate pupils with a communist attitude towards
labour, with a strong sense of responsibility and
cooperation and with a desire always to do their
best at work.   An inter-disciplinary approach is
likely to be at least as fully used as it is at
present.

Out-of-school Education.   What the child does
out-of-school is also not neglected by Soviet
educationalists nor is his spare time considered as
purely recreational.   It is thought of as being yet
another opportunity for education, frequently in
relation to work.   Out-of-school activity is
organised by a large number of institutions - the
school, the youth movement, inter-school production
combines and so on.   The provision of facilities
for children's out-of-school entertainment and
instruction is already extensive, but is rapidly

expanding.

In 1979 there were 4,785 Pioneer or Pupil Palaces or Houses in the USSR, an increase of just over 40 per cent over the number existing in 1965.[31] These buildings are clubs organised either by local schools or, more often, the youth movement (the Pioneers). The largest are called Palaces and they are to be found in the capitals of all the republics and in other important regional towns. In appearance and content they are indeed palatial and the Leningrad Pioneer Palace is even housed in a former palace on the Nevsky Prospect. Their aim is to 'develop the creative interests and individual abilities of children'.[32] Each House or Palace contains a variety of special interest clubs catering for enthusiasts in, say, chess, physics, aeroplane modelling, drama or sport. The work of the clubs often has a vocational bias and their activity is guided by trained adults.

In addition in 1979 there were 1,273 Young Technicians' and 793 Young Naturalists' Centres, an increase of 220.65 per cent and 175.34 per cent respectively over the 1965 figures. These, as their names suggest, are clubs for children with particular technical, botanical or zoological interests. Equipment and materials are supplied for the technicians to develop their creative skills and the young naturalists are encouraged to study their local flora and fauna. They also help with conservation work in their area and look after and observe small animals and birds.

Another interesting facility available for children in some parts of the Soviet Union and with a clearly potential vocational significance is the Children's Railway. There were 39 of these in 1979. In 1965 there were 33 showing that there has been a less dramatic increase here. Children's railways are staffed entirely by children who act as drivers, ticket sellers and collectors, planners and maintenance workers and so on.

Summer Pioneer Camps are the most numerous facility provided by the Soviet state for its children. In 1979 there were 57,763 of these, an increase of 138.6 per cent over the provision for 1965. Large numbers of children spend at least part of their three-month summer vacation at a camp. The camps are often under the aegis of a particular factory or institution so that a parent will obtain a place for his child through his work-place. Usually, children spend one month there and the average size of a camp is 500 children at any one

time.   The routine of camp life is strong and, like
Scout and Guide camps, has a distinct military
flavour.   The very routine helps to train in the
work-related virtue of discipline.   A variety of
clubs operate in the camp, modelling, musical, chess
and so on and the children spend time in sporting,
hiking and para-military activities.   These are often
competitive, so that the Pioneer camp in its
organisation backs up the work of the school in
preparing young people for the kind of social
organisation they will later meet in factory or on
collective farm.

Music, Art and Dance Schools are another facet
of the extracurricular opportunities available to
Soviet youngsters.   There were 7,364 of these in
1979, an increase of 160.3 per cent over 1965.
Similarly, there were 6,196 Sports Schools, an
increase of 144.41 per cent.   These figures do not
refer to the special schools attended full-time by
children with a particular artistic or sporting
talent.   They offer after-school facilities to
those with perhaps less outstanding ability.   Music
schools, for example, take children from the age of
seven.   Parents have to pay for the instruction
given and their children will be taken on only if
they pass a hearing and a musical aptitude test.
Many of the young people who attend these schools
two or three times a week, later enter musical
vocational colleges and become professional
musicians of some kind.[33]   Similarly, children who
have attended art, dance or sports schools not
infrequently end up in professions using the skills
that were developed there.

The overall number of facilities for children
to use in their spare time rose by approximately
100 per cent between 1965 and 1979.   Other
opportunities not mentioned above include children's
libraries, theatres and clubs organised by the armed
forces and by individual factories.

Out-of-school activity is important in two ways
as far as vocational education is concerned.   Firstly,
it gives children and opportunity to develop in a
more sophisticated way any particular talents or
interests that they may have and which the school
programme does not give full scope to.   Secondly,
it reinforces the work of the school in terms of
work values and habits.   At the Pioneer Club or
the Young Technicians' Centre the child will be
encouraged to respect work and to do it as
diligently as he can in the same way that he is
taught to do so at school.   It is likely that the

facilities will continue increasing and improving
in an attempt to restrict young people's exposure to
potentially different, even hostile, attitudes
towards work which they might come across at home or
on the street.

Technical-trade Schools. This section of Soviet
education and that which follows are those which
are concerned most exclusively with vocational
training. The intention here is to give a brief
outline of the structure of these two fields of
education and then to return to specific problems
and trends in their development after a consideration
of the role of higher education in vocational
training.

Technical-trade schools[34] cover the lower levels
of institutionalised vocational training. The
current Soviet trend is to give work training even
for an elementary type of job at an institution rather
than on-the-job. The institutions at which the
first levels of professional training are given are:

1. Technical-trade Schools (PTUs)
2. Secondary Technical-trade Schools (SPTUs)
3. Technical Schools (TUs)

For all such schools there is rarely an entry
examination. Pupils are selected on the basis of
their general school marks and a test is given only
when the specific job to be taught requires it.
Thus, for example, a drawing test may be given to
those wishing to enter the Leningrad school for
china-painters and a language examination to aspiring
type-setters. Certain applicants are given
preference: orphans, children from children's homes,
children of invalids, young people recommended to
the school by the enterprise or the collective farm
where they are already working, children of workers
at the factory or farm to which the school is
affiliated and young men just demobbed after their
National Service.

Pupils are given some material incentives to
attend such schools. Time spent studying there is
counted as work experience in future salary
calculations. Payment is given for work done in the
base enterprise while training. Hostels are
provided when the school accepts pupils from other
towns and all pupils are given free food and work
clothing. In agricultural technical-trade schools
pupils also receive a grant.

On graduation all pupils are given work in

their specialism and are expected to stay in that job for three years or at least until, if boys, they are called up. Graduates may be exempted from immediate work on production if they gain particularly high marks and would like to continue studying. They may, for example, enter a secondary specialised institution without taking an entrance examination or they can apply for a place on a daytime higher education course. If their aim is to be an 'engineer-pedagogue', the lofty name given to teachers of practical subjects in a technical school, then they are allowed precedence in entry to an appropriate higher educational institution.

The above conditions apply to all three types of technical-trade schools but there are also some differences between the training offered by these different institutions.

Technical-trade Schools (PTUs). These schools provide pupils with a basic work training but not with any general education. Often their main role is now not so much to run daytime classes but to give evening and shift courses so that workers can study at times compatible with their work shifts. In this way workers gain a qualification without leaving their jobs. Work-places cooperate in this by permitting study leave. To prepare for and sit examinations, workers are allowed 30 days off per year during which time they are paid 50 per cent of their average salary.

The length and level of courses offered by PTUs vary. PTU no. 19 in Leningrad offers evening courses for technical draughtsmen lasting 20 months and open only to those who have completed a full ten-year general education. PTU no. 71 in Leningrad, on the other hand, provides evening and shift courses of 7 months for railway attendants and these are open to applicants with a minimum of eight years schooling. Some PTUs, moreover, do not only give initial job training but also run courses enabling experienced workers to raise their qualifications.

Secondary Technical-trade Schools (SPTUs). These are schools which take pupils who have completed eight years at secondary school and provide them not only with a work training but also with the final two years of compulsory general education. If he passes his final examinations after three years of study and practical work, the pupil receives both a general education certificate and a diploma in, say, lathe-turning, tractor-driving or watch-repairing.

The network of secondary technical-trade
schools has grown very rapidly in recent years and
the authorities are anxious to persuade eighth class
school pupils that SPTUs form a worthy alternative
to the final two years at a general secondary school.
As has been seen, attending a vocational school
offers slight material advantages and pupils are
encouraged to feel that they are not abandoning
their chances of higher education if they leave the
general secondary school after the eighth class. It
will be seen later how far the incentives are
successful and the encouragements justified.

Technical Schools (TUs). These schools offer
full-time courses and are open only to pupils who
have completed ten years of secondary schooling.
They do not give general education classes. Like
pupils at agricultural PTUs and SPTUs pupils at all
technical schools are paid a basic grant. This is
usually 30-37 roubles but increases by 15 to 20 per
cent if excellent marks are achieved in all subjects.
Technical schools provide courses preparing pupils
to be, for example, house-painters, photographers or
waiters with knowledge of a foreign language for
Intourist hotels. Particularly successful graduates
of these schools are given preferential treatment if
they decide to apply for an evening or correspondence
course at a higher educational institution. Courses
in TUs usually last from a year to eighteen months.

Secondary Specialised Colleges. The technical-trade
schools described above are administered by the
State Committee on Vocational and Technical Education
which is responsible for all aspects of their courses
and planning. Secondary specialised colleges,[35] on
the other hand, come under the auspices of the
Ministry of Higher and Secondary Specialised Education.
They provide vocational training at a rather higher
level. They are subdivided in the Soviet literature
into technicums and colleges but the different name
signifies only the type of specialism offered by the
institution. Technicums train personnel for industry,
agriculture, construction and transport whereas
colleges (uchilishcha) mainly train specialists in
health, education and culture. Thus Leningrad has
57 technicums training, for example, ship-builders,
veterinary assistants and computer technicians and
36 colleges preparing nurses, upbringers for
pre-school institutions and cultural club organisers.
Some of the courses offered at these colleges
accept students who have completed only eight years

of school, whereas others stipulate a full
secondary education.   Students enrolled after only
eight years' schooling are expected to complete their
secondary education at the college itself or in an
evening school.   The length of courses varies with
both the type of specialism and with the educational
level of the student intake.   Leningrad's regional
medical college trains nurses and midwives in two
years ten months if they have eight years of
schooling and in one year ten months if they have
already completed their secondary education.   Radio-
constructors are similarly trained in either three
years ten months or in two years eight months.   Some
specialisms can be studied on evening or correspondence
courses run by these colleges.   Through evening
classes one can, for example, become a rubber
technologist, a choir leader or a nurse.   Nursing is
not available as a correspondence subject but many
technological and cultural professions are.

As well as in the level of their courses, these
colleges differ also from the technical-trade schools
in that applicants are selected on the basis of
special entry exams.   Those who have eight years of
secondary education and wish to enter a college to
study one of most of the available specialisms must
take a dictation test in Russian and an oral
mathematics exam.   Eighth class school-leavers who
apply for a music, art, theatre or other cultural
college, replace the mathematics test with an oral
examination in Russian language and literature.
There are three different sets of examinations for
applicants who already have a full secondary
education.   Candidates for all types of college must
do a written examination in Russian language and
literature but they will also have an oral test in
either mathematics, chemistry or the history of the
USSR, depending on what type of course they wish to
follow.

Anyone who has at least eight years of
secondary schooling may apply to do an evening or
correspondence course at a college but there is an
age limit of 30 years on applicants to full-time
courses.   Certain applicants are given precedence:
those who got excellent marks on leaving secondary
or technical-trade school;   those who have at least
two years of work experience in an area related to
the specialism applied for;   men who have just been
demobbed;   people directed to the college by the
factory or farm where they are already working and
orphans.

Many of the students at these colleges receive

grants, particularly if they are doing courses related to agriculture where there is felt to be an especial need for specialists. In less urgent fields they may receive a grant only if they have already two years of practical experience. All students are paid for any productive work they may do as part of their working practice and are given free working clothes.

On graduation all students are found work in their specialism and are expected to stay in that job for three years. Exceptions to this are those students who obtain excellent marks in all subjects and ten per cent of those who have a combination of excellent and good marks. These top graduates have the right immediately to enter the day department of a higher educational institution. Other graduates have the right to enter directly only the evening or correspondence departments of higher educational institutions.

More attention will be paid to the nature of the programmes at technical trade schools and secondary specialised colleges and to particular problems of their organisation and place in modern Soviet society after a brief discussion below of higher education.

Higher Education. Like other areas of education in the USSR, Soviet higher education has a strongly vocational flavour. Courses not only give students theoretical information but also train them to do specific jobs. Students of English at the Maurice Thorez Institute of Languages in Moscow, for example, do not merely study the language in depth, they also choose to train as either a translator or a teacher. Practical work forms a major part of the programme on any course.

Entry to higher educational institutions (whose courses usually last five years) is selective through an entrance examination. Attempting to be helpful to those who have left school some time previously, many institutes have now opened preparatory departments.[36] These were first set up at some institutes in 1969 to try to iron out social differences in opportunities and to give those who are already working the chance to raise their level of qualification to that of higher education. About one fifth of all students in their first year of study at many institutions now come from preparatory departments.[37] These have not proved quite so satisfactory as was hoped. Students who have come from preparatory departments tend to have a lower

124

success rate throughout their courses than do students who have come straight from school.[38] Moreover, the departments tend to be exploited by students who failed to get a place in higher education on first leaving school and who have worked the statutory two years before joining a preparatory department.[39] In other words, these departments are seen as an easy route to higher education rather than being used by workers who after some years of experience on the job wish to give their practical knowledge a stronger educational basis.

There is a lower level of competition for entry to evening or correspondence departments of higher educational institutions than to day departments. Many Soviet students take advantage of these opportunities for part-time study, combining work on production with studying for a degree. In the academic year 1979/80 there were 5,186,000 students in Soviet higher education of whom 653,000 (13 per cent) were in evening departments and 1,601,000 (31 per cent) were in correspondence departments.[40] It is accepted that the difficulties of combining work and study make a slightly lower standard of degree inevitable for those who are not studying full-time but, nevertheless, such students are felt to be valuable to the economy in that they give a more rational use of labour resources and also help to spread the skills provided by higher education throughout production.

An interesting type of higher educational institution found in the Soviet Union is a technical institute attached to a large industrial enterprise. These institutes are referred to as zavody-vtuzy.[41] The aim of these is to prepare engineers from among the workers already attached to the patron enterprise. The average period of study is five and a half to six years. Students also tend to receive a grant that is 15 per cent higher than that received by other students. The extra material incentive thus given to students at zavody-vtuzy is doubtless due to the important practical role they are felt to play in the economy through attracting those who already have strong practical knowledge of an enterprise into a scheme which will prepare them to be engineers of exactly the profile required by the enterprise in question.

Over the seventies there has been an increasing tendency in higher education, as at lower levels, to try to encourage more independence and creativity on behalf of the taught. This has made itself felt

at institutes through students - even at undergraduate
level - being encouraged to devise and carry out their
own small research projects.[42]   This is likely to be
a continuing trend as the authorities try to produce
a generation of more inventive and innovative
engineers and other specialists.

In one area in particular the higher educational
institution is blamed for not carrying out its
development of students' work values adequately. This
is in fostering any desire of the students to put what
they have learnt into practice on production after
graduation. Far more students aspire to do research
or design work than are needed by society and there
is a reluctance to go into work in industry.[43] Those
who are compulsorily sent to work on production after
graduation do so often with a bad grace and change
positions at the earliest opportunity.   Such
attitudes clearly are not likely to create a lively
productive atmosphere among those doing engineering
level jobs at the factory.

As a result the once high prestige of engineering
as a profession is declining. Komsomol'skaya Pravda
recently wrote with concern that there is now much
less competition for places at engineering institutes
and students of only poor quality are enrolled.   The
newspaper points out that this is certainly not
advantageous for society as a whole but it is
advantageous for certain groups.   Parents are glad
to see their offspring obtain an education.   The
young people concerned are only too happy to get a
diploma.   The institute staff find life easier if
they do not fail their students - how then can they
complain?   The factory director then gets skilled
manpower 'cost-free' and so why should he not use it
cheaply in place of technicians, foremen and sometimes
even workers while sending the hourly wage earners off
to help at vegetable depots, Pioneer camps or with the
mowing.[44]   Reports are also frequently heard of
engineers being sent off to bring in the harvest. It
would, thus, seem that it is not only the higher
educational institution which is to be blamed for not
instilling their students with an enthusiasm for work
on production but also the system is to be blamed for
not always using its engineers and their professional
training to the best possible advantage.   It is
probable that educational theorists will continue to
tell the institutes to improve their character
education work but the attitudes which are causing
concern are unlikely to alter unless there is a more
fundamental change in the organisation of labour at
the factory.

Higher education in the USSR is systematically and emphatically vocational, building as much practical work into the courses as is possible and finding different ways of encouraging those who already have work experience to study for a degree. Such students bring valued practical knowledge to their studies and they are also socially useful in that they demonstrate clearly that social mobility is possible through the Soviet system of education. Innovation is possibly easier to implement at the higher levels of education and certainly the current stress on more independent, creative work has been put into practice most quickly here. Work values are, however, probably harder to influence at this stage of development, although this is an area that is still causing some concern. Having outlined some of the main aspects of vocational training in relation to Soviet higher education let us now turn to consider some of the main preoccupations in connection with the vocational schools and colleges.

Problems and Trends in the Vocational Schools and Colleges

There are a number of problems and trends which relate to the process of labour training as a whole, or to the vocational schools and colleges in particular, which need further attention. These can be considered under the following broad headings:

1. Contingents of students doing different types of vocational training.
2. The prestige of vocational courses.
3. Teaching and content of vocational courses.
4. Vocational schools' relationship with other organisations.
5. Success of labour training process.

Contingents of Students Doing Different Types of Vocational Training.

At the age of fifteen the Soviet child either stays at the general school or else leaves to attend a secondary technical-trade school. Which path do most youngsters choose to follow?[45] In the 1979/80 academic year there were approximately 5,500,000 children in the ninth, tenth and eleventh forms of the general school (the eleventh form exists only in certain republics where the local language poses particular problems). In comparison there were 3,935,000 students in PTUs, of whom 2,069,000 were in schools giving a secondary course as well as a trade training. As has already been seen, some eighth-form leavers go straight to a

secondary specialised college although many of the
student body there have a full secondary education.
In the same academic year there were approximately
4,646,000 students in such colleges of whom 62.6 per
cent were on daytime courses, 11.2 per cent were in
evening departments and 26.2 per cent were in
correspondence departments.

If we compare these figures with those of only
nine years previously, the most dramatic change is
seen in the area of secondary technical-trade
education.   In 1970/1 there were only approximately
180,000 pupils in the day departments of secondary
PTUs.   Over the decade there has thus been an
increase of 1049 per cent.   The number of such
schools has risen over the same period from 615 to
4026, an increase of 555 per cent.   These striking
changes are simply due to the central decision to
develop this type of education in the early seventies
in order to create a generation of young people more
thoroughly trained for work than those who had
started work immediately after leaving the general
school.

A comparison of the numbers of students in
secondary specialised colleges over the same period
shows that numbers here have also risen, though less
sharply.   The total number of students in this
branch of education has increased by 5.9 per cent.
There has been a slight decline in the number of
evening students with only a very slight increase in
those doing correspondence courses.   The proportion
of those doing daytime courses has risen from 58 to
62 per cent.   The sociologist, Filippov, approves
this tendency in that the standard reached by day
students is inevitably higher.   Moreover, after
graduation it is easier to distribute day students
into those jobs for which there is the greatest need
for them.[46]

The increases noted above in the numbers of
those doing institutionalised vocational training
become even more striking when it is remembered that
the size of the school-leaving age-group which forms
the bulk of the student population has fallen
throughout the seventies.   Nevertheless it must not
be felt that there are hardly any young people left
going straight into work after leaving the general
school.   It has been estimated that approximately
two million school-leavers, one third of the total
age-group, go straight to a job receiving there
their basic training.[47]   This is felt by many
planners to be a problem both for the factories
which have to provide on-the-job training and for

the young workers who are less likely to experience
job satisfaction or to get a training which will
stand them in such good stead in their future
career.[48]   There is still scope, therefore, for the
expansion of the institutionalised vocational
training programme and it is certain that this will
continue developing in the eighties.
    Are the young people who attend vocational
schools or colleges, as opposed to going either
straight to work or to a higher educational
institution, typical of the population as a whole in
terms of sex and social background and are there
republican or urban/rural differences in the patterns
of labour education?
    As far as sex is concerned, there are
differences in the vocational education patterns of
boys and girls.   Women have an appropriate share of
the places in higher education (52 per cent) and a
rather favourable proportion of those in secondary
specialised colleges (56 per cent).[49]   They are a
small proportion of the pupils in PTUs, however;
they do not provide more than 30 per cent of the
intake there and in some republics their share is
substantially less.   It is not more than 1 to 3 per
cent in such schools in rural areas of Lithuania,
Estonia and Tadzhikistan.[50]   For those girls who
leave school and go straight to work without any
formal training the standard of on-the-job
preparation is felt to be particularly low.   In a
study of some machine-tools enterprises, it was found
that despite the fact that the average level of
schooling was slightly higher for girls than boys,
boys made much more rapid progress through the low
job grades, staying only 1.5 years in the first
grade, whereas girls stayed 4.6 years.[51]   The Soviet
writers commenting on these figures blamed the factory
authorities for undertraining the female members of
the work force and for neglecting the fact that women
are on average more disciplined and responsible in
relation to their work than men.   The not untypical
pattern emerges that women fare well in the
educational process, particularly at its higher
levels, but when it comes to their job experience
they are less likely to succeed than men are.
    A school-leaver's social background affects the
educational path he is likely to follow also.   The
higher the level of the educational institution and
the higher its status, the greater the proportion of
the children of the intelligentsia to be found
there.[52]   This does not, of course, mean that there
are no children of working or peasant origins at

Moscow University but their share of the student population does not correspond to their share of the total Soviet population of the appropriate age. At the lower levels of vocational education, workers' children participate fully. A study of students at secondary specialised institutions in Nizhni Tagil found that their social background was more or less equivalent to the distribution of social classes in the town as a whole.[53] The vocational school with the lowest status in the USSR is the agricultural PTU and it is there that the social group with the lowest prestige, the collective farm peasantry, is much more extensively represented than elsewhere.[54]

Geographical factors, as well as those of gender and social background, help to determine likely educational patterns. The development of PTUs has taken place in all the republics although it has been faster in those republics where there is an especial demand for qualified labour. The increase in numbers of PTU graduates over the last few years has been most marked in Uzbekistan, Georgia, Azerbaidzhan, Kirgizia, Tadzhikstan, Armenia and Turkmenistan. The average increase in output in the USSR between 1975 and 1978 was 8.4 per cent. The percentages for the above seven republics were 36, 20, 23, 17, 15, 38 and 50 per cent respectively.[55] The growth has been slowest in the Baltic republics where the system was more fully developed prior to 1975, and industry was already better supplied with qualified workers. Despite the increases noted above, the proportion of students in PTUs in Central Asia still falls below that of the Slav republics; in Central Asia only seven to eight per cent of the 16 to 18 age-group were in PTUs in 1978, when it was twice that proportion in Russia, the Ukraine, Belorussia or Kazakhstan.[56]

The urban/rural distinction is an extremely important one in the Soviet Union. There is a tendency for young people to want to move to the towns, causing a shortage of young labour in rural areas. Specialists are reluctant to return to work in country areas so that skilled workers (including teachers, doctors and so on) are also in regrettably short supply. Vocational schools are being built to train specialists in agriculture both to improve the efficiency of work done on the farms and also to raise the status of those working in agriculture. Building agricultural PTUs has not always reached its planned levels; in 1979, the chairman of the State Committee on Vocational and Technical Education, Bulgakov, insisted that each region must have its own

PTU preparing workers for collective and state
farms, adding that this aim had been achieved in the
Leningrad region and in the Mari ASSR but that many
areas were still deficient.[57]
    In conclusion, the contingents of students at
Soviet vocational schools and colleges are not
representative of the population as a whole in terms
of gender and social and geographical background.
This is causing concern for economic planners mainly
with regard to the urban/rural dimension but attempts
are also being made to create a more balanced system
within the union republics and to provide greater
opportunities for people of working origins in the
higher levels of the educational process (through
the establishment of preparatory departments, for
example).

The Prestige of Vocational Education.   Many of the
points made above relate very closely to the question
of the prestige of different types of educational
paths.   Generally speaking, the type of education
which enjoys the highest prestige is that where the
student body is primarily urban, from the
intelligentsia and in an industrially advanced
republic.
    The situation has changed in recent years,
however, in that the disproportionately high status
of the higher educational institution has
diminished.[58]   In the sixties and early seventies
80 to 90 per cent of school-leavers aspired to
higher education and many of these were inevitably
destined to disappointment.   Through the seventies
the prestige of other forms of institutionalised
vocational training has risen.   In a survey carried
out in 1979 among older schoolchildren it was found
that 33.5 per cent wanted to go straight into
higher education whereas 14.9 per cent wanted to
study in a technicum and 12.9 per cent wanted to go
to a technical-trade school.[59]   There are thus
going to be fewer disappointed school-leavers in the
next year or two.   This does not mean that the
aspirations of young people now fully correspond
with the plans of the state.   Filippov reports that
there is a serious lack of applicants for certain
types of technical-trade schools, for some technical
higher institutes and for certain departments of
teacher training colleges.[60]   The technical-trade
schools where there is a shortfall of applicants are
in particular those with an agricultural profile,
but the attempts to raise the status of agricultural
work have not so far been successful.

The other professional area with particularly
low prestige in the sixties and early seventies was
the service sphere.[61]   Here the position has changed,
if not for the reasons sought by the state.   Work in
a shop has now become an attractive job and pupils
are happy to attend schools training for such work.[62]
The shortage of certain products in Soviet shops
gives those who work in them a strong bartering
position as their access to scarce goods is so much
easier than that of the majority.
    To sum up, the higher educational institution
is still the most prestigious form of education in
the USSR but many school-leavers have now become
more realistic in their aspirations.   The establishment of a fuller system of institutionalised
vocational training has doubtless facilitated this
in that there are still very few school-leavers who
would like to go straight to work on production.[63]
Those who would once have opted for a university are
now content with a secondary specialised college or
even a technical trade school.

Teaching and Content of Courses.   There are a number
of problems concerned with the teaching and content
of courses at vocational schools and colleges.   It
is frequently pointed out that, although the
secondary PTUs are intended to give a general
education that is as good as that of the ordinary
secondary school, the standard of general education
there is not so high as in the ordinary school.[64]
This is partly because the best pupils stay at
school so that they can try the easiest route to
higher education and partly because the better
teachers of academic subjects prefer to stay in the
schools with the better children and the higher
status.
    What is the training for the teachers of
practical subjects in the technical-trade schools?
Usually they are people with a secondary
specialised education, less commonly a higher one,
and who have spent some time working on production.
Training of teaching staff for vocational
institutions takes place mainly in industrial-
pedagogical technicums and occasionally in
engineering-pedagogical departments attached to a
number of higher educational institutes.   In 1978
the first special institute devoted to training
engineer-pedagogues was opened.   This is located in
Sverdlovsk and it aims to give both an initial
training for teachers of practical subjects in
vocational schools and colleges and also to provide

courses for raising the qualifications of those who are already working in the field.   It is planned in future to open other institutes of this profile.[65] In this way it is hoped to raise both the standard and the status of teaching of vocational subjects. In comparison with teachers of other subjects, those involved in labour training have had a relatively low likelihood of having higher education and this has lowered the standing of the profession.

To turn to the content of courses at the vocational school, there is particular concern to give these a broad profile, so that students can transfer their skills to another related specialism without too many problems if changing industrial conditions necessitate this.   In this way PTU pupils are taught not only the subjects narrowly related to their own future job, they also learn the fundamentals of mechanics, electronics, technology and the organisation and economics of production.[66] It has been stated by the last Party Congress that improved methods of training in vocational schools are necessary to create a work force that can cope with the demands of technical progress and that will be able to raise labour productivity,[67] two of the particular problems of the contemporary Soviet economic situation referred to at the beginning of this chapter.   The programmes being developed to try to help overcome these difficulties include far more problem-solving and programmed learning.   In the new courses, pupils at secondary PTUs spend about 60 per cent of their 36 hour week on production training and subjects related to their profession.[68] Teachers are urged to link the information given in general education classes to the specific working qualification aimed at.   The priority is not, therefore, to make courses identical to those of the general secondary school.

Although it is protested that educational standards should not be reduced for those children who have left school after the eighth class, it is clearly felt that it is the vocational element that is of prime importance.   It would seem unlikely that the academic standards of the secondary PTUs will ever equal those of most general schools.   The basic aim of the SPTU is naturally more to train skilled workers than to ensure that its graduates are well-equipped to enter a higher educational institution. There are already more than enough aspirants for higher education leaving the secondary schools. While Soviet educationalists are proud that their system provides relatively easy access to all types

of learning for all those who might at any time
wish to take advantage of it, they are on the whole
more anxious about the quality and efficiency of the
future work force.

Vocational Schools' Relationship with Other
Organisations. Some problems are also arising from
the relationships of the vocational schools and
colleges with other organisations.   Their relations
with both local schools and factories are far from
simple.   The general school, for instance, is
often reluctant to lose its pupils to the SPTU, just
as the pupils are frequently unwilling to go, and so
the vocational schools do not always find it easy to
achieve their planned intake figures.[69]   In the
Russian republic in 1973 there was a shortfall of
18.5 per cent between the planned intake figure of
715,500 and the realised one of 583,000.   In the
Ukraine the shortfall was similar, at 18.6 per cent.
        Links with local factories are also problematic.
Some factories have refused to take PTU graduates,
saying that they do not remain long enough in a job.[70]
Training pupils so that they have a flexibility to
change jobs easily is perhaps having some rather
undesirable side-effects.   It is also felt by some
factories that vocational schools concentrate too
much on theory to the detriment of practical training.
Thus graduates may know quite advanced mathematics
but are scarcely able to hold a hammer.[71]   For many
factory foremen such a sense of priorities is faulty
and they would prefer to have workers who have learnt
their skills on-the-job, regardless of their level
of theoretical knowledge.   It would also seem
probable that vocational college graduates are not
always welcomed on the shopfloor in that they may
arrive at work with feelings of superiority over the
other workers and may criticise the established order
of things.

Success of Labour Training Programme.   Some final
problems and trends are highlighted if the question
of the overall success of the labour training
programme is examined.   It has been seen how Soviet
vocational education has three basic goals - moral
education, skill training and vocational guidance.
To what extent are these goals achieved?
        As far as moral education is concerned, there
are clearly problems.   In this area, as in many
other fields of life, the Soviet system invites
criticism by setting extremely high goals for itself.
Any failures to attain these goals are sometimes used

by hostile critics who jump at the opportunity to
judge the system on its own terms and denounce the
entire system regardless of any achievements it may
have made.

In the field of moral education the goals are
particularly high.   It is impossible to estimate
accurately overall levels of success in inculcating
the desired attitudes to work.   It is evident that
there are many weak spots.   One sociologist, for
example, reports too strong an element of what he
terms 'thingism', meaning that young people are too
concerned with possessions and not enough with
labouring for the good of society or even with working
for its own sake.[72]   Similarly, an unsatisfactory
level of discipline and responsibility towards one's
work is regularly bemoaned and alcohol as a factor
behind undisciplined, irresponsible behaviour at
college or work is often mentioned.   Delinquency
seems to be disproportionately high among PTU pupils
compared with their peers at school or at work.[73]
For many of those 'PTUshniki' who leave their
country home at 16 to go to technical-trade school
in the town the temptations of alcohol and petty
crime, offered by those older pupils sharing their
hostel accommodation, are too strong to resist.

One aspect of education in work values seems to
have met with a greater degree of success, namely
that of creating a respect for learning.   Although
fewer now aspire to higher education, the majority
of Soviet young people are eager to continue
studying in some way or another.   A survey of the
value orientations of young people in the agricultural
Kirov region, for example, showed that over 80 per
cent wished to go on studying.[74]   For some, of
course, the motivation to study is not so much to
improve society as to advance their own career, but
nevertheless it would seem that a respect for learning and a desire to study are values that have been
genuinely assimilated by many young people.

As far as any teaching of practical skills is
concerned there are also successes and weaknesses.
Young workers trained at SPTUs proceed through the
working grades faster than those who were trained
on-the-job.[75]   It has also been noted how PTU
graduates seem particularly inclined to change their
jobs quickly.   This shows a certain success in the
aim of creating flexible workers but the
consequences of this are double-edged for the
economy.   Movement between jobs is seen as positive
only when necessitated by changing economic
circumstances.

A major difficulty in the training of skills in a planned system lies in predicting accurately how many specialists of each variety are needed and then in producing the right numbers of each. There are inevitably failures both in prediction and in directing youngsters into the required professions. There have been complaints of too few masons and not enough house-painters, for instance. Agriculture has particularly suffered. Between 1965 and 1975 the output of industrial specialists from PTUs trebled, whereas the number of agricultural specialists rose only 1.8 times. There are too few tractor-drivers, for example, and there is an urgent need for skilled farmworkers of many other profiles.[76]

Despite the recent expansion of the structure of vocational guidance work, there are regular calls for improvements here. Indeed, poor work in this area is often blamed for the shortages of workers of certain types noted above. It is deplored that children frequently have a weak understanding of the nature of particular jobs even of those common in their own town.[77] The relatively insignificant role of the school reported by youngsters in influencing them in their choice of job is felt to be unsatisfactory. The systematisation of vocational guidance work through a variety of agencies is called for, but it is admitted that this is a complex problem and no quick answer is likely to be found.[78]

The vociferous concern noted throughout to improve all three aspects of Soviet vocational education shows the lack of official satisfaction with the current state of affairs. Schools and colleges are constantly urged to better their work here. The Utopian heights of the goals presented make success on all fronts improbable. Indeed, the goals aspired to contain contradictions that make success in achieving all the desired aims impossible. An expected norm of respect for institutionalised education is hardly compatible with an equal feeling of respect for unskilled work. Investigations of later job satisfaction have shown that those who failed to enter a higher educational institution were more content with their work than those who obtained a degree.[79] It would seem that the higher one's education the less likely one is to be satisfied with a menial job. One Soviet sociologist has pointed out that it is ridiculous to expect today's educated school-leaver to find his job as a loader noble and has suggested that the solution lies in automating industry as much as possible, ridding it of its tedious jobs and leaving only the more interesting work for people to perform.[80]   It would certainly seem that attitudes towards labour are conditioned at least as much by the actual working situation in society as by education.   Large numbers of young people are unlikely, for example, to go into agricultural work while the conditions of rural life contrast unfavourably with those in towns, despite attempts at persuasion by their teachers. Consequently improvements in work orientations will need to stem not merely from school textbooks, teachers' homilies and the other provisions outlined in this paper but also from changes in the organisation and content of work in the factory or on the farm.

NOTES

1.   L.G. Grinberg et al., Osnovy kommunisticheskoi morali (Moscow, 1980), p. 98.
2.   H. Marcuse, Soviet Marxism (Penguin, Harmondsworth, 1971), p. 19.
3.   F.A. O'Dell, Socialisation through Children's Literature: the Soviet Example (Cambridge University Press, 1978), pp. 36-9.
4.   S.P. Aksenov et al., (eds.), Rabochemu klassu - dostoinoe popolnenie (Moscow, 1981), pp. 22-3.
5.   Ministerstvo prosveshcheniya SSSR, Rekomendatsii vsesoyuznoi nauchnoprakticheskoi konferentsii 'Aktual'nye sotsial'nye ekonomisticheskie problemy razvitiya narodnogo obrazovaniya' (Moscow, 1979), p. 7.
6.   V.P. Tomin, Uroven' obrazovaniya naseleniya SSSR (Moscow, 1981), p. 117.
7.   D.S. Lane and F.A. O'Dell, The Soviet Industrial Worker: Social Class, Education and Control (Martin Robertson, London, 1978), pp. 56-64.
8.   F.R. Filippov, Sotsiologiya obrazovaniya (Moscow, 1980), p. 111.
9.   L.I. Muzhelevskaya and L.V. Russkova (eds.), Spravochnik po doshkol'nomu vospitaniyu (Moscow, 1980), pp. 377-80.
10.   Ibid., pp. 263-5.
11.   F.A. O'Dell, Socialisation, pp. 94-5.
12.   I.T. Ogorodnikova, Pedagogika shkoly (Moscow, 1978), p. 190.
13.   Ibid., p. 194.
14.   Deti v SSSR (Moscow, 1979), p. 29.
15.   V.A. Zhamin, Sotsial'no-ekonomicheskie problemy obrazovaniya i nauki v razvitom

sotsialisticheskom obshchestve (Moscow, 1979), p. 41.
16. A.I. Novikov, 'O proizvoditel'nom trude
podrostkov', Sotsiologicheskie issledovaniya, no. 3
(1981), p. 94.
17. Rodnaya rech' (Moscow, 1981), p. 3.
18. Programma vos'miletnei i srednei shkoly:
geografiya (Moscow, 1980).
19. Programma vos'miletnei i srednei shkoly:
istoriya (Moscow, 1980).
20. L.N. Tokareva et al., (eds.), Materialy k
leninskim urokam na inostrannykh yazykakh (Tashkent,
1977), p. 25.
21. G.Kh. Shakhnazarov et al., Obshchestvovedenie
(Moscow, 1980), pp. 310-2.
22. I. Markus', 'Teoriya bez praktiki',
Uchitel'skaya gazeta, 21 Oct. 1976.
23. V.F. Odintsov, 'Nekotorye rezul'taty
izucheniya professional'nykh orientatsii molodezhi
kirovskoi oblasti', Sotsiologicheskie issledovaniya,
no. 2 (1981), p. 113.
24. G.Bol'shakov, 'KPD shkol'nykh masterskikh',
Uchitel'skaya gazeta, 26 Mar. 1977.
25. N.K. Fomina, 'Primernoe tematicheskoe
planirovanie zanyatii po obsluzhivayushchemu trudu
v IV-VI klassakh', Shkola i proizvodstvo, no. 8, 1981.
26. Novikov, 'O trude', p. 93.
27. Ibid., p. 96.
28. I. Belonin et al., 'Iz opyta trudovoi
podgotovki shkol'nikov', Sovetskaya pedagogika,
no. 6 (1981), p. 67.
29. Ibid., p. 70.
30. Ibid., p. 74.
31. The figures throughout this section all
come from Narodnoe khozyaistvo v 1979 godu (Moscow,
1980), p. 492.
32. M. A. Denisova, Lingvostranovedcheskii
slovar' (Moscow, 1978), p. 105.
33. Ibid., p. 145.
34. The factual information in this section
comes from Professional'no-tekhnicheskie uchebnye
zavedeniya Leningrada: spravochnik dlya postupayushchikh (Leningrad, 1980).
35. The factual information in this section
comes from Tekhnikumy i uchilishcha Leningradskoi
oblasti: spravochnik dlya postupayushchikh
(Leningrad, 1980).
36. F.R. Filippov, Sotsial'nye peremeshcheniya
v razvitom sotsialisticheskom obshchestve (Moscow,
1979), p. 11.
37. Idem.
38. F.R. Filippov, Yu.N. Kozyrev and D.I. Zyuzin

(eds.), Obrazovanie i sotsial'naya struktura (Moscow, 1976), p. 65.
39. M.N. Rutkevich and F.R. Filippov (eds.), Vysshaya shkola kak faktor izmeneniya sotsial'noi struktury razvitogo, sotsialisticheskogo obshchestva (Moscow, 1978), p. 20.
40. Narodnoe khozyaist'vo v 1979 godu (Moscow, 1980), p. 492.
41. Denisova, Lingvostranovedcheskii, pp. 108-9.
42. V.T. Lisovskii and V.A. Sukhin, Kompleksnoe issledovanie problem obucheniya i kommunisticheskogo vospitaniya spetsialistov s vysshim obrazovaniem (Leningrad, 1980), p. 74.
43. Filippov, Sotsiologiya, pp. 126-7.
44. Komsomol'skaya pravda, 3 June 1981, p. 2.
45. Narodnoe khozyaistvo v 1979 godu (Moscow, 1980), p. 486, p. 489 and p. 492 for the statistical data in this section.
46. Filippov, Sotsiologiya, p. 120.
47. Tomin, Uroven', p. 111.
48. Idem.
49. Narodnoe khozyaistvo v 1979 godu (Moscow, 1980), p. 503.
50. Zhamin, Sotsial'no-ekonomicheskie problemy, p. 57.
51. D.N. Karpukhin and A.B. Shteiner 'Zhenskii trud i trud zhenshchin' EKO, no. 3 (1978), p. 43.
52. Lane and O'Dell, pp. 108-16 discusses this point more fully.
53. Filippov, Sotsiologiya, p. 121.
54. Sbornik prikazov i instruktsii Ministerstva prosveshcheniya RSFSR, no. 20 (Moscow, 1980), p. 3.
55. Tomin, Uroven', p. 113.
56. Zhamin, Sotsial'no-ekonomicheskie problemy, p. 57.
57. Tomin, Uroven', p. 114.
58. Filippov, Sotsiologiya, p. 110.
59. E.V. Belkin, 'Professional'no-tekhnicheskoe obrazovanie v zhiznennykh planakh molodezhi, Sotsiologicheskie issledovaniya, no. 2 (1981), p. 107.
60. Filippov, Sotsiologiya, p. 110.
61. V.V. Vodzinskaya, 'Orientations to occupations' in M. Yanowitch and W.A. Fisher, Social Stratification and Mobility in the USSR (International Arts and Sciences Press, New York, 1973), pp. 169-70.
62. Lisovskii and Sukhin, Kompleksnoe issledovanie, p. 16.
63. Filippov, Sotsiologiya, p. 109.
64. E.K. Vasil'eva et al., (eds.), Naselenie Leningrada (Moscow, 1981), pp. 59-60.

65. Filippov, Sotsiologiya, pp. 144-5.
66. Tomin, Uroven', p. 109.
67. Aksenov, Rabochemu klassu, p. 123.
68. Ibid., p. 124.
69. Tomin, Uroven', pp. 113-4.
70. Filippov, Sotsiologiya, p. 118.
71. Personal conversations.
72. V.T. Lisovskii et al., Zhit' dostoino
(Moscow, 1979), p. 85 and elsewhere.
73. V.O. Rukavishnikov et al., 'Podrostok v
shkole i doma', Sotsiologicheskie issledovaniya,
no. 2 (1981), p. 122.
74. Odintsov, Nekotorye rezul'taty, p. 113.
75. Filippov, Sotsiologiya, pp. 114-5.
76. Ibid., pp. 116-7.
77. Odintsov, Nekotorye rezul'taty, p. 113.
78. Filippov, Sotsiologiya, pp. 111-2.
79. I.S. Kon, Psikhologiya yunosheskogo
vozrasta (Moscow, 1979), p. 154.
80. M. Titma (ed.), Sotsial'naya i
professional'naya orientatsiya molodezhi v usloviyakh
razvitogo sotsialisticheskogo obshchestva v SSSR
(Tallin, 1977), p. 75.

BIBLIOGRAPHY

Aksenov, S.P. et al., (eds.), Rabochemu klassu -
    dostoinoe popolnenie (Moscow, 1981)
Belkin, E.V. 'Professional'no-tekhnicheskoe
    obrazovanie v zhiznennykh planakh molodezhi',
    Sotsiologicheskie issledovaniya, no. 2 (1981)
Belonin, I. et al., 'Iz opyta trudovoi podgotovki
    shkol'nikov', Sovetskaya pedagogika no. 6 (1981)
Bol'shakov, G. 'KPD shkol'nykh masterskikh',
    Uchitel'skaya gazeta, 26 Mar. 1977
Denisova, M.A. Lingvostranovedcheskii slovar'
    (Moscow, 1978)
Deti v SSSR (Moscow, 1979)
Filippov, F.R. et al., (eds.), Obrazovanie i
    sotsial'naya struktura (Moscow, 1976)
----- Sotsial'nye peremeshcheniya v razvitom
    sotsialisticheskom obshchestve (Moscow, 1979)
----- Sotsiologiya obrazovaniya (Moscow, 1980)
Fomina, N.K. 'Primernoe tematicheskoe planirovanie
    zanyatii po obsluzhivayushchemu trudu v IV-VI
    klassakh', Shkola i proizvodstvo, no. 8 (1981)
Grinberg, L.G. et al., Osnovy kommunisticheskoi
    morali (Moscow, 1980)
Karpukhin, D.N. and Shteiner, A.B. 'Zhenskii trud i
    trud zhenshchin' (EKO, no. 3, 1978)
Komsomol'skaya pravda

Kon, I.S. Psikhologiya yunosheskogo vozrasta
    (Moscow, 1979)
Lane, D.S. and O'Dell, F.A. The Soviet Industrial
    Worker: Social Class, Education and Control
    (Martin Robertson, London, 1978)
Lisovskii, V.T. et al., Zhit' dostoino (Moscow, 1979)
-----and Sukhin, V.A. Kompleksnoe issledovanie
    problem obucheniya i kommunisticheskogo
    vospitaniya spetsialistov s vysshim obrazovaniem
    (Leningrad, 1980)
Marcuse, H. Soviet Marxism (Penguin, Harmondsworth,
    1971)
Markus', 'Teoriya bez praktiki', Uchitel'skaya gazeta,
    21 Oct. 1976
Ministerstvo prosveshcheniya SSSR, Rekomendatsii
    vsesoyuznoi nauchnoprakticheskoi konferentsii
    'Aktual'nye sotsial'nye ekonomisticheskie
    problemy razvitiya narodnogo obrazovaniya'
    (Moscow, 1979)
Muzhelevskaya, L.I. and Russkova, L.V. (eds.),
    Spravochnik po doshkol'nomu vospitaniyu
    (Moscow, 1980)
Narodnoe khozyaistvo SSSR v 1979 godu (Moscow, 1980)
Novikov, A.I. 'O proizvoditel'nom trude podrostkov',
    Sotsiologicheskie issledovaniya, no. 3 (1981)
O'Dell, F.A. Socialisation through Children's
    Literature: the Soviet Example (Cambridge
    University Press, 1978)
Odintsov, V.F. 'Nekotorye rezul'taty izucheniya
    professional'nykh orientatsii molodezhi
    Kirovskoi oblasti', Sotsiologicheskie
    issledovaniya, no. 2 (1981)
Ogorodnikova, I.T. Pedagogika shkoly (Moscow, 1978)
Professional'no-tekhnicheskoe obrazovanie
Professional'no-tekhnicheskie uchebnye zavedeniya
    Leningrada: spravochnik dlya postupayushchikh
    (Leningrad, 1980)
Programma vos'miletnei i srednei shkoly:
    geografiya (Moscow, 1980)
Programma vos'miletnei i srednei shkoly:istoriya
    (Moscow, 1980)
Rodnaya rech' (Moscow, 1981)
Rukavishnikov, V.O. et al., 'Podrostok v shkole i
    doma', Sotsiologicheskie issledovaniya, no. 2
    (1981)
Rutkevich, M.N. and Filippov, F.R. (eds.), Vysshaya
    shkola kak faktor izmeneniya sotsial'noi
    struktury razvitogo sotsialisticheskogo
    obshchestva (Moscow, 1978)
Sbornik prikazov i instruktsii Ministerstva
    prosveshcheniya RSFSR (no. 2, Moscow, 1980)
Shakhnazarov, G.K. et al., Obshchestvovedenie

(Moscow, 1980)
Shkola i proizvodstvo
Srednee spetsial'noe obrazovanie
Tekhnikumy i uchilishcha Leningrada i Leningradskoi
    oblasti: spravochnik dlya postupayushchikh
    (Leningrad, 1980)
Titma, M. (ed.), Sotsial'naya i professional'naya
    orientatsiya molodezhi v usloviyakh razvitogo
    sotsialisticheskogo obshchestva v SSSR (Tallin,
    1977)
Tokareva, L.N. et al., Materialy k Leninskim urokam
    na inostrannykh yazykakh (Tashkent, 1977)
Tomin, V.P. Uroven' obrazovaniya v SSSR (Moscow,
    1981)
Uchitel'skaya gazeta
Vasil'eva, E.K. et al., (eds.), Naselenie Leningrada
    (Moscow, 1981)
Vodzinskaya, V.V. 'Orientations to Occupations' in
    M. Yanowitch and W.A. Fisher, Social Stratifi-
    cation and Mobility in the USSR (New York, 1973)
Zhamin, V.A. Sotsial'no-ekonomicheskie problemy
    obrazovanii i nauki v razvitom sotsialisticheskom
    obshchestve (Moscow, 1979)

Chapter 6

THE POLITICAL CONTENT OF EDUCATION IN THE USSR

John Morison

The Background

An important element of continuity between the
Tsarist and Soviet regimes has been the deliberate
use of education as a means of inculcating loyalty
in the population and of developing positive
political attitudes towards those in power.   So far
as Peter the Great and Catherine the Great were
concerned, in their attempts to create a national
system of education in Russia in the eighteenth
century, it was axiomatic that the state had the
right to attempt to influence, or rather to control
the thought patterns of the young.   Virtuous
attitudes and Christian piety alone were not enough;
devotion to the ruler was an essential ingredient of
the system of moral training which they strove to
develop.   Catherine's adviser, Betskoi, clearly saw
the schools as the institutions in which the new
Russian man, able and content to play his destined
role in an ordered society, could be formed in a
deliberate and premeditated process.[1]   This type of
attitude persisted through the nineteenth century,
although often the main concern seemed to be to
shield the young from harmful outside ideas.   To a
ruling class conditioned to believe that the essence
of Russian nationality was an instinctive loyalty to
the Tsar, the problem was to preserve and nurture
feelings that already existed rather than to create
positive attitudes towards the ruler from a void.
Thus, K.P. Pobedonostsev, lay head of the Russian
Orthodox Church from 1880 to 1905, argued that
education should be suited to the future calling of
its recipients.   It therefore should be minimal for
the large majority of the population, destined as they
were to a life of menial, manual toil.   They had to be
preserved from the 'mirage of illusory learning'
which corrupted the mind, and from the efforts of

modern enlighteners to dispel popular prejudices
and ignorance by the power of reason and logic.
Social stability demanded the reinforcement in the
ordinary man of opinions which he held upon faith
and from instinct. The simple and the weak had to
be protected from the subtlety of intellectuals
'under the pretext of guidance stealing the sheep
from the flock and leading or driving them into the
wilderness'.[2]
The Bolsheviks, after their seizure of power
in October 1917, were much more positive and
aggressive in their approach. Political education
was seen as an essential component in the campaign
to consolidate their position. The Civil War was
to them as much a political as a military struggle,
a campaign to win the allegiance of minds just as
much or even more than one to hold and gain territory.
Their enormous programme of political education was
not, however, just an attempt to eliminate old
tsarist or bourgeois attitudes in the population at
large. It was consciously motivated by the
aspiration to educate and mould a new and morally
superior type of being, one which would be capable
of living in a socialist and ultimately communist
society. This new man should be inspired by
collectivism, should put the public interest first
at all times, should be ready to aid his comrades,
and should be politically active and patriotic in a
socialist rather than bourgeois and chauvinistic
manner. Without this fundamental transformation of
attitudes, the new form of society for which the
revolution had been fought would be unattainable.
The Bolsheviks were never confident that this change
in popular consciousness would occur spontaneously
with the new economic structure; it was something
that required energetic direction from the
enlightened vanguard, namely the party itself.

Recent Developments
After over six decades of socialist education of the
population, and after Stalin's physical coercion and
elimination of remnants of the old order, one might
reasonably have expected that there would be less
emphasis than before on political education at the
beginning of the 1980s. The reverse, however, is
the case as the result of three recent authoritative
pronouncements, whose message has been incessantly
repeated in recent Soviet writings on education and
ideology.
The 25th Party Congress in 1976 devoted
considerable attention to questions of ideological

education.   In his report, Leonid Brezhnev stated,

> Comrades! The strength of our order lies in
> the consciousness of the masses.   And the party
> considers the inculcation of communist conscious-
> ness, the readiness, will and knowledge needed to
> build communism to be its constant concern.   In
> the period on which I am reporting (the previous
> five years), questions of ideological education,
> and the problems of the formation of the new man,
> a worthy builder of communism, have occupied a
> big place in all our work.

Although much had already been achieved, Brezhnev
warned against complacency.   Even though all schoolchildren and students were now mastering the fundamentals of political knowledge and 'the mass study of
Marxism-Leninism is the most important distinguishing
feature of the development of social consciousness at
the contemporary stage', he demanded greater
effectiveness in this work and the raising of its
theoretical level.   It was imperative for the
decisions of the Congress to be implanted deeply in
the minds of the population at large, and for
feelings of Soviet patriotism and socialist internationalism to be developed still further.[3]
The themes enunciated by Brezhnev at the 25th
Party Congress were further developed in a Central
Committee decree published on 26 April 1979, and
entitled 'On the further improvement of ideological
and political-educational work'.   This document
stated that the Communist Party of the Soviet Union
considered the communist education of the workers to
be an important aspect of the struggle for communism.

> The path of economic, socio-political and
> cultural development of the country, the full
> realisation of the possibilities of developed
> socialism, the realisation of the Leninist
> foreign policy course of the Soviet Union and
> the strengthening of its international position
> depend all the more on the success of
> ideological and political educational work.

All levels of the party were instructed to take
concrete measures to improve this part of their work,
to raise its effectiveness and quality, to ameliorate
its forms and methods, and to remove existing
deficiencies.   Such agitation and propaganda should be
at a high scientific level, be more concrete and
linked to the solution of economic and political tasks,

and take on a more aggressive character. Special
attention should be paid to work among young people.
'The duty of party and Komsomol organisations is to
implant in the young generation a feeling of
historical responsibility for the fate of socialism,
and for the well-being and safety of the Motherland.'
The Ministries of Education and associated bodies
were strictly enjoined to unify organically the
academic and upbringing processes '... and to ensure
high moral and political qualities and a love of
work'. Interest in political knowledge had to be
inculcated.[4]

In his speech to the 26th Party Congress on
23 February 1981, Brezhnev emphasised that the
Party's policies in this area had been clearly
stated in the decree of 26 April 1979, which was
expected to retain its validity for a long period.
On this occasion, Brezhnev was more concerned with
the inadequacies of journalists and party agitators
whose official tone and abstract turn of phrase
repelled their listeners and so undermined their
message. Political education and agitation had to
be conducted in lively language and to be firmly
connected to real issues of everyday life. Nevertheless, his firm endorsement of the earlier decree has
quickly been taken up by other spokesmen and
commentators as meaning that greater stress than ever
needs to be placed on the political content of
education.[5] At the congress itself, V.V. Grishin,
the first secretary of the Moscow City Committee of
the party, promised that the party organisation of
the capital would unceasingly aim to strengthen the
ideological education of the masses, and would
improve its work on the formation of the new man and
the consolidation of the socialist way of life.[6]
A.A. Smirnova, a rural schoolteacher from Kostroma
province, assured the delegates that she and her
colleagues would not only strive to impart deep and
accurate knowledge to their pupils, but also would
train them in firm ideological convictions,
patriotism, high moral principles, and readiness to
defend the Socialist Motherland. The aim of the
schoolteacher must be to train active and conscious
builders of Communism.[7] The Ministry of Education
of the USSR followed the Congress with a detailed
directive instructing all teachers to study the
decisions of the Congress with their pupils, and to
carry on ideological work in a lively and interesting
fashion, with concrete links to life and to
contemporary reality.[8] The Minister himself,
M.A. Prokof'ev, drove this latter point home in a

forceful speech in which he insisted that it was important to instil in school-children not just ideas, but also communist convictions and communist morals.[9]

It therefore seems certain that one of the important themes of Soviet education in the 1980s will be the need to make political education more effective and even more all-pervasive than before. The reasons for this throw an interesting light on some of the current preoccupations of the Soviet leadership. Firstly, there is a reaction against what is seen to be an increasing ideological threat from outside; secondly, a concern to eliminate attitudes which are inconsistent with the claim to have achieved a state of developed socialism; and thirdly, a desire to improve the population's attitude towards work with consequent beneficial effects on production levels.

Much attention has recently been devoted to what is alleged to be an increased ideological threat from without. In his speech to the 26th Party Congress, V.V. Grishin described it thus:

> World imperialism and its accomplices are extending their hostile propaganda directed at undermining the ideological foundations of socialism. Our class enemies are slandering the policy of the CPSU and of the Soviet state, are trying to influence unstable people and to implant in them views and moral traits which are alien to us.[10]

In his speech, Brezhnev also referred to increased propagandistic efforts by the class enemy, and to a strengthening of the latter's attempts to exert a corrupting influence on the consciousness of Soviet people.[11] Imperialism and its allies were systematically conducting a hostile campaign against the socialist countries, blackening their achievements and trying to turn people against socialism. The Soviet Minister of Education, M.A. Prokof'ev, followed him by warning against 'reactionary bourgeois pedagogical theories and concepts' which threaten to revive a 'petty bourgeois and nationalistic outlook' among ideologically immature pedagogues.[12] The then deputy chairman of the KGB, V.M. Chebrikov, added his voice to the chorus of concern in a detailed warning to young people published in the journal Young Communist in April 1981. He alleged that its enemies were conducting a 'psychological war' against the Soviet Union,

trying to create a rift between the Soviet people
and the Communist Party by discrediting the Soviet
state. Soviet youth were a principal target of
this subversion, it being hoped to attract them to
bourgeois ideology and to create in individuals an
apolitical, nihilistic and anti-social mood. The
USA had allocated 393 million dollars in its 1978-9
budget for this specific purpose. In a particularly
cunning move, 'revisionism' was being used (rather
than a direct attack), and the class enemy was
masking his attack in socialist or even Marxist
phraseology. Attempts were being made to turn the
youth against their elders, and to lead them to
attack the 'conservatism of old cadres' who were
allegedly obstructing the 'democratisation',
'liberalisation', and 'humanisation' of socialism.
'The aims of such ideological diversions are
obvious: to provoke political conflicts within the
socialist state, to undermine the trust of the youth
in the Communist party, and to discredit the
Komsomol'. They were trying to promote pluralism,
and to use 'traitors' who had posed as 'defenders of
human rights' in the 1970s. They were attempting
to stimulate bourgeois nationalist sentiments in
Soviet youth through the work of emigré Zionist,
Ukrainian, Lithuanian and other nationalistic
organisations. Such nationalism could lead to
criminal activity, specific reference being made to
the bombs planted in the Moscow metro by Armenians in
February 1979. Religion was also being used by
anti-communists in their ideological onslaught on
Soviet youth, as a means of disseminating nationalism.
Bourgeois specialists in psychological warfare were
also striving to inoculate Soviet youth with anti-
pathetic attitudes towards socialism by means of the
capitalist cult of consumerism, stress on living
standards, Western fashions and sexual freedom.
They were hoping to infect Soviet youth with the
anarchism prevalent among their Western counter-
parts.13
    There is no doubt that, as Chebrikov's article
stated, the Soviet leadership is especially concerned
about ideological challenges from within the
socialist camp. The open split with China,
following upon Stalin's break with Yugoslavia,
destroyed the Soviet Union's claim to undisputed
leadership of the Communist world, and opened the
way for the development of different roads to
socialism which, from a Soviet viewpoint, clearly
seemed to be leading in the opposite direction.
Czech attempts to 'humanise' socialism were forcibly

suppressed.   Recent developments in Poland are of
enormous concern, and are indirectly referred to in
Chebrikov's fulminations against revisionism.
Brezhnev was blunter in his speech to the 26th Party
Congress.

> In places where mistakes and miscalculations
> in internal policies are added to the under-
> mining activity of imperialism, a fertile soil
> arises for the activisation of elements
> hostile to socialism.   This happened in
> fraternal Poland, where the enemies of
> socialism, with the support of external
> forces, created anarchy and strove to turn
> the course of events in a counter-revolutionary
> direction.

He also warned against the Chinese distortions of
the principles of socialism which had been manifested
in international as well as in domestic policies.[14]
Their concern does, however, go deeper than
this.   Khrushchev's selective denunciation of
Stalin in 1956 undermined the myth of the infallible
party and opened the way for open criticisms of the
Soviet model of socialism.   It also created the
danger of scepticism developing amongst the
population about the claims of a regime which,
despite admitting some past errors, was reluctant to
drop the mantle of infallibility.   Increased contact
with the outside world, another consequence of
Khrushchev's policies, intensified the risk of the
spread of scepticism by exposing the fallibility of
some of the claims made by the regime.   The current
stress on political education is intended to counter
this.   Stalinist compulsion has been largely
replaced by persuasion.   Admission of past errors
has made it imperative for the regime to justify
itself and its policies, and actively to win popular
support.
Another factor which was prominent in the minds
of Brezhnev and his associates was their claim that
the Soviet Union has from the early 1960s passed
into the new and higher phase of 'developed
socialism'.   Brezhnev himself introduced this new
concept in 1967, and the idea has been elaborated
in the 1970s.   This new prolonged transitional
phase on the road to Communism is said to be marked
by high levels of production, the elimination of
class distinctions between manual and brain workers
and peasants, and by increased mass participation in
'socialist democracy' without, however, any

diminution of central control by the Party.[15] This
concept places high demands on the political
educators. On the one hand, the relics of
attitudes related to the past and to class distinct-
iveness must be eliminated if citizens worthy of the
stage of developed socialism are to be produced.
Nationalism and religion are obvious targets, but
Brezhnev himself obviously felt strongly about the
continued existence of 'recidivists of philistine
and petty bourgeois psychology'. The USSR's progress
into a new stage of development necessitates an
intensification of campaigns against 'deviations
from the socialist norms of morality. Money-
grubbing, private-property tendencies, hooliganism,
bureaucratism and callousness towards humanity
contradict the very essence of our order'.[16] Even
the growing Soviet fashion of owning pet dogs is
open to condemnation on these grounds at a time of
meat shortages.
      On the other hand, the concept of developed
socialism demands a raising of the level of
political consciousness of all members of the
population, if they are to be more active
participants in Soviet democracy in the manner now
demanded of them. According to the 1979 decree,
'an important source of the strength of the
socialist order lies precisely in the activity of
the masses'. The masses must be politically
educated to know in detail what the policies of the
party are, and at the same time they must be
indoctrinated to sympathise fully with these
objectives so that their activity goes only in the
desired direction and does not lead to conflict with
the central political authority.
      Behind this stress on mass activity, is clearly
an awareness not just of the need to stimulate
higher rates of economic productivity but also of
the implications of recent technological advance
described in the phrase 'the scientific-technical
revolution'. For the new technology to be
effective, a better educated work force is required,
and one capable of using initiative and imagination,
qualities largely suppressed by Stalinist controls.
Individual action should no longer be stifled by
unthinking collectivism, but it must still remain
within the general guidelines of collectivist goals
and not lapse into selfish individualism. Thus,
in his speech to the 25th Party Congress, Brezhnev
stated,

> In contemporary conditions, when the volume
> of knowledge necessary for man is growing
> sharply and quickly, it is already impossible
> to place the main stress on the mastering of
> a fixed sum of facts.   It is important to
> implant the skill of independently
> supplementing one's knowledge, and of
> orientating oneself in the violent flow of
> scientific and political information.[17]

In part, it is hoped that an increased stress
on education for work and work experience in schools
can help to develop a more positive attitude to work,
better work habits and an increase in productivity.
It is expected that a politically more aware work
force will see the need for renewed individual effort
and positive attitudes if the goals of the
collective are to be achieved.   Moreover, the fact
that individual initiative is now expected and that
the passive absorption of limited amounts of pre-
ordained information is no longer sufficient in new
conditions of rapid technological innovation
necessitates the development of a more sophisticated
system of ideological and political education.   The
goals of society can only be achieved if the
energies and imagination of the people are released
and enterprise encouraged, but this process must
take place within the parameters established by the
Party.   The task of the political educator is to
ensure that the creative energies of the population
are willingly directed towards collectivist rather
than individual goals.   Strong supervision and
direction are still needed, if the potential chaos
of a Polish-type situation is to be avoided.   The
problem is to combine these central controls with
spontaneous productive initiatives from the work
force.   The Soviet leadership obviously sees the
answer to this dilemma in an intensification of
ideological work among the population.   Children
have to be taught not just the techniques of work,
but also to respect unquestioningly the principle
of unstinting effort at the work place to achieve
the common goals.

An interesting example of the attempt to
stimulate mass activity in order to use public
initiative to eliminate waste, raise standards and
at the same time control deviationist tendencies has
been the establishment of organs of 'popular control'
in factories and higher educational institutions.
These bodies of activists, legitimised by Article 2
of the Constitution, may carry out raids on cafeterias

or production lines to check on standards and quality
of work, and to ensure that savings in electricity
are being implemented.   Members of the work force
are thus encouraged to check up not only on the work
of the administrators and of those in authority but
also, and one suspects more often in practice, on
that of their work-mates.   Even secondary schools
have their elected Pupils' Committees which help to
discipline fellow pupils, bringing social pressure
to bear on miscreants.

Implications for the Curriculum

The increased stress on political education and the
implications of the scientific-technical revolution
have been instrumental in bringing about certain
changes in the secondary school timetable.   In
response to the scientific-technical revolution, the
amount of time devoted to the natural sciences and
mathematics was increased in the early 1970s.
However, as a gesture to political education, new
subjects, Soviet State and Law and Social Studies
were introduced, despite pressures in favour of
subjects more obviously relevant to the economy.   A
certain amount of para-military training in the guise
of civil defence was also introduced.   More recent
readjustments have resulted in a year more of
foreign language study, and a doubling of the time
allocated to work training in the final two grades,
to four hours a week.
     Of more significance than timetable changes
have been alterations to the syllabus and the
introduction of revised or new textbooks, a process
which is still going on.   The general aim has been
to eliminate duplication of material between
subjects and to delete some material of secondary
importance, or considered to be unduly complicated.
Overburdening with facts has been seen as a fault
needing remedial action.   In an attempt to gain
the pupils' interest, a wide range of optional courses
has been introduced, a particular aim of which has
been to help pupils to make an intelligent choice of
career.   What is happening is not a clear reduction
in the overall work load, but rather a reorganisation
of the material, and in particular an attempt to
create meaningful coordination and links between the
syllabuses of different subject areas.   This
applies with special force to themes connected with
political education and with education for work
which are expected to permeate the whole curriculum.
Thus, Yu.Yu. Ivanov, an official in the USSR Ministry
of Education with responsibility for school

administration, argued in August 1980 that the improved curricula would have the advantage of coordinating the curriculum for each subject more closely with the current tasks of communist construction, or, in other words, with the needs of the economy. This was because of the considerably increased emphasis on a polytechnical orientation in all courses, with pupils being introduced to the 'leading branches of socialist economic construction', modern technology and questions relating to economics and the organisation of labour. Secondly, he lauded the increased social, or in other words political, orientation of school courses.[18]

It is realised that changes in curriculum alone will be insufficient to achieve the desired goals; teaching methods also must be made more effective. In the words of F.G. Panachin, First Deputy Minister of Education of the USSR,

> In our view, an unduly heavy school-pupil work load is often due less to the large volume of study material than to the existence of serious faults in the organisation of the teaching process, imbalance in homework assignments, and an insufficiently high level of teacher training in special field and teaching methods.[19]

What is expected is not just the use of new textbooks and new teaching aids, but also a different approach to the business of teaching itself. Instead of formal expositions, rote learning and the routine drilling of pupils in large quantities of prescribed material, teachers are to be expected to make the process of learning an active one. Children are to be encouraged to work things out for themselves, and to relate experiences from their own life to the theories being taught them. In other words, individual initiative is to be encouraged, and local features and examples are to be included in the syllabus. The need for politically competent teachers is recognised: 'The most important condition of the high effectiveness of this (political) work in the school is the deep ideological conviction and political competence of the teachers, the ability to evaluate facts and the phenomena of social life from a party position, and to answer convincingly questions arising from the pupils.'[20] Hence, it is stressed that there is an urgent need for special preparation and retraining of teachers in this respect. Many pedagogical institutes have responded by offering special courses

such as 'The Formation of the Communist World View
in the School Pupil', 'Inculcating in Pupils an
Activist Stance in Life', and 'The Education of
School Youth on the Basis of the Life and Activity
of V.I. Lenin'. Activism has to find expression in
the ability of pupils in the senior classes to
defend their convictions and viewpoints, and to argue
convincingly against the provocation of the Soviet
Union's ideological enemies. Such an approach
obviously depends on the active discussion of
politically unacceptable ideas, a dangerous process
in a country still as firmly controlled as the
Soviet Union. However, a recent authoritative
article has summoned schoolteachers to follow the
example of School no. 805 in the Zelenograd region
of Moscow province in organising special courses on
the 'peculiarities of the contemporary stage of
ideological struggle', or 'schools of counter-
propaganda'. After studying the two systems and the
ideological diversions, pupils should be trained to
conduct polemics on issues at the centre of
ideological struggle. Open and sharp political talks
should not be feared.[21] One suspects, though, that
the average teacher will respond more readily to the
Ministry of Education's recent summons to acquaint
all children with the content of the documents of
the 26th Party Congress in their classes in a lively
and interesting manner, with concrete links to life
and the facts of the contemporary world. Here they
are essentially being asked to explain and expound
party policy in the traditional manner, albeit in a
more lively fashion than in the past.[22] Whatever
methods may be used, it is no longer sufficient just
to receive knowledge; pupils must be convinced of
its truth and guided by it in their activities.[23]
    The political content of the syllabus in Soviet
schools and establishments of further and higher
education is supposed to be all-embracing. In
other words, all subject disciplines are intended to
be taught in a manner which is not only ideologically
acceptable, but also actively political in the sense
of inculcating a communist world outlook. Nevertheless, there are obviously some subject areas which
respond more readily than others to this treatment,
and which are specifically political in their
purpose and content. These are history, introduced
from the fourth class onwards, social studies, from
the eighth class, including a new course introduced
in 1977-8 on Soviet government and law, and military
training in the last two years. In higher education,
there are compulsory courses each year for all

students in all faculties on Marxism-Leninism in its
various aspects, the history of the Communist Party
of the Soviet Union and scientific communism.
Systematic instruction in 'scientific atheism' is
also introduced at this stage.

Education of the Younger Child
In the kindergartens and the first three years of
the general ten-year schools, there are no
specifically political lessons.   However, the
essential basis of a communist world outlook is laid
in these years.   In the kindergarten this is
achieved mainly through stories about Lenin and his
family, about his childhood and school years.   In
the first three years of the general school, this
knowledge about Lenin is extended to his career as
a revolutionary and leader of the first socialist
state in the world.   Lenin is portrayed as a
paragon of all the virtues, simple, modest, and
devoted to the people.   This message is reinforced
in art and music lessons.   Through study of Serov's
picture of Lenin among peasant intercessors, the
infants are supposed to be brought to perceive Lenin
through the eyes of the peasants and workers of his
day, as a humane and devoted leader accessible to the
people.   In music lessons, songs about Lenin and
revolutionary songs reinforce this message.   The
reading texts lead children on from stories about
Lenin to the introduction of more abstract concepts
such as 'the party' and 'communism'.   Children are
brought to master such phrases as: 'Lenin created
the Communist Party. The party continues the work
of Lenin.   It leads our people to a bright and
happy life;' and:

> The Communist Party is called the Leninist
> party because it was organised by Lenin.
> Vladamir Il'ich devoted all his strength to
> a struggle for the happiness of the people.
> The Communist Party is continuing the work of
> the great Lenin.   It is leading out people to
> a bright, happy life, to Communism.[24]

Children are taught to respond to the sight of
a portrait of Lenin with phrases such as 'Lenin
organised the party of communists.   He helped the
people to rid itself of the exploiters.   The workers
of the whole world know and love Lenin.'
One enthusistic teacher from Dagestan delights
in telling her pupils that the stars on the Kremlin
wall today shine brighter than all the stars in the

heavens, and that people go to Lenin's Mausoleum to speak with their leader, to open wide their souls before him, and to assure him that there is no force on earth capable of compelling the Soviet people to renounce the path bequeathed to them by Lenin.

In extolling Lenin, Soviet teachers are consciously putting him forward as a model for their pupils to follow, to stimulate in them respect for others, a wish to finish everything that has been started, to be economical with time, and to be organised and exact in their lives. In rejoicing in the victories of the Motherland, the children are taught to attribute them to the heroic work of the Soviet people and are hopefully inspired to strive to emulate their noble predecessors.[25]

Nor do the infants escape instruction about the benevolence of the party, and the basic outlines of its policies. Children are taught to associate themselves with the party and to realise that 'the party cares about children and all the Soviet people', it provides them with flats, looks after their health, and makes their Motherland still stronger to ensure that the world and the Soviet people will not know a new war.[26] The 26th Party Congress was followed keenly by these elementary classes, with special ceremonies to mark the event. More to the point, classes have been devoted to putting across the main lines of party policy in a simplified form. One Muscovite first-former is said to have succeeded in producing the following sentences:

> This year the new Five-year Plan has begun.
> In these five years many factories, schools, hospitals and kindergartens will be built.
> A metro will be constructed in Chertanovo.
> But for this to happen we must all work well, and children must study hard.

In school no. 304 in Moscow, the children watched the proceedings of the congress on television and all solemnly rose as one with the delegates when Brezhnev was seen to enter the hall, and also broke out in a 'stormy ovation' to greet him.[27] It is by means such as these that it is consciously intended that children should have achieved the rudiments of a communist world outlook by the end of their third year at school, should be proud of their country, and should emotionally be in sympathy with the policies of the party.[28]

Secondary Education

After the third year, the child is considered to
have finished the primary stage and to be ready to
embark on subject specialisation. In what is
described as a 'complex approach' to the problem,
each subject area is supposed to make its distinctive
contribution to the process of political education.
Rather than talk of the school as a location for a
systematic programme of such work, a recent article
insists that the school itself is in its entirety a
system devoted to the production of good communists
(vospitatel'naya sistema).[29] It is argued that even
the natural sciences and mathematics, not the most
obvious instruments of ideological enlightenment,
can serve this purpose. They can help pupils to
understand the development of natural phenomena and
their close relationship with the development of
society; they should lay the foundation for a
materialist view of the world. More specifically,
biology, through the study of human evolution,
should help to destroy religious views. More
generally, natural science subjects are considered
to lead to a scientific understanding of organic
and inorganic nature and to a view of man as the
crowning development of nature. Through science,
man can expect to dominate nature and his
environment and thereby achieve the state of
material abundance essential for the achievement of
communism.[30]

The study of foreign languages gives more direct
scope for politically inspired lessons. It gives
access to primary sources such as 'the speeches of
leaders of brotherly communist and workers' parties
of capitalist countries, and of progressive public
figures' and enables one to read 'progressive
foreign writers'. 'All this allows schoolchildren
to fill out their knowledge with facts which
convince them all the more of the advantages of the
socialist system over the capitalist one, and of the
necessity of struggle for the victory of communism'.
Inevitably, emotional texts about the life of
V.I. Lenin and Soviet achievements are included in
foreign language text books. These courses are,
however, particularly valuable for the opportunities
they give to mount a convincing counter-attack
against foreign enemies. Thus, an English textbook
for the ninth grade takes as one of its themes the
decision by the American artist Rockwell Kent to
donate his pictures to the Soviet Union. This text
contrasts the oppression of progressive artists in
imperialist countries with the benevolent and

munificent attitude of the Soviet system to its own
artists. Film strips showing how musicians play
and artists draw in chalk on the pavements of
capitalist countries in the hope of attracting alms
are used to reinforce the supposed contrast. As
one of their tasks designed to activate their command
of a foreign language pupils are required to compare
the situation of young people finishing school in
the USSR with those in capitalist countries.[31] A
new textbook called <u>Mastering English Through Talking
Politics</u> uses this contrastive method throughout in a
singularly tendentious manner. The section on
education is not untypical. On the one hand, it
is stated about Great Britain:

> Further and higher education are not free of
> charge. A student has to pay a tuition fee.
> Student grants are sometimes provided by local
> education authorities and companies for the most
> promising students. However, most of the
> students have to cover education costs on their
> own. As a rule only well-to-do families can
> afford to send their children to university.
> This clearly shows the class-oriented nature
> of higher education in Great Britain.

On the other hand, in the Soviet Union: 'Education
is free at all levels. Moreover, students of higher
schools get grants... The (sic) admission to the
(sic) institutions of higher education is competitive.
It is based on a system of entrance examinations.'[32]
Classes in Russian literature provide similar
opportunities, though here the stress lies more on
Soviet heroism and achievement as an aid to the
development of patriotic feelings, of anti-religious
sentiments and of the correct moral and social
attitudes.[33]
The central core of the political education
programme in the Soviet school is, however,
contained in the classes devoted to history and the
social sciences. History has long been openly
recognised as the most valuable academic instrument
for the indoctrination of the young in the USSR.
It is studied as a separate discipline from a
child's fourth year at school, right through to his
final year. New textbooks are aimed to give the
child a more systematic exposition of the works of
Marx, Engels and Lenin, and of the basic documents
of the Communist Party and of the Soviet State.
The works of Lenin, and latterly of Brezhnev himself,
feature prominently in the programme. History as a

158

subject is seen as essential in forming a communist world outlook in that it reveals to the pupils the laws of history, of human development and of the class struggle. It proves thereby that capitalism is inevitably doomed and that socialism will triumph everywhere. By associating the 'national liberation movements' with this process, it shows the Soviet child his internationalist duty to aid such movements on a world-wide scale. Right from the fourth class, children are introduced to abstract concepts such as 'inequality', 'exploiter', 'serf order', 'capitalist', 'revolution' and so on in concrete historical contexts. In the fourth class a capitalist is thus defined as 'a rich man who exploits hired workers'.

By pointing out that the USSR was the first country to achieve socialism, and thereby is the natural leader and hope of progressive mankind, the study of history helps to instil a feeling of patriotism in the Soviet child. In Tsarist times, a Russian national was officially deemed by definition to be loyal to the Tsar. In Soviet Russia, a determined and consistent effort is made not only to develop patriotic feelings among the population but also clearly and inextricably to associate the Communist Party with national successes, and thereby to make it the leading symbol of Soviet patriotism. Thus, a study of Soviet successes in the Second World War (known as the Great Fatherland War in its phase after 1941) is stressed as being essential to the development of patriotism in the young. At the same time, it helps to develop a feeling of hatred towards the enemies of socialism, in the first instance the German fascists, but, by process of transference, also the imperialist powers of the contemporary world.

> While imperialism exists, while hundreds of millions of people on earth remain the slaves of capital, each of our children must be ready for a bloody conflict on the field of battle. It is necessary to transmit to the young generation not only all the strength and depth of our patriotism but also the white-heat of our hatred for fascism, and for the imperialists - the tyrants over mankind. The war against fascist Germany was a war between two opposed socio-economic systems, a struggle that still continues. A burning love for the Motherland is inseparable from the deepest hatred towards its enemies.[34]

The study of history is also considered to be
essential in the struggle to eliminate attitudes
associated with the old order. Religion is thus
shown to be historically a weapon in the class war
of exploiters against the mass of the population.
The reactionary role of the church in the development
of culture has to be shown. In later classes, texts
from Lenin are used to demonstrate the positive
attractions of atheism. By the tenth class, children
should have been convinced that religious morality is
unscientific and incompatible with the norms of life
of the Soviet people. 'Religion obstructs the
inculcation of hatred towards the exploiters and
towards the enemies of the workers; by preaching
universal love and forgiveness, it supports outmoded
customs in the family and in life.'[35] Additionally,
history is used to combat 'chauvinistic bourgeois
nationalism' and to promote in its place the concept
of proletarian internationalism, and to preach the
need for the fraternal union of the proletariat of
all nations in the struggle for the common aim of
socialism and communism. Thus, for instance, the
study of the Civil War in the ninth class is used
to provide a definition of a patriotism of a higher
type, namely Soviet patriotism. This kind of
patriotism does away with simple national loyalties.
This is the patriotism of all on the Red side,
whether they were Russians, Ukrainians, Czechs,
Belorussians or others, in the struggle against the
class enemy in defence of the new, progressive order.
Patriotism on the White side, on the other hand, was
manifested in bourgeois nationalism, and in attempts
to restore the old capitalist order. The victory
of the Reds was the victory of the world proletariat
over the combined efforts of international capitalism.
It is admitted that nationalistic prejudices still
exist; the task of teachers of Soviet history is
to eliminate them by demonstrating 'the brotherly
collaboration of the peoples of the USSR in the
construction of socialism', and by proving that the
Soviet people represents a new historical community
of peoples of different races.[36]
    The classes in social studies reinforce and
expand the political message obtained in the history
classes. The new course on 'the fundamental
principles of the Soviet State and Law' introduced
into the eighth class is of particular interest.
This is designed firstly to make the theoretical
point that Soviet law is qualitatively different
from bourgeois legal systems, and secondly, on a
more practical plane, to promote law-abiding habits

amongst Soviet youth. Whereas in bourgeois
societies, laws are designed to protect property
and the interests of the ruling classes, in the USSR
laws and the constitution defend the common good and
guarantee basic human rights, such as that to work,
to free education, to decent cheap accommodation,
and so on. This is in stark contrast to capitalist
countries like Britain where in 1978 it is said that
almost 100,000 people were without a flat at a time
when over 100,000 flats in London alone were empty
because they were too expensive for ordinary people.[37]
It is further alleged that, 'in a series of
capitalist states, imperialist circles inflame a
military psychosis and connive at propaganda of a
man-hating ideology. In our state, propaganda in
favour of war, nationalism, racial hostility and
discord is a criminal activity.'[38] It is hoped
that knowledge of the laws themselves, and in
particular of the penalties for breaking them, will
discourage young people from crime. Moreover, it
is emphasised that it is the task of each Soviet
citizen to play an active role in fighting against
crime, since inactivity or passivity can lead to
harm to the state. The rights of Soviet citizens
demand for their realisation a clear acknowledgement
of their obligations to the state. These extend
from observance of the law to positive attitudes
towards work. The right to work guaranteed in the
USSR demands as its converse the obligation of each
citizen to work properly. It is no accident that
this new course places emphasis in its content on
the labour laws, and on the need for work discipline
and respect for socialist (i.e. state) property.

The social studies course in the tenth class
expands the range of the political concepts gained
from the classes in history, and is intended to give
a deeper understanding of the role of the Soviet
Communist Party at home and abroad. The underlying theme is the superiority of socialism over
capitalism and the consequent inevitable victory of
the former. Additionally, pupils are warned against
the snares of revisionist Marxists and are exhorted,
on leaving school, to help to raise productivity
through the effectiveness and quality of their own
work. Marxist-Leninist theory is supposed always
to be supported by empirical evidence. Thus, in
the section of the course entitled 'from capitalism
to socialism', much information is produced to
illustrate the crisis of contemporary capitalism and
what is made out to be the serious military threat
from the West, and in particular from the USA, the

'world exploiter and gendarme, the irreconcilable
enemy of liberation movements'. In this context,
the impossibility of peaceful coexistence in the
sphere of ideology is emphasised. In lessons on
the 'Soviet socialist state', the new Constitution
of 1977 is used as a basic text for detailed study.[39]
Great stress is laid on the material of the 25th and
26th Party Congresses, and recent party decrees. The
autobiographical trilogy of Brezhnev is strongly
recommended as ideal material for study. This
section of a pupil's course is thus, in effect, a
detailed exposition of current policies of the Soviet
leadership in their historical context expounded in
laudatory tones calculated to win positive support
for them.

Higher Education
In higher education, the extent of political content
in a student's course depends on his particular
subject specialisation. Thus, there is an extremely
high political emphasis in history, but a
relatively low one in natural sciences. For many
students, therefore, political education comes
essentially in courses throughout their period of
study, in dialectical and historical materialism,
scientific atheism, history of the CPSU, the
development of capitalism and socialism according
to the principles of Marxism-Leninism, which are
compulsory for all subject specialisations. Since
all of these are examinable and have to be passed,
it means that all Soviet students are forced to
memorise the required texts and can at very least
repeat the ideological phrases required of them.
Essentially these courses develop at a more
sophisticated level the material already presented
in the secondary school, although scientific atheism
has been introduced as a subject in its own right
instead of just being an adjunct to other courses.
The main outline of the programme is determined
centrally, but the individual institutions are able
to introduce material appropriate to their
particular specialisation, in accordance with
Lenin's dictum that the propagandist should adjust
his approach to suit his particular audience. A
mining institute will thus dwell on the miners'
experiences in its course on the history of the
Communist Party.[40] Teachers of political economy
courses are encouraged to use local examples to show
how individual initiative and socialist competition
can increase production.[41] Patriotism is stimulated
by visits from local heroes of the Great Patriotic

War, and graphic accounts, for instance, of the activities of local groups of partisans in the war.[42] It is realised that students after graduation will often become responsible for groups of workers, and that therefore it is important for them to be able to expound clearly and effectively their communist convictions and to counter ideological diversions. Students may therefore be required not just to prepare papers for presentation, but also to participate in mock press conferences. In this context, the recent introduction of 'Faculties of Social Professions' (FOPs) into the majority of higher education institutions is of importance. These faculties are designed to attract students on all courses to ideological work and so turn out specialists who will additionally be able to organise cultural and political work among the population at large.[43]

The political education process in the educational system is not confined to the classroom or lecture hall. A variety of voluntary activities are organised to reinforce the implantation of desired attitudes. Special trips to Lenin museums are organised, essay competitions organised and conferences held on Lenin and political themes. 'Lenin corners' are devoutly tended in schools, and wall newspapers prepared. Pressure is put on pupils and students to volunteer to join groups of young lecturers 'to prepare and give lectures on political themes not only to their fellows, but also to the population at large in factories, on construction sites and at other such places.'[44] The multitude of newspapers and journals published specially for children and young people are liberally sprinkled with articles of a political nature. Patriotism is encouraged by laudatory features on Soviet heroes such as the cosmonaut Gagarin, whose thirst for knowledge, ceaseless activity and hard work apparently led him to his pinnacle of fame. In other words, the qualities which the leadership wishes the ideal Soviet man to display are featured prominently in these character studies, for emulation by the young readers. Stories of legendary pioneer heroes who killed over twenty Hitlerites in their first battle are designed to stimulate patriotism, whilst negative attitudes towards foreign imperialist powers are fostered by articles such as the one on the murder of John Lennon in which it was claimed that no Western newspapers condemned a society 'in which even a madman can buy a pistol or rifle in any arms shop'.[45] Pioneer Truth

on 8 May 1981 published an article on Northern
Ireland, accusing English imperialism of stirring
up discord between Protestants and Catholics in
order to maintain its grip over Ulster, and
portraying the hunger strikers as patriots fighting
for their motherland against British enslavement.
The contrastive approach is used in an account of a
Soviet sportswoman's visit to Spain, to show how,
in contrast to the USSR, most Spanish children are
denied sports facilities because their parents
cannot afford to pay the huge fees demanded.   The
USSR is said to trade honestly and always keep its
contracts, whereas the USA uses international trade
to impose political pressures, as in the recent
grain embargo.[46]   Heroic tales from Afghanistan
about progressive peasant boys with hand grenades
point the political moral that what is going on there
is a class struggle against the feudal order of
exploiters, and in particular for the right of young
people to education.   The troops are alleged to be
concentrated on the frontiers, day and night trying
to prevent the incursion of armed bands in the pay
of foreign espionage services.[47]

Youth Organisations

The mass youth organisations, whether they be the
Octobrists for the first three classes, the Pioneers
for the next three, and then the Komsomol from the
seventh grade onwards, all continue to organise a
plethora of activities consecrated to reinforcing
the formal programme of political education.   Of
particular importance in this context are the summer
camps for pioneers, and work detachments for senior
pupils and students.   Much of the activity of the
pioneer camps is purely recreational, but a
conscious attempt is made to form the right
attitudes through pressure of the collective, and
political sessions are a regular feature.   Labour
becomes a more prominent feature as children become
old enough to join the detachments which go out to
help gather the harvest, or to engage in construction
projects and the like.   This work is of economic
significance, for instance, over 30 per cent of the
total tomato harvest being picked annually by
students in the Astrakhan region, but it is also
supposed to instil collectivist attitudes and
correct work habits in the participants. * In
theory it heightens the youth's consciousness and
approval of the goals of the party; in practice,
one suspects that those engaged in tasks like
lifting sugar beet may sometimes feel that they are

being used as cheap labour.[48]

This chapter has concentrated deliberately on political education within the formal educational system. However, for the Soviet leadership, this process is of much wider application, affecting the whole population virtually from birth to the grave, and involving the family, the place of work, leisure activities from the arts to sport, and all the mass media. All of this activity has been intensified in response to directives from the centre. It is, however, very difficult to form a realistic assessment of how successful this programme has been and is likely to be in the 1980s. Western commentators tend to be sceptical about its efficacy. To take three recent examples, Hill and Frank state that the results of the special lecture programme seem to be 'far from what might be desired by the leaders' and point to Soviet complaints about the negative elements which remain in Soviet society. Carrere d'Encausse argues that Soviet educational policy has failed to achieve its main goal, the creation of a homogeneous Soviet society. With specific reference to the native peoples of Siberia and to the Soviet Moslem population, she concludes that local elites still look to their ethnic group as a manifestation of a growing feeling of national identity. Powell has argued that atheistic education in both school and university has aroused little interest in either pupil or teacher and so has been ineffective.[49] References in the Soviet press are easily found to support this view, whether they be cryptic references to bad behaviour by children on summer camps or more specific analyses of failings in the formal educational programme. In the answers to one questionnaire, 60 per cent of an eighth year class failed to realise that the international duty of a Soviet citizen is supposed to include all-sided support to national liberation movements. A recent Soviet source says that only a small percentage of children in senior classes in another survey considered that religion brought any harm even though they did not see any advantages to it either. Studies of the Komsomol have pointed to a passive attitude by many of its members towards its activities, including a reluctance to become involved in socially useful work.[50] Sociology has only relatively recently come into favour as an academic discipline in the USSR. Polling of attitudes on various subjects has begun, recent studies, for instance, showing that the level of religious belief is nearly three times as high in

the countryside compared with the town in Penza province and that one in ten families now has a religious
upbringing, even if the actual level of religious
belief among the educated urban youth is very low
indeed.[51]   However, these polls have tended to be
on specific issues in particular areas and to
generalise on the basis of them is, as a recent
article in Pravda has pointed out, dangerous. Alarmed
by events in Poland, this article indicates that the
Soviet leadership sees the urgent need for more
systematic and extensive testing of public opinion.[52]
If this takes place, and is published, it may become
possible to assess the degree of success or failure
of the Soviet political education programme.   In
the meantime, the best that one can do is to point
to Soviet criticism of inadequacies, and to the very
fact of the recent intensification of the programme,
to support the view that success so far has been
limited.   However, in so doing, one should not
underestimate the degree of passive acceptance of the
general objectives of the regime, except perhaps in
some of the national republics.   What would seem to
be lacking is general popular enthusiasm expressed in
active participation in activities directed towards
achievement of these goals.

Looking Towards the Future
It seems clear that a continued feature of Soviet
educational policies throughout the 1980s will be a
considerable and probably increased stress on the
political education of the population.   This is for
a combination of political and economic reasons.
The loss of the USSR's undisputed ideological leadership of the Communist world has led to a series of
challenges, and to presentation of alternative models
which might hold some attraction for sections of the
Soviet population if allowed to infiltrate undisputed.
There is no sign of any abatement of these
challenges.   Recent developments in Poland,
emphasising the dangers resulting from the vanguard
party becoming isolated from the popular masses,
have only highlighted the need for a forceful and
positive campaign actively to engage the political
loyalty of the Soviet people to the party.   The
obvious connection between religious sentiments and
nationalist feeling in republics like Lithuania, and
the spectre of Muslim fundamentalism spreading to
the USSR have made essential an intensive campaign
against nationalist separatist sentiments.   In late
Tsarist Russia, the Orthodox church was seen as the
cement binding together a multinational Empire.

Communist ideology and Soviet patriotism are used as the modern equivalents. The necessity to prove that the laws of history are being fulfilled and that therefore the USSR is well on the way to achieving Communism has made ideologically imperative the more active involvement of the citizen in the affairs of society. The economic need to revitalise the economy and to utilise technological innovations to the best advantage has underlined the urgency of obtaining the active commitment of the people at large to the objectives set for them by the Party. Physical coercion has been largely abandoned with the renunciation of much of Stalinist methodology; it is anyway too crude an instrument to be effective in an advanced technological society. The bored repetition of standard phrases is no longer sufficient for political education. An active and intelligent defence of Communist principles as defined by the Soviet leadership is required, together with an ability decisively to reject alternatives posed by other sources. More than that, active commitment to these principles has to be manifested in the individual's way of life and his attitude to work. These objectives are obviously not going to be easy to achieve, and carry with them certain dangers. The more stimulating and active studies demanded allow scope for independence of approach and entail discussion, albeit in a negative fashion, of heretical concepts. Although official ideology does not allow the possibility of a divergence of interest between the Soviet people and their rulers, the latter are obviously concerned lest the unthinkable may happen. In order to prevent this, not only do the people have to be convinced positively that they are at one with the Politburo, but also the latter has increasingly to ascertain and to take account of popular aspirations. To satisfy these, a more productive economy is essential, but this in itself demands a more energetic commitment from the population, with greater initiative from below and less of the inertia that has been the inevitable legacy of the years of Stalinist coercion. The programme of political education, for all its intentions, seems still all too often to repeat set formulae redolent of the past; its future full success remains open to doubt.

THE POLITICAL CONTENT OF EDUCATION IN THE USSR

NOTES

1. J.L. Black, Citizens for the Fatherland (Columbia University Press, New York, 1979), pp. 80-81.

2. K.P. Pobedonostsev, Reflections of a Russian Statesman (University of Michigan Press, Ann Arbor, 1965), p. 84.

3. L.I. Brezhnev, 'Otchet tsentral'nogo komiteta KPSS i ocherednye zadachi partii v oblasti vnutrennei i vneshnei politiki', Materialy XXV s"ezda KPSS (Izdatel'stvo politicheskoi literatury, Moscow, 1976), pp. 71-81.

4. O dal'neishem uluchshenii ideologicheskoi, politiko-vospitatel'noi raboty. Postanovlenie TsKKPSS ot 26 aprelia 1979 goda (Politizdat, Moscow, 1980), pp. 3-15.

5. L.I. Brezhnev, 'Otchet tsentral'nogo komiteta KPSS XXVI s"ezdu kommunisticheskoi partii Sovetskogo Soyuza i ocherednye zadachi partii v oblasti vnutrennei i vneshnei politiki', XXVI s"ezd kommunisticheskoi partii Sovetskogo Soyuza. Stenograficheskii otchet (Izdatel'stvo politicheskoi literatury, Moscow, 1981), pp. 94-98.

6. XXVI s"ezd, p. 113.

7. Ibid., pp. 372-373.

8. M.A. Prokof'ev, 'Shkol'nikam - o XXVI s"ezde KPSS', Vospitanie shkol'nikov, 1981, no. 3, p. 2.

9. 'Kachestvo i eshche raz kachestvo: Doklad ministra prosveshcheniya SSSR M.A. Prokof'eva na godichnom sobranii APN SSSR', Uchitel'skaya gazeta, 26 May, 1981, p. 3.

10. XXVI s"ezd, p. 113.

11. Ibid., pp. 94, 26.

12. Prokof'ev, 'Shkol'nikam', p. 3.

13. V.M. Chebrikov, 'Bditel'nost' - ispytannoe oruzhie', Molodoi kommunist, 1981, no. 4, pp. 28-34.

14. XXVI s"ezd, pp. 26-27.

15. Alfred B. Evans Jr., 'Developed Socialism in Soviet Ideology', Soviet Studies, vol. XXIX, no. 3 (July 1977), pp. 409-428.

16. Materialy XXV s"ezda KPSS, pp. 77-78.

17. Ibid., p. 77.

18. Elaine V. Harasymiw, 'Civic Education in the Soviet Union. A Model for Political Socialisation', Canadian Slavonic Papers, vol. XXII, no. 1 (March 1980), pp. 52-54; F.G. Panachin, 'The Party's School Programme in Action', Soviet Education, vol. XXIII, no. 5 (March 1981), pp. 63-75 (from Sovetskaya pedagogika, 1979, no. 12, pp. 3-9); Yu.Yu. Ivanov, 'Pedagogical Support for Universal

Secondary Education', Soviet Education, vol. XXIII, no. 5 (March 1981), pp. 7-16 (from Sovetskaya pedagogika, 1980, no. 8, pp. 3-7).
   19. F.G. Panachin, 'The Party's School Programme in Action', p. 70.
   20. A.I. Gavrikov, Ya. Zhalud and P.N. Reshetov, 'Vospitanie molodezhi v usloviyakh sovremennoi ideologicheskoi bor'by', Sovetskaya pedagogika, 1981, no. 5, p. 35.
   21. Ibid., pp. 35-36; V.K. Rozov, 'Socio-economic Issues of Teacher Education and Increasing the Effective Utilisation of Pedagogical Cadres', Soviet Education, vol. XXIII, no. 5 (March 1981), pp. 57-58 (from Sovetskaya pedagogika, 1980, no. 2, pp. 97-102).
   22. Prokof'ev, 'Shkol'nikam', p. 2.
   23. M.T. Studenikin (Ed.), Kommunisticheskoe vospitanie uchashchikhsya na urokakh istorii, obshchestvovedenia i osnov sovetskogo gosudarstva i prava (Prosveshchenie, Moscow, 1981), p. 15.
   24. M.S. Vasil'eva, 'O kommunisticheskoi partii na urokakh chteniya', Nachal'naya shkola, 1981, no. 4, pp. 23-24.
   25. 'Rastim Iunykh Lenintsev. Iz opyta', Nachal'naya shkola, 1981, no. 4, pp. 25-36.
   26. Vasil'eva, 'O kommunisticheskoi partii', p. 23.
   27. N.A. Gorokhov, P.I. Shpital'nik, N.I. Volkus, D.F. Kondrat'eva and L.I. Taktaeva, 'Shkoly v dni XXVI s"ezda KPSS', Nachal'naya shkola, 1981, no. 4, pp. 5-10; Prokof'ev, 'Shkol'nikam', p. 3.
   28. M.S. Vasil'eva, 'O formirovanii nachal kommunisticheskogo mirovozzreniya mladshikh shkol'nikov v protsesse obucheniya', Sovetskaya pedagogika, 1981, no. 5, pp. 43-47.
   29. T.A. Kurakin and L.I. Novikova, 'Kharakteristika sovremennoi shkoly kak vospitatel'noi sistemy', Sovetskaya pedagogika, 1981, no. 5, p. 37.
   30. I.T. Ogorodnikov (Ed.), School Pedagogy, in Soviet Education, vol. XXII, nos. 9-10 (July-August 1980), pp. 132-134.
   31. A.D. Klimentenko, 'Formirovanie kommunisticheskogo mirovozzreniya shkol'nikov pri obuchenii inostrannym yazykam', Voprosy pedagogiki, 1981, no. 4, pp. 35-40.
   32. I.I. Panova, Iu. M. Revtovich, G.I. Beryozka, Mastering English Through Talking Politics (Vysheishaya Shkola, Minsk, 1981), pp. 58-65.
   33. Ogorodnikov, School Pedagogy, p. 134; see also N.N. Shneidman, Literature and Ideology in Soviet Education (D.C. Heath and Co., Toronto and London, 1973).

34. 'Privivat' chuvstvo otvetstvennosti za sud'by sotsialisma, za prosvetanie i bezopasnost' Rodiny', Vospitanie shkol'nikov, 1981, no. 1, pp. 9-11.
35. Studenikin, Kommunisticheskoe vospitanie, p. 31.
36. Ibid., pp. 47-71; see also L.N. Bogolyubov, Ideinoe vospitanie na urokakh istorii (Prosveshchenie, Moscow, 1981).
37. N.G. Suvorova, 'Obrazovatel'no-vospitatel'-naya rol' izucheniya Konstitutsii SSSR' in Studenikin, Kommunisticheskoe vospitanie, p. 177.
38. A.F. Kovaleva and A.A. Galkina, 'Formirovanie pravovogo soznaniya uchashchikhsya' in Studenikin, Kommunisticheskoe vospitanie, pp. 165-166.
39. Studenikin, Kommunisticheskoe vospitanie, pp. 17-28 and 116-146; Prokof'ev, 'Shkol'nikam', pp. 2-9; Ogorodnikov, School Pedagogy, pp. 135-137; Obshchestvovedenie. Programma dlya srednei obshcheobrazovatel'noi shkoly i srednikh spetsial'nykh uchebnykh zavedenii (Politizdat, Moscow, 1980).
40. F.S. Pavlov and E.I. Shashenkova, Sviaz' prepodavaniya istorii c profilem vuza (Vysshaya shkola, Moscow, 1981), pp. 8-9 and 19-40.
41. V.V. Korochkin, 'V kurse politicheskoi ekonomii', Vestnik vysshei shkoly, 1981, no. 5, p. 61.
42. V.G. Goleva and S.P. Bezzubek, 'Na slavnykh traditsiyakh', Vestnik vysshei shkoly, 1981, no. 5, pp. 54-55.
43. E.N. Tsygankova, 'Spetskurs po nauchnomu kommunizmu', Vestnik vysshei shkoly, 1981, no. 5, p. 68; A.M. Korshunov and A.V. Mironov, 'Uluchshat' raboty FOP-ov', Vestnik vysshei shkoly, 1981, no. 4, pp. 51-54.
44. G.V. Kiselev, 'Opyt shushenskikh shkol po vospitanii uchashchikhsya', Sovetskaya pedagogika, 1981, no. 4, pp. 21-23; M.B. Liga, 'OPP v narodnom muzee', Vestnik vysshei shkoly, 1981, no. 4, pp. 56-57; I.V. Strokov, 'Optimiziruem obuchenie v Sh.M.L.', Vestnik vysshei shkoly, 1981, no. 3, pp. 65-66; M. Naidich, 'Lektorskaya gruppa starsheklassnikov', Vospitanie shkol'nikov, 1981, no. 3, pp. 35-37; V.M. Savel'ev and V.I. Burmistrov,'Primenyaya raznoobraznye metody', Vestnik vysshei shkoly, 1981, no. 3, pp. 67-68; V.K. Taunek and A.P. Savotkin, 'Privivaem navyki lektorskogo masterstva', Vestnik vysshei shkoly, 1981, no. 4, pp. 54-56.
45. Pioner, 1981, no. 5, pp. 3-5 and 28-29.
46. Pionerskaya pravda, no. 37, 8 May 1981, no. 41, 22 May 1981 and no. 44, 2 June 1981.
47. Andrei Sakharov, 'Konets Zhandi Guliama',

Pioner, 1981, no. 4, pp. 41-46;   Pavel Penezhko,
'Tri goda bor'by i pobedy, Pioner, 1981, no. 4, p. 47.
    48. V.M. Ryzhkov, 'Studencheskim otryadam -
vnimanie i zaboty', Vestnik vysshei shkoly, 1981,
no. 5, pp. 50-52;   L.V. Alieva and I.G. Gordin,
'Pioneriya na marshe.   Iz pionerskoi letopisi',
Nachal'naya shkola, 1981, no. 5, pp. 5-8; Yu. Burakov,
'Pionerskii lager - shkola vospitaniya aktiva',
Vospitanie shkol'nikov, 1981, no. 3, pp. 49-51.
    49. Ronald J. Hill and Peter Frank, The Soviet
Communist Party (George Allen and Unwin, London, 1981),
p. 78; Hélène Carrere d'Encausse, 'Political
Socialization in the USSR with Special Reference to
non-Russian Nationalities', Slavic and European
Education Review, 1981, no. 1, pp. 1-10;   David E.
Powell, Anti-Religious Propaganda in the Soviet Union
(MIT Press, Cambridge and London, 1975), pp. 56-57.
    50. K. Bykov, 'I pervye mozoli', Znamya Yunosti,
Minsk, 16 July, 1981, p. 2;   Studenikin,
Kommunisticheskoe vospitanie, pp. 27, 108-109;
K.G. Stolypina, 'Vospitanie aktivnoi sotsial'noi
pozitsii starshikh shkol'nikov', Voprosy pedagogiki,
1981, no. 4, p. 43.
    51. V.D. Kobetskii, 'Study of the Process of
Overcoming Religiosity and of the Dissemination of
Atheism', Soviet Sociology, vol. XIX, no. 1 (1980),
pp. 50-62.
    52. R. Safarov, 'Obshchestvennoe mnenie:
izuchenie i deistvennost'', Pravda, 25 September,
1981, pp. 2-3.

NEW MODEL CURRICULUM FOR SOVIET PRIMARY, EIGHT-YEAR AND SECONDARY SCHOOLS, 1981/2 (1977/8 in parentheses, where different)

Periods per week per form

SUBJECTS	I	II	III	IV	V	VI	VII	VIII	IX	X	Total
1. Russian language	12	11	10	8	6	4	3	2	–	–	54
2. Literature					2	2	2	3	4	3	18
3. Mathematics	6	6	6	6	6	6	6	6	5	5/4(5)	57.5(58)
4. History						2	2	3	4	3	18
5. Soviet State and Law								1			1
6. Social Studies										2	2
7. Nature Study		1	2	1(2)							4(5)
8. Geography						3	2	2	2		11
9. Biology					2	2	2	2	1	2	11
10. Physics							2	3	4	4/5(5)	15.5(16)
11. Astronomy									–(1)	1	2(3)
12. Technical Drawing							1	1	–		2
13. Chemistry							2	2	3	3	10
14. Foreign Language				4(–)	3(4)	2(3)	2(3)	1(2)	1(2)	1(2)	14(16)
15. Art	1	1	1	1	1	1	1				6
16. Music and Singing	1	1	1	1	1	1	1				7
17. Physical Education	2	2	2	2	2	2	2	2	2	2	20
18. Labour Training	2	2	2	2	2	2	2	2	4(2)	4(2)	24(20)
19. Elem. Military Training									2	2	4
TOTAL COMPULSORY PERIODS	24	24	24	27(24)	29(30)	29(30)	**29**(30)	30(31)	32	32	280(281)
20. Options					2		2	3	4	4	13

Source: Byulleten' normativnykh aktov Ministerstva prosveshcheniya SSSR, 1980, no. 12, pp. 27–30. Note: The 1977/8 periods are for the RSFSR (from Sbornik prikazov i instruktsii Ministerstva prosveshcheniya RSFSR, 1977, no. 7, p. 27).

Chapter 7

SOVIET PHYSICAL EDUCATION

James Riordan

Theory
'The Soviet education system shall serve communist
upbringing and the spiritual and physical development
of young people.'[1]

> 'Marxism-Leninism is the ideological basis of
> the Soviet theory of physical education. Marx,
> Engels and Lenin scientifically substantiated
> the principle that the main objective of
> communist education is all-round development
> and training for labour and defence of one's
> country. Physical education is a component
> part of all-round education.'[2]

Although this paper will concentrate on
physical education in Soviet schools, an introductory
word is necessary on the overall framework of
education and physical culture within which the
Soviet authorities view school PE. The following
three key principles help to explain the Soviet
approach to PE and the essential differences with
Western theory and practice.

The Concept of Physical Culture
In Soviet physical education we are dealing with a
philosophy - notably of physical culture - that
differs fundamentally from that which we in the West
normally associate with physical education,
competitive sport or recreation. Physical culture
is the parent whose children are games, outdoor
recreation, PE and competitive sport - even health,
hygiene, civil defence and artistic expression.
The acquisition of their culture is said to be an
integral process that accompanies a person through
life, in home, nursery, school, college, factory,
office and farm. Accordingly, physical culture in

the USSR is by no means a matter merely of fun and games, something you can take or leave as you please. Someone who neglects the physical side of his development is seen as only half a person, like one who neglects the education of his mind.

To Westerners accustomed to the idea that sport is the garden of human activities, and often a private garden at that, the approach to sport or physical culture in modernising societies like the USSR may be difficult to understand. It is a serious business, controlled by the State, with serious functions to perform: it is associated with health, defence, patriotism, integration, productivity, international recognition, even nation-building. That is why, it is claimed, physical culture could not be allowed to develop haphazardly, as in the West. In any case, there has been no leisure class to develop sport for its own disport.

Physical and Mental Development

In Soviet conceptualising, since the human organism develops and changes under the influence of external conditions, including the social environment, subjection to physical exercise not only develops that part of the body to which it is directed, but also has an effect on the whole psychosomatic system - on the personality. A strong bond exists, then, between social and individual development and between the physical and mental development of the individual. Hence the emphasis on parity between physical and mental culture in human development, both for the all-round development of the individual and, ultimately, for the health of society.

The principles of this outlook are ascribed in Soviet writing mainly to four men: Marx, Lenin, Lesgaft and Pavlov.

Karl Marx (1818-83). At the time Marx was writing, metaphysics was in the grip of a dualism that separated mind from matter and, under the influence of Christian theology, often exaggerated a distinction into an antagonism; in such a world-view, body and soul were seen as warring parties with the body cast as the villain of the piece. This led to a concern with things of the mind at the expense of bodily activities. Marx rejected the dualist philosophy and stressed that not only was there an intimate relationship between matter and mind, but that the former largely determined the latter. He looked forward to the education system of the future

that would 'combine productive labour with
instruction and gymnastics, not only as a means of
improving the efficiency of production, but as the
only way to produce fully-developed human beings.'[3]

Vladimir Lenin (1870-1924).   Unlike Marx, who
personally abhorred any physical exercise,[4] Lenin
was an active practitioner of physical fitness in
his own life.   Like Marx, Lenin's educational
philosophy favoured a combination of the training of
the mind and body:

> It is impossible to visualise the ideal of a
> future society without a combination of
> instruction and productive labour, nor can
> productive labour without parallel instruction
> and physical education be put on a plane
> required by the modern level of technology and
> scientific knowledge.[5]

But Lenin added an emphasis on character-
training that was absent from Marx.   He recognised
the effects that sport and PE might have, for
instance, upon the development of qualities of
character valuable to individuals and society, upon
the social behaviour of citizens and upon the
promotion of health.   One can imagine Lenin's ideal
young people (not unlike the heroes of Kingsley's
Westward Ho and Hughes's Tom Brown's Schooldays)
drawn in glowing colours, adorned with every sort of
athletic accomplishment and displaying the
excellence of simple understanding and the urge to
serve the cause.   The resolution passed by the
Third All-Russia Congress of the Russian Young
Communist League (October, 1920) - at which Lenin
spoke - surely reflected his views on the functions
of physical education:

> The physical education of the younger
> generation is an essential element in the
> overall system of the communist upbringing of
> young people, aimed at creating harmoniously-
> developed people, creative citizens of
> communist society.   Today, physical education
> also has direct practical aims: 1) preparing
> young people for work; and 2) preparing them
> for military defence of Soviet power.[6]

This, the first clear-cut official statement on
the aims of physical education, makes no bones about
its rational use for work and defence.   It does,

however, hint that, once the society is on its feet
and socialism is moving towards communism,
utilitarian-instrumental aims will give way to
self-realisation.

Lesgaft (1837-1909). The figure who is said to
have made the most lasting impression on Russian
and Soviet physical education was Pyotr Lesgaft,
biologist, anatomist, educationalist and social
reformer - the founder of the new discipline of PE
in tsarist Russia. Several major tenets of his
theory and system today underlie Soviet PE: ideas
of harmonious development, of social awareness
through PE, of the principle of step-by-step,
consistent training, of belief in a biological
justification for exercise and games in general, of
women's social emancipation through the bodily
liberation of physical activity, and of the strict
observance of age, sex and individual characteristics
of children when engaging in physical exercise.
Training and teaching in the USSR are still largely
guided by Lesgaft's views on mastering bodily
movements by stages, starting from the learning of
correct forms of movement in the nursery and
gradually increasing the load up to the
elaboration of spatial and temporal orientation. On
the other hand, his hostility to competitive sport,
public displays and victory rituals, while finding
ready accord in the 1920s, came to be rejected
totally with the onset of full-scale industrialisation
and the widespread application of incentives throughout the economy.[7]

Pavlov (1849-1926). If Lesgaft 'was the founder of
the scientific system of physical education',[8] the
work of 'the great Russian physiologist, Pavlov,
forms the basis of the entire system of physical
education in the Soviet Union'.[9] In fact, the
physiological studies of Ivan Pavlov and others were
to have a considerable impact on Soviet PE and
sport, including national fitness programmes (the
GTO), sports training methods and physical exercises
at work (proizvodstvennaya gimnastika). By means of
numerous experiments with animals, Pavlov concluded
that the human organism and its environment were
connected by conditioned reflexes - 'temporary
connections of the nervous system that constantly
appear, grow strong and then disappear'.[10]
According to this theory, 'the conditioned reflex is
the basis of all of our higher nervous activity'.[11]
This theory had several implications for Soviet PE.

Primarily, it meant that exercise was highly
salutary for the central nervous system: systematic
participation in a variety of games, gymnastics and
sports improves the general functioning and capacity
both of the physical organism and of the mind; hence
the need for regular physical activity by all
citizens, for the good of society as well as of the
individual.

Giftedness

If the culture of the body is regarded as just as
vital as that of the mind for the harmonious development of the individual and of society, it would
follow that talent in physical culture should be
treated no differently from talent in art, music or
science.   In other words, promising young gymnasts,
say, should be regarded in the same way as promising
ballet dancers: they have to be given every
opportunity to develop their ability.   What is more,
unlike the earlier administrators of amateur sport
in the West, the Soviet leadership has never been
constrained by the notion that sport is an unworthy
profession or career.   Given this outlook, it is
logical that the USSR should have an extensive
screening system in schools and clubs designed to
sift out talent at an early age.
     Despite the ideological desires of Soviet
leaders, the forms of physical culture which developed
in Soviet society have not always coincided with the
predictions of Marxist writers about the society of
the future.   In a vast multinational land that has
witnessed disorientingly rapid change, physical
culture, with its broad relevance to education,
health, culture and politics, and its capacity to
mobilise people (predispose them towards change),
has uniquely served the state as a vehicle of social
change and an adjunct to the policy of building a
strong nation-state.

Organisation

'Soviet physical education represents a unity of
ideological and scientific principles, as well as
of organisations and institutions which implement
and control the physical education of Soviet
citizens.'12
     The administration of physical culture came
under the aegis of the state after the October 1917
Revolution, and the entire PE and sports movement has
since been fully integrated with the political system.
Over the past nearly 65 years, physical culture has
therefore been state-controlled, encouraged and

shaped by specific utilitarian and ideological
designs.
    Where Soviet schools differ from their Western
counterparts in the teaching of physical education is
in the explicitness and directness of the application
of their aims to practice, and in their standardisation of curricula and syllabuses.   A detailed
syllabus for every nursery, school and college in
the country is laid down by the USSR Ministry of
Education, although each Republican ministry has a
certain degree of freedom in establishing the form,
hours and marking of the subject: 'These syllabuses
are mandatory state documents compiled for each age
group;   they are not subject to arbitrary changes by
teachers or school heads.'[13]   In a highly centralised
society like the Soviet Union's, it is regarded as
desirable to have a single syllabus laid down from
above.   Each educational level is linked so that
'the syllabus for primary classes is a continuation
of that for children of pre-school age in nurseries
or at home.   At the same time, it is a necessary
step in preparing children for PE in the senior
forms.'[14]
    All the same, as we shall see below, theory
and practice do not always coincide.   It is well to
remember that much depends in practice on existing
facilities, on attitudes and priorities of senior
educators (especially school heads) and, most of all,
on the individual teacher's enthusiasm and creativity,
experience and initiative, sense of humour and love
for children;   such imponderables are not reflected
in official prescriptions.

History
The 1920s.   Like other areas of social action
immediately after the 1917 Revolution, education went
through a period of experimentation, principally with
progressive educational theories.   In many schools,
physical education was replaced by a study of hygiene
and health, seen in their relation to a factory, a
market, a bakery, and so on.   Such was the school
PE syllabus drawn up by the Education Research
Section of the State Academic Council (GUS) that was
in operation in schools between 1923 and 1927.   This
'GUS Syllabus' was 'a complex syllabus, not one by
subject, in which various subjects, including physical
education, were combined'.[15]
    Physical education, as a subject in its own
right, received little encouragement from the new
syllabus covering the years 1927-9 ('Syllabus of
Physical Exercises for Labour Schools').   The

178

Scientific and Technical Committee attached to the
Supreme Council of Physical Culture, responsible for
PE syllabuses in schools, believed that PE should be
'an integral part of the education process and not
something tacked on superficially to the curriculum.'[16]
Its Chairman, A.A. Zigmund, wrote that 'the existence
of physical education instructors is a sign of
pedagogical illiteracy'.[17]

Despite a number of resolutions and programmes,
it was not until 1929 that PE actually became a
compulsory subject in schools and colleges, with an
allotted weekly quota of two hours.

As industrialisation got under way, a strict
regimen was evolved for all Soviet schools, and a
full programme of compulsory PE was introduced in
1933. Nonetheless, the 1923 'GUS' syllabus and the
1927 PE syllabus did lay a basis for school PE,
particularly the preparation of detailed plans of
each lesson by doctors and educationalists in a
central research institute; during the 1930s, these
were passed on to every school for compulsory
application. The instructions given to PE teachers
in the 1927 syllabus included the following aims for
school PE:

> To fortify and maintain health, to enhance the
> organism's resistance to illness, to counteract
> the 'industrial diseases' of school life, to
> cultivate dexterity, suppleness, speed,
> coordination, precision, the ability to use
> one's strength rationally, to develop a sense
> of balance, rhythm and attentiveness, to
> inculcate moral values and form good social
> habits.[18]

These aims were to be pursued by employing
natural forms of movement which human beings have
used throughout their evolution: walking, running,
jumping, throwing, balancing, swimming, skating,
skiing, sledding, climbing, classical and folk
dancing, excursions and nature rambles.[19]

Little mention was made of using equipment,
since hardly any existed. Besides PE lessons,
exercises were recommended for out-of-school time,
particularly early morning exercises. In 1929, a
daily morning broadcast began (and has continued to
the present day) with 'keep fit' lessons for the
population at large. No mention was made in either
of the two PE syllabuses produced in the 1920s of
team and combat sports like soccer, rugby, basketball,
boxing and wrestling - partly because facilities were

179

lacking, but mainly because the educational body
concerned with PE in schools was preoccupied with
the bodily functions of games for improving health
and opposed team and combat sports as potentially
deleterious to mental and physical health.

The 1930s.   The new PE syllabus introduced in 1933
laid down the guidelines for each PE lesson, which
was to be distinct from lessons in other school
subjects.   Like its predecessor, it stressed the
health side of PE, but added three new elements:
1) first aid;   2) sports theory;   and 3) training
for the new nationwide sports programme, the BGTO
(Be Ready for Labour and Defence) - children had to
meet one standard in form 1 at the age of seven, two
in form 2, eight in form 3 and nine in forms 4-7.
The time allotted to PE was to be two-and-a-half
hours in forms 1-4, and three hours in forms 5-10,
spread over the then 10-day school 'week'.
     With the encouragement of competition and
organised sports in the country at large, the PE
syllabus was formalised in the latter part of the
1930s in order to incorporate inter-school
competition.   In the new syllabus set for 1937,
gymnastics was included for the first time and made
the basis of the PE lesson: exercises were
prescribed using the rings, parallel bars, horse and
horizontal bars.   No longer was the material
classified according to basic motor movements, but
now by specific sports;   gymnastics, athletics,
skiing, team games such as volleyball and basketball,
and swimming.   The time devoted to PE was, however,
reduced to one hour per week for all classes, with
no time allowed separately for games - as a
concomitant of the growing emphasis on formal
academic lessons.
     With war clouds gathering, another syllabus was
introduced in 1940, which inserted military training
(drilling and hand-to-hand combat) into the
curriculum for the senior forms.

The 1940s and 1950s.   In the new syllabus scheduled
for 1947, the stated aim was to improve children's
health.   Back came the classification by motor
skills rather than by sport and the virtual
elimination of team games.   All PE teachers received
detailed instructions on how to conduct each lesson,
their attention being drawn to the biological and
psychological requirements of children, particularly
the physically weak.   Yet the amount of time
allotted in school hours was small: 33 hours a year

for forms 1-2 and 8-10, and 66 hours for forms 3-7.

The Party decision of 1948 to campaign for
improved skill in all sports and the earlier
decision to compete on a wide scale in international
sport were bound to affect school physical education.
A radically new syllabus was drawn up for 1954 which
again changed the orientation from motor skills to
competitive sports, and instructed schools to 'teach
the basic skills in gymnastics, sports and team
games.'20   For the first time since the 1937-41 PE
syllabus, physical education in schools was to be
centred on the nationwide fitness programme, the
GTO (Ready for Labour and Defence), and it was
intended that each pupil completing the seventh form
(at the age of 14 or 15) would gain his BGTO badge,
and each pupil completing the tenth form (at the age
of 17) would gain his GTO Stage 1 badge.

At colleges and universities, compulsory
physical education in the first two years of the
students' courses (instituted in 1929) was, from
1947 to 1948, made subject to an examination which,
if failed, could hold the student back a year.

The 1960s and 1970s.   Following the 1958 law 'On
Strengthening the Connection between School and Life
and the Further Development of the Education System
in the USSR', a new physical education syllabus was
introduced in 1960 that differed radically from its
predecessor.   The 1954 syllabus had reflected the
contemporary all-out campaign to shine internationally,
and PE had been geared to achieve this end:
individual sports were practised intensively,
potential stars were given special attention (often
to the detriment of the mass of children), precise
standards of achievement at each form level were
established, and schools were obliged to take part in
a large number of competitions (which further
exacerbated the bias towards the best pupils).   The
1960 syllabus (which lasted until 1967) did away
with the compulsory standards for each form except
for the top classes, the number of inter-school
contests was reduced, and the content of the syllabus
was divided into two parts: Part 1 (forms 1-4,
ages 7-11) was common for all schools and consisted
of gymnastics, athletics, skiing and team games (72
hours a year);   Part 2 (forms 5-8, ages 11-15)
consisted of two sections, one which was common to
all schools, the other offering an option: each
school could select a sport in which it wished to
specialise (depending on climatic conditions,
available facilities and the teacher's specialism and

interests). In addition, children were taken for a whole day once every two months to the local stadium for athletics contests and team games or were taken skating and skiing, according to season. These were officially known as 'Health Days' and they were supplemented by ten planned school tournaments during the school year; in fact, five of the 'Health Days' coincided with tournament days, so children were to have approximately 11-12 complete sports days off from school each year.[21]

Standards of achievement in the 1960 syllabus were related to the BGTO norms. At the end of each school year, pupils were awarded marks (out of five) for their PE and games performance and knowledge. In 1963, the RSFSR Education Ministry further enhanced the status of PE by including it in the school-leaving certificate. Subsequently, some other republics followed suit.

In 1967, the old PE syllabus was replaced. With the gradual transition from the 8-year school to the 10-year school (the school-leaving age was set for 17 by 1970) and the revision of the school curriculum, the attention devoted to academic subjects initially increased somewhat at the expense of PE, with the optional sports section being removed. Gymnastics remained the basis of the PE lesson, with athletics (for forms 5-10), skiing and team games (mainly basketball, handball and volleyball) making up the 70 hours a year for each form. Although the subject lost status between 1967 and 1971 by being excluded from the school-leaving certificate, it subsequently regained its former position among school subjects and in the mid-1970s was marked out of five (as with all subjects) - a pupil might be kept down if he failed his end-of-year PE examination - it again featured in the school-leaving certificate and had homework prescribed for it (twice a week, to last some 15 minutes on each occasion).

With the launching of a new and upgraded GTO programme in 1972,

> The GTO became the basis of Soviet physical education in terms of syllabus and qualifying standards; its aim is to help shape the moral and spiritual outlook of Soviet people, their all-round harmonious development, to maintain good health and creative activity over a long lifetime, and to prepare the population for highly-productive labour and defence of their country.[22]

In so far as the GTO is today the basis of physical education, it is important here to say a few words about it.

The GTO National Fitness Programme.   The national fitness programme Gotov k trudu i oborone (GTO), 'Ready for Labour and Defence', was instituted in 1931, setting targets for all-round ability in a number of sports and knowledge of the rudiments of hygiene, first aid and civil defence, for which token gold and silver badges are awarded.   Its objective was to extend the scope of sports participation, give everyone something to aim for - that is, set modest targets whose attainment brought some honorific recognition - and make regular physical exercise a normal feature of the Soviet way of life.   Between 1934 and 1972, the BGTO ('Be Ready for Labour and Defence') existed for schoolchildren, covering 16 sports and theoretical subjects.

Today, the GTO programme has five stages, determined by age, which all necessitate a certain minimum performance in running, jumping, throwing, shooting, skiing and gymnastics.   The programme (which is revised every ten years on average) set in March 1972 had the following five stages:

1.   boys and girls aged 10-13;
2.   boys and girls aged 14-15;
3.   boys and girls aged 16-18 (see Appendix 1);
4.   women aged 19-34, men aged 19-39;
5.   women aged 35-55, men aged 40-60 (older people may compete only with a doctor's permission).

GTO planning quotas are set for every club, sports society, region and school, and tests are held throughout the year.   The target at the end of the 1970s was for every fit schoolchild to obtain a GTO badge for his age group; pupils have to meet the standards of each of the first three GTO stages over a period of a year.   Each stage consists of two sections.   The first, theoretical, part consists of a knowledge of Soviet physical culture (history, structure, aims) and international sport, of personal and public hygiene (knowing the effect of exercise on the organism; rudiments of first aid; ill effects of smoking, alcohol and drugs; self-control in terms of checking on one's weight, sleep, eating, pulse, breathing) and of civil defence.   Boys aged 16-18, for example, have to undergo an initial military training programme, while 16-18-year-old girls have

183

to acquire the basic rules of civil defence (including wearing a gas mask for an hour).

The second, practical, part of the GTO programme involves exercises that promote physical qualities like speed, stamina, strength and skill, and exercises for acquiring applied motor habits, like running for speed and stamina, jumping for height and length, throwing, skiing, swimming and weightlifting. Stages 3-5 also include hand-grenade throwing and shooting. The practical norms for Stage 3, for example, are based on athletics, gymnastics, skiing and skating (cycling or cross-country running in snow-free regions), swimming, shooting, outdoor pursuits and orienteering; each 16-18-year-old is also expected to achieve a set (higher) standard or ranking in the sport of his choice.

This, then, is the basis of the school physical education programme today.

The 1980s. At the beginning of the 1980s, the only major change in school PE was the inclusion of swimming in the curriculum (as part of the campaign to teach every pupil to swim). As the PE calendar below shows, the syllabus consists of theoretical instruction on the GTO, gymnastics, athletics, skiing, swimming, team games (mostly handball or basketball in forms 4-8, with volleyball added in forms 9-10), wrestling (for boys) and modern rhythmic gymnastics (for girls). The typical PE syllabus operating in 1980 is shown in Table 1.

As Table 1 indicates, all pupils are allocated 70 hours of PE a year. Of the senior school curriculum of 36 hours per week, two periods of 45-minutes are devoted to physical education - which is about the average for Western schools.[23] In forms 9-10, lessons are held separately for girls and boys, in so far as 'at that age boys considerably surpass girls in strength and stamina development.'[24] A further reason is that young men are taught applied military skills in the PE lesson. Attendance at the Soviet PE lesson is compulsory, even for those pupils with a doctor's note (though they need not participate).

The two deficiencies that have constantly hampered the implementation of PE plans have been lack of physical facilities and qualified teachers. The simple fact is that most schools built prior to 1970 do not have even the most rudimentary grounds suitable for games; by no means every school has proper accommodation even for indoor exercises.

Table 1: Physical Education per School Year: Forms 1-10, 1980

Form	GTO Theory	Gymnastics	Wrestling[a] or Mod.Gyms.[b]	Athletics	Skiing	Swimming	Team Games[c]
1	–	28	–	–	12	–	30
2-3	–	30	–	–	12	–	28
4	2	10	–	10	14	26	8
5	2	18	–	18	16	–	16
6	2	20	–	18	16	–	14
7	2	14	8	16	16	–	14
8	2	14	8	16	16	–	14
9	2	10	$10^a/8^b$	$16^a/18^b$	16	–	16
10	2	10	$10^a/8^b$	$16^a/18^b$	16	–	16

Note: a. Boys; b. Girls; c. Consists of handball or basketball up to form 8, then eight hours of volleyball and eight of either handball or basketball in forms 9-10.

Source: USSR Ministry of Education, Programmy vos'miletnei i srednei shkoly. Fizicheskaya kul'tura dlya I-X klassov, (Minsk, 1980), pp. 5-6.

Although in recent years many schools have had
special sports wings built on to the main building
and there are projects for constructing area sports
centres to be used jointly by several schools,
schools are still, by West European and North American
standards, underequipped. The then Soviet Deputy
Minister of Education, M.I. Kondakov, at an All-union
conference on improving physical culture among
schoolchildren, held in March 1968, reported that
some 80 per cent of all secondary schools had no
sports grounds, 75 per cent had no gymnasiums,
50 per cent did not have even the equipment necessary
for conducting PE lessons according to the state
syllabus, and some 40 per cent of PE teachers were
unqualified.[25]   In primary schools, the situation
was even worse: of the 85,000 primary schools,
80,000 were understaffed and underequipped for
physical education and games.[26]
   It was this situation that mainly gave rise in
the early 1970s to campaigns to improve school
sports facilities, and brought forth a set of
minimum standards for new schools in 1970. At the
same time the authorities launched a campaign to
teach all children to swim and several small pools,
called lyagushatki ('tadpole pools'), were built;
the first prefabricated pools (25 m long, 12.5 m
wide and 1.2 m deep) went into production in 1973 for
schools and Young Pioneer camps. It was claimed
somewhat generally in 1981 that 'more and more
schools now have their own swimming pools, and
practically every school has its gym, running track
and sports ground.'[27]

Other School Programmes

There are other developments which deserve attention
in order to gain a fuller picture of Soviet physical
education. They are 1) additional physical
activities for schoolchildren and 2) specialised
schools.

Additional Physical Activities. Besides the set PE
lesson, the school is responsible for a number of
other physical activities. The education authorities
urge that all children should engage in 15-20 minutes
setting-up exercises every morning at home or school.
Since this is entirely at the discretion of parents
and teachers, it is sometimes neglected. A survey in
Siberia in the mid-1970s revealed that 39 per cent of
the boys and 41 per cent of the girls in Khabarovsk,
and 45 per cent of the boys and 43 per cent of the
girls in Komsomol'sk-on-Amur actually did their

morning exercises regularly.[28]

Teachers are also urged to conduct exercises throughout the day, particularly in the breaks between lessons - whenever the opportunity arises to insert a fizkul'tminutka.

In out-of-school time, many schoolchildren spend at least a fortnight of their summer holiday in a camp, often under canvas in a forest or by the sea or a river. It was stated in 1971 that 'virtually one in three schoolchildren will be in a Young Pioneer school, sport or tourist camp during the summer of 1971.'[29] However, according to official figures, about one in four-five children were actually being served by Young Pioneer camps.[30] At such camps children take part in a variety of educational activities - nature study, orienteering, hiking, canoeing, rock climbing, swimming, and social or local studies.

Young people who wish to pursue a particular sport and take part in competition may do so in the school sports section, the Young Pioneer clubs, sports societies, local stadiums, parks or the courtyard of their block of flats; all are free of charge. However, the pupil can also buy a season ticket for enrolment in such popular sports sections as figure skating, swimming and tennis. All school pupils are urged to take part in the All-Union Spartakiad of Schoolchildren - it is claimed that over 7,000 participated in the 16th Spartakiad in July 1981.[31] Others may take part in such nation-wide individual sports contests as the kozhany myach ('leather ball'), zolotaya shaiba ('golden puck') and belaya lad'ya ('white pawn'). The official assertion is that each year some 40 million children (of the 45 million pupils) take part in various sports tournaments.[32] On the other hand, local surveys reveal that not more than a quarter of all children pursue a sport regularly, partly because of the counter attraction of television, a lack of sports facilities and the refusal of sports societies to admit the casual young enthusiast.

It is clear, nonetheless, that schoolchildren make up a substantial proportion of the country's sports participants. In 1974, school sports sections constituted nearly half the country's sports groups and provided as many as 43 per cent of the regular athletes, over half the GTO badge-holders and a sizeable proportion of the ranked athletes.[33]

Not all PE teachers are happy about official exhortations to higher sports proficiency. They argue that it militates against developing the very principles of mass participation, collectivism and comradeship that physical education is supposed to nurture. One teacher writes that she tries to teach three principles to her PE class of 23 girls:

> To develop an appreciation of beauty, to value friendship and to be fond of hard work. But what would the district inspector say? He would probably ask me how many girls gained a sports ranking at the end of the year. That's the trouble: we gallop after rankings without stopping to think what we are doing. Scarcely is a child out of the cradle than we fix his fate as a Master of Sport. Yet how many children are thrown overboard in our race for results?[34]

This is a fairly common complaint among PE teachers, who so often find themselves in the invidious position of striving to sustain the interest of their charges with few facilities and a hostile or indifferent head, yet being judged by results measured in terms of the success of the few.

Specialised Schools. Young people who wish to pursue a sport seriously and to develop their talent may do so in one of several types of school (see Fig. 1).

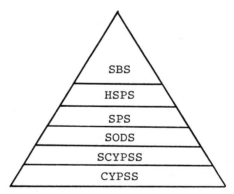

Figure 1   Schools for talent

SBS = sports boarding school; HSPS = higher sports proficiency school; SPS = sports proficiency school; SODS = sport-oriented day school; SCYPSS = specialist children's and young people's sports school; CYPSS = children's and young people's sports school.

At the base of the pyramid is the children's and young people's sports school (CYPSS) which young people can attend outside their normal school hours (they are in fact 'clubs' in the Western sense). There were over 5,000 such schools with a membership of 1.75 million children in 1980.[35]   An attempt is made to spread the net as widely as possible, both to catch all potential talent and to distribute facilities fairly evenly among the republics. Belorussia, for instance, is divided into six regions, each of which has some 35 such schools with an average of 50 coaches per school.   Each school caters for an average of six sports.   For example, the Republic School of Olympic Reserves in Minsk (which I visited in 1978 and September 1981) has some 800 children in six sections: water polo, handball, tennis, gymnastics, volleyball and chess (the chess section having six separate groups under three instructors).

Children are normally considered for a CYPSS on the recommendation of the school PE teacher or at the request of their parents.   Attendance and coaching are free.   Although most of the schools take children at 11 years of age, for some sports they may accept them earlier or later.   For example, entrants to swimming sections may be taken in at 6 or 7, while cyclists and speed skaters are usually admitted at 13 or 14.   On the other hand, in 1977, the Moscow Dinamo CYPSS started up a gymnastics section for children between four and six, who attend three times a week;   and the Minsk Dinamo 'soccer nursery' takes young boys at 6 and 7.

Originally, it was intended that each CYPSS should cultivate up to ten sports, but today most concentrate on no more than three, some on only a single sport.   The single-sport schools are known as specialist children's and young people's sports schools (SCYPSS).   For example, each leading soccer club runs its own soccer SCYPSS, which provide a full course of training for promising young footballers.

The aim of these schools is to make the best use of the limited facilities available in the USSR to give special coaching to young people in a particular sport so that they may become proficient, gain a ranking and graduate to a Republican, city or Soviet national team.   They are regarded as one of the keys to Soviet sporting success, especially in the Olympics.   In fact, of the 35 sports pursued in the schools in 1980, only six were outside the Olympic programme: acrobatics, chess, modern

gymnastics, handball, tennis and table tennis. The
sports most practised were athletics, basketball,
gymnastics, volleyball, swimming and skiing.

The organisations responsible for financing and
administering the schools are the local education
authorities, the trade union sports societies (such
as Spartak, Lokomotiv) and the big sports clubs run
by Dinamo and the armed forces. Of the 2772 CYPSSs
that existed in 1967, the education authorities were
responsible for just over half, the TU societies for
a third and Dinamo and the armed forces for the
remainder.[36]

It is possible, from the age of 7, to attend a
full-time 'sport-oriented' school, which combines a
normal school curriculum with sports training (on
the model of the 'foreign language'-oriented schools).
They provide pupils with extra instruction in sport
and possess facilities that are superior to those
available at 'normal' secondary schools.

Above these schools in specialist training come
the sports proficiency schools and the higher sports
proficiency schools, which provide both extra-
curricular training for schoolchildren and students
and short-term vacation courses. The distinction
between them is normally one of age: students
between 16 and 18 attend the former, those 18 and
over the latter.

At the apex of the pyramid are the sport
boarding schools, of which there were 26 in 1980.[37]
The USSR opened its first sports boarding school on
an experimental basis in Tashkent in 1962; this was
modelled on similar schools that had been established
in the German Democratic Republic in 1949. It was
not until 1970 that a special government resolution
set an official seal of approval on their existence;
hitherto they had been given virtually no publicity.
While some concentrate on a single sport, others
cultivate a range, though usually no more than four.
Significantly, only sports in the Olympic programme
are taken up by the sports boarding schools.

They follow other special boarding schools in
adhering to the standard Soviet curriculum for
ordinary schools, but their timetables allow for an
additional study load in sports theory and practice.
Their aim is to permit pupils to obtain their
school-leaving certificate in addition to acquiring
proficiency in a particular sport. Boarders are
accepted between 7 and 12 years of age, depending on
their sport, and they stay on until 18 - a year
longer than at normal schools.

The motive for the establishment of these sports

boarding schools has been the conviction that talent in sport has to be developed at an early age if it is to have an opportunity to blossom to the full.   It is therefore regarded as advantageous to bring children with an instinctive aptitude for sport into the 'controlled' environment of a residential school, where they are provided with the best coaches and amenities, nurtured on a special diet, supervised constantly by doctors and sports instructors and stimulated by mutual interest and enthusiasm.   Moreover, early specialisation, especially in such sports as athletics, swimming and gymnastics (which make up two-thirds of all Olympic medals) is regarded as essential to the attainment of high standards and success in present-day inter-national competition.

Some Comparisons and Future Trends

Comparatively speaking, there are a number of similarities between Soviet and Western systems and aims of physical education.   Several countries stress the development of the whole child.   The term 'harmonious development' is used by Denmark and Norway.   Other typical statements are 'the develop-ment of the whole person, both physically and mentally' (Austria);   'essential contribution to the making of the whole person' (Belgium);   and 'to educate the whole person as an individual through physical education' (West Germany and the United States).   The aim of physical fitness and health for improving working capacity is included in the PE programmes of Norway, Israel and Egypt. Physical fitness as a requirement for potential military service in the national interest holds true both for Israel and Taiwan, and is implicit in the PE system of some other countries where military service is compulsory.   In fact, when PE (or, rather, PT) was first introduced for boys into British elementary schools after the 1870 Education Act, it took the form of military drill and was taught by drill sergeants from the War Office;   it was intended, in the words of the Act, 'to teach the boys habits of sharp obedience, smartness, order and cleanliness'.[38]
       On the whole, however, a recent comparative study of PE lessons for the French- and German-speaking countries of Europe showed that the lessons were today based on educational, psychological, physiological and social considerations, and the trend was away from 'industrious' activities for physiological effects mainly.   Moreover, PE was

severing its ties with the military and medical professions and was allying itself more with education. This change had been accelerated by the strong attraction of sports to the young people of these countries.[39]

By contrast, the teaching of PE in the Soviet Union tends to be rather formal with a stress on skill and perfection rather than play and fun. Prescribed activities are taught and physiological outcomes are emphasised. A typical class will start with a short warm-up period; then the teacher will go into the instructional part of the lesson to develop physical and motor capacities or new skill techniques before concluding with a tapering-off activity. Class control and discipline are rather strict.

Nonetheless, Soviet physical education today shows certain discernible trends that mark it off from the past. First of all, the PE syllabus contains a greater range of activities than ever before. Second, although physical educators still believe that a well-rounded programme cannot exist with sports alone and that developmental exercises must be included, the trend would seem to be away from gymnastics and drill towards specialised courses in sports so that pupils can develop their aptitudes and interests, and become proficient in a particular sport (rather than mediocre in three). Third, although the teaching of physical education still emphasises skill and perfection for utilitarian ends (labour and defence), there seems to be a significant, though still weak, trend away from formal exercises done in unison towards attempts to meet the individual needs of the pupils.

There are a number of reasons behind these trends. One obvious reason is the increasing availability of facilities to cope with more sports - especially swimming and athletics, and, within school sports sections, even such diverse pursuits as rugby, field hockey, badminton and archery. Another reason is the less urgent need today to concentrate on building up health and the shift of attention to developing sports proficiency. However, as with the education system generally, it is changes in society and the population's response to them, as well as the leadership's current priorities, that have most influenced current trends in physical education.

Historically, political manipulation of physical culture characteristically resulted from centralised planning and administration designed to subordinate

areas of social life such as physical activities to
the political and economic tasks of building a strong
state.   In recent years, however, certain internal
forces within Soviet society have encouraged a
dismantling of previously well-entrenched institutions
and values in the field of physical culture.
Individuals have increasing free time and prosperity,
and an ever wider range of amenities and equipment
to pursue the leisure activities of their choice,
particularly in a non-institutional setting.   As a
result, how an individual spends his leisure-time is
becoming less ruled by the official utilitarian-
instrumental approach - despite official attempts to
regulate the use of increasing free time - and more
governed by the notion that an outdoor pursuit or
indoor activity, a game or a pastime of any kind is
desirable in itself, for its own sake.
     To give one example, people are tending to form
smaller (family) groups for recreation and holidays
(going on family rather than individual subsidised -
putyovka - or Pioneer camp trips).   Moreover, there
appears to be an increasing desire to 'get away from
it all' rather than to 'get together'.   On the
whole, the leadership has, in the past, tried to see
to it that the facilities available to the population
at large have predisposed them toward some form of
public, collective recreation - mainly through the
school sports section, trade-union, public park or
play-centre behind a block of flats.   Now that most
families have a long weekend away from work (and
sometimes a family car), these formally-based
facilities no longer suit them because they are
'ill-adapted to family forms of free-time activity
or to the active leisure-pursuits of a small group
linked by personal-and-friendly rather than formal
relations'.[40]   There is, therefore, a trend away
from 'public and mass' recreation towards 'individual,
domestic, family and passive leisure', especially
watching television.[41]
     All these factors are evoking a response from
the educational authorities in revising provision
for physical education.   The Chairman of the USSR
Committee on Physical Culture and Sport, Sergei
Pavlov, would like to see an 'increase in the amount
of physical education in the school timetable'.   It
is proposed,

>   to introduce a long break of 90 minutes in the
>   school day for all manner of physical activities
>   (a kind of daily auxiliary PE lesson);   there
>   should be weekly outdoor recreation periods;

school holidays should be more frequent and shorter, and rationally used in the interests of better health and sound physical development.[42]

Pavlov is aware that 'foreign critics of Soviet physical education often claim that it has a utilitarian character and aims at preparing young people for labour which, they contend, runs counter to free development of the individual'.[43]

He would like to see less State-controlled, work- and military-oriented physical education, and more individual- and family-centred activities. For this to happen changes must be made,

enabling the family better to supervise physical education, producing more portable sports goods for family use, basing more sports clubs on the home and the community, and building more out-door recreation centres.[44]

Whether these proposals ever see the light of day remains to be seen; certainly other educators have in the past put up considerable resistance to any increase in physical education in the school curriculum, especially at the expense of 'academic' subjects. Furthermore, the more conservative members of the political establishment have up till now been disinclined to shift away from structured exercises for rational ends towards games for pure enjoyment and relaxation. What does seem reasonable to predict is that pressure from pupils, parents and PE teachers will increasingly force the education authorities to seek a more acceptable balance between didactic functions in physical training and a more stimulating, interesting and diversified games period.

Appendix 1

GTO - Stage 3:

'Sila i muzhestvo' ('Strength and Courage')
(for Boys and Girls 16-18)

Academic requirements (to be examined)

1.   To have a knowledge of the subject
'Physical Culture and Sport in the USSR'.
2.   To know and carry out the rules for
personal and public hygiene.
3.   To master the programme for initial
military training (including the section on the
protection from weapons of mass destruction) and
to wear a gas mask for one hour, or undergo
specialist training in a DOSAAF organisation, or
obtain an applied technical speciality (for boys).
Girls should know the basic rules of civil defence
and wear a gas mask for one hour.
4.   To be able to explain the importance of
and perform a set of morning exercises.

Physical exercises: qualifying standards

		Boys		Girls	
	Type of exercise	Silver Badge	Gold Badge	Silver Badge	Gold Badge
1.	Run 100 m (sec)	14.2	13.5	16.2	15.4
2.	Run 500 m (min/sec)	–	–	2.00	1.50
	1000 m (min/sec)	3.30	3.20	–	–
	or				
	Skate 500 m (min/sec)	1.25	1.15	1.30	1.20
3.	Long jump (cm)	440	480	340	375
	or				
	High jump (cm)	125	135	105	115
4.	Hurl a hand-grenade of				
	500 gm (m)	–	–	21	25
	700 gm (m)	35	40	–	–
	or putt the shot of				
	4 kg (m/cm)	–	–	6.00	6.80
	5 kg (m)	8	10	–	–

Cont'd

Appendix 1 (Cont'd)

Type of exercise	Boys		Girls	
	Silver Badge	Gold Badge	Silver Badge	Gold Badge
5. Ski 3 km (min)	-	-	20	18
5 km (min)	27	25	-	-
or 10 km (min)	57	52	-	-
In snow-free regions: Run cross country				
3 km (min)	-	-	20	18
6 km (min)	35	32	-	-
or cycle cross country				
10 km (min)	-	-	30	27
20 km (min)	50	46	-	-
6. Swim 100 m (min/sec)	2.00	1.45	2.15	2.00
7. Press-ups	8	12	-	-
Pull-ups	-	-	10	12
8. Fire a small-bore rifle at 25 m (points)	33	40	30	37
or at 50 m (points)	30	37	27	34
or fire a heavy weapon	Satis-factory	Well	Satis-factory	Well
9. Tourist hike with test of tourist knowledge and orienteering	1 hike of 20 km or 2 hikes of 12 km	1 hike of 25 km or 2 hikes of 15 km	1 hike of 20 km or 2 hikes of 12 km	1 hike of 25 km or 2 hikes of 15 km
10. Obtain a sports ranking in: (a) motor car, motor boat, motor-cycle, gliding, parachuting, aero-plane, helicopter, sub-aqua or water sports, biathlon, pentathlon, pistol shooting, radio sport, orienteering, wrestling or boxing;	-	III	-	III
(b) any other sport	-	II	-	II

Note: For the Gold Badge, one must complete not less than 7 qualifying standards at Gold Badge level and 2 standards at Silver Badge level (except item 10). Girls who have completed a first-aid training course may forego item 10 for their Gold Badge.

NOTES

1.   USSR Constitution, Article 25.
2.   D.V. Khukhlaeva, Teoriya i metodika
fizicheskogo vospitaniya detei doshkol'nogo vozrasta,
2nd edn. (Prosveshchenie, Moscow, 1976), p. 6.
3.   K. Marx, Capital (3 vols., Foreign Languages
Publishing House, Moscow, 1961), vol. 1, pp. 483-484.
4.   Y. Kapp, Eleanor Marx (2 vols., Lawrence
and Wishart, London, 1972), vol. 1, p. 193;   the only
game Marx seemed to enjoy was chess (p. 26), although
Engels was 'an enthusiastic rider to hounds, a
mighty walker and a deep drinker' (p. 108).
5.   V.I. Lenin, Polnoe sobranie sochinenii,
6th edn. (64 vols., Politizdat, Moscow, 1968), vol.
11, p. 485.
6.   I.D. Chudinov (ed.), Osnovnye postanovleniya
i instruktsii po voprosam fizicheskoi kul'tury i
sporta, 1917-1957 (Fizkul'tura i sport, Moscow, 1959),
pp. 43-44.
7.   See J. Riordan, 'Pyotr Franzevich Lesgaft.
The Founder of Russian Physical Education', Journal
of Sport History, vol. 4, no. 2 (1977), pp. 229-241.
8.   F.I. Samoukov (ed.), Istoriya fizicheskoi
kul'tury (Fizkul'tura i sport, Moscow, 1964), p. 230.
9.   Khukhlaeva, Teoriya i metodika, p. 6.
10.   I.P. Pavlov, Polnoe sobranie sochinenii
(12 vols., Akademiya Nauk SSSR, Moscow, 1951),
vol. 2, p. 245.
11.   Ibid., p. 246.
12.   Khukhlaeva, Teoriya i metodika, p. 8.
13.   V.M. Kachashkin, Metodika fizicheskogo
vospitaniya (Fizkul'tura i sport, Moscow, 1972), p. 54.
14.   Ibid.
15.   Samoukov, Istoriya fizicheskoi kul'tury,
p. 284.
16.   Vestnik fizicheskoi kul'tury (1925), no. 3,
p. 2.
17.   Fizkul'tura i sport (1925), no. 2, p. 17.
18.   Fizicheskaya kul'tura v shkole (1969),
no. 9, p. 4.
19.   Ibid., p. 5.
20.   Fizicheskaya kul'tura v shkole (1967)
no. 9, p. 7.
21.   T.N. Vasil'eva et al. (eds.), Fizicheskaya
kul'tura v V-VIII klassakh (Prosveshchenie, Moscow,
1967), p. 242.
22.   Kachashkin, Metodika fizicheskogo
vospitaniya, p. 54.
23.   See B.L. Bennett, M.L. Howell, U. Simri,
Comparative Physical Education and Sport (Lea &

Febiger, Philadelphia, 1975), p. 43.
24. G.V. Roshchupkin, Fizicheskaya kul'tura shkol'nikov 9-10-kh klassov, 2nd edn. (Zdorov'ya, Kiev, 1979), p. 50. Elsewhere in Europe, PE classes are normally non-coeducational after 11-12.
25. M.I. Kondakov, 'Osnova osnov' in V.A. Ivonin (ed.), Velenie vremeni (Fizkul'tura i sport, Moscow, 1969), p. 26.
26. Teoriya i praktika fizicheskoi kul'tury (1970), no. 8, p. 59.
27. Sport v SSSR (1981), no. 3, p. 2.
28. V.P. Kashirin, 'Razvitie fizicheskoi kul'tury i sporta v obshcheobrazovatel'nykh shkolakh' in G.I. Kukushkin et al., Planirovanie fizicheskoi kul'tury i sporta (Fizkul'tura i sport, Moscow, 1974), p. 86.
29. Sovetskii sport, 1 July 1971, p. 2.
30. Narodnoe khozyaistvo SSSR v 1970 g (Statistika, Moscow, 1971), pp. 633, 636.
31. Sport v SSSR (1981), no. 3, p. 2.
32. Sport v SSSR (1981), no. 7, p. 2.
33. Fizkul'tura i sport (1975), no. 9, p. 3.
34. Fizicheskaya kul'tura v shkole (1967), no. 9, p. 26.
35. V.M. Vydrin (ed.), Sport v sovremennom obshchestve (Fizkul'tura i sport, Moscow, 1980), p. 159.
36. N. Makartsev and P.A. Sobolev, Govoryat tsifry i fakty (Fizkul'tura i sport, Moscow, 1969), p. 40. I was told in Moscow in September 1981 that by a new resolution the t-u DYUSS were to concentrate mainly on talented children, the Ministry of Education DYUSS on casual enthusiasts.
37. See Chap. 4 in J. Riordan, Soviet Sport (Basil Blackwell, Oxford, 1980).
38. See P.C. McIntosh, Physical Education in England Since 1800 (G. Bell & Sons, London, 1972), p. 109.
39. R. Decker, 'Plan of a Physical Education Lesson', Gymnasion, vol. 6 (Winter 1969), pp. 17-18.
40. L.A. Gordon and N.M. Rimashevskaya, Pyatidnevnaya rabochaya nedelya i svobodnoe vremya trudyashchikhsya (Statistika, Moscow, 1972), p. 115.
41. Ibid., pp. 38-39.
42. S. Pavlov, 'Physical Culture and Sport in Socialist Society' in The USSR: Sport and Way of Life (Social Sciences Today, Moscow, 1980), pp. 14-15.
43. Ibid., pp. 8-9.
44. Ibid., p. 15.

Chapter 8

ACCESS TO HIGHER EDUCATION IN THE SOVIET UNION

George Avis

Introduction
The importance of access to higher education for the
economic, social and political structures of
industrialised nations can hardly be disputed. The
way in which a society defines and implements such
access tells us something about the role it assigns
to higher education and about the broader ideological
principles that society adheres to.   Consequently,
the primary purpose of higher education is viewed in
different ways.   For some it is essentially the
pursuit of knowledge entailing high academic
standards and research excellence; for others it is
more the training of highly qualified personnel for
the national economy; and others still regard higher
education as a means of social levelling and
democratisation which opens up knowledge, power and
status to as many people as possible.   Such goals,
of course, are not mutually exclusive and may be
pursued simultaneously, given a sufficiently high
level of resources to do so.   However, most systems
of higher education tend to give priority to one of
these basic approaches, and this structures the aims
and procedures of admissions policy.
      Soviet higher education follows the 'training'
model.   The pursuit of knowledge for its own sake
or the right to education for individual self-
development rather than collective purposes has not
hitherto been recognised as a main aim.   Overall
coverage in higher education is high but entry
policies are strictly selective, designed to pick
out the academically able for specialised advanced
training which will prepare them for servicing the
economy.   Yet from time to time strong egalitarian
pressures challenge the prevailing utilitarian
assumptions.
      In the next decade or so universities and other

higher education institutions in Europe and around
the world will be faced with problems of demographic
decline, graduate unemployment, falling aspirations
for higher education among young people, loss of
income and prestige, and reduced admissions. Indeed,
these problems already beset them. Access is no
longer a matter of opening up higher education to the
formerly deprived but more a problem of filling
empty lecture halls. Traditional roles and
procedures are now being questioned and opportunities
for new flexible study programmes to attract a wider
and non-traditional clientele are being explored.
Higher education in the Soviet Union also faces some
of these problems. What form they have taken and
how they have affected access in the seventies, as
well as what developments are likely in the near
future, are the sort of questions we shall be
examining in this essay.
     In what follows limitation of space precludes
discussion of important relevant issues such as
demographic change, population movement and manpower
planning. Some preliminary remarks will be made
about enrolment figures and general trends in student
recruitment in the 1970s. But the main focus of
attention will be on three aspects of access which
have traditionally concerned politicians,
educationalists and sociologists, namely the extent
to which a person's sex, nationality, and social
background determine his chances of obtaining higher
education. In recent years Western scholars have
taken a keen interest in the impact of social class
on educational opportunity in the Soviet Union but
they have tended to concentrate on Soviet research
relating to the late 1960s. By contrast, we shall
be looking below at recently published materials from
sociological surveys carried out in the 1970s with
the intention of presenting a more up-to-date, though
necessarily incomplete, picture of the situation.

Enrolment Statistics
The quantitative features of enrolments in the past
two decades are summarised in Table 1.   The
expansion in students numbers is striking,
particularly in the sixties. Official emphasis on
part-time higher education during the Khrushchev
reform period is reflected in the relative decline
in the proportion of full-time day students up to
1965.   From then on the policy was reversed as part
of a campaign to improve overall 'product quality'
via the full-time mode of study. In effect, this
tended to reduce access to what has been traditionally

Table 1: Numbers of Students in Soviet Higher Education and Rates of Increase, 1960 to 1980

	All (thousands)	%	Day (thousands)	%	Correspondence (thousands)	%	Evening (thousands)	%
(a) Total numbers								
1960	2,396	100	1,156	48	995	42	245	10
1965	3,861	100	1,584	41	1,708	44	569	15
1970	4,581	100	2,241	49	1,682	37	658	14
1975	4,854	100	2,628	54	1,582	33	644	13
1980	5,236	100	2,979	57	1,608	31	649	12
(b) Percentage increase (1960 = 100)								
1960	100		100		100		100	
1965	161		137		172		232	
1970	191		194		169		269	
1975	203		227		159		263	
1980	219		258		162		265	
(c) Percentage change within 5-year periods								
1960–65	161		137		172		232	
1965–70	119		141		98		116	
1970–75	106		117		94		98	
1975–80	108		113		102		101	

Source: Narodnoe khozyaistvo SSSR v 1979 g. (Statistika, Moscow, 1980), p. 492; Narodnoe khozyaistvo SSSR v 1972 g. (Statistika, Moscow, 1973), p. 637; SSSR v tsifrakh v 1980 godu (Finansy i statistika, Moscow, 1981), p. 209.

regarded as a 'second chance' track for those who miss the opportunity of entering full-time higher education in the usual way after school.   The rise in enrolments outstripped population growth with the result that the number of students per 10,000 inhabitants rose from 111 in 1960 to 196 in 1979 - one of the highest participation rates among industrialised countries.[1]

However, in the late sixties the pace of expansion began to slow down considerably (see Table 1(a) and (b)), coming almost to a halt in the seventies and only marginally keeping ahead of the population rate.[2]   The proportion of the 20- to 24-year-old age group undertaking full-time higher education also rose dramatically from 7.1 per cent in 1960 to 13.1 per cent in 1970, then fell to 11.7 per cent in 1975 - plain enough evidence of retrenchment.[3]   This slowing down occurred at a time when more and more Soviet young people were acquiring a full secondary general or secondary specialised education - the necessary qualifications for application to enter a VUZ (higher education institution).[4]   Thus, in 1971 the number of students admitted to all types of higher education was nearly 28 per cent of the total number gaining the above qualifications, yet by 1980 this figure had slumped to just under 21 per cent.[5]   Despite the fact that at the beginning of the seventies the 'bulge' in the school age population had still to work its way fully through the senior grades, expansion in student recruitment was not allowed to keep pace with the greater numbers.   How the Soviet authorities and young people themselves coped with this situation is examined next.

Trends in Student Recruitment in the 1970s
The seventies were years of challenge, paradox and change for student recruitment.   At the beginning of the decade the Soviet authorities embarked upon what appeared to be quite contradictory policies; on the one hand, implementation of universal full secondary education for a burgeoning school population and, on the other, retrenchment in VUZ admissions.   Attitudes of parents, teachers and pupils, who regarded the secondary school as primarily a preparation for eventual higher education and the alternative vocational channels as inferior options, seemed then to be immovable.   And there was a reduction in relative terms of part-time higher education opportunities which might have acted as a safety valve for disappointed applicants

to full-time courses.   Furthermore, despite evidence
that in the sixties working-class and peasant children
succeeded less well in school and found it harder to
compete for VUZ places with the children of white-
collar workers,[6] school attainment was made a formal
criterion for suitability for VUZ entry.[7]
     As it happened many of the conflicts anticipated
by both Western and Soviet commentators did not
materialise.   Measures taken to redirect the
educational and career orientations of Soviet school
children   proved surprisingly successful.   The
prestige of the PTU (professional'no-tekhnicheskoe
uchilishche - trade school) and the tekhnikum
(technical college) was raised by enriching their
vocational programmes with a much larger element of
general education,[8] and by powerful campaigns of
vocational guidance in the media.   Some local
authorities transformed many of their PTUs into
'secondary PTUs', which provide a full secondary
general education as well as trade training, and
set quotas for the number of eighth-grade leavers
who would have to enter them.[9]   This, combined with
a greater realism amongst pupils about the prospects
of obtaining a VUZ place led to a sweeping change in
their educational aspirations.   Pupils completing
the eighth and tenth grades were attracted to the
new secondary PTUs and post-secondary courses in
tekhnikums.   After decades in which it had enjoyed
unrivalled prestige among Soviet youth higher
education began to lose some of its attraction.   In
particular, there occurred a generalised swing away
from formerly popular courses in engineering,
technology, mathematics and physics.   Their place
in the prestige rankings has been taken by the
humanities and the arts.[10]
     The reorientation or 'cooling out' process,
designed to give priority to the training of
skilled manual workers and technicians, proved so
efficient that a serious problem of inadequate
recruitment (nedobor) arose in certain specialities,
particularly those connected with heavy industry,
mining, metallurgy, mineral and oil extraction.
Throughout the seventies frequent emergency changes
have been made in the official VUZ entry regulations
in order to make it easier for secondary school
pupils and tekhnikum graduates to gain admission to
courses in these subject areas.[11]   The term
ostrodefitsitnyi (in short supply), normally
associated with scarce consumer goods, has come to
be applied to those specialisms and occupations in
which there is a great deficiency of trained

graduates.[12] A further consequence of the drop in
applications was a deterioration both in the quality
of entrants to technical VUZs and in student academic
performance.[13] And allied to this is the
increasingly serious decline in firm vocational
orientation among students who had already commenced
an expensive and prolonged course of specific
professional training.[14] Nevertheless, Five-year
Plan targets for student intake and graduations were
still achieved throughout the decade; indeed, they
were overfulfilled.[15] But the worrying imbalances
in recruitment which developed still remain to be
solved.

In view of anticipated severe pressure for
places in higher education at the end of the sixties,
certain categories of recruits were accorded special
concessions or privileges in admissions arrangements.
A separate quota of places was retained for workers
from production; rural school leavers from remote
areas were given facilitated entry to pedagogical,
medical and cultural institutes. The latter
measure is intended to help combat the high turnover
of teachers, doctors and librarians seconded to these
areas from economically and culturally developed
parts of the country.[16] A more radical innovation
has been the creation in most VUZs of so-called
Preparatory Divisions (podgotovitel'nye otdeleniya).
These provide full-time courses of eight to ten
months duration for leading manual workers, kolkhoz
workers and demobbed servicemen who must be
recommended by their work place or unit commander.
On completing the preparatory course satisfactorily
these students receive priority admission to the
VUZ proper without taking any competitive
examinations.[17] It is intended that the injection
into the student milieu of mature activists from
the working class will improve the social
composition of the intake as well as provide leadership and a good example to a student population
which has been getting younger and younger.[18]

Differences in Access Between the Sexes
It is possible to say now at the beginning of the
1980s that Soviet women suffer no overall lack of
access to higher education. Indeed, the Soviet
Union is one of the very few countries in the world
where virtual parity of representation with men has
been secured both in student numbers and in the
proportion of graduate specialists in the working
population.[19] What is a real problem affecting
secondary specialised and higher education alike is

the overrepresentation of women among students
studying certain subjects and disciplines, and their
underrepresentation in others (see Table 2). Over
a long period of time female students have dominated
enrolments in faculties and institutes in the
humanities, medicine and education, but are much less
inclined than men to enter engineering and
agricultural VUZs. This pattern of preferences has
become a source of considerable concern in recent
years. At a time of acute labour shortage such
imbalances in the supply and training of manpower
are seen as economically damaging.[20]

The problem has its roots in traditional Soviet
notions about 'male' and 'female' occupations which
continue to exercise a powerful influence on the
educational orientations and choices of girls during
their school careers. Many researches have shown
that Soviet schoolgirls are relatively reluctant to
train for skilled manual trades in PTUs after
completing the eighth grade of the general education
school.[21] They prefer to stay on in the senior
grades which offer a surer path to higher education
or to the post-secondary training for intermediate
nonmanual professions provided in the tekhnikums
Consequently, the senior grades of secondary schools
and, hence, potential cohorts of VUZ entrants have
become 'feminised', while able boys are rejecting
the academic general-education track in order to
obtain trade training and eventually swell the already
predominantly male ranks of the skilled manual working
class.[22] The latter tendency is particularly strong
in industrial areas. One Urals researcher, for
example, records a decline in the proportion of boys
in the ninth and tenth grades of secondary schools
in Nizhnyi Tagil from 44.5 per cent in 1968 to
38 per cent in 1976. Yet this centre of heavy
industry desperately needs a locally-based supply of
graduate engineers to organise and supervise
production.[23] Filippov, a leading Soviet
educational sociologist, cites overall national
figures for 1970/1 to show that in grades one to
four of Soviet schools there were the expected
48 to 49 per cent of girls, yet in the senior grades
there were 56 per cent, a proportion which increased
to 58 per cent in urban settlements and rose to as
high as 62 per cent in the Baltic republics and to
two-thirds in industrially developed regions of the
country.[24] And among a select sample of 4,500
tenth-graders included in the All-Union Survey of
1973/4 the researchers found some 58 per cent were
girls.[25]

Table 2: Percentage of Female Students in Soviet Higher and Secondary Specialised Institutions, 1970 to 1979

Type of Institution	Higher Education			Secondary Specialised Education		
	1970/1	1975/6	1979/80	1970/1	1975/6	1979/80
All	49	50	52	54	54	56
Industrial, Construction, Transport & Communication	38	40	41	40	41	43
Agriculture	30	33	34	37	37	37
Economics, Law	60	62	66	83	85	85
Medicine, Physical Education & Sport	56	56	57	87	88	89
Education, Art, Cinematography	66	68	69	81	82	84
USSR population	53.9	53.6	53.4	53.9	53.6	53.4

Source: Narodnoe khozyaistvo SSSR v 1979 g. (Statistika, Moscow, 1980), p. 503; Naselenie SSSR: Po dannym Vsesoyuznoi perepisi naseleniya 1979 goda (Politizdat, Moscow, 1980), p. 16; Narodnoe khozyaistvo SSSR v 1975 g. (Statistika, Moscow, 1975), p. 8.

The exacerbation of this process in the seventies is obviously an unintended consequence of the highly successful campaign, referred to above, whereby the Soviet authorities have diverted young people away from higher education by upgrading vocational education opportunities. Much of the skill training given in the new PTUs is aimed at 'male' trades, so that they have not attracted eighth-grade girls.[26] It might indeed be claimed that Soviet boys have been 'cooled out' to excess. Once they have taken up PTU or tekhnikum courses they seem to abandon higher education ambitions, even though the new general-education component of the curricula supposedly keeps open the chance of eventual VUZ entry. Perhaps this is not so surprising, as several Soviet commentators have pointed out, when skilled manual workers are as much in demand as graduate engineers and can command wages as high as, or even higher, than the latter.[27] Moreover, the standard of teaching and attainment in the general-education part of PTU programmes is acknowledged to be much inferior to that in regular secondary schools and hardly constitutes an adequate preparation for entry to higher education.[28] Because of these considerations, not to mention the obligation on PTU and tekhnikum graduates to complete a compulsory work assignment after training or to be subject to military call-up, the vocational track effectively rules out or considerably reduces the chances of acquiring higher education after it.

A corollary to this is that, in general, a smaller proportion of boys than girls now apply to VUZs. And since girls tend to prefer non-technical specialities, institutions of higher technical education have been experiencing serious recruiting problems.[29]

Ottenberg claims that PTUs recruit largely from early leavers, the majority of whom are boys, so that in the early seventies only 25 to 28 per cent of PTU students were girls.[30] Tekhnikums recruiting at the post-secondary level were, also, reported to be subject to intense 'feminisation'. In his Gorky study in 1968 Zyuzin found that three-quarters of these tekhnikum students were female. He attributes this in part to the fact that male secondary school graduates are liable to be conscripted, but he makes it clear that tekhnikum courses are simply not attracting boys, except, perhaps, the sons of collective farm workers.[31] As a result of this trend there have been calls for the authorities to find some way of retrieving the males 'lost' to PTUs

by offering on graduation easier access to courses
in technical VUZs in the same field as their trades,
particularly those connected with heavy industry.[32]
Conversely, it has been urged that the network of
secondary PTUs catering for branches of the economy
which employ mainly female labour should be expanded
in order to attract girls away from the ninth grades
of schools.[33]

The question arises: if there are more females
among potential recruits for higher education, then
should women not be better represented all-round in
Soviet VUZs than they are now? One answer is that
some equalising takes place at the stage when the
decision to apply to a VUZ is made. Those boys
who remain in the senior grades of the general
school are said to be a select group who from the
outset are more determined to enter higher education
than the girls.[34] The same source of this suggestion also points out that men tend to predominate in
those categories of recruits for which the admission
rules provide privileged entry arrangements
(production workers, ex-servicemen, Preparatory
Division students).[35] There is, too, hearsay
evidence that pedagogical institutes discriminate
unofficially in favour of male applicants, so urgent
is their need to increase the number of men teachers
in the schools.

The extreme 'feminisation' of certain subject
areas in Soviet higher education poses problems in
both a direct and indirect way.[36] It reinforces
occupational stereotypes, takes girls of high
ability away from subject areas of importance to
the economy, and tends to intensify competition for
entry to certain types of VUZ, thus keeping out some
capable aspirants.[37] A number of Baltic sociologists found in the late seventies that women
students are less prone than men to drop out during
their course with the result that by the final year
the female percentage in the student body increases.
This aggravates the situation in institutions where
'feminisation' of the intake is already pronounced.[38]
In technical and agricultural VUZs, however, the
higher attrition among male students does bring
about a better representation for their female
counterparts.[39] Nevertheless, the alarm aroused by
these trends has led to serious suggestions being
made that in future some regulation of the sex
composition of VUZs should take place at the time of
entry.[40]

It would be a mistake to deduce from the above
observations that it is Soviet men who are

discriminated against in access to higher education.
There are other indices of participation in higher
education which demonstrate that women still lag
behind.   For example, while it is true that in the
working population in 1979 there were only 4 per
cent less female graduates than male graduates,
among the population as a whole the gap widens to
17 per cent.[41]   And in a number of Central Asian
and Caucasian republics, according to 1970 Census
data, there were marked differences in the
proportions of men and women with higher education.
In Azerbaijan, Turkmenia, Uzbekistan and Tadzhikistan
there were from 50 to nearly 100 per cent more men
graduates.   These huge gaps are attributed to
historical reactionary attitudes to women in those
republics.[42]   More pertinent, perhaps, is the fact
that in three of these republics - Azerbaijan,
Tadzhikistan and Turkmenia - the gap between the
numbers of male and female graduates actually
worsened from 1959 to 1970.[43]   As for women in the
main national group of each of these republics they
make up only from 22 to 33 per cent of VUZ
enrolments.[44]   It remains to be seen when the 1979
Census data are published whether these negative
features have been alleviated in the seventies.

Regional and Ethnic Differences in Access

The investigation of social and economic development
in the different regions and among the different
ethnic groups of the Soviet Union has given rise to
much Western scholarly writing in recent years.[45]
Most commentators emphasise that spectacular progress
has been made during the Soviet period in opening up
higher education to all indigenous nationalities.[46]
Indeed, the major ethnic groups often match or
surpass many advanced industrial nations of the
world in numbers of students and graduate specialists.
The focus of our attention here, however, will be on
existing differences and inequalities between regions
and nationalities.   For the sake of brevity, we shall
delimit the scope of our examination by confining it,
in the main, to the union republics and their titular
nationalities, and to just a few broad quantitative
indicators of achievement in higher education.

Union Republics

The most up-to-date general measure of comparative
access is provided by annual statistics for the
number of students in each republic per 10,000
inhabitants.   Table 3 shows these for the last
decade and a half and gives the percentages of the

Table 3: Number of Students per 10,000 Inhabitants by Union Republic, 1965 to 1980

	1965/6	%	1970/1	1975/6	1979/80	%
USSR	166	100	188	190	196	100
Russian Federation	185	111	204	212	219	112
Lithuania	155	93	180	188	205	105
Latvia	145	87	171	182	188	96
Armenia	174	105	214	190	187	95
Belorussia	120	72	154	170	181	92
Ukraine	151	91	170	169	175	89
Uzbekistan	159	96	192	174	173	88
Azerbaijan	144	87	191	173	172	88
Estonia	165	99	161	163	172	88
Georgia	170	102	189	168	170	87
Kazakhstan	120	72	151	152	169	86
Kirgizia	123	74	162	151	154	79
Tadzhikistan	119	72	149	144	141	72
Moldavia	108	65	124	115	127	65
Turkmenistan	103	62	131	122	121	62

Source: <u>Narodnoe khozyaistvo SSSR v 1979 g.</u> (Statistika, Moscow, 1981), p. 498.

USSR average for 1965/6 and 1979/80, ranking the
republics in descending order in the latter year.
Clear inequalities between the republics persist
throughout the period indicated.   Some progress
seems to have been made before 1970 to reduce the
wide discrepancy between the USSR figure and the
rates of the worst off republics - Turkmenistan,
Tadzhikistan and Moldavia.   But in the period from
1970 to 1979 the gains were lost.   These republics
now find themselves just as far below the national
average as they were in 1965.   Kirgizia and
Kazakhstan, though still lagging well behind the
USSR for numbers of students, improved their
position in relative terms;   Kazakhstan quite
substantially narrowed the gap from 28 per cent in
1965 to 14 per cent in 1979.   But several republics
- Georgia, Estonia, Armenia, Uzbekistan and the
Ukraine - lost considerable ground.   If one
compares the ranking of all republics in 1965/6 with
that of 1979/80 it can be seen that Belorussia,
Lithuania and Latvia have dramatically improved
their position, while Georgia and Estonia have
slipped from third and fourth places, respectively,
to tenth and ninth.
　　These adverse trends might be attributed in
part to geographical and economic factors which
influence the distribution of higher education
establishments.   Certainly, overall figures for
large areas can conceal considerable differences in
provision within each area.   Filippov estimates, for
example, that in 1973, despite a total of 207
students per 10,000 population for the Russian
Federation as a whole, the figures within the
republic vary widely, from 826 in the country's
largest VUZ centre, Moscow, to 202 in industrial
Sverdlovsk Region, and to only 113 in rural Moscow
Region.   But even in predominantly rural regions
higher education can be stimulated by making it a
priority, which probably explains the very high
figure for Novosibirsk Region of 299 students.[47]
　　Some explanation might be sought, too, in the
retrenchment of the seventies or demographic
movements.   Yet the consistent effect one might
expect here is not observable.   It is true that the
three Central Asian republics which have not
improved on their 1965 position had a 28 to 31 per
cent increase in their total population in the
seventies.   But Georgia and Estonia whose relative
standing in relation to the national average
actually worsened between 1965 and 1979 experienced
only a slight increase in their populations.[48]

Moreover, it might be argued that a centrally
prescribed policy of retrenchment in student
enrolments could, and should, have excluded the
republics at the bottom of the table.[49] In fact,
it was not these but other republics such as
Belorussia, Latvia and Kazakhstan which made great
leaps forward. The bottom three remain where they
were originally. Clearly a multiplicity of factors
is at work here within each republic. Nevertheless,
the fact of differential provision must still be
recognised.

To put the above comments into proper
perspective it is necessary to point out that the
number of students in Turkmenistan - the lowest-
ranking of all the republics in 1979 - comes very
close to the 1975 figures for the United Kingdom,
Ireland and West Germany, and is indisputably higher
than those for Switzerland, Portugal, Greece, Hungary
and Romania.[50]

Quantitative comparisons between republics
prompt other questions: Do they offer a similar range
and quality of higher education? Do seemingly
respectable participation rates conceal inferior
standards or lack of opportunity to study certain
subjects?

Comparative standards are difficult to assess.
In theory, all diplomas awarded to Soviet students
on graduation denote a similar level of academic
attainment, whatever and wherever the VUZ attended.
But it is generally conceded that academic standards
inevitably vary between different VUZs according to
such traditional criteria as average ability of
student intake, quality of staff, research output,
and financial resources. Universities, indeed,
are officially accorded leading status, and part-time
higher education establishments are acknowledged to
be worse than full-time VUZs both in teaching and
student performance. An adequate analysis of these
qualitative differences is beyond the scope of the
present paper, but it would be fair to say that VUZs
in most economically underdeveloped areas of the
country (for example, the North, Eastern Siberia,
parts of Central Asia), particularly new VUZs, provide
an inferior higher education to that offered by
established VUZs in the European and Caucasian
republics.

The range of higher education available must also
depend to some extent on the economic structure and
level of development of any given republic. In the
industrially well-developed regions such as the
Russian Federation, the Ukraine, Latvia, Belorussia,

Estonia, Georgia and Armenia between 33 and 40 per cent of all students are enrolled in VUZs which train specialists for industry. In the other republics the proportions are much less.[51] On the other hand, in 1975/6 as many as 68 per cent of all students in Tadzhikistan and 54 per cent in Turkmenistan were following teacher training courses, compared with just 25 per cent in the Russian Federation.[52] Undoubtedly, higher education provision in some republics is much narrower than in others. Hence, for many years now measures have been taken to compensate for this through a system of student secondments from 'peripheral' republics to VUZs in European republics which bypasses normal entrance examinations. The scale of this and other forms of interrepublican co-operation in student exchange is comparatively small. In the period 1967 to 1976 Russian Federation VUZs offered a mere 25,000 places to other republics, and the Ukraine - only about 7,000.[53]

Major Ethnic Groups. It is probable that regional measures overestimate the higher education opportunities enjoyed by ethnic groups.[54] Unfortunately, up-to-date information on the acquisition of higher education by nationalities within republics will not be available until publication of the relevant 1979 Census results. In the meantime scholars must rely on earlier census and other statistical materials relating to 1970/1 and 1976/7. These are utilised in a recent study to show what proportion of the population of each nationality over the age of ten years in 1970/1 had received a complete or incomplete higher education. There are substantial divergences from the USSR average of 5.5 per cent, ranging from superior levels of 39.9, 10.5, 7.5 and 5.9 per cent for Jews, Georgians, Armenians and Russians, respectively, to 4.0 per cent for Belorussians, 3.8 for Kirgiz, and even less for Uzbeks, Tadzhiks and Turkmen, while the figure for Moldavians is as low as 2.2 per cent.[55]
    The same study adduces 1970 data which make it possible to compare the proportion of each nationality within the total Soviet population and its share of total VUZ enrolments. Not surprisingly, in the light of the graduate statistics just cited, the nationalities which prove to be very much over-represented among students as a whole are Jews, Russians and Georgians; Azerbaijanis and Armenians are also overrepresented, though to a lesser degree; Kazakhs, Kirgiz, Lithuanians and Estonians in Soviet

VUZs broadly match their representation in the
population at large. But the remaining major
ethnic groups are all underrepresented in the
statistical sense.[56]
   Another way of looking at access to higher
education is to apply the standard measure of number
of students per 10,000 members of each nationality.
Here again, our estimates indicate that in 1970 the
overall USSR figure of 188 students is greatly
exceeded by Jews (492), Georgians (271), Russians
(212), Armenians (229), and just surpassed by
Azerbaijanis (196) and Kazakhs (189). Nationalities
falling well below the average are Belorussians and
Turkmen (144), Tadzhiks (132), Bashkirs (119),
Moldavians (114), Chuvash (94), and Mordvins (92).[57]
When these estimated data for ethnic groups are
compared with analogous 1970 data for the republics
in which they are the main indigenous nationality
(see Table 3), some interesting discrepancies come
to light. Thus, while the republic of Georgia in
1970 could boast 189 students per 10,000 inhabitants,
the comparable figure for students of Georgian ethnic
origin in all Soviet VUZs was as high as 271.
Similar improvements on their republics' rates are
to be seen for the following groups: Kazakhs (189
compared to 151), Kirgiz (182 to 162), Estonians
(178 to 161), Armenians (229 to 214), Turkmen (144
to 131), Russians (212 to 204), Lithuanians (187 to
180) and Azerbaijanis (196 to 191). On the
negative side, unfavourable correlations between
nationality and republican rates exist for Uzbeks
(164 and 192), Latvians (152 and 171), Ukrainians
(152 and 170), Tadzhiks (132 and 149), Belorussians
(144 and 154) and Moldavians (114 and 124).[58]
   Much of this variation, whether positive or
negative, can probably be accounted for by the
extent to which these titular groups participate in
the higher education of their republics. Table 4
shows for each republic the degree of participation
both by the main ethnic group and by Russians. The
sort of divergences in representation that we have
already highlighted are faithfully reflected here.
The three major Caucasian nationalities, together
with Estonians, Lithuanians, Kazakhs and Kirgiz
occupy more than their fair share of the VUZ places
in their respective republics at the expense of
non-indigenous groups; in Georgia, Armenia and
Estonia even Russians are underrepresented. But
in those republics where the indigenous nationality
is considerably underrepresented in VUZs (Latvia,
Ukraine, Uzbekistan, Tadzhikistan, Belorussia and

Table 4: Proportions of Main Ethnic Group and of Russians in the Total Population and VUZ Enrolments of Union Republics, 1970/1

	Percentage of Main Ethnic Group in		Percentage of Russians in	
	Population	VUZ Enrolments	Population	VUZ Enrolments
Russian Federation	82.8	83.8	82.8	83.8
Lithuania	80.1	84.0	8.6	10.4
Latvia	56.8	47.1	29.8	39.1
Armenia	88.6	96.2	2.7	2.6
Belorussia	81.0	63.7	10.4	24.5
Ukraine	74.9	59.9	19.4	32.9
Uzbekistan	65.5	56.8	12.5	18.8
Azerbaijan	73.8	78.9	10.0	12.2
Estonia	68.2	72.1	24.7	21.8
Georgia	66.8	82.2	8.5	6.5
Kazakhstan	32.6	39.9	42.4	42.6
Kirgizia	43.8	47.3	29.2	35.1
Tadzhikistan	56.2	49.5	11.9	20.4
Moldavia	64.6	59.2	11.6	17.6
Turkmenistan	65.6	64.6	14.5	21.1

Source: Estimated from: Itogi Vsesoyuznoi perepisi naseleniya 1970 goda. Tom 4 (Statistika, Moscow, 1973), pp. 12-15; Narodnoe obrazovanie, nauka i kul'tura v SSSR (Statistika, Moscow, 1971), pp. 197-204.

Moldavia), it is striking that all or much of the
shortfall parallels the extent of overrepresentation
of Russians. By comparison with similar indicators
for 1960/1, however, the general trend appears to
have been a small decline in the proportion of
Russians in non-Russian VUZs. This is particularly
marked in Moldavia, Georgia, and in the Central
Asian republics of Uzbekistan and Turkmenistan.
The opposite, however, is true of the Ukraine,
Belorussia and the Baltic republics, where the
titular nationalities are relatively worse off in
1970/1, while the Russian section of their
populations has improved upon its share of student
enrolments.[59]
     It is difficult to gauge changes in VUZ access
in the seventies as far as Soviet nationalities are
concerned. Certainly, some data for 1976/7 have
been published giving numbers of students in higher
education by nationality. But the lack of
population statistics for national groups for the
same year means that actual representation in higher
education (whether in percentage terms or in number
of students per 10,000 population) can be estimated
only approximately by employing as parameters the
relevant population data from the 1970 and 1979
Censuses.[60]   Such estimates indicate that since
1970 Georgians and Jews have fared badly in both
absolute and relative terms.   In fact, the number
of Jewish students slumped so dramatically from
106 thousand to 67 thousand that charges made by
Western scholars of anti-Jewish discrimination in
VUZ admissions received further strong statistical
backing.[61]   Nevertheless, in the late seventies, as
before, the children of both these nationalities,
as well as those of Russians, Armenians and Kazakhs
were undoubtedly overrepresented in the Soviet
student body.   Also between 1970 and 1976 larger
than average increases in student numbers are
recorded for Kirgiz, Tadzhiks, Uzbeks, Belorussians
and Turkmen, but these were probably insufficient
to ensure their proper representation.[62]
     It is easier to establish the existence and
persistence of differences in access between
nationalities than to account for them.   Various
explanations have been advanced in the literature
(see Notes 45, 46 and 54) ranging from political
favouritism and strategic considerations to language
obstacles and cultural backwardness.   Few of them,
however, are supported by detailed argument and most
lack consistency of application.   One powerful
factor is said to be urbanisation.[63]   It is true

that for many nationalities a strong positive
correlation can be demonstrated between numbers of
students and graduate specialists and the extent to
which the national group has become urbanised.
Highly urbanised nationalities such as Jews, Russians
and Armenians produce more VUZ graduates and
students than, say, the mainly rural Moldavians,
Tadzhiks and Turkmen.   On the other hand, this
criterion cannot explain the achievements in higher
education of Georgians and Azerbaijanis, a majority
of whom are rural dwellers.[64]   Nor does it explain
why Kazakhs and Kirgiz have proportionately more
students than Belorussians, when the latter have been
subject to a much greater degree of urbanisation.[65]
Similar anomalies are observed if one contrasts the
number of graduates in the rural population of each
nationality or attempts to use level of development
as a variable.[66]   The search then for a general
explanation has proved unsuccessful.   A more
promising, if onerous, approach which remains to be
tested is one which treats each nationality as a
particular case and explores in depth a broad set of
possible factors.
     There appears to be little prospect of
improvement in the relative position of republics
and ethnic groups in their access to higher education
in the next decade.   No expansion in student
numbers is envisaged in the Five-year Plan up to
1985.[67]   For most republics declining population
growth may bring about some slight statistical gains
in the sort of population-student indices we have
been examining.   For republics with rapidly
expanding populations - and these tend to be those
with relatively worse higher education enrolment
ratios - the opposite effect is more probable.   The
Soviet Minister of Higher Education has emphasised
that henceforth VUZs will be operating in a climate
of some economic stringency.[68]   And no indication
has been given that the resources required to
eradicate existing inequalities between republics in
higher education will be made available.

Social Class and Access to Higher Education
Access to higher education in the Soviet Union, as
in other countries, has been shown to be largely
determined by processes of selection and
differentiation occurring at earlier stages of
schooling.   The results of Soviet empirical research
in the late sixties demonstrate that the path to
higher education, starting from the earliest stage
of a pupil's progress and career plans in the

eight-grade school, is rendered more difficult for
some social groups than for others.   After the
failure of the Khrushchev educational reform in the
mid-sixties there developed a situation of mass
demand and fierce competition for VUZ places.   Such
conditions, given the rather inflexible and traditionally academic selection procedures of Soviet VUZs,
favoured candidates from more cultured and
intellectual homes.   Measures were introduced to
mitigate further pressure on higher education
stemming from the policy of universal secondary
education, including early and more intensive
vocational guidance of school pupils, the upgrading
of PTUs, and the identification and nurturing of
academically bright children in special schools and
classes.   An increasing gap between the standards
of school tuition and VUZ entry requirements led to
the expansion of pre-VUZ preparation courses and
private coaching.   All these developments tended to
reduce the chances of 'lower' socio-economic groups
obtaining a higher education. [69]
     The exposure of persisting systematic
inequalities between social groups in their enjoyment
of higher education provoked controversy among
Soviet sociologists in the late sixties and early
seventies. [70]   The evidence showed that the children
of the manual working class and kolkhoz peasants
were seriously underrepresented in the senior grades
of the general education school and were less likely
to aspire to advanced studies. [71]   Cohorts of
applicants and entrants to most VUZs proved to be
numerically dominated by the offspring of what might
be termed the Soviet middle classes. [72]   Such factual
inequality was enough to cause concern, but the
prospect of the situation worsening led to arguments
as to the priorities to be adopted and the methods
to be employed in a socialist society in order to
eradicate the imbalances revealed.
     Two basic views were expounded by sociologists
and other academics.   One was that inequality in
access to higher education is the inevitable price
to be paid for pursuing the primary purpose of the
tertiary sector, namely to select and train the
most able young people to service the national
economy.   Relaxation of entry standards and the
granting of special entry privileges to particular
social groups would, therefore, be economically
damaging and probably infringe the constitutional
rights of others. [73]   Proponents of the second view
placed greater stress on egalitarian principles and
the need for positive discrimination in regulating

the social composition of VUZs.[74]

During the seventies research continued in this area. Major surveys were conducted at republican and national level to investigate the role of higher education in forming the social class structure of Soviet society.[75] More data were made available by official statistical offices; even figures for the social background of all VUZ entrants nationally, hitherto not published, found their way into print. But on the whole the academic argument became muted. Access seemed to become less urgent a problem in the general sense. Yet the evidence of a definite pattern of class differences in higher education continued to accumulate. In the following section we shall examine briefly a few of the materials which have been published most recently on the representation of various social strata in the student bodies of Soviet VUZs.

The Social Class Composition of VUZ Students. Most empirical data on the social composition of Soviet students are taken from official VUZ statistical returns (see Tables 5 and 6). For the purpose of investigating the family background of VUZ recruits these official figures suffer from annoying imprecision.[76] Nevertheless, unlike survey samples, they do encompass the whole student body and are collected on the same basis throughout the country. They can, therefore, provide a useful broad indication of trends.

Table 5 reveals a definite tendency in the 1970s for the proportion of working-class students in full-time higher education to rise at the expense of those from peasant and non-manual backgrounds. In most cases these movements are not large. And they should be seen, too, in relation to changes in the social structure of the population at large over the same period. (Thus, while the percentage of non-manual workers in the population remained roughly constant between the 1970 Census and 1976, manual workers increased their share from 57 to 62 per cent and that of kolkhoz peasants dropped from 20 to 16 per cent.)[77] The USSR (All) figures for 1976/7 do not distinguish between manual workers and peasants; it is clear that taken together these groups have achieved a stable level of representation of about 61 per cent, and this continues until the end of the decade.[78] This general pattern for all VUZs is reflected almost exactly in other data for the seventies

Table 5: Social Composition of First-Year Students in Higher Education Institutions of USSR and Selected Republics, 1970 to 1976 (per cent)[a]

Area and Social Background[b]	Total Population (1970 census)[c]	1970/1	1971/2	1972/3	1973/4	1974/5	1975/6
USSR (All)							
1.	22.6	44.0	53.1	—	38.9	—	(38.7)[d]
2.	56.7	41.7	36.2	—	43.1	—	{61.3
3.	20.5	14.3	10.7	—	18.0	—	
USSR (Six Regions)							
1.	—	53.3	50.3	48.8	49.1	48.0	47.0
2.	—	37.7	39.8	42.4	44.4	45.4	45.5
3.	—	9.0	9.9	8.8	6.5	6.6	7.5
Estonia							
1.	26.6	50.3	47.4	47.0	46.1	41.4	42.7
2.	60.1	39.9	43.3	45.5	47.0	51.8	51.1
3.	13.1	9.8	9.3	7.5	6.8	6.8	6.2
Latvia							
1.	25.5	48.6	49.8	49.7	48.8	48.8	49.7
2.	56.6	39.9	39.2	40.4	42.5	42.7	42.9
3.	17.6	11.5	11.1	9.9	8.7	8.6	7.4
Kazakhstan							
1.	23.5	43.6	—	41.4	—	40.8	
2.	68.1	45.6	—	49.9	—	52.6	
3.	8.2	10.8	—	8.7	—	6.6	

Cont'd .....

Table 5 Continued

Notes:

a. Based on official VUZ statistics which combine social origins and pre-VUZ
    occupational status (full-time day students).

b. The following categories are used: 1. Non-manual worker, 2. Manual worker,
    3. Collective farm worker/peasant.

c. Excludes a fraction of one per cent of respondents belonging to other social
    groups or not indicating their social group.

d. 1976/7 data cited, with bracketed figures obtained by subtraction.

Source: USSR and Estonia – M.N. Rutkevich and F.R. Filippov (eds.), Vysshaya
shkola kak faktor izmeneniya sotsial'noi struktury razvitogo sotsialisticheskogo
obshchestva (Nauka, Moscow, 1978), pp. 66, 110, 141; The Times, 23 November 1972;
Bulleten' MV i SSO SSSR, 1977, no. 2, p. 7; Latvia – M.E. Ashmane, 'Sotsial'nye
istochniki formirovaniya kontingenta studentov Latviiskoi SSSR' in M.E. Ashmane
(ed.), Vysshaya shkola i sotsial'naya struktura razvitogo sotsialisticheskogo
obshchestva (Zinatne, Riga, 1981), p. 14; Kazakhstan – M.N. Rutkevich et al.,
'Protsessy vosproizvodstva sotsial'noi struktury sovetskogo obshchestva' in
M.N. Rutkevich and F.R. Filippov (eds.), Sotsial'naya struktura razvitogo
sotsialisticheskogo obshchestva v SSSR (Nauka, Moscow, 1976), p. 191; 1970 Census
– Itogi Vsesoyuznoi perepisi naseleniya 1970 goda. Tom 5 (Statistika, Moscow,
1973), pp. 8–15.

relating to pedagogical institutes in the Russian Federal Republic (not reproduced here).[79]   The Kazakhstan figures suggest that collective farm peasants do quite well;   in Latvia non-manuals actually improve their share to nearly half the total VUZ intake.   A similar small improvement in the latter group's representation was also reported in a study of Lithuanian VUZs in the mid-seventies.[80] By and large, however, the basic differences noted in the 1960s remain unchanged, with middle-class entrants taking up from one and a half to two times more VUZ places than their proportion in the population might entitle them to, and with the other two groups substantially underrepresented.

More localised data for full-time entrants are set out in Table 6.   Here the same pattern of change between the proportions of manual and non-manual workers is evident.   Non-manual decline can be seen in four VUZ centres.   It is steeper in Moscow than elsewhere;   in Kharkov it is slight, while Odessa escapes it altogether.   Although Gorky VUZs exhibit a small increase in students from non-manual backgrounds in the years shown, when 1969 is used as the baseline this increase becomes a slight drop.[81]   In almost all areas collective farm workers receive a statistically fair share and more. Their percentage in Moscow VUZs is particularly impressive.   It is true that the capital recruits students from all over the Soviet Union, but the peasant figures there and in other centres do suggest that the policy of encouraging rural candidates to apply to pedagogical, medical and cultural institutes has had some effect.

The overall trends illustrated in the two tables are confirmed by other studies.[82]   Working-class students have apparently improved their access to higher education to some extent.   Within groups of VUZs much of this improvement seems to be concentrated in technological institutes.[83]   The children of collective farm workers tend to be generally underrepresented.   Middle-class representation in some areas has not changed since the late sixties, but it has suffered some decline overall.   Despite this, the non-manual worker group, especially highly qualified specialists and intellectuals, retains its traditional relative superiority in access to higher education.[84]

How do Soviet sociologists and educationalists react to statistical data of this kind?   In the sixties there was a tendency for researchers to ignore the implications of such findings and to

Table 6: Social Composition of First-Year Students in Selected Major VUZ Centres, 1970 to 1976 (per cent)[a]

VUZ Centre and Social Background[b]	Region Working Population (1970 Census)[c]	1970/1	1971/2	1972/3	1973/4	1974/5	1975/6
Moscow							
1.	32.7	63.4	63.4	56.5	58.3	57.4	54.3
2.	66.6	32.0	32.0	39.1	38.1	38.8	40.4
3.	0.6	4.6	4.6	4.4	3.6	3.8	5.1
Sverdlovsk							
1.	27.7	54.0	49.6	46.5	47.9	47.4	48.4
2.	70.5	42.4	47.7	49.2	49.7	49.5	49.1
3.	1.7	3.6	2.8	4.4	2.4	3.1	2.1
Novosibirsk							
1.	29.8	51.7	49.0	49.8	45.9	46.2	46.2
2.	64.4	36.3	34.5	38.4	48.7	48.6	48.0
3.	5.7	12.0	16.7	11.9	5.4	4.2	5.8
Odessa							
1.	25.7	31.6	30.1	33.5	35.3	32.6	31.6
2.	46.2	45.5	48.2	44.5	44.9	46.8	46.4
3.	27.7	22.9	21.7	22.0	19.8	20.6	22.0
Kharkov							
1.	29.1	35.8	34.0	35.5	32.2	32.3	—
2.	58.6	49.4	52.4	51.5	54.5	55.3	—
3.	12.1	14.8	13.6	13.0	13.3	12.4	—
Gorky							
1.	25.6	—	39.2	—	45.7	—	41.8
2.	63.2	—	52.5	—	48.8	—	52.6
3.	11.0	—	8.3	—	5.5	—	5.7

Cont'd ....

Table 6 Continued

Notes:

a. Data based on official VUZ statistics which combine social origins and pre-VUZ occupational status (full-time students).

b. The following categories are used: 1. Non-manual workers, 2. Manual workers, 3. Collective farm workers/peasants.

c. Excluding a fraction of one per cent of respondents belonging to other social groups or not indicating their social group.

Source: For Moscow, Sverdlovsk, Novosibirsk and Odessa – M.N. Rutkevich and F.R. Filippov (eds.), Vysshaya shkola kak faktor izmeneniya sotsial'noi struktury razvitogo sotsialisticheskogo obshchestva (Nauka, Moscow, 1978), p. 141; Kharkov – I.I. Sheremet, 'Sotsial'nyi sostav studenchestva', Sotsiologicheskie issledovaniya, no. 2 (1977), p. 77; Gorky – S.S. Balabanov et al., 'Problema regulirovaniya sotsial'nogo sostava studenchestva' in A.A. Terent'ev (ed.), Sotsiologiya i vysshaya shkola [Vyp 6] (Gorky University, Gorky, 1978), p. 90; 1970 Census – Itogi Vsesoyuznoi perepisi naseleniya 1970 goda. Tom 5 (Statistika, Moscow, 1973), pp. 34–41.

declare that the problem of inequality of access for different social groups was being solved and that the social composition of students was approaching that of the population.[85]   Nowadays they are more circumspect, occasionally even pessimistic.[86]   The evidence we have presented in the tables does appear to demonstrate that Soviet higher education has become more open to working-class and peasant children.   Yet some reservations must be made.   To begin with, progress in this direction is not always consistent, as we have noted; nor is it very marked.   Furthermore, information on the distribution of social class groups within the catchment areas of VUZs is not available, so that comparison between student bodies and populations they come from cannot be very accurate as far as the seventies is concerned.

A crucial factor, however, in assessing recent developments must be the role played by the new Preparatory Divisions (see p. 204 above).   In 1975/6 some 97,000 students entered full-time VUZ courses from these Divisions.   It has been estimated that the influx of this new type of entrant accounts for nearly 80 per cent of the growth in full-time student numbers since 1970.[87] This being so, Preparatory Divisions either mask a swing from higher education or they must have created fiercer competition for entry among ordinary applicants - a situation in which the middle-class candidate tends to be more successful. In any case, the sizeable contribution to VUZ intakes which the Divisions' graduates represent - all of them former manual workers, collective farm workers or demobbed servicemen who could not, or would not, enter higher education in the normal way - must inevitably have some impact on the social class composition of students.   Indeed, this was one of the reasons why the Divisions were set up and why they have been praised.   Not only is their influence to be observed in the results reviewed in Tables 5 and 6 but also in the apparent success rates in entry competitions of applicants from working-class backgrounds.   Studies in the 1960s always showed that there were proportionately more middle-class children among successful entrants than among applicants, that is they performed better in the entrance examinations.[88]   But in the 1970s some research has indicated that it is now working-class candidates who tend to increase their share among entrants - not because of examination success but because Preparatory Division graduates are excused from the entry competition and enter the first year of VUZs directly.[89]

Now, if the introduction of nearly 20 per cent of workers, peasants and servicemen into the annual intake of VUZs[90] results in only a small improvement in the overall representation of these social groups in the student body, as we have seen, then the basic underlying trend may have been a worsening of access opportunities for working-class children coming from the schools. Of course, there are more complex implications to be considered here, particularly those connected with the general swing from higher education, but the point is, we believe, a significant one.

In 1973/4 the Soviet Academy of Sciences' Institute of Sociological Research carried out a most comprehensive study of the social composition of students in six regions of the country. This All-Union Survey attempted to avoid the ambiguities in official statistics by looking at the social origins as well as the occupational status of students in its sample. In line with other recent Soviet sociological research it also examined mothers' occupations as well as those of fathers. A selection of results is offered in Table 7. Despite unsatisfactory aspects of their published present-ation,[91] they provide an interesting snapshot of VUZ recruitment in the mid-seventies.

The picture of student intakes presented by the Survey is one of considerable imbalances between the various social strata. The children of manual workers make up less than 40 per cent of the student body in all centres except Sverdlovsk. In Moscow and Odessa their share is notably low. Highly qualified specialists comprise the overwhelming bulk of the non-manual fathers and outnumber the other occupational categories in all areas except, again, Sverdlovsk. This particular social group clearly enjoys undiminished superior access to higher education; if non-manual representation has declined slightly from 1969, it has been at the expense of routine workers.[92] Most significant of all, perhaps, is the finding that three-quarters of all students have mothers in non-manual jobs. The conclusion of the Survey's organisers is that the social make-up of VUZ students has drawn closer to that of Soviet society as a whole. Preparatory Divisions are acknowledged to have been influential in this process of equalising access, yet, curiously enough, no details of their impact emerge from the Survey report.[93]

In the last decade Soviet sociologists have

Table 7: Social Origins of First-year Students in Selected Major VUZ Centres by Parental Occupations,[a] All-Union Survey 1973/4 (per cent)

	Moscow %	Sverdlovsk %	Novosibirsk %	Odessa %	Tallin/Tartu %	Voronezh %	All Centres %
Father (i)[b]							
1. }	56.7	43.4	43.4	44.3	44.3	36.6	44.8
2. }	24.1	36.5	34.3	32.4	32.4	29.0	31.2
3.	3.4	3.6	6.6	9.6	9.5	13.4	8.4
4.	15.8	16.5	15.7	13.8	13.8	18.0	15.6
5.	—	—	—	—	—	—	—
Father (ii)[c]							
1.	61.2	42.6	—	35.5	40.0	— }	48.0
2.	3.8	3.0	—	6.8	6.9	—	37.3
3.	28.5	47.7	—	33.4	36.2	—	14.7
4.	6.5	6.6	—	24.3	16.9	—	—
5.	—	—	—	—	—	—	—
Mother[c]							
1.	62.6	47.4	—	40.9	40.9	— }	74.9
2.	20.7	27.1	—	27.4	34.4	—	14.2
3.	11.4	21.1	—	11.7	12.3	—	10.9
4.	5.3	4.5	—	20.0	12.3	—	—
5.	—	—	—	—	—	—	—

Notes: a. The following categories are used: 1. Highly qualified non-manual. 2. Routine non-manual. 3. Manual worker. 4. Agricultural worker. 5. Residual categories (pensioners, servicemen, etc.) and non-response. b. Source specifically includes category 5. c. These data exclude category 5, but how they have been estimated is unclear. Source: Father (i) data - M.N. Rutkevich, Intelligentsiya v razvitom sotsialisticheskom obshchestve (Politizdat, Moscow, 1977), p. 61; all other data - M.N. Rutkevich and F.R. Filippov (eds.), Vysshaya shkola kak faktor izmeneniya sotsial'noi struktury razvitogo sotsialisticheskogo obshchestva (Nauka, Moscow, 1978), pp. 111, 136-7.

become more aware that the problem of social
inequality in higher education is not solved simply
by ensuring adequate representation of different
social groups in VUZ intakes. Several researches
have revealed that weak attainment and dropout of
students during VUZ courses tend to be socially
biased.[94] As a consequence, the social composition
of first-year students is often quite different from
that of final-year students. And recent official
attempts to regulate social composition by lowering
academic standards at entry can prove to be
counterproductive. For the improved chances of
working-class and peasant candidates at the
admission stage are nullified by academic wastage
before graduation.[95]

Trends in the 1980s
Student recruitment and problems of access in the
1980s will be dominated by two factors. The first
is an acute shortage of skilled manpower in the
Soviet economy. Government economic planners and
managers are faced with the vital task of harnessing
all available human resources for work in production.
The second factor is a worsening demographic
situation which has brought about a sharp fall in
the numbers of school leavers and thus fewer
potential recruits for higher education.[96]
     In their main guidelines for the national
economy in the next five years and beyond the party
and government propose that a total of about 10
million specialists should be trained in higher and
secondary specialised education sectors.[97] Of
these 4 million will be VUZ graduates, a figure
which represents a standstill in student numbers;[98]
no expansion, but no contraction either such as is
taking place in Western higher education. Steady
student numbers and a declining age group will
enhance, statistically speaking, the chances of
Soviet young people entering a VUZ. But the VUZs
themselves will be operating in something akin to a
buyers' market and are likely to experience some
difficulty in fulfilling intake quotas, particularly
for those courses which have hitherto been less
popular.[99] To ensure, therefore, that the higher
education system continues to meet its obligations
to the economy certain measures affecting admissions
have been projected.
     To begin with, priority in recruitment will be
given to economically vital courses, and this may
entail a reduction in student numbers in those
specialisms which are already producing too many

graduates for the country's needs.[100] Previous policy on part-time higher education will be reversed and a certain amount of expansion will be allowed here - not primarily for reasons of social equity, it should be said, but to make up likely shortfalls in full-time admissions. This provision will be used, too, to boost the qualifications and competence of tekhnikum graduates working in those industries and regions of the country where the shortage of VUZ specialists is most felt.[101] Thirdly, the usual rather haphazard approach to the forward planning of student intakes and graduate output is being tightened up, that is made more realistic and efficient.[102] To this end, VUZ authorities will be concerned not merely with recruitment but also with eliminating weak student performance and dropout which have prevented the achievement of graduate targets in the past. Finally, VUZs are being encouraged to recruit more purposively in the secondary schools.[103] Closer co-operation between schools and VUZs will probably lead to more vigorous propagandising among parents and pupils of the merits of higher education, in general, and of engineering and technical subjects, in particular. And within schools one can expect to see a greater degree of control and direction exercised over the vocational and educational choices of pupils earlier on in their school careers.[104]

The sort of measures outlined will have a definite impact on the access to higher education of certain groups. The increased availability of VUZ places will not necessarily mean easier entry. The Soviet authorities are anxious to avoid a drop in the quality of recruits - hence an emphasis on earlier selection and preparation of able pupils. It would be consistent with such a policy to envisage special tuition, preparation courses or coaching for selected pupils organised by VUZ staff via formal agreements with schools. At any rate, it seems probable that existing special schools and classes will receive further development since they already send considerable numbers of talented pupils into the higher education system.[105] Judging by past experience, sponsoring of able pupils on these lines tends to benefit children from more cultured homes, whose parents are well educated. Such pupils are less susceptible to the pressures of school and media vocational guidance, whereas children whose parents are less knowledgeable and experienced in matters of educational choice are more likely to be persuaded not to pursue the goal of higher education. It is probable that vocational counselling will be used to persuade academically promising boys to remain in the general education school rather than transfer to a PTU or tekhnikum. Girls, on the other hand, will no doubt be urged to switch to vocational training for the service industries in larger numbers than in the past. Such reorientation of attitudes among schoolgirls away from the academic track may be assisted by some curtailment of intakes to VUZs which are currently popular with them.

If the foregoing is largely informed speculation, it is quite certain that access to higher education will become easier for graduates of PTUs and tekhnikums, provided they have qualified and have work experience in specified trades and specialisms.[106]   Moreover, VUZs have been instructed to respond more directly to the needs of the economy by adapting their curricula to the reality of production requirements and by setting up teaching branches inside enterprises to offer advanced instruction to the workers in subjects relevant to their work.[107]   One consequence of these proposals is that more working-class students are likely to be found in Soviet VUZs than in the past.

Overall then, some widening of access to higher education can be expected in the near future. There is a certain irony in this situation.   For decades the social problems of unequal access have been accorded less importance than economic objectives.   In the 1980s, however, due to manpower shortages, it is the need to achieve economic goals which could bring about a greater degree of equality and democratisation in the composition of the student bodies of Soviet VUZs.

NOTES

1.   Narodnoe khozyaistvo SSSR v 1972 g. (Statistika, Moscow, 1973), p. 643; Narodnoe khozyaistvo v 1979 g. (Statistika, Moscow, 1980), p. 498;   U. Teichler, 'Trends in Higher Education with Respect to Student Population', Higher Education in Europe, vol. 5, no. 2 (1980), p. 26.
2.   B. Von Kopp, Probleme der Hochschulzulassung im Internationalen Vergleich (Deutsches Institut für Internationale Pädagogische Forschung, Frankfurt am Main, 1981), p. 58.
3.   Ibid., p. 61.
4.   The Russian term VUZ denotes any type of

ACCESS TO HIGHER EDUCATION IN THE SOVIET UNION

higher education establishment, whether university
or specialised institute. Following accepted
practice it will be used throughout this paper in
anglicised nominal and adjectival forms, i.e. VUZ,
VUZs.
    5. Estimate from Narodnoe obrazovanie, nauka
i kultura v SSSR (Statistika, Moscow, 1977), pp. 17,
246; SSSR v tsifrakh v 1980 godu (Finansy i
statistika, Moscow, 1981), pp. 203, 209.
    6. For a review of this evidence see G.H. Avis,
'Social Class and Access to Full-time Higher
Education in the Soviet Union', unpublished MSc
dissertation, University of Bradford, 1977, pp. 19-26,
55-6, 112-31.
    7. Byulleten' MV i SSO SSSR, no. 5 (1972),
p. 11.
    8. For relevant legislation see A.A. Abakumov
et al. (comps.), Narodnoe obrazovanie v SSSR,
obshcheobrazovatel'naya shkola: sbornik dokumentov
1917-1973 g.g.(Pedagogika, Moscow, 1974), pp. 129-30,
240-3.
    9. Izvestiya, 26 May 1974, p. 3.
    10. See e.g. D.I. Zyuzin, Kachestvo podgotovki
spetsialistov kak sotsial'naya problema (Nauka,
Moscow, 1978), p. 44; F.R. Filippov et al.,
'Orientatsiya shkol'nikov na vysshee obrazovanie' in
M.N. Rutkevich and F.R. Filippov (eds.), Vysshaya
shkola kak faktor izmenenyia sotsial'noi struktury
razvitogo sotsialisticheskogo obshchestva (Nauka,
Moscow, 1978), pp. 103-4; M.Kh. Titma, Vybor
professii kak sotsial'naya problema (Mysl', Moscow,
1975), p. 116; A.S. Shuruev and F.S. Ryabkov,
'Dinamichnoe razvitie vysshego obrazovaniya',
Vestnik vysshei shkoly, no. 9 (1976), p. 15.
    11. Byulleten' MV i SSO SSSR, no. 10 (1975),
pp. 16-25; Byulleten' MV i SSO SSSR, no. 6 (1977),
pp. 3-9; Byulleten' MV i SSO SSSR, no. 12 (1978),
p. 3; Byulleten' MV i SSO SSSR, no. 9 (1979),
pp. 3-4, 7-8, 11-12; Pravda, 5 July 1981, p. 3.
    12. Byulleten' MV i SSO SSSR, no. 5 (1980),
pp. 19ff.
    13. See note 11 for concessions made in entry
requirements for technical VUZs. The low quality
of VUZ training has been the subject of academic
and press discussion: see, for example,
S.S. Balabanov, 'Dvizhenie studencheskikh
kontingentov' in A.A. Terent'ev and V.I. Turanskii
(eds.), Sotsiologiya i vysshaya shkola, Vypusk 4
(Gorky University, Gorky, 1975), p. 72; A.K.
Grigor'ev, Vysshaya shkola: problemy vospitaniya
(Lenizdat, Leningrad, 1981), pp. 39-42; Pravda,

6 April 1979, p. 3; Pravda, 5 Jan. 1980, p. 3;
Pravda, 10 Dec. 1980, p. 4; Komsomol'skaya pravda,
3 June 1981, p. 2.
    14. V.T. Lisovskii and A.V. Dmitriev, Lichnost'
studenta (Leningrad University, Leningrad, 1974),
pp. 48-61; Yakobsoo et al., 'Opyt issledovaniya
vybora spetsial'nosti i professii budushchikh
uchitelei' in Kh. Kalder et al. (eds.), Uluchshenie
podbora kontingenta·studentov i povyshenie effektivnosti uchebnogo protsessa. Problemy vysshei shkoly 3
(Tartu University, Tartu, 1979), pp. 56-64; M.Kh.
Titma and L.Ya. Rubina, 'Sotsial'no-professional'naya
orientatsiya studenchestva' in Rutkevich and
Filippov, Vysshaya shkola kak faktor, p. 182.
    15. Shuruev and Ryabkov, 'Dinamichnoe razvitie',
p. 14; D.I. Chuprunov, 'Obsuzhdaya programmnyi
dokument partii', Vestnik vysshei shkoly, no. 1
(1981), p. 4.
    16. See the official regulations published in
Byulleten' MV i SSO SSSR, no. 6 (1969), pp. 10-12.
For a general summary of entry privileges see
V.P. Elyutin, Vysshaya shkola obshchestva razvitogo
sotsializma (Vysshaya shkola, Moscow, 1980),
pp. 316-21.
    17. Byulleten' MV i SSO SSSR, no. 10 (1969),
pp. 1-4.
    18. For a detailed commentary on the
establishment and progress of Preparatory Divisions
see G.H. Avis, 'Preparatory Divisions in Soviet
Higher Education Establishments: Ten Years of
Radical Experiment', Soviet Studies (forthcoming).
    19. Teichler, 'Trends in Higher Education',
p. 29; Narodnoe khozyaistvo 1979, p. 33.
    20. Yu. N. Kozyrev et al., 'Tendentsii
izmeneniya sotsial'nogo sostava studenchestva' in
Rutkevich and Filippov, Vysshaya shkola kak faktor,'
p. 125; V.P. Tomin, Uroven' obrazovaniya naseleniya
SSSR (Finansy i statistika, Moscow, 1981),
pp. 140-1.
    21. N. Ottenberg, 'Izmenenie professional'noi
struktury rabochikh kadrov i trebovaniya k ikh
podgotovke' in D.I. Valentei (ed.), Obrazovatel'naya
i sotsial'no-professional'naya struktura naseleniya
SSSR (Statistika, Moscow, 1975), p. 58; F.R. Filippov,
Vseobshchee srednee obrazovanie v SSSR (Mysl', Moscow,
1976), pp. 110-11.
    22. Filippov et al., 'Orientatsiya shkol'nikov',
p. 104; see also references in Note 21.
    23. Yu P. Petrov, 'Sistema srednego
obrazovaniya: tendentsiya odnorodnosti v
sotsial'nom sostave uchashchikhsya (na primere

krupnogo promyshlennogo goroda)' in N.A. Aitov (ed.), Sotsial'naya struktura gorodskogo naseleniya SSSR (Ufa, 1978), p. 155.

24. Filippov, Vseobshchee srednee, p. 110.

25. Kozyrev et al., 'Tendentsii izmeneniya', p. 126. This sample of tenth-graders were intending to enter VUZ.

26. Filippov, Vseobshchee srednee, p. 110.

27. Pravda, 7 June 1981, p. 3; Komsomol'skaya pravda, 3 June 1981, p. 2.

28. Filippov, Vseobshchee srednee, pp. 112-13.

29. See Notes 10, 11 and 12.

30. Ottenberg, 'Izmenenie professional'noi struktury', p. 58.

31. D. Zyuzin, 'Sotsial'no-demograficheskie usloviya povysheniya kachestva podgotovki spetsialistov srednego zvena' in Valentei, Obrazovatel'naya, p. 42.

32. See, for example, Petrov, 'Sistema srednego', p. 156. For the implementation of admission concessions for PTU graduates see Byulleten' MV i SSO SSSR, no. 9 (1979), pp. 4-5, 11-12.

33. Ottenberg, 'Izmenenie professional'noi struktury', p. 58; Filippov, Vseobshchee srednee, p. 111.

34. Kozyrev et al., 'Tendentsii izmeneniya', p. 126.

35. Ibid., pp. 126-7.

36. Titma, Vybor professii, pp. 134-5.

37. Filippov et al., 'Orientatsiya shkol'nikov', p. 104.

38. A.K. Shimkene, 'Nekotorye otritsatel'nye posledstviya otseva studentov' in Yu. Leonavichyus (ed.), Problema adaptatsii studentov (Ministry of Higher and Specialised Education of the Lithuanian SSR, Vil'nyus, 1978), p. 135; M.E. Ashmane, 'Sotsial'nye istochniki formirovaniya kontingenta studentov Latviiskoi SSR' in M.E. Ashmane (ed.), Vysshaya shkola i sotsial'naya struktura razvitogo sotsialisticheskogo obshchestva (Zinatne, Riga, 1981), p. 17.

39. Ashmane, 'Sotsial'nye istochniki', p. 17.

40. M.Kh. Titma and P.O. Kenkmann, 'Regional'nye osobennosti komplektovaniya vysshei shkoly' in Rutkevich and Filippov, Vysshaya shkola kak faktor, p. 147; Ya. Ya. Krutskikh, 'Vysshee pedagogicheskoe obrazovanie – istochnik popolneniya pedagogicheskikh kadrov respubliki' in Ashmane, Vysshaya shkola, p. 84.

41. Tomin, Uroven' obrazovaniya, pp. 87, 89.

42.   Ibid., p. 88.
43.   Estimated from data in Tomin, Uroven' obrazovaniya, pp. 85-6.
44.   Narodnoe obrazovanie, nauka i kultura v SSSR (Statistika, Moscow, 1971), pp. 200-3. Percentages cited are for 1970/1.
45.   See, for example, E. Goldhagen (ed.), Ethnic Minorities in the Soviet Union (Praeger, New York, 1968); J. Pennar et al., Modernization and Diversity in Soviet Education, with Special Reference to Nationality Groups (Praeger, New York, 1971); E. Allworth (ed.), The Nationality Question in Soviet Central Asia (Praeger, New York, 1973); J.R. Azrael (ed.), Soviet Nationality Policies and Practices (Praeger, New York, 1978).
46.   M.M. Shorish, 'Who Shall Be Educated: Selection and Integration in Soviet Central Asia' in Allworth, The Nationality Question, pp. 86-99; T. Rakowska-Harmstone, 'The Dialectics of Nationalism in the USSR', Problems of Communism, vol. 23, no. 3 (1974), p. 6; N. Kravetz, 'Education of Ethnic and National Minorities in the USSR: a Report on Current Developments', Comparative Education, vol. 16, no. 1 (1980), pp. 13-23.
47.   F.R. Filippov, 'Sovershenstvovanie, sistemy obrazovaniya i preodolenie sotsial'nykh razlichii' in Rutkevich and Filippov, Vysshaya shkola kak faktor, p. 66.
48.   Naselenie SSSR: Po dannym Vsesoyuznoi perepisi naseleniya 1979 goda (Politizdat, Moscow, 1980), p. 4.
49.   A claim that Soviet budgetary policy fails to compensate for or redress social inequalities in union republics is made by P. Zwick, 'Ethnoregional Socioeconomic Fragmentation and Soviet Budgetary Policy', Soviet Studies, vol. 31, no. 3 (1979), pp. 380-400.
50.   Teichler, 'Trends in Higher Education', p. 26.
51.   Zyuzin, Kachestvo podgotovki, p. 44.
52.   Estimated from data in Narodnoe obrazovanie, nauka i kultura 1977, pp. 232-42, 244.
53.   V.T. Petrov, 'Sotrudnichestvo i vzaimopomoshch' v podgotovke spetsialistov', Vestnik vysshei shkoly, no. 5 (1979), pp. 8-9.
54.   B. Silver, 'Levels of Sociocultural Development Among Soviet Nationalities: A Partial Test of the Equalization Hypothesis', American Political Science Review, vol. 68, no. 4 (1974), pp. 1636-7.
55.   Kravetz, 'Education of Ethnic and National

Minorities', p. 16.
    56.   Ibid., pp. 15, 20.
    57.   Estimated from nationalities population
statistics in Naselenie SSSR, pp. 23-4, and student
data in Narodnoe obrazovanie, nauka i kultura 1971,
p. 196.
    58.   See Note 57.
    59.   Indicators for 1960/1 are estimated from
1959 Census population data for republics given in
Itogi Vsesoyuznoi perepisi naseleniya 1970 goda.
Tom 4 (Statistika, Moscow, 1973), pp. 12-15, and
from student numbers in Narodnoe obrazovanie,
nauka i kultura 1971, pp. 197-204.
    60.   Student data for 1976/7 are taken from
Narodnoe khozyaistvo SSSR za 60 let (Statistika,
Moscow, 1977), p. 588. Census data on national-
ities for 1970 and 1979 are available in
Naselenie SSSR, pp. 23-4.
    61.   N. DeWitt, The Status of Jews in Soviet
Education (American Jewish Congress, Commission on
International Affairs) New York, 1964; Pennar
et al., Modernization and Diversity, pp. 333-4;
Kravetz, 'Education of Ethnic and National
Minorities', pp. 19-20.
    62.   Kravetz, 'Education of Ethnic and
National Minorities', pp. 15, 20.
    63.   Ibid., p. 17.
    64.   Ibid., pp. 16-17, 20.
    65.   Ibid., p. 17. In 1970 the numbers of
students per 10,000 population were 189, 182 and
144 respectively, for Kazakhs, Kirgiz and Belorussians - see Note 57.
    66.   Itogi Vsesoyuznoi perepisi. Tom 4,
pp. 393-404. The numbers of graduates in the rural
populations of nationalities vary widely.
Surprisingly enough, all the Central Asian ethnic
groups, except Tadzhiks, have considerably higher
figures than European nationalities such as Russians,
Ukrainians and Belorussians. For a ranking of
union republics according to growth and level of
development in 1966 see Rakowska-Harmstone,
'The Dialectics of Nationalism', p. 4.
    67.   Chuprunov, 'Obsuzhdaya programmnyi
dokument', p. 4.
    68.   V.P. Elyutin, 'Zadachi vysshei shkoly
v svete reshenii XXVI s"ezda KPSS, Vestnik vysshei
shkoly, no. 5 (1981), p. 9.
    69.   The published literature on this topic
is extensive. Recent lengthy commentaries are to
be found in R.B. Dobson, 'Social Status and
Inequality of Access to Higher Education in the USSR'

in J. Karabel and A.H. Halsey (eds.), Power and Ideology in Education (Oxford University Press, New York, 1977), pp. 254-75; M. Yanowitch, Social and Economic Inequality in the Soviet Union: Six Studies (Martin Robertson, London, 1977), pp. 58-99; see also Avis, 'Social Class and Access', passim.
70. Yanowitch, Social and Economic Inequality, pp. 73-96; G.H. Avis, 'The Sociology of Soviet Higher Education: A Review of Recent Empirical Research' in B. Harasymiw (ed.), Education and the Mass Media in the Soviet Union and Eastern Europe (Praeger, New York, 1976), pp. 58-9.
71. Avis, 'Social Class and Access', pp. 19-96.
72. Avis, 'The Sociology of Soviet Higher Education', pp. 40-51.
73. See, for example, M.N. Rutkevich and F.R. Filippov, Sotsial'nye peremeshcheniya (Mysl', Moscow, 1970), pp. 139-52; V. Shubkin, 'Nachalo puti: rasmyshleniya o problemakh vybora professii', Novyi mir, no. 2 (1976), pp. 200-1.
74. See, for example, V. Mishin, Obshchestvennyi progress (Volgo-Vyatskoe Izd., Gorky, 1970), pp. 242-9; A.V. Zelepukin, 'Formirovanie i sotsial'nye funktsii sovetskoi intelligentsii' in I.N. Chikhichin (ed.), Sotsial'no-klassovaya struktura i politicheskaya organisatsiya sotsialisticheskogo obshchestva (Saratov University, Saratov, 1971), pp. 105.
75. E.G. A. Sukamyagi et al. (eds.), Vysshaya shkola i sotsial'no-professional'naya orientatsiya uchashcheisya molodezhi, I (Tartu University, Tartu, 1975); Titma, Vybor professii; Rutkevich and Filippov, Vysshaya shkola kak faktor; Kalder et al., Uluchshenie podbora; Ashmane, Vysshaya shkola.
76. Figures for students' social background in VUZ records are compiled from responses provided by entrants themselves on initial registration. Those coming straight from school must state the occupational status of their parents (usually the father); those in employment prior to entry must put their own occupational status, even if they were employed for only a short period of time. Of the latter group, of course, some will have a different occupational status from that of their parents, so that their real social background is not obvious. As for entrants coming straight from school, some will be unable to classify their father's occupation or may prefer to put their mother's occupation for reasons of their own. See M.E. Ashmane, 'Sotsial'nyi sostav studencheskoi Latviiskoi

SSR' in P.V. Laizan (ed.), Sotsial'nye aspekty
obrazovaniya, (Uchenye zapiski, Latviiskii
gosudarstvennyi universitet, vol. 158) (Latvian
State University, Riga, 1972), pp. 16, 18.
77.   Itogi, Vsesoyuznoi perepisi naseleniya
1970 goda. Tom 5 (Statistika, Moscow, 1973), p. 9;
Narodnoe khozyaistvo za 60 let, p. 8.
78.   Byulleten' MV i SSO SSSR, no. 2 (1978),
p. 8; Byulleten' MV i SSO SSSR, no. 4 (1980), p. 8.
79.   V.F. Pugach, 'Nekotorye resul'taty
faktornogo analiza sotsial'nykh aspektov
formirovaniya studencheskikh kontingentov pedvuzov'
in F.R. Filippov (ed.), Sotsial'nye problemy
formirovaniya popolnenii intelligentsii (USSR Academy
of Sciences, Institute of Sociological Research,
Moscow, 1980), p. 29.
80.   A. Matulyonis, 'Osobennosti formirovaniya
molodogo popolneniya intelligentsii v Litovskoi SSR'
in F.R. Filippov (ed.), Obrazovanie i sotsial'naya
struktura (USSR Academy of Sciences, Institute of
Sociological Research, Moscow, 1976), p. 145.
81.   S.S. Balabanov et al., Problema
regulirovaniya sotsial'nogo sostava studenchestva'
in A.A. Terent'ev (ed.), Sotsiologiya i vysshaya
shkola [Vypusk 6] (Gorky University, Gorky, 1978),
p. 90.
82.   See, for example, L.V. Topchii, 'Na poroge
vuza' in V.A. Yadov (ed.), Molodezh' i sovremennost'
(Obshchestvo Znanie, Leningrad, 1975), p. 100;
Lisovskii and Dmitriev, Lichnost' studenta, p. 48.
83.   In Kharkov the percentages of working-
class students in different types of VUZ in 1974 were
as follows: arts - 32.2, medical - 44.5,
construction - 58.8, and transport - 62.1 (I.I.
Sheremet, 'Sotsial'nyi sostav studenchestva',
Sotsiologicheskie issledovaniya, no. 2 (1977),
p. 76).   In all Sverdlovsk Region VUZs Filippov
records a total of 46.5% working-class students,
but in the university only 34.3% (Filippov,
Vseobshchee srednee, p. 86).
84.   In the All-Union Survey it was found
that between 1969 and 1973 the relative decline of
students from non-manual backgrounds could be
accounted for almost entirely by a drop in the
representation of routine non-manual workers'
children.   See Rutkevich and Filippov, Vysshaya
shkola kak faktor, p. 144.
85.   E.g. B. Rubin and Yu. Kolesnikov,
Student glazami sotsiologa (Rostov-on-Don University,
Rostov-on-Don, 1968), pp. 65-6; M.N. Rutkevich,
'Intelligentsiya kak sotsial'naya gruppa i ee

sblizhenie s rabochim klassom' in Ts. A. Stepanyan and V.S. Semyonov (eds.), Klassy, sotsial'nye sloi i gruppy v SSSR (Nauka, Moscow, 1968), pp. 157-8.
86.   M.N. Rutkevich et al., 'Protsessy vosproizvodstva sotsial'noi struktury sovetskogo obshchestva' in M.N. Rutkevich and Filippov (eds.), Sotsial'naya struktura razvitogo sotsialisticheskogo obshchestva v SSSR (Nauka, Moscow, 1976), p. 190; A.V. Koop, 'Ob osnovnykh funktsiyakh obrazovaniya v usloviyakh razvitogo sotsializma' in Kalder, Uluchshenie podbora, pp. 9-15.
87.   See Note 18.
88.   Avis, 'The Sociology of Soviet Higher Education', pp. 40-3.
89.   E.g. Sheremet, 'Sotsial'nyi sostav studenchestva', p. 77; G.A. Zhuravleva, 'Vuzovskaya orientatsiya molodezhi i formirovanie kontingenta studentov' in Filippov, Sotsial'nye problemy formirovaniya, p. 111.
90.   See Avis, 'Preparatory Divisions', Table 1.
91.   The two authoritative sources of these results adduce apparently conflicting data for some findings.   Residual social categories and non-response are generally not included in the published results, yet their contribution appears substantial enough to introduce bias in conclusions which ignore them.   Moreover, comparison with official statistics of VUZ social composition is rendered difficult since all agricultural workers, (whether employed on state or collective farms) are put into a single category, as are all non-manual specialists, including those working on collective farms.
92.   See Note 84.
93.   Titma and Kenkmann, 'Regional'nye osobennosti', p. 150.
94.   L.Ya. Tubina, 'Sotsial'nyi sostav studentov-pervokursnikov i tendentsii ego izmeneniya v usloviyakh krupnogo ekonomicheskogo raiona', in Filippov, Obrazovanie i sotsial'naya struktura, pp. 76-7; S.S. Balabanov, 'Sotsiologicheskie aspekty otseva studentov' in Filippov, Obrazovanie i sotsial'naya struktura, pp. 91-5.
95.   Shimkene, 'Nekotorye otritsatel'nye posledstviya', p. 135.
96.   Elyutin, Vysshaya shkola obshchestva, pp. 411-412.
97.   Chuprunov, 'Obsuzhdaya programmnyi dokument', p. 4.
98.   Elyutin, 'Zadachi vysshei shkoly', p. 8.
99.   Chuprunov, 'Obsuzhdaya programmnyi

dokument', p. 5.
100. Ibid.
101. Izvestiya, 9 July 1981, p. 3;
Elyutin, 'Zadachi vysshei shkoly', p. 6.
102. Elyutin, Vysshaya shkola obshchestva,
pp. 406-13; Pravda, 22 March 1981, p. 3.
103. Pravda, 10 Dec. 1980, p. 4; Pravda,
3 April 1981, p. 3. Zyuzin, Kachestvo podgotovki,
pp. 45-6.
104. Elyutin, Vysshaya shkola obshchestva,
pp. 324-7; Pravda, 5 Jan. 1980, p. 3; Pravda,
9 June 1980, p. 3.
105. In the All-Union Survey of 1973/4 nearly
17% of the total sample of students had attended a
special school or class giving advanced tuition in
particular subjects. By region the proportions
ranged from as many as 28.4% in Estonia to 8.3% in
Odessa (see Titma and Kenkmann, 'Regional'nye
osobennosti', p. 151). It is generally
acknowledged that these special schools recruit
mainly from among the children of specialists and
other non-manual workers (see e.g. Titma, Vybor
professii, p. 58; Filippov, 'Sovershenstvovanie
sistemy', p. 65).
106. Pravda, 5 Jan. 1980, p. 3; Pravda,
5 July 1981, p. 3. For existing VUZ entry
privileges for this category of applicant see
Note 11.
107. Pravda, 9 June 1980, p. 3; Pravda,
8 Sept. 1980, p. 3; Pravda, 24 Feb. 1981, p. 7.

Chapter 9

SOVIET SOCIOLOGISTS AND SOVIET ECONOMISTS ON SOVIET
EDUCATION

Janusz Tomiak

I am concerned in my paper with the views which
Soviet sociologists and Soviet economists hold on
Soviet education. While the theme seems to be an
important and an interesting one, one should stress
the difficulties inherent in a study of this kind.
One concerns the time element involved. Although
more penetrating and analytical studies concerned
with the social and economic aspects of education in
the USSR are of relatively recent origin, one can
identify significant statements and comments
referring explicitly to education which were made
earlier on, in the 1920s and 1930s, by those whose
primary concern was the study of either economics
or sociology. They should not be forgotten or
ignored, but their relevance to the studies of
problems of Soviet education in the 1960s, 1970s
and now, the 1980s, has largely been removed by the
growing complexity of the educational system of the
Soviet Union. The other difficulty arises in
connection with the arbitrary character of the
decision to draw - in connection with this kind of
inquiry - valid lines of division between the
different sub-divisions of sociology and economics
as more comprehensive and composite fields of study.
It is, of course, quite significant that in the
course of the last twenty years or so the concepts
of sociology of education and of economics of
education gained, first of all, a formal recognition
and subsequently, wider circulation, so that today
they constitute in the USSR significant sub-divisions
of their respective fields in their own right.
However, it must be emphasised that the comments
coming from those who work in such specialised areas
as e.g. the sociology of work, sociology of the
family, sociology of leisure, or, economic planning
and economics of industry or agriculture, have quite

frequently had direct relevance - and sometimes a direct impact - upon educational developments and the formulation of educational policy.

Soviet Sociologists on Soviet Education

Studies of social structure, social stratification and social mobility in the USSR began to emerge some time after the death of Stalin. They expanded under Khrushchev and the Soviet Sociological Association came into being in 1958, though Soviet sociologists started to participate in the meetings of the International Sociological Association in a more pronounced way only in the 1960s. More than eighty Soviet sociologists took part in the Sixth Congress of the ISA in 1966 at Evian, in France; some four hundred in the Seventh Congress in Varna, Bulgaria, in 1970; about a hundred attended the Eighth Congress in Toronto and the Ninth Congress in Stockholm in 1974 and 1978, respectively. Meanwhile, sociological investigations of all kinds began to be undertaken in the USSR in specialised sociological research institutes, the Party sociological institutions, numerous universities and other higher education establishments. Although the specialised sociological scientific periodical, a quarterly, Sotsiologicheskie issledovaniya (Sociological Research) only began to be published in 1974, many articles within the field had previously appeared in several other papers and periodicals, such as Pravda, Izvestiya, Literaturnaya Gazeta, Voprosy Filosofii, Filosofskie nauki or Novyi Mir.[1]

A long way back, in the 1950s, some Soviet studies pointed out the connection between general improvement in socialist culture and the increasing - albeit slowly at that time - standards of education of the Soviet working class, in terms of both general education and vocational training. In the years 1958/9, sociological research carried out in the field of education was largely connected with the proposed reconstruction of the educational system. In the following years, sociological investigations increased further, linked to Nikita Khrushchev's expansionist and reformist zeal and his attempt to establish closer links between school and life. Some negative features of the educational set-up were brought to light. Attention was thus drawn to the contradiction between the objective needs of socialist society and the aspirations of many young people, as well as to some major faults in the organisation of vocational training in secondary schools and the socio-economic consequences of these phenomena. One example was the discovery of the fact that a very small number of leavers from secondary schools with vocational training were able to obtain jobs for which they had been trained. In the summer 1978 issue of Current Sociology, journal of the International Sociological Association, two top Soviet sociologists, G.V. Osipov and M.N. Rutkevich,[2] in an attempt to sum up the substance of Soviet investigations, examined sociological research in the USSR in the decade 1965-75. Section VI, entitled 'Sociological research into problems of spiritual life in society' contained a sub-section 'Educational sociology' and tried to identify the principal interests and the substance of investigations undertaken in that field in the Soviet Union. Osipov and Rutkevich stressed that although there was a long tradition of investigating sociological problems of education in the country, the relatively independent discipline of sociology of education was only established in the 1960s and suggested that concern with sociological aspects of education at that time was far from accidental. In the 1960s there was - what they call - a leap forward in education, brought about by scientific and technological changes as well as radical changes in socialist social relations, linked - in the Soviet political rhetoric - to the Soviet Union entering the stage of developed socialism. Indeed, looking back, in the 1960s studying became an important form of social activity for a rapidly growing number of people in the USSR. In the 1950s, the number of individuals enrolled in all forms of full-time courses had been stable, about 37-39 million people; in the 1960s it grew quickly, reaching 57 million in 1970.

Sociology of Education as a Field of Study. It was F.R. Filippov who defined the subject matter of sociology of education as a field of study in its own right in the USSR in the following words:

> Sociology of education studies the system of education as a social institution. The subject matter of sociology of education is in this sense the interaction of the system of education with its own sub-systems, as well as its interaction with the global social systems, above all, with the systems 'science-technology', 'classes and social strata', 'culture' and 'ideology and politics'.[3]

In his opinion, a comparative analysis of the
social functions of the system of education as a
whole and its individual sub-systems, makes it
possible to estimate their impact upon the character
of social relations as well as the peculiarities of
the division of labour. Filippov also believes
that in the Soviet Union, in contrast to the situation
in many other countries, sociology of education has
been developing somewhat faster than other branches
of sociology. This - he believes - is, partly at
least, because of relatively easy access to objects
of research by Soviet sociologists, many of whom are
educationists, for example, school teachers or
teachers in specialised or higher educational
establishments. The core constituent of sociology
of education is, according to Filippov, consideration
of structural changes in the system of education and
their interaction with production and the social
structure of population. The scientific and
technological revolution, the changes in social
relations and the development of the system of
education itself, put continually new problems and
dilemmas before sociologists. Among them, probably
the most complicated is the problem of forecasting
in the long term the development of education as an
institutional system in interaction with global
social systems; hence the concentration of
attention upon this aspect of social change, which
is given special consideration by a number of
scientific bodies operating under the overall
guidance of the Institute of Sociological Research
of the USSR Academy of Sciences.[4]
In response to official encouragement, but
also very much due to the increasing conviction on
the part of individual investigators that research
of this kind was important and worthwhile,
interesting sociological investigations were carried
out in the late 1960s in Sverdlovsk and Novosibirsk
into large numbers of children in older classes in
respect of their aspirations and their subsequent
educational and vocational careers. There were
some differences and divergencies in the methods of
tackling the problem between the two groups of
investigators. The Sverdlovsk sociologists
approached the problem from the point of view of the
manifested tendencies in development of the social
structure of Soviet society. The Novosibirsk
sociologists concentrated their attention
principally on the occupational structure of Soviet
population, which attracted criticism.[5]

243

Studies of Student Aspirations and Social Mobility.
The first major work devoted to the sociological
problems of education was published in Sverdlovsk
Pedagogical Institute under the title Sotsiologicheskie
problemy narodnogo obrazovaniya (Sociological Problems
of People's Education) in 1967, edited by
G.N. Korostolev. Its contents matched the issues
identified by Filippov. At the same time L.N. Kogan
and T.S. Mochulskaya examined the problem of what
influences were instrumental in stimulating the
desire for education among students. There came
extensive studies of sociological problems of
education in Leningrad. The main topics which
received attention there were the aspirations of
young people and their job placements, an important
issue spotlighted earlier by a well-known Soviet
sociologist V.M. Shubkin. A.G. Zdravomyslov and his
associates examined the attitudes of young people to
work in the book Chelovek i ego rabota (Man and his
Work), which came out in Leningrad in 1967. Two
years later S.N. Ikennikova and V.T. Lisovskii
published their study of the self-portrait of youth:
Molodezh o sebe, o svoikh sverstnikakh (Youth about
Itself and Its Peers). V.T. Lisovskii produced
also independently Eskiz k portretu - zhiznennye
plany, interesy, stremleniya sovetskoi molodyozhi
(Sketching the Portrait of Soviet Youth - Life
Plans, Interests and Aspirations) in Moscow in 1969.
    A group of Novosibirsk sociologists published
in 1969 an important work Sotsiologicheskie i
ekonomicheskie problemy obrazovaniya (Sociological
and Economic Problems of Education). This in many
ways tended to reflect the relatively open and
scientifically more sophisticated atmosphere of the
Siberian branch of the Academy of Sciences of the
USSR, as the work on sociological problems of
education continued there with some vigour,
culminating at the time in Vladimir N. Shubkin's
Sotsiologicheskie opyty (Sociological Problems),
which appeared in 1970 and where the author
elaborated a mathematical model for forecasting the
chances of young people receiving higher education.
It was not, however, that the work received a general
acclaim, as critical comments were made from the
methodological point of view, stressing that the
author, a man of high repute and distinction, failed
to take into account possible fluctuations in the
number of vacancies in first year courses and
ignored the possibilities of changes in the rules
applying to entry into a VUZ.[6]
    Attention turned to examining the socio-economic

aspects of school environment.   V.N. Turchenko and
his team examined in the early 1970s the development
of general secondary education and the availability
of teachers in rural areas in their book Nauchno-
tekhnicheskaya revolyutsiya i revolyutsiya v
obrazovanii (Scientific-technological Revolution
and the Revolution in Education), which came out in
1973.
    That substantial discrepancies between young
people's plans for the future and their subsequent
realisation in life in respect of both study and
work depended upon the social background of pupils
as well as their area of residence, was revealed
quite clearly by a number of investigators in the
late 1960s.   Included in this group of studies
should be several reports basing their evidence upon
concrete empirical evidence: Zhiznennye plany
molodezhi (Life Plans of Youth) by Ya.M. Tkach,
Molodezh i trud (Youth and Work) by V.A. Yadov and
V.I. Dobrynina, as well as the investigations by
very well known senior Soviet sociologists
O.I. Shkaratan, V.O. Rukavishnikov and M.N.
Rutkevich.[7]   In the 1970s they were supplemented by
more substantial and analytical studies by
V.V. Vodzinskaya and E.K. Vasil'eva, whose detailed
study of Leningrad youth gained wide reputation.
Her book Sotsial'no-professional'nyi uroven'
gorodskoi molodezhi (Socio-vocational Level of Urban
Youth), published in 1973 was based upon three
social surveys involving several thousands of
Leningrad's pupils and young workers and looked very
seriously at the dilemma of how to reconcile young
people's vocational aspirations with the manpower
needs determined by the state.   Employment prospects
for the eight-year school leavers were sharply
contrasted with those of the ten-year school leavers,
the reasons for vocational preferences and choices
were scrutinised by the writer, while the frequent
changes in the redistribution of the original work
placings revealed the existence of underlying
difficulties and problems.

Studies of Linkages between Social Structure and
Education.   Sociologists in Sverdlovsk and in Nizhny
Tagil examined at the end of the 1960s and the
beginning of the 1970s the connection between the
social structure of a mature socialist society and
the system of education.   Special attention was
given to the role of education as a factor bringing
different social groups of Soviet society closer
together and facilitating the social mobility of the

younger generation.[8]

The study by M.N. Rutkevich and F.R. Filippov
Sotsial'nye peremeshcheniya (Social Mobility),
Moscow, 1970, led to prolonged debates at the First
All-Union Scientific Conference on Changes in the
Social Structure of Socialist Society in Sverdlovsk
in February on the subject of movement between the
different social strata of Soviet society. Similar
studies were undertaken at that time in other Soviet
Republics.   M.Kh. Titma from Tartu University and
Yu.I. Leonavichius from Kaunas Polytechnical
Institute examined the aspirations of the young in
Estonia and Lithuania.[9]   At the same time the
influence of education on the upward social mobility
of young workers was studied in the Bashkir Autonomous
People's Republic under the direction of N.A. Aitov.[10]
Stress was put on the contribution of education to
increasing productivity and an interesting contradiction was discovered between improvements in the
educational standards of working youth and the
continued needs of industry for unskilled labour.
This led to vigorous debates and made some experts
express their doubts as to the need for the speeding
up of educational progress.

1973/4 saw the first inquiry in the USSR into
the role of higher education establishments as a
means of changing the social structure of the
developed socialist society.   It was an interesting
longitudinal study, carried out simultaneously in
six areas: Moscow city, Moscow region, Novosibirsk,
Sverdlovsk, Odessa and the Estonian Republic.   It
involved observations of about 50,000 individuals,
namely school pupils in the first, eighth and tenth
classes and in the first and final years in higher
education.   The study revealed that:

(1)   there was a change in the social composition
of the school population as one advanced from the
junior classes to the school leavers;

(2)   the social composition of the pupil/student
population depended upon the particular character of
each region, the social orientation of the pupils,
the young people's ambitions, their aspirations for
higher education and the realisation of such
aspirations;

(3)   the make-up of contingents of students was
connected with the educational background of their
parents, with the provision for their material needs,
the character of their work and also with the social
homogeneity or heterogeneity of the family.[11]

The problems and achievements of Soviet sociology of education were examined in retrospect, as mentioned before, by G.V. Osipov and M.N. Rutkevich. Their summary conclusion was that sociological research in the 1960s and 1970s has shown that education is a powerful factor for change in the social structure of a developed socialist society, in which the social condition of the people depends to an increasing extent on the character of their work, access to which is determined by their education. That research also revealed other regularities characteristic of socialism: a massive increase in general education, especially of young people and the development of vocational training of various standards and content, closely connected with the all-round development of the individual and the creation of a harmoniously developed citizen of communist society.[12]

While summary comments of this kind provided little insight into the theoretical aspects and methodological considerations arising in connection with the on-going research, it was gradually becoming clear that many Soviet sociologists were carefully giving consideration to Western sociological analyses and investigations. This can be demonstrated by reference to the writings of some of the well known Soviet sociologists, such as for example F.R. Filippov. He has devoted particular attention to the linkages between the social structure of society and the system of education in the USSR. In his view, the relative autonomy of the system of education, that is its relative independence of production is either over-looked or else rendered absolute by Western educationists and sociologists. Thus, in his opinion, writers such as Philip H. Coombs and Talcott Parsons tend either to overestimate the significance of society's expenditure on education, or else to argue that the interconnection between science and education and technological progress ought to be seen as arising from a general growth in demand for skilled personnel in an expanding economy. In his view, contrary to what he calls 'technological determinism', the educational system reacts to the demands of the scientific and technological revolution by changes in the structure of its institutions, in as much as the scientific and technological revolution brings about changes in division of labour and, subsequently, in the social structure. The transformed educational system, in turn, produces a corresponding effect on the social structure and the division of labour and, through

them, on scientific and technological progress. Thus,
the completion of transition to universal secondary
education makes it possible to continuously narrow the
gulf between different social groups, for example, the
urban and rural population. While there is a
tendency for the different social groups to gradually
draw together, Filippov clearly states that social
homogeneity has not, as yet, been achieved in Soviet
society and certain social distinctions remain in
existence. Such distinctions are observed not only
in the differing levels of education of the rural and
urban population, but also in the character of labour
and the level of education of the working class and
the collective farmers on the one hand and the
intelligentsia, on the other.[13]
    Two other arguments put forward by F.R. Filippov
should be noted. One concerns the interpretation of
the fact that a growing proportion of workers in
large scale industrial enterprises has been able to
complete secondary education as one moves through
time and examines records over the last decade or so.
Filippov sees this as proof that manual and brain
work are gradually drawing closer together, because
of what he defines as intellectualisation of manual
labour on the one hand and technicalisation of brain
work, on the other. Postulating the crucial
importance of overall tendencies of such kind and
magnitude seems, however, to contradict the
pronounced tendency in the Soviet economy to demand
large numbers of semi-skilled and even unskilled
workers for a range of industrial sectors. The
other argument concerns the share of students with a
working class background studying at higher education
establishments. Filippov based his argument that
that share was increasing - and increasing rapidly -
upon the figures concerning one region (Sverdlovsk)
only and over the period 1968-72. More recent data
concerning the whole country tend to put that
argument in doubt, not so much in respect of the
tendency as such, but in respect of the speed with
which it progresses.[14]
    Today, the number of Soviet sociologists working
in the fields of sociology of education, sociology of
youth and sociology of work is quite substantial.
There are also many who work in the related areas of
sociology of the family, sociology of leisure and
sociology of social relations. Of great interest
are the investigations concerning women's work,
careers and leisure budgets by A.G. Kharchev.
Basing his research on Lenin's principle that to
effect women's complete emancipation and make them

truly equal with men it is necessary to enable them
to participate fully in productive labour, he has
stressed the role of education in the process. On
the other hand, his studies have revealed the fact
that married women's incomes are very much lower
than those of their husbands in numerous industries
and that the relative proportions of women working
in the economy vary quite substantially from one
Republic to another and, in general, inversely to the
birth rates in the population of the given Republic.[15]
Comparative studies of spare-time budgets have
been made by V.D. Patrushev. Although they were
based upon evidence collected in the late 1960s in
selected cities representing a small number of
countries, and revealed a surprisingly high
proportion of spare-time spent on education and
self-education by both Soviet men and women in
comparison with other countries, they also offered
interesting evidence in some other respects. Thus
they confirmed the fact that there were enormous
differences between Soviet men and women in this
respect and that the total amount of spare time for
the former greatly exceeded that for the latter.[16]

Interdisciplinary Co-operation. More recently, as
Soviet sociologists of education continued their
research and inquiries into the different aspects of
educational development, efforts were made to examine
the more complex issues through interdisciplinary
cooperation. In February 1979 the USSR Academy of
Pedagogical Sciences, jointly with the quarterly
Sotsiologicheskie issledovaniya, sponsored a
Round-table Discussion on the Sociological Problems
of Education between the educational experts and the
sociologists of education. A number of participants
presented their views on the issues which in their
opinion constituted study areas that were common to
both pedagogy and sociology.[17] Indeed, R. Gurova,
Sector Head of the Scientific Research Institute of
General Problems of Upbringing of the USSR Academy
of Pedagogical Sciences, stressed particularly
strongly the growing interaction between sociology
and pedagogy in the analysis of problems in
education.[18]
Among the important sociologists present in the
1979 Round-table Discussion were A.G. Kharchev,
chief editor of Sotsiologicheskie issledovaniya,
N.S. Mansurov, head of the Department of Sociological
Research on the Ideological Processes at the
Institute of Sociological Research of the USSR
Academy of Sciences and F.R. Filippov, as the head of

the Department of Sociological Problems of Youth and
Education, at the Institute of Sociological Research
of the USSR Academy of Sciences. While the
discussions touched upon many important issues and
problems, attention concentrated upon some of the
issues connected with the evident lack of concrete,
scientifically based, social education programmes
for specific groups in the population and for
combatting certain negative phenomena among youth
such as for example alcoholism. Mention also was
made of the need for more experimentation, proper
analysis and summary of results of particular
investigations which would open up the way for
further research work, and for greater concentration
on vocational guidance, labour education and
training, so that through programmes of joint
research, the relevant data within a unified
sociological, pedagogical and psychological context
could be successfully analysed. Suggestions were
made to the effect that the upper grades of secondary
schools should be made more vocationally oriented and
that the teaching in vocational-technical schools
should become more genuinely polytechnical in
character; particular attention was drawn to the
fact that the new type of school, that with a
prolonged day, had become an important feature of
the system; in schools of this kind children were
spending not four, five or six, but eight to ten
hours, which meant a new kind of home-school
relationship. Arguments were advanced to the
effect that sociological theories in the new sub-
divisions of sociology such as the sociology of the
family or the sociology of youth, should be used in
programmes of integrated research operated jointly
by educationists and sociologists of education.
Reference was made in discussions to the
preoccupation among teachers and other people with
'protsentomaniya', that is a tendency to award high
grades, and to the proceeding feminisation of the
teaching profession and its possible consequences
for the pupils, particularly the boys.[19] Problems
common to many other countries were mentioned:
instances where it was evident that the overall
knowledge of the pupils exceeded that of the
individual teacher and occasions where some pupils
were better informed than a teacher in the
teacher's own subject. Linked to this was the
challenge for all teacher training establishments
to modify their programmes and prepare the future
teachers to face a situation where a constantly
increasing flow of information was a permanent

feature of the system. Other comments brought under
consideration the dilemma of dysfunctional growth of
the educational system; as was stressed by one of
the speakers, the present state of the industrial
production pattern required almost one-third of all
jobs in the Soviet economy at the level of semi-
skilled or even unskilled labour, while at the same
time efforts were being made to ensure that all young
men and women completing their education acquired a
definite trade or occupation.[20]
　　Contradictions of a different kind were
identified by F.R. Filippov. He pointed out the
fact that the teaching and upbringing processes were
profoundly influenced by the real contradictions
inherent in the movement of Soviet society towards
complete social homogeneity. People from different
social backgrounds were all receiving a uniform kind
of education, in a formal sense. In practice,
however, education varied considerably in quality,
between for example, the urban and rural areas or the
day and evening courses. This contradiction
continually reproduced the dialectical interaction
of two contrary tendencies - the obliteration and
reproduction of social differences, even though the
former tended to dominate the latter.
　　Taking a realistic rather than an ideological
stand, Filippov mentioned yet another problem rooted
in the existence of 'unequal labour' under socialism,
as under any other system. The differentiation of
types of vocational education oriented towards
differentiated types of work and professional
proficiency, were making it necessary that in
preparing the younger generation to choose an
occupation intelligently, an interest in the socially
diversified types of work as well as an acceptance
of its inevitable hierarchical character had to be
instilled in school leavers. Although they had to
be oriented towards the possibility of social
advancement through the course of their lives and
in consequence, given the opportunity of moving on
from the less to the more complex type of labour,
clashes in making decisions concerning individual
pupils in respect of vocational guidance and
allocation to specific forms of training were bound
to occur.[21]
　　Other forms of dysfunctional relationship were
identified by N.A. Aitov and R.T. Nasibullin in a
recent article on the vocational mobility of the
intelligentsia.[22] Their research, conducted in
the sociological laboratory in the Ufa Aviation
Institute, revealed that in general about a third

of higher education graduates whose subsequent careers had been investigated, were not working in the area of their specialisation. The implication was that if this was true of the country as a whole, some one out of three billion rubles spent on higher education in the USSR was misinvested, if not simply wasted.

Table 1: Graduates Employed and Not Employed in their own Specialisation

(% of all surveyed specialists in Neftekamsk, Sterlitamak and Naberezhnye Chelny)

Specialisation	Employed in their specialisation	Not employed in their specialisation
Instructor in humanities and social sciences	79.4	20.6
Instructor in natural and exact sciences	80.9	19.1
Planning engineer	76.5	23.5
Physician	90.8	9.2
Mechanical engineer	44.3	55.7
Production engineer	56.7	43.3
Electrical engineer	65.8	34.2

Source: Sotsiologicheskie issledovaniya, no. 2, April/June 1980, p. 107.

Equalisation of Educational Opportunities. The more fundamental kinds of resistance to the equalisation of educational opportunities, particularly at the level of vocational-technical education have recently been discussed by M.N. Rutkevich.[23] In his opinion the statistical information available indicates that the convergence of the Union Republics in terms of social class structure has been proceeding quickly over the last two decades. However, there still remains the problem of equalisation among the Republics in respect of the highly skilled stratum of

the working class and the engineering and technical
intelligentsia working in industry.

Table 2: Number of Workers and Office Employees
working in Industry per 10,000 of Population

Union Republic	1960	1975
RSFSR	126	159
Ukraine	93	135
Belorussia	67	127
Uzbekistan	42	60
Kazakhstan	54	81
Georgia	64	81
Azerbaidzhan	55	60
Lithuania	75	138
Moldavia	40	83
Latvia	127	162
Kirgizia	48	71
Tadzhikistan	35	44
Armenia	75	111
Turkmenia	41	40
Estonia	132	161
USSR average	103	133

Source: Sotsiologicheskie issledovaniya, no. 2,
April/June, 1981, p. 19.

According to Rutkevich, the differences in
terms of general education levels among the various
nationalities living in Central Asiatic Republics
have been declining more rapidly in the course of
the last few decades than the differences in
vocational training levels. Accepting that location
of industry is in itself determined by the unequal
concentration of natural resources in certain areas,
differentiation in the levels and character of
vocational training is likely to persist given the
relative geographical immobility of many Central
Asiatic Republics' populations.

Problems associated with the declining birth-
rates in many Soviet Union Republics (apart from those
in Soviet Central Asia) have naturally also been
discussed from the educational point of view.
I.S. Bolotin has stressed the fact that the number of
pupils in grades four to eight decreased by 1.6
million between 1965 and 1977, but that in grades one
to three declined by 2.7 million in the same period.
The real impact of this kind of change should

seriously affect vocational training and the supply
of trained labour for Soviet industry only in the
course of the Eleventh Five-year Planning Period
(1981/5). At the level of higher education, while
the admissions to VUZy increase all the time, the
competition for admission to day-time divisions of
higher education establishments in the USSR
declined, on average, from 269 applicants per 100
vacancies in 1970, to 255 per 100 in 1975. However,
as the author stresses, individual preferences have
also been changing: while the pressure for admission
to VUZy in the fields of industry in general,
transport and communications tended to ease up in the
1970s, the numbers of applications for admission to
the VUZy specialising in health, physical culture,
art and cinematography tended to increase (for
example in the last mentioned specialisation from
319 to 407 per 100 vacancies, between 1970 and
1975).[24]

Studies of Attitudes and Orientation of Youth.
Assessing the attitudes and orientation of Soviet
youth seems to be important. V.T. Lisovskii's
attention in recent times has centred around
establishing principles for typologies of
contemporary studentry. In an article under the
title 'Printsipy i kriterii tipologizatsii
sovremennego studenchestva' (The Principles and
Criteria of Typology of Contemporary Studentry),
he suggests analysing and measuring on a scale 1-16,
depending upon the intensity involved, the following
four key groups of qualities which should characterise
most adequately the Soviet student today, as well as
his role in communist society:

    (1) orientation towards studies, research and
profession;
    (2) orientation towards socio-political
activity and activist life-stance;
    (3) orientation towards culture;
    (4) orientation towards the collective.[25]

    A scale of this kind may tell us something
about the order of desirable qualities as envisaged
by the needs of the system, but it would be difficult
to judge the sociological significance of this kind
of approach without knowing much more about the
details of the proposed scale and the way it is to
be administered by the researchers.
    V.A. Smirnov in an article 'Problema
formirovaniya u rabochei molodezhi soznatel'nogo

otnosheniya k trudu' (The Problem of Formation of a
Conscious attitude towards Labour among the Working
Youth), tackles the same problem, proposing to find
out by a sociological inquiry among different groups
of young workers whether the following socio-political
and moral qualities do in fact characterise Soviet
youth today:

- a communist ideological orientation;
- a communist attitude towards labour;
- professional mastery of a profession or
  occupation;
- labour discipline;
- a feeling of being a master of production;
- personal participation in the management of
  production;
- socio-political activism;
- social responsibility expressed in an
  activist stance in life;
- Soviet patriotism;
- socialist internationalism;
- collectivism;
- a cultured outlook;
- an implacable attitude towards vestiges of
  the past in thought and deed.[26]

The list reminds one of the Moral Code of the
Builders of Communism, but it would be interesting
to see both empirically established deviations from
the expected norms and values and the significant
variations as conditioned by ethnic origin,
educational background or place of habitation.

Summing up. Looking back on what the Soviet
sociologists of education have been attempting to
do, the American writers Harold J. Noah and Beatrice
B. Szekely have commented:

> The sociology of education is a new field in
> the USSR, emerging from the upsurge of interest
> in sociology itself, that has taken place in
> Soviet research during the past fifteen years.
> The state of the art is, as yet, undeveloped.
> Definitions and goals for educational sociology
> are still being set and the results of the
> first research studies are current news.[27]

The relative newness of the sociology of
education as a field of study in its own right in the
USSR is, of course, clear. Taking the publication
of the first substantial contributions in the field

as a starting point, it is now some fifteen years old. Conceptual development of the subject, that is the debates concerning definitions of the basic concepts and objectives and their reformulation from time to time, may be seen yet as an essential element of the continuous development of the subject itself and, therefore, a never ending process. However, if the objectives are based upon the assumption that their fundamental function is to accumulate enough evidence in order to confirm some basic laws of social development, which are generally accepted as given and are not to be challenged under any circumstances, then the character of the subject is in itself quite different from what it is elsewhere, in other countries and other systems, where an open-ended discussion prevails. In so far as the older and, no doubt, more influential and powerful Soviet sociologists of education are concerned, there is little evidence of any significant shift from the position of accumulating data in order to confirm the laws of development accepted a priori and derived from a fixed and rigid philosophical outlook, towards an open analysis of problems and a rigorous examination of alternative forms of their solution. Inflexible conceptual frameworks inevitably tend to exercise a limiting influence as powerful forces of operational constraints. Clearly, when one is bound to function within a system which is characterised by a universal acceptance of predetermined 'objective laws', regulating all social and economic phenomena, one has to proceed with caution.

On the other hand, many, particularly younger, Soviet researchers in the field of sociology of education have been busy collecting and classifying important and relevant empirical and observable data of different kinds. The point, however, is that the nature of hypotheses to which they are being linked is still very much circumscribed by the constraints which reflect the basic assumptions of the system as a whole. Yet, a critical examination of the existing forms of educational organisation and procedures requires a definite absence of restriction in the formulation of hypotheses, in order to pave the way for reform and to lead to the necessary improvements, which may require a conscious abandoning of the fixed canons of prevailing doctrines. Such evidence as there is, suggests, however, that an approach based upon any such considerations, is as yet unlikely to come to dominate the field of sociological inquiries into educational structures and processes in the USSR in the immediate future.

Nevertheless, the investigations of several Soviet sociologists into their own system of education and upbringing - even when explicitly designed to confirm the basic socio-economic propositions now considered as very much out of date elsewhere - have in several instances revealed inconsistencies and incongruencies of a very interesting kind. The realisation of the existence and the actual dimension of the gap between what is and what ought to be the case, is in itself an inescapable consequence of the ongoing research work which is worth noting. The significance of it, bearing in mind the character and the present stage of development of Soviet society, may be of quite fundamental importance.

Soviet Economists on Soviet Education

Early Studies in Economics of Education.

Turning now to what the Soviet economists have been saying about Soviet education, we ought to first briefly look back to the early years of Soviet Russia and identify a man who did say several things about the relationship between the economy and education. Strumillo Petrashkevich Stanislav Gustavovich Strumilin (1877-1974), was a Soviet economist and statistician, member of the Academy of Sciences of the USSR since 1931 and member of the CPSU from 1923. He was a delegate to the Fifth Congress of the Russian Social-Democratic Labour Party held in London in 1907. In the years 1921-37 and 1943-51 he worked in the Gosplan, becoming a member of the Praesidium and deputy to the chairman. He taught in the Moscow State University in the years 1921-23 and in the Moscow State Institute of Economics between 1931-50. From 1948 he was for four years the head of the division of history of the national economy in the Institute of Economics of the Academy of Sciences of the USSR. Between 1948 and 1974 he worked in the Academy of Social Sciences at the Central Committee of the CPSU. He was the author of several works on economics: Bogatstvo i trud (Wealth and Work), published in 1905; Problemy ekonomiki truda (Problems of the Economics of Labour), published in 1925 and republished in 1957; Ocherki sovetskoi ekonomiki (Essays on the Soviet Economy), published in 1928; Promyshlennyi perevorot v Rossii (The Industrial Revolution in Russia), which appeared in 1944.[28] In April 1962 he wrote his famous article on the effectiveness of education in the USSR in Ekonomicheskaya gazeta (The Economic

257

Gazette).[29]
It was Stanislav Strumilin who, in the 1920s,
began to give serious consideration to the economic
returns from expenditure on school education, in
connection with his work in the State Planning
Commission. In the periodical Planovoe khozyaistvo
(Planned Economy) Strumilin published in 1924
probably the first clearly reasoned analysis of the
importance of the system of education for the
development of the national economy under the title
Khozyaistvennoe znachenie narodnogo obrazovaniya
(The Economic Significance of People's Education),
whose two sections on physical work and school
learning and on mental work and educational
qualification were designed to demonstrate the value
of investing in education and training. This was
directly related to the draft ten-year school
development plan formulated in 1924 to provide
universal, free and compulsory education for all
children, starting with four years of elementary
education. The argument was that rudimentary
instruction gained in one single year of elementary
education was bound to result in increases in
productivity largely exceeding the benefit of a
similar period of apprenticeship in a factory.
Strumilin's work seems to have been largely neglected
and even forgotten until the 1950s, when he produced
a new edition of his book Problemy ekonomiki truda.
In this he restated his earlier arguments, providing
more detailed calculations, justifying further
heavy investment in education for economic reasons.
Thus, he argued, after four years of primary education
a worker's output - and output related wages - were
79 per cent higher than those of a worker of first
category, who had had no schooling; after seven
years of study, this rose to 235 per cent; after
nine years of study to 280 per cent and after a
full course of study in higher education to 320 per
cent. In his later calculations he estimated that
because of greatly improving educational opportunities
in the USSR, the productivity of labour increased
from 1940 to 1950 by 52 per cent and just about
doubled between 1950 and 1960.[30]
It may be useful to indicate at this stage that
the beginnings of rigorous studies of the economic
aspects of education are of relatively recent
origin. Interestingly enough, the first decisively
important contributions came from the comparative
educationists working in the 1950s in London
University. The Year Book of Education of 1954,
published by Evans Brothers, London, in association

with the University of London Institute of Education and the Teachers College, Columbia University, New· York under the joint editorship of Robert King Hall, Nicholas Hans and Joseph Lauwerys, marked the beginning of a sustained interest in the economic aspects of education. Devoted explicitly to an analysis of the relationship between education and technological development, it contained, among others, sections on the aims, objectives and implications of technological development, cultural change, and planning and education.

The Year Book of Education of 1956, published two years later, examined, by drawing together into one volume contributions from many distinguished specialists in the field, the connection between education and the economy.

In the late 1950s and in the early 1960s there appeared in the United States a number of important books, drawing attention to the importance of education for economic growth and development. Important contributions came from Edward Denison, who published his Contribution of Education to Economic Growth in the USA in 1959 and The Sources of Economic Growth in the United States and the Alternatives before Us in 1962; from Seymour Harris, whose Higher Education - Resources and Finance came in 1962 and Harbison and Myers, who published their Human Resources, Education and Economic Growth in 1963 and their Education, Manpower and Economic Growth in 1964.

In Britain John Vaizey's The Economics of Education appeared in 1962 and in the middle and late 1960s came important studies of the productivity and efficiency of education and of mathematical models in educational planning, as well as the OECD reports of the study group in the economics of education. In 1964 there appeared another important work, Economic Aspects of Higher Education, with contributions from Frank Bowles, Seymour Harris, Dolfe Vogelnik,· Nicholas DeWitt, Friedrich Edding, William G. Bowen, Gotfried Bombach and Claude Vimont.

Economics of Higher Education. In the USSR, it was the economist L.I. Tul'chinskii, working at that time in the Finance Research Institute of the USSR Ministry of Finance, the author of Finansovye problemy professional'nogo obrazovaniya v SSSR (Financial Problems of Vocational Education in the USSR) published in Moscow in 1968, who made the first attempt to specify the subject matter of what was of very great interest to him, i.e. the economics

259

of higher education:

> Under the concept we include a complex of issues
> concerned with the management and internal
> structure of higher education establishments,
> their material, technical, educational and
> research facilities, problems of work and wages,
> the system of planning, financing, accounting
> and reporting.[31]

He justified the importance of research in this
field by stressing the fact that Soviet higher
education establishments today are not only
educational institutions involved in teaching and
research, but due to the scale of their operations,
are also large and **highly diversified** economic units
which possess numerous direct links with the
commodity and monetary systems. Several universities
and establishments of higher learning command vast
material resources that are worth far more than those
of many large industrial units of production and
include not only hundreds of buildings and thousands
of expensive machines and instruments, but also
workshops, experimental farms and complex training
facilities. The annual budget of all higher
education establishments, in fact, well exceeds one
billion rubles. As a result, it was necessary that
proper attention was paid to the management of every
VUZ in the country.[32]
As Tul'chinskii revealed in his article, the
Finance Research Institute of the USSR Ministry of
Finance conducted a study of the economic aspects of
management of 96 VUZy in 14 Union Republics in the
early 1960s, which indicated that many higher
education establishments in the USSR paid little
attention to such aspects. Organisational and
administrative weaknesses resulted in an enormous
waste of resources. In more specific terms, the
inquiry criticised the existence of small and
uneconomic departments in many VUZy; high drop-out
rates; wide differences in the student-teacher
ratio from one VUZ to another; the use of
inappropriate indicators in respect of individual
teachers' work (for example taking into account only
the number of hours put in by a teacher when
calculating the effectiveness of his work);
surprisingly low teaching loads in certain
establishments and very complicated and over-elaborate
planning procedures, consuming too high a proportion
of time which could be spent more profitably on
research.[33]

Economics of Education as a Field of Study. While
Tul'chinskii's article marked an interesting
beginning in the opening up of debates on all aspects
of the economics of education in the USSR, the first
Soviet economist of great reputation to publish a
substantial book under the title Ekonomika
obrazovaniya (Economics of Education) was V.A. Zhamin,
then a research scholar from the Institute of
Economics of the USSR Academy of Sciences. The book
appeared in 1969 and it consisted of fifteen chapters,
dealing in succession with: economics of education
as a subject of study; the principal stages of
development of the Soviet economy and of the Soviet
system of education; the organisation and the legal
framework of the educational system; interconnections
between education and the economy; the organisation
and planning of general education; preparation of
skilled workers and specialists in the USSR; the
material-technical basis of the educational system;
the preparation of teachers, their remuneration and
the organisation of teachers' work; financing
education; the structure of expenditure on education;
economic problems of the further development of the
national system of education and the efficiency of
education.
     According to Zhamin, the economics of education
as a subject is facing the difficult task of deciding
the optimal allocation of resources for educational
purposes from a long term point of view. This
necessitates taking into account the contribution of
education to complex forms of human development in
scientific and cultural fields as well as to the
physical wellbeing and health of the people, which
are all of enormous importance, though they cannot
be measured easily.
     In 1970 V.A. Zhamin and S.L. Kostanyan published
their work Ekonomika i obrazovanie (Economics and
Education). The book was interesting in that the
two authors, after painstaking calculations came to
the conclusion that in 1964 the education and skills
mastered by the labour force accounted for 28.5 per
cent of the national income of the USSR.[34]
     Characteristic of the study of economic aspects
of education was the approach of S.L. Kostanyan, who
in a book Predmet i metod ekonomiki obrazovaniya
(Subject Matter and Method of Economics of Education)
argued that economic laws in the sphere of education
reveal themselves as law-trends, even though - as
such - they only determine the basic direction of
development, since the presence of a large number of
specific features and conditions attaching to

particular situations cannot be ignored. He argued
that it was possible to identify some laws
characteristic of the period of developed socialism,
namely: 1) the law of planned development; 2) the
law of value, based on Karl Marx's proposition that
manpower costs are a part of the system of values
expended on its production.[35]
    It seems, however, doubtful if laws of this kind
have any operational value or instrumental
significance in discussing educational developments,
even in the Soviet Union.

    A penetrating analysis of the costs of study at
the level of higher education and, particularly, of
the actual costs of the alternative forms of study:
full-time, part-time and by correspondence, was
undertaken in the USSR in the late 1960s by
Beniamin Remennikov in his book Ekonomicheskie
problemy vysshego obrazovaniya v SSSR (The Economic
Problems of Higher Education in the USSR). Having
studied in detail the cost of education per student
in three universities (one in the RSFSR, one in
Belorussia and one in Uzbekistan), he was in a position
to point out the fact that the cost of study by
correspondence or on a part-time basis was not at all
a small proportion of the cost of study on a full-time
basis. According to his calculations, in the mid-
1960s the cost of education per student per year on
a full-time course was 970 rubles, on an evening
course - 290 rubles and on a correspondence course
- 80 rubles, excluding capital expenditure. While
these were the figures in respect of university
students, the cost of study in other higher education
establishments showed very considerable variations:
1685 to 827 rubles for full-time courses and between
110 to 69 rubles for corresponding courses. A
critical examination of the above data however, led
Remennikov to rather different conclusions concerning
the supposed relatively inexpensive study on a
part-time basis. His argument was that it was
imperative that proper corrections should be
included in the real cost of educating students on
part-time courses of study. Thus, while nominally
full-time courses might have appeared ten times more
expensive in the universities than study by
correspondence (that is 970 rubles over five years
= 4850 rubles; 80 rubles over six years = 480 rubles),
in fact, when proper allowances were made for time off
production taken by part-time students, study leave
before examinations, high drop-out rates and the
fact that many students took much more time than the
prescribed minimum to complete their course when

studying by correspondence, the latter was almost half as expensive as full-time study. Remennikov's work, no doubt, was a solid example of a realistic critical reappraisal of the existing assumptions in respect of the effectiveness of study at the level of higher education in the Soviet Union.[36]

The First All-Union Conference on Economics of Higher Education. In December 1971 there took place at the University of Kazan the first All-Union Scientific Conference on the Economics of Higher Education in the USSR. Its detailed proceedings were published two years later and have subsequently come to be seen as important for assessing the work already done in this area in the past and to be undertaken in this field in the future.[37] The more precise purpose of the Conference was to discuss and identify the research tasks in the field and to adopt recommendations in order to integrate efforts towards the earliest possible and the most effective execution of crucial investigations into economic aspects of higher education.

The principal areas which received attention were:

- problems in the theory and methodology of the economics of higher education;
- planning, effectiveness of training and utilisation of specialists with higher education;
- planning and effectiveness of scientific investigations at higher education establishments;
- the financing of higher education establishments and the effective use of their funds and facilities.[38]

Professor Zhamin, probably the most important participant, stressed the fact that scientific and technological progress caused changes in the structure of secondary specialised and higher education. Two trends, in fact, became apparent: (1), differentiation based upon a greater division of labour; (2), integration, based upon a higher level of general preparation in the humanities and in technical subjects, which was specially valuable for specialists employed in management in economic enterprises, social institutions or government agencies.

Effective training required continuous up-dating and improvement of the content of the specialist training, scientific planning of educational progress and incorporating scientific organisation of labour

into the system of higher education. He argued that
the raising of the level of engineering training in
economics and mathematics was of particular
importance under the modern conditions of production,
saying that today knowledge of economics was essential
for both persons directly employed in the production
sphere and for research engineers, designers and
planners. Methods used in the calculation of long-
term personnel requirements needed further elaboration.
Particularly essential was the need to render more
precise the method of determining 'saturation
coefficients', which were the crucial consideration
in calculating the numbers of specialists to be
trained.

He criticised the distribution of the country's
scientific research workers in the late 1960s.
There were then 34.4 per cent of them in the
universities and establishments of higher learning,
59.0 per cent in scientific research and development
institutions and only 6.6 per cent in enterprises of
a different kind, planning organisations and
industrial management. He called for the provision
of better links among all these three sectors and
between them and the different ministries, as well
as for improved population forecasting as the basis
for compiling labour balances. In addition, he
argued, attention should be devoted to the
elaboration of a model for the development of
education, which should include the analysis and
determination of the basic changes and improvements
which might occur in the system of education at all
its levels due to the specification of new goals set
for education in a given planning period.[39]

M.T. Nuzhin, in a paper on the role and
importance of the universities in the period of
scientific and technological revolution stressed the
growing relative importance of the universities as a
sector of higher education in the USSR. Over the
period of thirty years 1945-75, the number of
students in all higher education establishments in
the country increased 5.6 times, while the number of
students in the universities increased 6.6 times.
The latter have become very large institutions in
comparison with other institutions at this level:
for example in the academic year 1970/1 the average
enrolment in a VUZ, excluding the universities was
5,603 students; that in the universities - 9,804
students.[40]

V.F. Semenov from the University of Kazan, in a
paper on the concentration, structure and location
of higher education institutions dealt with the cost

of capital expenditure in this field. He made the argument, that there were important economies of scale to be considered: buildings providing facilities for 2,000 students constituted in practice as much as 83 per cent of the cost of providing facilities for 10,000 students. There was a trend for the higher education establishments to grow in size in any case (from an average of some 1,000 students in 1940/1 to approximately 5,700 in 1969/70) and the expansion was particularly rapid in the Central Asiatic Republics where the starting base had been very low, but was 'gigantomania' a sensible thing? What was, in fact, the optimum size for an establishment of higher learning? Apparently, this ought to vary according to the kind of specialisation of each institution. But it was an important issue, as in the period 1950-70 enrolment had increased in higher education 3.7 times and the cost of capital investment 7.9 times. Important related questions were connected with the optimal degree of concentration of VUZy in each area. Rational siting of new higher education establishments should be based upon 'zoning', in an attempt to create a properly construed network of institutions of this kind.[41]

The attempts to create a modern network of schools, based upon the principle of rationalisation of effort in the period of transition to complete secondary education for all, were illustrated more recently by I. Vybrik in respect of the current organisational changes in the Krymskaya oblast'.[42] The rapid decline in the number of primary schools has been accompanied there by a similar decline in the number of eight-year schools and a very considerable increase in the number of ten-year schools, which can be seen from the following table:

Table 3: Number of pupils and schools in Krymskaya oblast'

| Year | Total number of pupils | Number of schools | | |
		primary	eight-year	secondary
1966	225,000	432	284	174
1971	258,000	244	272	234
1978	251,000	41	159	320

Source: I. Vybrik, 'O ratsyonalizatsii shkol'noi seti', Narodnoe obrazovanie, no. 5, 1980, pp. 22-5.

Issues in Teacher Education. In so far as the
examination of problems of teacher training goes,
attention in recent years has concentrated upon the
evidence of improving standards among the teaching
staff in pedagogical institutes in the USSR. The
fact that the number of lecturers and instructors
there increased from some 45,300 in 1975 to 48,500
in 1979, while the number of teaching staff with
the higher qualifications of doctorates in science
and those with the qualifications of candidates of
science increased more slowly, indicates that
progress in qualitative terms was not matching that
in quantitative indices.[43]
    Another aspect of concern with the effectiveness
of the teaching profession in the process of educating
the young generation in the Soviet Union has been
investigations connected with the attestation of
teachers in service. The 1972 law on attestation
of teaching qualifications specified that this
should take place every five years. In fact, the
process began in 1976 and the first attestation
cycle was completed in 1980; in 1981 the second
cycle began and it will continue until 1985. The
returns covering the first four years indicated that
on the whole, the speed of the operation matched the
envisaged schedules in the RSFSR and Azerbaidzhan
and exceeded it in Latvia and Moldavia. Progress
in the attestation of teachers in service was
particularly good in Lithuania, Mordovska ASSR,
Stavropol'sky Krai, Moscow, Leningrad and Pskov.
However, progress in the Central Asiastic Republics
was much slower and left much to be desired.[44]
    Linked to this was the concern that there were
still regions where the supply of teachers was
inadequate. Some schools were experiencing a
definite shortage of teachers of mathematics and
foreign languages. Schools in the rural areas
were in a particularly difficult position. Training
a teacher and sending him or her to a village was
not enough. Many simply went back to the urban
environment as soon as their three years of
compulsory posting in the countryside expired.[45]
    The significance of rising educational standards
in the USSR for labour productivity has been again
discussed in economic journals. A.G. Sozykin,
Chairman of the RSFSR State Committee on Labour,
writing in Ekonomika i organizatsiya promyshlennogo
proizvodstva (Economics and Organisation of
Industrial Production) emphasised recently that
according to numerous economic surveys, the
productivity of workers with secondary education

substantially exceeded that of workers with lower educational standards. Further improvement depended very much upon the fulfilment of plans for constructing vocational schools. There were however serious delays in this respect, for example in the RSFSR, where in 1978 only 59 per cent of the plan was fulfilled. In addition, difficulties were being encountered in finding enough young people willing to enter industrial production. Among many adolescents jobs in offices, in laboratories and in administration enjoyed much greater popularity. In a period when the number of school leavers was declining in any case due to long-term fluctuations in the birth rate, there were real dilemmas facing several branches of production.[46]

The Effectiveness of Educational Research. At least three articles published in Sovetskaya pedagogika in 1981, dealt with a problem which clearly has of late become an important one, namely the effectiveness of educational research. The discussion on the subject was, in fact, initiated much earlier, in 1976, by V.M. Polonskii and very much expanded by the contributions from Mikhail Skatkin, of the Scientific Research Institute on General Pedagogy of the USSR Academy of Pedagogical Sciences and L.D. Kvirtiya and other writers in the subsequent years.[47] It is interesting, however, to observe that recently general remarks concerning the need to render educational research projects more effective and relevant to the manifested needs, have been replaced by specific proposals for introducing specially construed measuring devices to assess the importance of particular research works with a greater precision.

V.M. Polonskii in two articles on methods of determining the innovative character of completed pedagogical research projects,[48] proposed that the following criteria should be introduced to measure the significance of research:

aktual'nost' - topicality
nauchnaya novizna - scientific novelty
metodologicheskaya i teoreticheskaya
obosnovannost' - methodological and theoretical
foundations
kompleksnost' - complexity
koordinatsiya - coordination
vsestronnost' - comprehensiveness
populyarnost' - popularity
adekvatnost' metodicheskogo instrumentariya -

adequacy of methodological refinement
    kontseptual'nost' - conceptualisation
    <u>klassnost'</u> - high level
    <u>prakticheskaya znachimost'</u> - practical
significance
    vseobshchnost' - universality
    gotovnost' k vnedreniyu - readiness for adoption

The results of a particular research work should
be judged - Polonskii suggests - <u>'iz naukometricheskikh</u>
<u>informatsionnykh i ekonomicheskikh pozitsii'</u> - from
the scientificometric, informative and economic points
of view. He further suggests assessing research
works from the standpoint of the following requirements

    1) <u>semanticheskaya opredelennost'</u> - semantic
clarity
    2) <u>konstruktivnost'</u> - constructiveness
    3) <u>teoreticheskaya znachimost'</u> - theoretical
significance
    4) <u>prakticheskaya znachimost'</u> - practical
significance
    5) <u>effektivnost'</u> - effectiveness

Each of these is seen as a concept synthesising
other criteria, for example, theoretical significance
is constituted of the following elements: novelty,
topicality, prospects for future use, conceptual-
isation and demonstrable significance for theory
and practice. Each of the constituent elements is
assessed on a scale from 0 to 3; by averaging the
constituent elements one can assess theoretical
significance, understood as a potential influence
upon theoretical concepts in the field of
education and upbringing:

    rating 0 - repetition of known concepts, ideas
and laws;
    rating 1 - concretisation of ideas already
known;
    rating 2 - development of known ideas;
    rating 3 - introduction of new ideas and
concepts.

Similarly, one can assess the effectiveness of
research work in the following way:

    rating 0 - research work which produces
effectiveness no higher than as at present;
    rating 1 - research work which increases
effectiveness by up to 10 per cent;

rating 2 - research work which increases
effectiveness by 10-30 per cent;
rating 3 - research work which improves
existing performance by more than 30 per cent.[49]

Measuring the effectiveness of educational
research and its value and relevance to educational
practice is obviously quite important and an
objective assessment of these considerations ought
to be given a high priority. The scheme outlined
above may, however, gratuitously import methodologic-
ally significant subjective judgments into ostensibly
objective scales of measurement. Any concrete
attempts to apply the scheme in practice are likely
to demonstrate the difficulties arising in real life
in connection with the strategy proposed.

Looking Ahead. Looking at the position in which
the economics of education finds itself in the USSR
at the present time, one may observe that there are
fewer well established and renowned experts in this
field than in the area of sociology of education
who tend to be primarily concerned with the
confirmation of established 'laws of development',
derived from the prevailing ideology. Economic
investigations in education have spotlighted many
existing trends, identified several dysfunctional
relationships, revealed the existence of serious
dilemmas and problems and suggested some possible
solutions. Any macro-economic constraints have
proved themselves less powerful than the socio-
political ones and as a result the debates in this
field have been more open and more vigorous. They
are likely to lead to further research in the subject.
However, the application of the conclusions of the
ongoing investigations into educational practice and
any more significant shifts in policy, depend not so
much upon the research work itself, but rather upon
a much more complex pattern of power relations in the
USSR in the years to come and upon the order of
priorities which still attaches primary importance
to ideological imperatives.

NOTES

1.   The character and substance of
sociological research in the USSR in the 1960s were
examined in some detail by Zev Katz of the Russian
Research Centre at Harvard University in an article
'Sociology in the Soviet Union', in Problems of
Communism, (Washington, May-June, 1971), pp. 22-40.

269

Comprehensive and useful bibliographies of Soviet
sociology in general are Elizabeth Weinberg's The
Development of Sociology in the Soviet Union (London
and Boston, 1974) and Mervyn Matthews's and
T. Anthony Jones's Soviet Sociology, 1964-75: A
Bibliography (Praeger, London, New York, 1978).
    2. Gennaidy Vasil'evich Osipov, born in 1928,
graduated from the Institute of International
Relations in Moscow in 1952, professor and head of
Sociological Research Institute of the USSR Academy
of Sciences, vice-president of the Soviet
Sociological Association; Mikhail Nikolaevich
Rutkevich, born in 1917, graduated from the University
of Kiev in 1939, member of the Academy of Sciences of
the USSR, deputy head of the Division of Scientific
Communism of the Academy of Social Sciences of the
Central Committee of the CPSU.
    3.   F.R. Filippov, 'Social Structure of Society
and System of Education', paper presented to the
Eighth World Congress of Sociology in Toronto (Moscow,
1974), p. 18.
    4.   Ibid., pp. 18-20.
    5.   G.V. Osipov and M.N. Rutkevich, 'Sociology
in the USSR: 1965-75', in Current Sociology vol. 26,
no. 2 (International Sociological Association, Paris,
1978), p. 53.
    6.   Ibid., p. 54.
    7.   O.I. Shkaratan and V.O. Rukavishnikov,
'The Impact of the STR on Social Differentiation
and Integration in the Soviet City', paper presented
to the Eighth World Congress of Sociology in Toronto
(Moscow, 1974), 17 pp; M.N. Rutkevich, Klassy,
sotsial'nye sloi i gruppy v SSSR, (Moscow, 1968);
M.N. Rutkevich, O perspektivakh razvitiya
intelligentsii, (Moscow, 1971); M.N. Rutkevich,
'Razvitie novykh form sotsial'noi integratsii v
sotsialisticheskom obshchestve', paper presented to
the Eighth World Congress of Sociology in Toronto
(Moscow, 1974), 23 pp.
    8.   M.N. Rutkevich (ed.), Zhiznennye plany
molodezhi, (Ural'skii gosudarstvennyi universitet
im. Gorkogo, Sotsiologicheskie issledovaniya,
Sverdlovsk, 1966); F.R. Filippov, 'Social Structure',
pp. 10-11; M.N. Rutkevich, 'Razvitie novykh form',
pp. 9-12.
    9.   M.Kh. Titma and K.A. Pyarna, 'Controlling
the Choice of Occupation in Developed Socialist
Society', paper presented to the Eighth World
Congress of Sociology in Toronto (Moscow, 1974),
16 pp; Yu.I. Leonavichius et al. (eds.), Lichnost'
studenta, (Kaunas, 1970); Yu.I. Leonavichius et al.

(eds.), Student v uchebnom protsesse (Kaunas, 1972).
    10. N.A. Aitov, 'Vliyanie obshcheobrazovatel'-
nogo urovnya rabochikh na ikh proizvodstvennuyu
deyatel'nost' in Voprosy filosofii, no. 11, (1966),
pp. 23-31; N.A. Aitov also presented two interesting
papers to the Eighth World Congress of Sociology in
Toronto: 'Social Shifts in the USSR' (Moscow, 1974),
18 pp., and 'Planning of Urban Social Development in
the USSR' (Moscow, 1974), p. 16 pp.
    11. G.V. Osipov and M.N. Rutkevich, p. 56.
    12. Ibid., p. 57.
    13. F.R. Filippov, pp. 1-4.
    14. Ibid., pp. 6-10.
    15. A.G. Kharchev, 'Women's Career Work and
Family' in Soviet Sociological Association,
Sociology and the Present Age, collection of Papers
by Soviet Scientists presented to the Eighth World
Congress of Sociology in Toronto (Moscow, 1974),
pp. 172-84.
    16. V.D. Patrushev, 'Socio-economic Problems
of Time under Socialism' in Soviet Sociological
Association, Sociology, pp. 185-206.
    17. 'Sotsiologicheskie problemy vospitaniya i
obucheniya (kruglyi stol' zhurnala Sotsiologicheskie
issledovaniya i Akademii pedagogicheskikh nauk SSSR)',
in Sotsiologicheskie issledovaniya, no. 3, (1979),
pp. 53-74.
    18. Ibid., p. 64. R.G. Gurova had argued for
a closer integration between sociology and pedagogy
much earlier, in her book Sotsiologicheskie problemy
obrazovaniya i vospitaniya (Moscow, 1973).
    19. 'Sotsiologicheskie problemy', pp. 62-5.
    20. Ibid., pp. 64-9.
    21. Ibid., pp. 70-1.
    22. N.A. Aitov and R.T. Nasibullin,
'Professional'naya mobil'nost' intelligentsii', in
Sotsiologicheskie issledovaniya, no. 2, (Moscow,
1980), pp. 106-11.
    23. M.N. Rutkevich, 'Sblizhenie natsional'nykh
respublik i natsii SSSR po sotsial'no-klassovoi
strukture', in Sotsiologicheskie issledovaniya, no. 2,
(Moscow, 1981), pp. 14-24.
    24. I.S. Bolotin, 'Vozdeistvie demograficheskoi
situatsii na sredniyu i vysshuyu shkolu', in
Sotsiologicheskie issledovaniya, no. 4 (1979),
pp. 127-8.
    25. V.T. Lisovskii, 'Printsipy i kriterii
tipologizatsii sovremennego studenchestva', in
Sotsiologicheskie issledovaniya, no. 3 (1980),
pp. 130-5.   See also V.T. Lisovskii 'Social Goals
of Higher Education in Developed Socialist Society',

paper presented to the Eighth World Congress of
Sociology in Toronto (Moscow, 1974), 12 pp.
    26. V.A. Smirnov, 'Problema formirovaniya u
rabochei molodezhi soznatel'nogo otnosheniya k trudu',
in Sotsiologicheskie issledovaniya, no. 4 (1978),
pp. 80-6.
    27. Soviet Education, vol. XXIII, no. 6 (1981),
p. 3.
    28. Bol'shaya sovetskaya entsiklopediya,
vol. 24, (Moscow, 1976), pp. 606-7.
    29. S.G. Strumilin, 'Effektivnost' narodnogo
obrazovaniya v SSSR', in Ekonomicheskaya gazeta,
2 April, 1962, pp. 28-30.
    30. Ibid., pp. 28-30.
    31. L.I. Tul'chinskii, 'Voprosy ekonomiki
vysshego obrazovaniya (zametki ekonomista)', in
Vestnik vysshei shkoly, no. 4, (1964), p. 27; see
also L.I. Tul'chinskii, 'Eshche raz ob ekonomike
vysshego obrazovaniya', in Vestnik vysshei shkoly,
no. 5 (1965), pp. 72-7.
    32. L.I. Tul'chinskii, 'Voprosy ekonomiki,
p. 27.
    33. Ibid., p. 28.
    34. V.A. Zhamin and S.L. Kostanyan, Ekonomika
i obrazavanie (Moscow, 1970), p. 12. V.A. Zhamin
extended his analysis into socio-economic aspects
of educational developments in his recent book
Sotsial'no-ekonomicheskie problemy obrazovaniya i
nauki v razvitom sotsialisticheskom obshchestve
(Moscow, 1979).
    35. S.L. Kostanyan, Predmet i metod ekonomiki
obrazovaniya (Moscow, 1976), pp. 15-23.
    36. B.M. Remennikov, Ekonomicheskie problemy
vysshego obrazovaniya v SSSR (Vysshaya shkola,
Moscow, 1968), pp. 105-114.
    37. Ekonomika vysshego obrazovaniya (Materialy
Vsesoyuznoi nauchnoi konferentsii po ekonomike
obrazovaniya) (Kazanskii gosudarstvennyi universitet
im. Lenina, 1973); several sections of it were
translated into English and appeared in Soviet
Education, vol. XVIII, no. 1, (1975), pp. 5-111.
    38. Soviet Education, vol. XVIII, no. 1 (1975),
p. 6.
    39. Ibid., pp. 7-29.
    40. Ibid., pp. 30-43.
    41. Ibid., pp. 44-58.
    42. I. Vybrik, 'O ratsionalizatsii shkol'noi
seti', in Narodnoe obrazovanie, no. 5 (1980),
pp. 22-5.   See also A.M. Novikov, 'Nekotorye
pedagogicheskie i sotsial'no-ekonomicheskie problemy
ratsionalizatsii seti shkol', in Sovetskaya pedagogika,

no. 12 (1980), pp. 100-6.
  43. E. Kozhevnikov, 'Sovetskii uchitel' -
aktivnaya tvorcheskaya sila', in Narodnoe obrazovanie,
no. 10 (1980), pp. 2-7.
  44. G. Rebenko, 'Attestatsiya uchitelei i ee
effektivnost', in Narodnoe obrazovanie, no. 2 (1980),
pp. 33-6.
  45. Pravda, 12 August, 1980.
  46. A.G. Sozykin, 'Kadry dlya Sibiri:
potrebnost' i rezervy (k sibirskoi konferentsii)',
in Ekonomika i organizatsiya promyshlennogo proizvodstva, no. 5 (71), (Sibirskoe otdelenie Akademii
nauk SSSR, Novosibirsk, 1980), pp. 3-17.
  47. V.M. Polonskii, 'Otsenka effektivnosti
pedagogicheskikh issledovanii i razrabotok', in
Sovetskaya pedagogika, no. 11 (1976), pp. 75-84.
M.N. Skatkin, 'Osnovnye napravleniya issledovaniya
problemy izucheniya, obobshcheniya i ispol'zovaniya
peredovogo pedagogicheskogo opyta', in Sovetskaya
pedagogika, no. 2 (1979), pp. 13-20; L.D. Kvirtiya,
'Problemy klassifikatsii i effektivnosti
pedagogicheskikh issledovanii', in Sovetskaya
pedagogika, no. 10 (1979), pp. 108-14; M.N. Skatkin,
'O kriteriyakh effektivnosti i kachestva
zavershennykh nauchno-pedagogicheskikh issledovanii',
in Sovetskaya pedagogika, no. 5 (1980), pp. 71-6.
  48. V.M. Polonskii, 'Metody opredeleniya
novizny rezul'tatov pedagogicheskikh issledovanii',
in Sovetskaya pedagogika, no. 1 (1981), pp. 64-70;
V.M. Polonskii, 'Kriterii kachestva i effektivnosti
zavershennykh nauchno-pedagogicheskikh issledovanii',
in Sovetskaya pedagogika, no. 9 (1981), pp. 70-6.
See also S.Ya. Batyshev, 'K voprosu o povyshenii
effektivnosti pedagogicheskikh issledovanii', in
Sovetskaya pedagogika, no. 9 (1981), pp. 61-9 and
for a comparative analysis: M.B. Kol'chugina and
V.S. Mitina, 'Novye podkhody k probleme effektivnosti
obrazovaniya v vedushchikh kapitalisticheskikh
stranakh', in Sovetskaya pedagogika, no. 10 (1981),
pp. 78-84.
  49. M.V. Polonskii, 'Kriterii kachestva',
pp. 70-5.

BIBLIOGRAPHY

Aitov, N.A. 'Planning of Urban Social Development in
    the USSR', paper presented to the Eighth World
    Congress of Sociology in Toronto (Moscow, 1974),
    16 pp.
Aitov, N.A. 'Social Shifts in the USSR', paper
    presented to the Eighth World Congress of

SOVIET SOCIOLOGISTS AND ECONOMISTS ON SOVIET EDUCATION

Sociology in Toronto (Moscow, 1974), 18 pp.
Aitov, N.A. 'Vliyanie obshcheobrazovatel'nogo
    urovnya rabochikh na ikh proizvodstvennuyu
    deyatel'nost', Voprosy filosofii, no. 11, (1966),
    pp. 23-31
Aitov, N.A. and Nasibullin, R.T. 'Professional'naya
    mobil'nost' intelligentsii', Sotsiologicheskie
    issledovaniya, no. 2, (Moscow, 1980), pp. 106-11
Batyshev, S.Ya. 'K voprosu o povyshenii effektivnosti
    pedagogicheskikh issledovanii', Sovetskaya
    pedagogika, no. 9,(1981), pp. 61-9
Bolotin, I.S. 'Vozdeistvie demograficheskoi situatsii
    na sredniyu i vysshuyu shkolu', Sotsiologicheskie
    issledovaniya, no. 4, (1979), pp. 127-8
Ekonomika vysshego obrazovaniya (Materialy Vsesoyuznoi
    nauchnoi konferentsii po ekonomike obrazovaniya)
    (Kazanskii gosudarstvennyi universitet im.
    Lenina, 1973), Soviet Education, vol. XVIII,
    no. 1, (1975), pp. 5-111
Filippov, F.R. 'Social Structure of Society and
    System of Education', paper presented to the
    Eighth World Congress of Sociology in Toronto
    (Moscow, 1974), 18 pp.
Filippov, F.R. Vseobshchee srednee obrazovanie v
    SSSR: sotsiologicheskie problemy (Moscow, 1976)
Gurova, R.G. Sotsiologicheskie problemy obrazovaniya
    i vospitaniya, (Moscow, 1973)
Katz, Z. 'Sociology in the Soviet Union', Problems
    of Communism, vol. XX, (Washington, May-June,
    1971), pp. 22-40
Kharchev, A.G. 'Women's Career Work and Family',
    Soviet Sociological Association, Sociology and
    the Present Age, Collection of Papers by Soviet
    Scientists presented to the Eighth World
    Congress of Sociology in Toronto (Moscow, 1974),
    pp. 172-84
Kol'chugina, M.B. and Mitina, V.S. 'Novye podkhody
    k probleme effektivnosti obrazovaniya v
    vedushchikh kapitalisticheskikh stranakh',
    Sovetskaya pedagogika, no. 10, (1981), pp. 78-84
Kostanyan, S.L. Predmet i metod ekonomiki
    obrazovaniya (Moscow, 1976)
Kozhevnikov, E. 'Sovetskii uchitel' - aktivnaya
    tvorcheskaya sila', Narodnoe obrazovanie, no.
    10, (1980), pp. 2-7
Kvirtiya, L.D. 'Problemy klassifikatsii i
    effektivnosti pedagogicheskikh issledovanii',
    Sovetskaya pedagogika, no. 10, (1979),
    pp. 108-14.
Leonavichius, Yu.I. et al. (eds.), Lichnost'
    studenta, (Kaunas, 1970)

SOVIET SOCIOLOGISTS AND ECONOMISTS ON SOVIET EDUCATION

Leonavichius, Yu.I. et al. (eds.), Motivatsiya
   zhiznedeyatel'nosti studenta, (Kaunas, 1971)
Leonavichius, Yu.I. et al. (eds.), Student v
   uchebnom protsesse (Kaunas, 1972)
Lissovskii, V.T. 'Printsipy i kriterii
   tipologizatsii sovremennego studenchestva',
   Sotsiologicheskie issledovaniya, no. 3, (1980),
   pp. 130-5
Lissovskii, V.T. 'Social Goals of Higher Education
   in Developed Socialist Society', paper presented
   to the Eighth World Congress of Sociology in
   Toronto (Moscow, 1974), 12 pp.
Matthews, M. and Jones, T.A. Soviet Sociology,
   1964-75: A Bibliography, (Praeger, London,
   New York, 1978)
Novikov, A.M. 'Nekotorye pedagogicheskie i
   sotsial'no-ekonomicheskie problemy ratsionalizatsii seti shkol', Sovetskaya pedagogika,
   no. 12, (1980), pp. 100-6
Osipov, G.V. and Rutkevich, M.N. 'Sociology in the
   USSR: 1965-1975', Current Sociology, vol. 26,
   no. 2, (International Sociological Association,
   Paris, 1978), pp. 1-160 (whole issue)
Patrushev, V.D. 'Socio-economic Problems of Time
   under Socialism', Soviet Sociological
   Association, Sociology.... pp. 185-206
Polonskii, V.M. 'Kriterii kachestva i effektivnosti
   zavershennykh nauchno-pedagogicheskikh
   issledovanii, Sovetskaya pedagogika, no. 9,
   (1981), pp. 61-9
Polonskii, V.M. 'Metody opredeleniya novizny
   rezul'tatov pedagogicheskikh issledovanii',
   Sovetskaya pedagogika, no. 1, (1981), pp. 64-70
Polonskii, V.M. 'Otsenka effektivnosti pedagogicheskikh
   issledovanii i razrabotok', Sovetskaya pedagogika,
   no. 11, (1976), pp. 75-84
Pravda, 12 August, 1980
Rebenko, G. 'Attestatsiya uchitelei i ee effektivnost',
   Narodnoe obrazovanie, no. 2, (1980), pp. 33-6
Remennikov, B.M. Ekonomicheskie problemy vysshego
   obrazovaniya v SSSR (Vysshaya shkola, Moscow,
   1968)
Rutkevich, M.N. Klassy, sotsial'nye sloi i gruppy v
   SSSR, (Moscow, 1968)
Rutkevich, M.N. O perspektivakh razvitiya
   intelligentsii, (Moscow, 1971)
Rutkevich, M.N. 'Razvitie novykh form sotsial'noi
   integratsii v sotsialisticheskom obshchestve',
   paper presented to the Eighth World Congress of
   Sociology in Toronto (Moscow, 1974), 23 pp.
Rutkevich, M.N. 'Sblizhenie natsional'nykh respublik

i natsii SSSR po sotsial'no-klassovoi strukture',
Sotsiologicheskie issledovaniya, no. 2 (Moscow,
1981), pp. 14-24
Rutkevich, M.N. Zhiznennye plany molodezhi (Ural'skii
gosudarstvennyi universitet im. Gorkogo,
Sotsiologicheskie issledovaniya, Sverdlovsk,
1966)
Shkaratan, O.I. and Rukavishnikov, V.O. 'The Impact
of the STR on Social Differentiation and
Integration in the Soviet City', paper presented
to the Eighth World Congress of Sociology in
Toronto (Moscow, 1974), 17 pp.
Skatkin, M.N. 'O kriteriyakh effektivnosti i
kachestva zavershennykh nauchno-pedagogicheskikh
issledovanii', Sovetskaya pedagogika, no. 5,
(1980), pp. 71-6
Skatkin, M.N. 'Osnovnye napravleniya issledovaniya
problemy izucheniya, obobshcheniya i
ispol'zovaniya peredovogo pedagogicheskogo
opyta', Sovetskaya pedagogika, no. 2, (1979),
pp. 13-20
Smirnov, V.A. 'Problema formirovaniya u rabochei
molodezhi soznatel'nogo otnosheniya k trudu',
Sotsiologicheskie issledovaniya, no. 4, (1978),
pp. 80-6
'Sotsiologicheskie problemy vospitaniya i obucheniya
(kruglyi stol' zhurnala Sotsiologicheskie
issledovaniya i Akademii pedagogicheskikh nauk
SSSR)', Sotsiologicheskie issledovaniya, no. 3,
(1979), pp. 53-74
Sozykin, A.G. 'Kadry dlya Sibiri: potrebnost' i
rezervy (k sibirskoi konferentsii)', Ekonomika
i organizatsiya promyshlennogo proizvodstva,
no. 5 (71), (Sibirskoe otdelenie Akademii nauk
SSSR, Novosibirsk, 1980), pp. 3-17
Strumilin, S.G. 'Effektivnost' narodnogo
obrazovaniya v SSSR', Izbrannye proizvedeniya
(Moscow, 1965), pp. 265-77
Strumilin, S.G. 'Obshchestvennyi progress v SSSR
za 50 let', Voprosy ekonomiki, no. 11, (1969),
pp. 57-73
Strumilin, S.G. Promyshlennyi perevorot v Rossii
(Moscow, 1944)
Strumilin, S.G. 'The Economics of Education in the
USSR', Economic and Social Aspects of
Educational Planning, (UNESCO, Paris, 1964)
Titma, M.Kh. and Pyarna, K.A. 'Controlling the
Choice of Occupation in Developed Socialist
Society', paper presented to the Eighth World
Congress of Sociology in Toronto (Moscow, 1974),
16 pp.

Tul'chinskii, L.I. 'Eshche raz ob ekonomike vysshego
    obrazovaniya', Vestnik vysshei shkoly, no. 5
    (1965), pp. 72-7
Tul'chinskii, L.I. 'Voprosy ekonomiki vysshego
    obrazovaniya (zametki ekonomista)', Vestnik
    vysshei shkoly, no. 4 (1964), pp. 27-32
Vybrik, I. 'O ratsionalizatsii shkol'noi seti',
    Narodnoe obrazovanie, no. 5 (1980), pp. 22-5
Weinberg, E. The Development of Sociology in the
    Soviet Union, (London and Boston, 1974)
Zhamin, V. 'Aktual'nye problemy ekonomiki narodnogo
    obrazovaniya', Sovetskaya pedagogika, no. 1
    (1965)
Zhamin, V. 'Ekonomika i obrazovanie', Voprosy
    ekonomiki, no. 2 (1967), pp. 48-56
Zhamin, V. Ekonomika obrazovaniya, (Moscow, 1969)
Zhamin, V. and Kostanyan, S.L. 'Education and Soviet
    Economic Growth', International Review of
    Education, UNESCO Institute for Education,
    no. 2, vol. XVIII, (1972), pp. 155-71
Zhamin, V. Sotsial'no-ekonomicheskie problemy
    obrazovaniya i nauki v razvitom sotsialisticheskom
    obshchestve, (Moscow, 1979)

Chapter 10

NATIONAL SCHOOLS IN THE YAKUTSKAYA ASSR: SOME
LANGUAGE ISSUES

Frances Cooley

Introduction
This paper attempts to view some of the developments
which have been taking place concerning national
schools in the Yakutskaya ASSR (Autonomous Soviet
Socialist Republic) during recent years and to
identify trends which may be of significance in the
next few years. Attention is given wholly to
schools for children of Yakut nationality. (Because
of certain difficulties in rendering their names in
English, representatives of the different nationalities mentioned in this paper will be referred to as
the Yakut, the Evenk, the Even, the Chukchi and the
Yukagir.) Though they are by no means the only
group of native people in the Republic the Yakut
constitute the largest one; the other peoples are
considerably fewer in number and for various other
reasons, which include their geographic distribution,
are in a rather different situation in the respects
to be discussed. National schools are schools
where instruction is offered on or through a native,
non-Russian language. Mainly because of this extra
commitment they follow a curriculum which differs
somewhat from that of the ordinary Soviet, or
Russian, school. National schools for Yakut
children in the Yakutskaya ASSR, which will sometimes be referred to as Yakut schools, constitute a
large section of the total number of schools in the
Republic. In 1966-67, 63.9 per cent of all schools
there either conducted education through the medium
of Yakut or offered classes where such courses could
be followed.[1] Figures for the year 1970-1 indicate
that 41.7 per cent of all school children were then
receiving instruction through Yakut[2] which is a
sizeable proportion considering that in 1970 only
43 per cent of the population of the Republic claimed
to be Yakut by nationality and 43.6 per cent (which

278

includes some members of other native peoples and some Russians) claimed Yakut as their native tongue.[3]
The issues which are touched upon are mainly concerned with language, the role of the Yakut language and Russian in the school, being perhaps the most crucial to the national school. However, the treatment of this subject is by no means comprehensive and there are other important aspects of the national school which are not discussed here. The questions examined are all ones which have been raised in works on education in the Republic by local (and native) education experts. Only aspects of the general education school and particularly the primary years (the first three classes of the incomplete, or eight-year, school or of the full secondary, or ten-year, school) are dealt with. These are areas of the education system which come under the Ministry of Education of the Yakutskaya ASSR. (Higher and secondary specialised education come under the control of the Ministry of Higher and Secondary Specialised Education of the RSFSR, Russian Soviet Federative Socialist Republic, in Moscow.)
First of all, however, to put the recent situation of the Yakut school into a fuller setting, an attempt will be made to describe briefly the more significant events in the history of the education of the native population of the Yakut Republic from its beginning to the present day.

Background

The Yakutskaya ASSR occupies a vast area in northeast Siberia, stretching about 2000 kilometres from the shores of the Arctic Ocean southwards to a point level with the top of Lake Baikal and about 2500 kilometres from the Kolyma River in the east to the uplands separating the Yenisey and Lena valleys in the west. Its capital, Yakutsk, is on approximately the same parallel as the northernmost Faeroe Islands. The climate is severe with very long cold winters and short summers which in central Yakutiya can be quite hot. The terrain is characterised by large mountain ranges and plateaux and a dense network of rivers. Taiga vegetation covers about 80 per cent of the territory with mainly larch, spruce and birch forests. Treeless or tundra vegetation characterises the north.
The Yakut form the largest group within the native population of the Republic. These are a people with a Turkic language. It is thought that they are descended from groups who migrated to this

area only a few hundred years ago from further south
and possibly from around Lake Baikal and who merged
with the peoples already inhabiting the valley of
the River Lena, the central artery running almost
due north to the Arctic Ocean. Elements in the
language speak of close contact also with Tungus and
Mongol peoples. The main livelihood of the Yakut
is traditionally horse and cattle breeding and, to
a lesser extent, fishing and hunting. Originally
concentrated in an area in central Yakutiya between
the Lena, Vilyuy and Aldan river valleys, they have
now also spread further north where they have come
into closer contact with the peoples indigenous to
those parts, often taking up their traditional
occupations. The latter (frequently referred to as
'northern peoples' or 'peoples of the Far North')
include the Evenk (or Tungus, as they were formerly
known), Even (Lamut), Chukchi (Luoravetlan) and
Yukagir (Odul). The distribution of these peoples
on the whole extends far beyond the boundaries of
the Yakutskaya ASSR and some have their own national
territories. Not all related in language, their
traditional occupations range from hunting and
reindeer husbandry inland to fishing and sea-mammal
hunting on the rivers and coasts. In 1926 northern
peoples comprised only 5 per cent of the population
of the Republic.[4] Now, even though their overall
numbers have increased, they form only just over
2 per cent and the numbers of at least one nationality among them have dropped.[5]
     Russians penetrated as far as Yakutiya at the
beginning of the seventeenth century. Yakutsk was
founded in 1632. The first people to come to the
area included Cossacks and traders. The Russian
advance so far north and east was primarily one made
in search of furs. The posts set up by the first
arrivals were then gradually reinforced by more
stable elements: peasants and clergy. Native
peoples, with the exception of the Chukchi, showed
little resistance to the Russians and to the fur
tribute which the latter extracted from them. Later,
Yakutiya became the destiny of many criminals and
political exiles sent from central Russia. Under
the Russians, the territory, covering a somewhat
larger area than it does now, passed from being an
almost independent entity to form part of larger
administrative units. Finally, in 1852 a governor
was appointed. The Yakutskaya ASSR was formed in
1922.
     By 1926 the total population of the Yakutskaya
ASSR was approximately 289,000, of which the Yakut

comprised 82.3 per cent, Russians 10.5 per cent and the northern peoples 5 per cent.[6]

Native Education before 1917

The foundations for developments during the Soviet period in terms of the use of the native language in schools in the Yakutskaya ASSR were to a considerable extent laid down before the Revolution and particularly during the nineteenth century. Schools were very slow to appear. However, Yakut children it seems had access to some of the few which were established in the course of the eighteenth century, though these were primarily the children of the more prominent Yakut families. In 1801 a school for native children, _inorodcheskaya shkola_, was eventually founded at the Spasskii Monastery in Yakutsk. This was followed by a number of other schools, _prikhodskie shkoly_, parish schools, (of which there were eventually several dozen) and a couple of seminaries or similar establishments initiated by the church.[7] A system of schools under the control of the Russian Ministry of Education developed from 1808; by the end of the century these numbered about 16.[8] Added to these were a number of schools or classes run by individuals, including some political exiles. Their pupils also often included Yakut children. Much attention has been given to the latter establishments in Soviet literature which emphasises their important influence on the growing class of educated natives. All the above, however, had formed only the bare skeleton of a school network, both approval and disapproval of the idea of drawing native peoples into schools being voiced at one time or another by officials. By 1917 there was a total of about 173 schools in the territory with approximately 5,400 pupils, of which Yakut pupils comprised at least three-fifths. This may have been only one-tenth the total number of children of school age.[9]

The Yakut language was officially approved for use in schools only in 1913. The Russian Minister of Education issued 'Rules concerning primary schools for non-Russian peoples' permitting one- and two-class schools to have the native language as a compulsory taught subject and instruction in other subjects through the native language during the first two years of school.[10] Until then, those Yakut children who were in schools received the same education as their Russian peers, which would basically have been in Russian reading and writing, arithmetic and religious instruction. However, it is said that a number of teachers, especially in rural districts, did know Yakut and would use it during lessons, though this did not necessarily lead to successful results, particularly when there was little or no application outside the school for what the children learnt.

There was similarly no concerted effort until the beginning of the twentieth century to select and make official one transcription for the Yakut language, or to publish material in it. The church again made the first moves in this direction, apart from notes recording the language made by travellers and other observers. A priest Georgii Popov in 1818-21 translated the Short Catechism into Yakut. The archpriest Dmitrii Khitrov, author of a Yakut grammar published in 1858, was at the head of a commission for translating religious works into Yakut. At the end of the century the Kazan' Missionary Society was responsible for a school primer in Yakut which was published in 1895 and reissued three more times after that. There were other works of this nature compiled by various individuals throughout the course of the century and there must have been others that are unknown or forgotten. All those mentioned so far are works in which the Cyrillic script was used as a basis for transcriptions of Yakut. The most successful and scholarly contribution in this sense is presented in the grammar produced by the German Sanskrit scholar Otto Böhtlingk and published in 1851. The transcription he devised, also based on the Cyrillic script, was to become the most accepted and was basically that used for a number of publications up to the time of the Revolution. The nineteenth century and the beginning of the twentieth also witnessed the appearance of a large number of works devoted to the Yakut people and their territory. These were written as a result of expeditions, by scholars, certain political exiles, teachers and others, Russians, Yakut and people of other nationalities.

It has frequently been remarked that the Yakut, on the whole, were keen to enter actively into the opportunities offered by Russian society and, for instance, to receive an education. Individual wealthy Yakut made themselves responsible for petitioning for schools to be set up or for providing the money or buildings to this end. A report on the schools of the Ministry of Education states, apropos the negative attitude of certain teachers imported to teach at the secondary school in Yakutsk, that 'the percentage of Yakut in this establishment is very small' but that 'the best pupils in it, as though on purpose, are Yakut'.[11] Several Yakut pupils went on to receive a teacher's training, for example, in Irkutsk. The first teacher of Yakut nationality, a certain Nazar Borisov, was appointed in 1826. Although this was not always the story - some parents were reluctant to let their children attend schools, even if there were one somewhere in the vicinity, and the schools did not always produce the same positive results - this eagerness must have contributed to the appearance, by the end of the nineteenth century, of the nucleus of a native intelligentsia and a strong sense of national identity. The first works of Yakut literature were produced at about this time. Cultural and educational societies were organised such as Syrdyk (Light) and the nationalistic and educational society Sakha Aymakh (The Yakut People). The latter society was instrumental in causing the first school primer to be published in 1917 in a newly devised script based upon the Roman alphabet. As well as being numerically dominant in their territory, the Yakut seem also to have been quite strong culturally, linguistically at least. The writer I.A. Goncharov, travelling through the Yakutskaya Oblast[12] in the 1850s, remarked on cases of Russians conversing between themselves in Yakut.[13] An important consequence of this and of all that has been described here is that in the first years of the Revolution when a new order was being created for the country there were already people among the native, Yakut, population enthusiastic to take up places in local organisations.

Native Education since 1917
Embracing the policies put forward by the Bol'shevik party on the right to organise education in the native language, local bodies took a number of measures including the decree of 12 August 1922 issued by the Sovnarkom (Soviet of the Peoples' Commissars) of the Yakutskaya ASSR 'On the introduction of the Yakut language in all schools of the Republic'. Most importantly, this declared that the first year in all schools with a composition predominantly of Yakut children should be taught in Yakut and that thereafter the language should be taught as a subject to all children with a speaking knowledge of it and to all students in certain specialised institutions.[14] Dates for the completion of the introduction of

teaching of all subjects through the native
language in the first four years of education were
set for 1929-30, and for the same within the scope of
the seven-year school to begin in 1933-34.[15] Figures
published in 1936 indicate that by that time there
were 418 schools (including 340 four-year and
78 seven-year schools) where instruction was given
in Yakut to 32,368 pupils, or more than 70 per cent
of the total number of pupils in the Republic. The
figures also show that national schools represented
the overwhelming majority of schools there at that
time.[16]

The whole of this period, though not without
its troubles and setbacks, was marked by great zeal
in questions of education, literature and language.
1917 had seen the promotion of a new transcription
for the Yakut language based upon the International
Phonetic Alphabet. This remained the accepted
transcription, after certain amendments and with
adjustments to bring it closer to those of other
Turkic peoples, until 1938 when a transcription based
on the Cyrillic script was made official. Plans to
'yakuticise' schools went beyond the mere use of
Yakut as the medium of instruction and as a taught
subject but included also basing the content of
lessons primarily on material drawn from the pupil's
own environment and culture. These intentions,
however, were hampered by problems such as the lack
of guidance to teachers, insufficient numbers of
native teachers, or teachers with a knowledge of
Yakut, deficiencies in teaching materials and textbooks, and so on. The process was also interrupted
by the 1941-45 war. This radically reduced the
numbers of teachers who had to be replaced partly by
relatively untrained cadres.

By the 1940s Yakut, as a subject, occupied quite
a substantial section of the curriculum, at least in
the primary classes, by comparison with that which
had been allotted to it in the early 1920s.[17] By
then the promotion of Russian, which had actually
been well represented in the curriculum of the Yakut
school initially, was also in progress. In 1938 it
had become a compulsory subject in the curriculum
throughout the country. In the late 1940s further
directions were given for the improvement of Russian
teaching and for increasing the number of hours
devoted to it.[18]

The Yakutskaya ASSR since the war presents a
very different set of circumstances from that which
revolutionary zeal encountered. Of not least
importance is the expansion of industry resulting

from exploitation of the local, mainly mineral, resources. From a Republic with a predominantly rural population (89.9 per cent of the population was dependent upon agriculture in 1926, and only 5.3 per cent was urban)[19] it has become one with a significant urban population comprising 61 per cent of the total population in 1979.[20] More detailed figures published in 1976 show that in 19 central regions of the Republic the urban population was 43.9 per cent of the total, whereas it comprised 60.5 per cent in the northern and more remote regions.[21] Another significant change accompanying this is the increase in the proportion of Russians to the native population. From being 7 per cent of the population as noted in 1911, the Russians have become the majority group and in 1980 comprised 50.4 per cent of the whole.[22] These changes have naturally brought certain consequences to the cultural face of the Republic and to the organisation and nature of schooling as one element of this.

THE NATIONAL SCHOOL IN THE LATE 1960s AND 1970s

Reforms: Russian and Yakut

Since the early 1960s attention has been directed, amongst other goals, towards achieving univeral complete secondary education. A call was also made for improvements in the content of education: in the curriculum and textbooks; in teaching and upbringing work. One concern was that pupils' education should keep abreast with the demands of contemporary scientific and technological progress. There was also concern over levels of achievement in schools and the desire to tackle the problem of pupils repeating classes. The latter question has been examined thoroughly also in the Yakutskaya ASSR.[23] One source gives figures for 1965-6 and 1971-2 which indicate that it is a problem felt more keenly by the autonomous republics of Siberia than others.[24]

One of the resulting reforms in the Soviet school was the reduction of the primary stage of education from four to three years. The implementation of this reform in the Yakutskaya ASSR, for instance, required special attention and experimentation, particularly where the national school was concerned.[25] This was mainly because, with the reading and writing of two languages to master during the primary stage, Yakut pupils had more to cope with than their Russian peers. Before the transition was effected, this was already quite a load.[26]

At the same time, changes were made in the teaching of Russian. Discussions in the early 1960s focused on the stage at which pupils learning in their native Yakut should begin to learn to read and write Russian. Until then this would have been introduced in class II with some lessons in class I being devoted to helping them to attain a command of spoken Russian. (The reading and writing of Yakut would be introduced over six or seven months of class I.) There was evidently a move to promote the teaching of Russian and to improve the standards which pupils were reaching in it by proposing an earlier start to the teaching of reading and writing skills in Russian. Some considered that pupils in class I would have difficulty in dealing simultaneously with learning to read and write in two languages.[27] After some experimental work, however, which proved that this could be done with some success, from 1964/5 pupils began to be taught to read and write Russian from class I.[28] At the same time, experiments began on national schools or classes where pupils would be taught through the medium of Russian from class I.

Similar experiments were started in the same year on native language teaching in the primary classes. As a result, it was found that children in class I could master reading and writing skills in Yakut in the four or five months of the first half of the school year, which left the second half for concentrating on Russian.[29] The information in Table 1 is taken from a timetable proposed for the primary classes, which appeared in a work published in 1972 and was approved by the Ministry of Education of the RSFSR.

There have been some indications of developments in the native language and Russian courses since the early 1970s. In recent years attention has been given to raising the level of both native and Russian language learning in schools as a measure towards improving methods of teaching.[30] However, in order to make an assessment of the courses and developments within them, a detailed study of textbooks and associated literature is required. Considerable effort and thought is put into the preparation of textbooks for both languages. Over the past decade they have apparently been revised regularly every other year. Programmes, textbooks and teachers' handbooks are written specifically for the Yakut school, with the exception of textbooks of Russian for classes IX and X which are standard

NATIONAL SCHOOLS IN THE YAKUTSKAYA ASSR

Table 1: Hours per Subject per Week in the Primary
Classes I-III of Yakut Schools, as published in 1972

Subjects	I	II	III
Yakut Language	10[a]	8	5
Russian Language	4	7	9
Mathematics	6	6	6
Physical Education	2	2	2
Drawing, Labour Singing, Nature Study	3	4	5
Total	25	27	27

Note: a. The number of hours given for lessons in
class I are for the first half of the year. If the
indications given in a school programme for Yakut
lessons in the primary classes, published a few years
later, applied at the beginning of the decade also,
the number of hours given to Yakut lessons would be
reduced in the second half of the school year. It is
assumed that this may be to allow an increase in the
number of hours given to Russian lessons at that
point. The basis for this assumption is the
example of some details of a timetable published in
1947 and indications given in a more recent
publication.

Sources: P.I. Shadrin, Osnovnye problemy nachal'nogo
obrazovaniya v yakutskoi ASSR, (Yakutsk, 1972), p. 29.

N.V. Egorov and I.I. Karataev (comps.), Nachal'nay
oskuola programmalara. Sakha tyla. I-III kylaastara,
(Yakutsk, 1976), p. 35.

D.V. Muksunov, "Obshchii obzor programm nerusskikh
nachal'nykh shkol na 1947-1948 uchebnyi god",
V pomoshch' uchitelyu, vyp 2 (1947).

V.M. Anisimov, "Za razvitie nauchno - pedagogicheskoi
mysli v respublike", in Anisimov, Borisov and Egorov,
Voprosy vospitaniya i obucheniya v shkolakh Yakutii,
(Yakutsk, 1973), pp. 7-8.

throughout the RSFSR.[31]

Pre-School Education

Preparatory classes for six-year old children had been introduced into national schools (by a decision of the Soviet of Ministers of the RSFSR) back in 1947 as a measure to bring the curriculum of national schools into line with that of Russian schools. For one reason or another, and partly because it caused children attending those schools to finish their education there one year later than their Russian contemporaries, the preparatory classes were dropped. In the Yakutskaya ASSR they had been abandoned by 1959 but since the late 1960s they have been revived again. It is felt that the preparatory class could ensure that all children would receive the same amount of preparation before starting in the primary classes, that it would ease the burden that especially children in national schools have to cope with, having two languages to learn, and thirdly it would contribute to the pupils acquiring a better grasp of Russian:

> The fundamental tasks of the present preparatory classes are connected with the social and economic transformations which are defining the demographic processes of today. A not unimportant role amongst these is played by the aspiration of people of different nationalities towards the best possible mastery of the Russian language, written and spoken.[32]

Though still in the stages of finding its optimum form, the preparatory class is described in the same work as one which will become an integral part of the national school. In it the curriculum would consist of the native language, Russian, mathematics, drawing, music, physical education and labour, that is the same subjects as taught in class I, though lessons would be shorter and interspersed with other activities to suit the capacity of children of such young age to learn and concentrate. The advantage the preparatory class has over pre-school establishments in this respect is that, universally implemented, it would involve all native children, whereas attendance at pre-school institutions, at present, is optional.[33]
There is constant concern, emanating largely from language problems, to bring the national school on to an equal footing with the Russian school. Even

after the introduction of new curriculum plans and
textbooks, some children in Yakut classes or schools
are apparently still not achieving the same levels of
success as Russian children in Russian schools or
classes, even when their attainments in their
respective native languages are compared. Reasons
given for the shortcomings of Yakut schools are that
some teachers have not been included in retraining
courses; that there is a low level of theoretical
qualification among teachers of Russian and
mathematics in Yakut schools; that the methodology
of teaching Russian and the native language in Yakut
schools has been poorly developed or inadequately
mastered; that control over the work of teachers
using new programmes is unsatisfactory.[34]
      At the same time, however, quite a number of
Yakut pupils are very successful and go on to
university and other forms of further education.
Figures for the academic year 1969-70 show that
during that year approximately 6,200 Yakuts were
attending higher education establishments in the
whole of the USSR, which is equivalent to 209 people
to every 10,000 of the entire Yakut population of
the country. By comparison, the number of students
of Buryat nationality in higher education during the
same year was 10,700 (or 340 to every 10,000 members
of that nationality). To every 10,000 people of
Komi nationality in the USSR in that year there were
127 Komi attending higher education establishments.
A comparison of the numbers of students from the
same backgrounds at secondary specialised educational
establishments gives a slightly different picture.
According to a publication of 1977 there were
18 secondary specialised educational establishments
in Yakutiya then, preparing students for professions
in teaching, medicine, agriculture, industry,
finance, water transport, trade and culture.[35] In
1969-70, 149 out of every 10,000 of the Yakut
population of the USSR were at such institutions
over the whole country; the equivalent proportion
within the Buryat population was 181 to every
10,000 and the proportion of the Komi population in
secondary specialised education in the same year was
189 to every 10,000.[36] Concern is expressed by one
writer about the need for specialists with secondary
education in fields such as energy, construction and
economics. He refers to another articles of 1974.
It indicates that: 'persons of the indigenous
population form a very small proportion of specialists with secondary education...of the 39.9 thousand
specialists with secondary education, 10,000 or

26.8 per cent are indigenous inhabitants of Yakutiya.[37]   It may be that 'indigenous inhabitants' here also includes Russians whose families have lived in the area for generations - often called Yakutyane.

Language of Instruction

The related questions of the point at which Russian might be introduced into the national school as the language of instruction, for which subjects, or whether it should be introduced at all in this capacity, are ones which have been the subject of much discussion.   During the late 1940s 'yakutisation', or korenizatsiya,[38] was implemented as the teaching of all subjects within the seven-year school, with the possible exception of Russian language and literature, through the medium of Yakut.   A directive of the Minister of Education of the RSFSR of 18 November 1948 'on the state of education in the Yakutskaya ASSR' ordered that 'the unswerving fulfilment of the tasks of the korenizatsiya of the school be ensured, establishing the instruction of pupils in the foundations of the sciences (osnovy nauk) through the native language as far as class VII inclusively.'[39] At the same time, though, in some seven-year and secondary schools, certain subjects were beginning to be taught in Russian in classes V-VII.[40]

At present, judging from textbooks available in the different subjects, the situation as regards language of instruction is as follows: in Yakut schools all teaching in the primary classes, apart from lessons of Russian language and literature which are taught throughout the school predominantly in Russian, is performed through the medium of Yakut; from class IV onwards all subjects are taught in Yakut until class VIII with the exception of the foreign language (introduced in class V), physics, chemistry and mathematics from class VI, and geography and history from class VIII, inclusively. (Mathematics, until class VI, and geography and history until class VIII, are taught through Yakut, whereas physics and chemistry are only taught through Russian.)   Yakut language is taught as a subject from class I to VIII and Yakut literature until class X inclusively.[41]

The role of Yakut, and consequently that of Russian, in schools in Yakutiya has often been the subject of comment and one on which not all are in agreement.   According to one scholar, towards the 1940s, there were three main opinions on the subject of the language of instruction: one group felt that eventually a transition should be made to instruction

through the medium of Russian and using the
programme for Russian schools; a second group
proposed that, with all other subjects continuing
to be taught in Yakut, mathematics, physics and
chemistry should be taught in Russian in class
V-VII; the third group was for extending
korenizatsiya to all secondary and higher education
as well.[42]
Differing points of view on the form national
schools should take have been voiced over the past
decade as well. One authority on education in the
Republic is cited as giving support to the idea of
transferring to Russian as the language of
instruction throughout the school, after a gradual
transition during the first one-and-a-half to two
years. He advocates this particularly for schools
in rural areas and the Far North.[43] He is also the
initiator of some research into the education of
Yakut children in rural schools through Russian,
which has been successful.[44] Another presents the
argument that children should be educated, primarily
at least, in the language in which they have been
brought up and learnt to think, whether this is
their native language or not. He illustrates this
with the example of some Evenk children, whose
difficulties at school, it was felt, were attributable
largely to their being taught in a language other than
their mother tongue.[45] Both parties refer to the
importance of the expressed wishes of Yakut parents
in these respects, which vary; some would like an
education in Russian for their children and others
would prefer their children to have an education
through the medium of Yakut. Since 1958, parents
have had the right to choose in which language they
would like their children to be taught, whether in
their mother tongue or Russian, in this case. An
optional form of national school has developed since
then - schools, or classes, where instruction is in
Russian from the beginning. In at least some such
schools, children can study Yakut as a subject.
Thus various alternatives are open.
The following lengthy quotation on the subject
of the language of instruction, with particularly
the primary stage in mind, is from a publication of
1972:

One should explain to those parents, who,
enjoying the right to determine the language
through which their children are taught,
attempt to put their child in a school where
instruction is given not through the native

291

language, under what conditions this is
acceptable. If, for instance, a Yakut child
on entering school has no command of the
Russian language he would undoubtedly find it
easier to begin to learn through his native
language until he has a fluent knowledge of
Russian. To enter a school, though, where
teaching is performed through Russian places
an insurmountably hard task before him - that
of mastering a second language and
simultaneously learning to think in it...
It is quite another matter when a Yakut child
on entering school has an already fluent
knowledge of Russian. It would even be better
for him to enter a school where the teaching is
in Russian. He could only win by doing this,
since sooner or later, at some stage of learning,
he will have to transfer to Russian as the
language of instruction.[46]

The period since the Second World War is
identified as one of growing bilingualism in Yakut
and Russian in the Yakutskaya ASSR (and of
bilingualism and multilingualism for the peoples of
the Far North) - a more rapid process among the urban
than among the rural population.[47] There is a
slowly increasing number of native Russian speakers
in the Republic, mostly Russian in nationality
(54.68 per cent of the total population according
to the figures for 1980 as compared with 51.85 per
cent in 1970) and a more rapidly increasing number
of native peoples with fluent Russian as a second
language (55.13 per cent of all Yakut in the
Republic in 1980 claimed to have such a knowledge[48]
of Russian as opposed to 40.84 per cent in 1970).
With the exception of certain courses, all further
education in the Republic is conducted through
Russian. For pupils wishing to study or work in
other parts of the Soviet Union, a good knowledge of
Russian would be an advantage. The importance of
Russian, also, in some areas of production and as a
channel of communication with other nationalities and
of access to other cultures is often referred to.[49]
One important task of the national school is seen
to be 'to contribute actively towards the pupils
mastering their native and the Russian languages,
towards the formation of harmonious bilingualism'...[50]
In practical terms this would lead to children being
equipped for situations where either language might
be required. The broader significance of
bilingualism within Soviet society is connected also

with the encouragement of mutual exchange between
cultures, the rapprochement of nationalities, in
which Russian plays a large role. A discussion of
these policies would throw more light on this
subject.

The Changing School Network

A large proportion of schools in the Republic has
been offering education in the native, Yakut,
language. In the 1966/67 school year these
comprised 63.9 per cent of the total of 626 schools.
Such schools are of two kinds. The first kind
comprises schools where all pupils are receiving
education through their native language. These,
for the reason that the Yakut-speaking population
lives predominantly in rural settlements, some of
them very small indeed, a mere handful of people,
were, and are likely still to be, small, primary or
eight-year schools.   289, or 46.2 per cent of all
schools were of this sort in that year. The second
kind of schools are those which have parallel classes
with some pupils learning through Yakut (in one set
of classes) and others learning through Russian (in
another set).   Such schools are predominantly in
the larger settlements and towns where the population
is mixed in nationality.   (In 1970 only 14.07 per
cent of the urban population of the Republic claimed
Yakut as their native language, as opposed to
85.93 per cent of the rural population.)[51]   Consequently, these tend to be larger schools.   In
1966/67 there were 111 mixed schools, constituting
17.7 per cent of all schools and 80 per cent of
these were ten-year schools with an average number of
366 pupils per school compared with 145 pupils per
school with Yakut as the medium of instruction.
The remaining types of schools are those teaching
purely through Russian to Russian-speaking pupils
(there were 223 of these in 1966/7, of which a
quarter were ten-year schools and just under one-half
were primary schools) and three schools where some
instruction in Even was given.
By 1970/1 the picture has changed slightly in
that the number of mixed schools (with two languages
of instruction) has increased to 133, or 22.5 per
cent of a decreasing total number of 590 schools.
The number of pupils attending the former has
increased by 31.3 per cent by comparison with 1966/7
figures and constituted just over one-third of the
total number of pupils in the Republic.   The number
of single-language schools has decreased by just over
one-tenth (though at the expense of which schools is

not stated), yet the number of pupils attending them
has increased slightly (see Table 2). A further
figure published in 1976 gives the proportion of
mixed schools as 18 per cent of the total, which
shows the previous increase in decline.[52]   It would
be interesting to know more details of the nature of
the changes indicated above, particularly with
respect to the language of instruction.
Changes have been taking place in the structure
of the school network in the Soviet Union in general.
The implementation of universal compulsory eight-
year education, and more recently of universal
secondary (ten-year) education, has caused an increase
in eight-year and ten-year schools and a reduction in
the numbers of primary schools.   Table 3 shows the
pattern which has evolved in the Yakutskaya ASSR.
Another reason for this development is the need to
reduce, for economic and pedagogical reasons, the
number of 'dwarf' schools suffering difficulties
through having a very small number of pupils.   The
number of teachers in a school is determined by the
number of pupils.   Thus the situation becomes very
difficult for the teacher when, in a very small
primary school, he or she has to take two or more
classes.   This becomes even more complicated in
such schools where children are learning in two or
more different languages.   One source states that
in 1968/9 there were apparently only 13 primary
schools out of a total of 238 in the Yakutskaya
ASSR where teachers were taking the equivalent of one
class at a time and through the medium of one
language.[53]   A similar situation existed in some
eight-year schools also.   The aim has been, wherever
possible, to close down such schools or to amalgamate
them or even merge them with larger schools.   This,
however, is not always practicable for reasons which
have been investigated at length by local education
experts and which are quite complicated.   One
scholar presents proposals in two works for the
reorganisation of the school networks of six
different regions in the Republic.[54]   Three of
these are in the north and three are central.   One
reason he gives for maintaining a school in a
sparsely populated area is the fact that the school
provides a cultural base for the community and that
to remove it might cause a settlement to disband
when, from the point of view of its role in the
economy, it might be more expedient to help preserve
it.   This has been suggested, for instance, in the
case of settlements established at production bases
of state farms specialising in cattle or horse

Table 2: Schools According to Language of
Instruction in 1936[a] and in the 1966/7 and 1970/1
School Years in the Yakutskaya ASSR

Language of Instruction	1936[a]	1966/7	1970/1
Yakut	418	289	454
Russian	No data	223	
Yakut/Russian	No data	111	133
Other	No data	3	3
Total	520	626	590

Note: a. The information given as for 1936 was
published in that year; the precise date it refers
to is not given.

Sources:

G. Okoemov, 'Rodnoi yazyk v yakutskoi shkole',
Sovetskaya Yakutiya, no. 1, (1936), p. 50.

P.I. Shadrin, 'Set' obshcheobrazovatel'nykh shkol
yakutskoi ASSR' Yakutskii gosudarstvennyi
universitet: Trudy istoriko-filologicheskogo
fakul'teta, vyp. 2, (1969), p. 310.

P.P. Borisov, 'O yazyke obucheniya i o prepodavanii
rodnykh yazykov v natsional'nykh shkolakh Yakutii'
in V.M. Anisimov, P.P. Borisov and P.I. Egorov (eds.),
Voprosy vospitaniya i obucheniya v shkolakh Yakutii,
(Yakutsk, 1973), p. 101.

Table 3:   Numbers of Schools of Different Levels
in the 1958/9, 1966/7 and 1973/4 School Years in
the Yakutskaya ASSR

Schools	1958/9	1966/7	1973/4
Primary	296	250	131
Incomplete (eight-year) Secondary	176 (est.)	238	248
Complete (ten-year) Secondary	90 (1959)	138	196
Total	562	626	575

Sources:

P.I. Shadrin, 'Set' obshcheobrazovatel'nykh shkol
yakutskoi ASSR', Yakutskii gosudarstvennyi
universitet: Trudy istoriko -filologicheskogo
fakul'teta, vyp. 2, (1969), pp. 304, 307, 308, 309.

P.I. Shadrin, Osnovnye problemy nachal'nogo
obrazovaniya v yakutskoi ASSR, (Yakutsk, 1972), p. 4.

N.D. Neustroev, 'Struktura sel'skoi vos'miletnei
shkoly;shkol'nyi mikrorayon' in V.F. Afanas'ev and
D.A. Danilov (eds.), Sotsial'no - pedagogicheskie
problemy narodnogo obrazovaniya (Yakutsk, 1977),
p. 74.

breeding in the central regions.[55]   Climatic
conditions might also justify maintaining a small
primary school.[56]   Culture and language are also
factors.   Concern is shown for the effect on the
children of indigenous nationalities who have to
leave a school in familiar surroundings to attend a
school in an urban or very different environment.
The author cites the example of children in the far
north-eastern Nizh nekolymskii rayon[57] who come to
finish their ten-year education in the regional
centre, Cherskii, from rural eight-year schools.   He
gives the fact that 'in Cherskii they confront a
completely different environment and a different way
of life' as the reason why only a few odd ones
actually finish the course.[58]   Concerning the
question of language, it is discovered that the school
in the centre of the neighbouring Srednekolymskii
rayon, Srednekolymsk, does not suffer the same
problems as that in Cherskii;   there are Yakut classes
in the former which there are not in the latter.[59]
    Another strong motive for reorganising the
school network is the simultaneous reorganisation of
the local economy and the settlements based upon it.
The case is given of the central Megino-Kangalasskii
rayon, one of the more densely populated areas.
Cattle and horse breeding and some horticulture are
the main occupations there.   The population, 23,000
strong, in 1973/4 was spread over 72 settlements
(excluding the centre, Maya) almost two-thirds of
which had less than 200 inhabitants each.   It is
predicted that by 1990 this population will be
concentrated in only 30 settlements, 22 of which
will be quite large (having up to 2,500 inhabitants)
and the remainder one tenth that size.   The number
of schools would be correspondingly reduced from
11 ten-year, 14 eight-year and 6 primary schools
(as of 1973/4) to 11 ten-year, 11 eight-year and
4 primary schools.[60]
    Horse and cattle breeding being mainly Yakut
preserves it is most likely that the inhabitants of
the smaller settlements particularly are predominantly, if not exclusively, Yakut in nationality.   It
is predicted that the existing (in 1973/4) structure
of the school network in terms of language of
instruction will remain more or less the same.   Thus
one secondary school will offer instruction purely
through Russian, two secondary and one eight-year
schools will have parallel Russian and Yakut classes
and the remaining 22 schools will offer instruction
through Yakut.   (This implies also, contrary to the
situation in 1966/7, that there may now be ten-year

297

Yakut schools.) The one difference, it is suggested, will be 'that national classes with Russian as the medium of instruction may appear in individual schools'.[61]

Conclusion
In the preceding pages it has been attempted to point to a few recent developments concerning questions of language in Yakut school and to assess contemporary trends in this respect as far as this is possible. A number of measures have been taken recently, and are being taken, to raise levels of achievement in schools. One important target is improvement of the standards of Russian and native language learning in the school. An examination of textbooks and other relevant materials would give a more comprehensive picture of such developments. The preparatory class, universally implemented, would avail pupils of the opportunity of more training in Russian, as well as in the native language, and in more standardised form than can other present pre-school establishments. Encouragement has been given for some parents to send their children to national schools with instruction through the medium of Russian. At present, apparently, these are not very many in number.[62]

In considering the role of the national school, one is also aware of there being considerable differences between the urban and rural Yakut populations and between the rural population of the central rural rayons and the northern, remoter areas of the Republic. (Compare the Megino-Kangalasskii rayon, already mentioned, where in 1973/4 there were 73 settlements to an area of 12,400 square kilometres[63] and the Olenekskii rayon where reindeer husbandry is the predominant occupation and where, in the late 1960s, there were only 5 schools serving an area of 344,200 square kilometres and just under 600 pupils.[64]) The differences that this suggests might exist between communities in different areas of the Republic are significant. In central rural regions it seems that there will be little difference to the structure of the school network in terms of language of instruction; the differences there could be, might include transferring children from smaller schools to larger ones and a reduction in the numbers of pupils having to board at school. In northern and remoter regions, which it has not been possible to look at within the scope of this paper, these changes could mean much more. There, nomadism still exists to a certain degree and there is far

more dependence, consequently, on boarding
facilities. The problem of providing education
through the native language is already exacerbated
by the sparseness of the rural population over the
territory (about O.03 persons per square kilometre
on average)[65] and the mixture of nationalities
within that. Thus schools are frequently multi-
national and the language of instruction - either
Russian or Yakut - depending on the lingua franca
of the particular community. In these parts also
a greater difference exists between the urban and
rural populations and settlements.

Other nationalities living in the Yakutskaya
ASSR are in a different situation from the Yakut in
the respects discussed. The sparseness of their
numbers and distribution, in comparison with the
dense Yakut populations in some central rayons, have
much to do with this. Articles written in the
early 1970s have discussed the problems of their
education. The Even, for one, have three schools
(possibly more by now) where instruction is offered
in their native language in the first two or three
classes, and it has been proposed that more be done
for them and the other nationalities.[66] Indeed in
most recent years a good deal of attention has been
devoted to them, and other northern peoples, in
various ways.

NOTES

1. P.I. Shadrin, 'Set' obshcheobrazovatel'nykh
shkol yakutskoi ASSR' in Yakutskii Gosudarstvennyi
Universitet, Trudy istoriko-filologicheskogo
fakul'teta, vyp. 2, (1969), p. 310.
2. P.P. Borisov, 'O yazyke obucheniya i o
prepodavanii rodnykh yazykov v natsional'nykh
shkolakh Yakutii' in V.M. Anisimov, P.P. Borisov and
P.I. Egorov (eds.), Voprosy vospitaniya i obucheniya
v shkolakh Yakutii (Yakutskoe knizhnoe izdatel'stvo,
Yakutsk, 1973), p. 102.
3. Itogi Vsesoyuznoi perepisi naseleniya
1970 goda (Statistika, Moscow, 1973), tom 4, p. 150.
4. V.N. Antipin and others (eds.), Istoriya
yakutskoi ASSR. Tom 3. Sovetskaya Yakutiya,
(Izdatel'stvo Akademii Nauk SSSR, Moscow, 1963),
p. 11.
5. Vestnik statistiki, no. 7, (1980), p. 50.
6. Antipin, Istoriya yakutskoi ASSR, p. 11.
7. V.F. Afanas'ev, Shkola i razvitie
pedagogicheskoi mysli v Yakutii, (Yakutskoe knizhnoe
izdatel'stvo, Yakutsk, 1966), pp. 107, 109.

8. P. Gadzyatskii and N. Prelovskii (comps.), Deyatel'nost' Ministerstva narodnogo prosveshcheniya v dalokom yakutskom krae, (Irkutsk, 1893), p. 10.

9. Afanas'ev, Shkola i razvitie pedagogicheskoi mysli, p. 161.

10. Ibid., p. 126.

11. Gadzyatskii and Prelovskii, Deyatel'nost' Ministerstva narodnogo prosveshcheniya, p. 26.

12. An administrative district both in pre-revolutionary Russia and in the USSR.

13. I.A. Goncharov, Polnoe sobranie sochinenii, 3-e izd., (9 tomov, Izdanie Glazunova, St. Petersburg, 1896), Tom 7, p. 455.

14. G.P. Basharin (ed.), Kul'turnaya revolyutsiya v Yakutii (1917-1937 gg.) Sbornik dokumentov i materialov, (Yakutskoe knizhnoe izdatel'stvo, Yakutsk, 1968), p. 101.

15. G. Okoemov, 'Rodnoi yazyk v yakutskoi shkole' in Sovetskaya Yakutiya, no. 1, (1936), pp. 53, 54.

16. Ibid., p. 50.

17. An article of 1947 proposed that in the 1947/8 school year the following hours be devoted to Yakut lessons in the first three classes of the primary school (excluding the preparatory class which would have 14 hours weekly, in the first half of the year, and 8 in the second): class I - 14 hours weekly (10 in the second half of the year); class II - 12 hours weekly; class III - 10 hours weekly. See D.V. Muksunov, 'Obshchii obzor programm nerusskikh nachal'nykh shkol na 1947-1948 uchebnyi god', V pomoshch' uchitelyu, vyp. 2, (1947), pp. 12-3. By comparison, the curriculum of 1922/3 proposed 8,2 and 2 hours weekly for lessons of Yakut in the first three classes of school respectively. See Afanas'ev, Shkola i razvitie pedagogicheskoi mysli, p. 183.

18. I.I. Vinokurov, 'Nachal'noe obuchenie ustnoi russkoi rechi v yakutskoi shkole'in V pomoshch' uchitelyu, vyp. 2, (1947), pp. 56-7.

19. F. Lorimer, The Population of the Soviet Union: History and Prospects, (League of Nations, Geneva, 1946), p. 69.

20. O predvaritel'nykh itogakh Vsesoyuznoi perepisi naseleniya 1979 goda (Statistika, Moscow, 1979), p. 8.

21. D.A. Danilov, Sotsial'no - pedagogicheskie osnovy organizatsii shkol'noi sistemy v avtonomnykh respublikakh Sibiri, (Yakutskoe knizhnoe izdatel'stvo, Yakutsk, 1976), p. 123.

22. Vestnik statistiki, no. 7, 1980, p. 50.

23. See, for instance, P.P. Borisov, 'Didakticheskie prichiny vtorogodnichestva i puti ikh ustraneniya' in Rabota po novym programmam v shkolakh Yakutii (Doklady nauchno-prakticheskoi konferentsii po problemam povysheniya effektivnosti uroka v usloviyakh perekhoda na novye programmy), (Yakutskoe knizhnoe izdatel'stvo, Yakutsk, 1974), pp. 20-30.

24. D.A. Danilov, 'Sotsial'no-pedagogicheskie aspekty osushchestvleniya vseobshchego obucheniya v natsional'nykh respublikakh Sibiri' in Afanas'ev and Danilov, Sotsial'no-pedagogicheskie problemy, p. 10.

25. P.I. Shadrin, Osnovnye problemy nachal'nogo obrazovaniya v yakutskoi ASSR (Yakutskoe knizhnoe izdatel'stvo, Yakutsk, 1972), p. 7.

26. Ibid., p. 21.

27. V.M. Anisimov, 'Za razvitie nauchno-pedagogicheskoi mysli v respublike' in Anisimov, Borisov and Egorov, Voprosy vospitaniya i obucheniya, p. 7.

28. Ibid., p. 7.

29. Ibid., pp. 4-6, 8.

30. G.P. Veselov, 'O sostoyanii i merakh po dal'neishemu uluchsheniyu obucheniya rodnym i russkomu yazykam v natsional'nykh shkolakh RSFSR v svete reshenii XXV s"ezda KPSS' in N.A. Baskakov (ed.) and others, Puti razvitiya natsional'no-russkogo dvuyazychiya v nerusskikh shkolakh RSFSR (Izdatel'stvo 'Nauka', Moscow, 1979), pp. 21-28.

31. Ibid., p. 27.

32. D.A. Danilov, Sotsial'no-pedagogicheskie osnovy, p. 201.

33. Ibid., pp. 207, 210-11.

34. P.S. Skryabin, 'Ob osnovnykh problemakh povysheniya effektivnosti uroka v usloviyakh perekhoda na novye programmy', in Rabota po novym programmam, pp. 6-7.

35. P.I. Shadrin, 'Nekotorye aspekty vseobshchego srednego obrazovaniya v yakutskoi ASSR' in Afanas'ev and Danilov, Sotsial'no-pedagogicheskie problemy, pp. 38-9.

36. Numbers per 10,000 population have been calculated from figures given in: Narodnoe khozyaistvo SSSR v 1969g. Statisticheskii ezhegodnik (Izdatel'stvo 'Statistika', Moscow, 1970), p. 690; Narodnoe khozyaistvo SSSR v 1970g. Statisticheskii ezhegodnik (Izdatel'stvo 'Statistika', Moscow, 1971), p. 16.

37. Shadrin, 'Nekotorye aspekty', p. 43.

38. The process of 'introducing the native language of children into the practical work of

instruction and upbringing in the national school'.
I.A. Kairov and others (eds.), Narodnoe obrazovanie
v SSSR (Izdatel'stvo Akademii pedagogicheskikh nauk,
Moscow, 1957), p. 261.
  39. V pomoshch' uchitelyu, vyp. 5-6 (1949),
p. 145.
  40. V pomoshch' uchitelyu, vyp. 4 (1948), p. 11.
  41. This information is deduced from the
availability of the following textbooks in Yakut:
Bukvar' (Primer); Sakha tyla (Yakut Language), for
classes I-VIII; Törööbüt sangabyt (Our Native
Speech), for classes I-III; Törööbüt literaturabyt
(Our Native Literature), classes IV-VI; Sakha
literaturata (Yakut Literature), classes VII-X;
Ayylgha üöreghe (Nature Study) for classes II-IV;
Botanika (Botany), classes V-VI; Zoologiya (Zoology)
for classes VI-VII; history textbooks for classes
IV-VII; geography textbooks for classes V-VII;
mathematics textbooks for classes IV-V. All the
textbooks listed here, except those on Yakut language
and literature, are translated from the equivalent
Russian textbooks.
  42. Afanas'ev, Shkola i razvitie pedagogicheskoi
mysli, pp. 258-9.
  43. Borisov, 'O yazyke obucheniya', pp. 92-3.
  44. Anisimov, 'Za razvitie nauchno-pedagogicheskoi mysli', p. 11.
  45. Borisov, 'O yazyke obucheniya', p. 97.
  46. Shadrin, Osnovnye problemy nachal'nogo
obrazovaniya, pp. 47-8.
  47. P.G. Samsonov, 'Bilingvizm i etapy ego
razvitiya v yakutskoi ASSR' in Baskakov and others,
Puti razvitiya natsional'no-russkogo dvuyazychiya,
pp. 128-131.
  48. Itogi Vsesoyuznoi perepisi naseleniya
1970 goda, Tom 4, p. 150. Vestnik statistiki, no. 7
(1980), p. 50.
  49. Danilov, Sotsial'no-pedagogicheskie
osnovy, p. 100.
  50. R.K. Chernikov, 'Osnovnye problemy
formirovaniya i razvitiya dvuyazychiya u uchashchikhsya
natsional'noi shkoly' in Baskakov and others, Puti
razvitiya natsional'no-russkogo dvuyazychiya, p. 29.
  51. Itogi Vsesoyuznoi perepisi naseleniya 1970
goda, Tom 4, pp. 150-1.
  52. Danilov, Sotsial'no pedagogicheskie
osnovy, p. 181.
  53. Shadrin, Osnovnye problemy nachal'nogo
obrazovaniya, p. 9.
  54. D.A. Danilov, Organizatsionno-pedagogicheskie problemy obshcheobrazovatel'noi shkoly na

krainem severe. (Yakutskoe knizhnoe izdatel'stvo, Yakutsk, 1969).
55. Danilov, Sotsial'no-pedagogicheskie osnovy, pp. 137-8.
56. Ibid., p. 137.
57. An administrative area within a larger unit such as an autonomous republic or an oblast'.
58 Danilov, Organizatsionno-pedagogicheskie problemy, p. 37.
59. Danilov, Sotsial'no-pedagogicheskie osnovy, p. 117.
60. Ibid., pp. 134-5, 147.
61. Ibid., p. 146.
62. Ibid., p. 181.
63. Ibid., p. 134.
64. Shadrin, 'Set' obshcheobrazovatel'nykh shkol', p. 310. F. Donskoi, 'Na smenu Chumam i Yarangam', Polyarnaya zvezda, no. 5 (1974), p. 107. Chums and Yarangas are both tent-like dwellings used by nomadic peoples in north-east Siberia.
65. Donskoi, 'Na smenu Chumam i Yarangam', p. 107.
66. V.M. Anisimov and V.S. Keimetinov, 'Nekotorye voprosy izucheniya rodnogo yazyka v evenskoi shkole' in Anisimov, Borisov and Egorov, Voprosy vospitaniya i obucheniya, pp. 156-161.

BIBLIOGRAPHY

Afanas'ev, V.F. Shkola i razvitie pedagogicheskoi mysli v Yakutii, (Yakutskoe knizhnoe izdatel'stvo, Yakutsk, 1966)
Afanas'ev, V.F. and Danilov, D.A.(eds.) Sotsial'no-pedagogicheskie problemy narodnogo obrazovaniya (Yakutsk, 1977)
Afanas'ev, V.F. 'Yazyk druzhby i bratstva', Polyarnaya zvezda, no. 6, (1975)
Anisimov, V.M. and Keimetinov, V.S. 'Nekotorye voprosy izucheniya rodnogo yazyka v evenskoi shkole', Anisimov, Borisov and Egorov Voprosy vospitaniya i obucheniya v shkolakh Yakutii (Yakutskoe knizhnoe izdatel'stvo, Yakutsk, 1973)
Anisimov, V.M. 'Za razvitie nauchno-pedagogicheskoi mysli v respublike', Anisimov, Borisov and Egorov Voprosy vospitaniya i obucheniya v shkolakh Yakutii
Antipin, V.N. and others (eds.), Istoriya yakutskoi ASSR. Tom 3. Sovetskaya Yakutiya (Izdatel'stvo Akademii Nauk SSSR, Moscow, 1963)
Basharin, G.P. (ed.) Kul'turnaya revolyutsiya v Yakutii (1917-1937 gg.). Sbornik dokumentov i

materialov (Yakutskoe knizhnoe izdatel'stvo, Yakutsk, 1968)

Baskakov, N.A. and others (ed.) Puti razvitiya natsional'no-russkogo dvuyazychiya v nerusskikh shkolakh RSFSR (Nauka, Moscow, 1979)

Borisov, P.P. 'O yazyke obucheniya i o prepodavanii rodnykh yazykov v natsional'nykh shkolakh Yakutii', Anisimov, Borisov, Egorov (eds.) Voprosy vospitaniya i obucheniya v shkolakh Yakutii (Yakutskoe knizhnoe izdatel'stvo, Yakutsk, 1973)

Boyko, V.I. (ed.) and others, Sotsial'naya struktura naseleniya Sibiri (Nauka, Sibirskoe otdelenie, Novosibirsk, 1970)

Danilov, D.A. Organizatsionno-pedagogicheskie problemy obshcheobrazovatel'noi shkoly na krainem severe (Yakutskoe knizhnoe izdatel'stvo, Yakutsk, 1969)

Danilov, D.A. Sotsial'no-pedagogicheskie osnovy organizatsii shkol'noi sistemy v avtonomnykh respublikakh Sibiri (Yakutskoe knizhnoe izdatel'stvo, Yakutsk, 1976)

Donskoi, F. 'Na smenu Chumam i Yarangam', Polyarnaya zvezda, no. 5 (1974) pp. 107-10

Egorov, N.V. and Karataev (comps.) Nachal'nai oskuola programmalara. Sakha tyla. I-III Kylaastara (Yakutsk, 1976)

Gadzyatskii, P. and Prelovskii, N. Deyatel'nost' Ministerstva narodnogo prosveshcheniya v dalokom yakutskom krae (Irkutsk, 1893)

Goncharov, I.A. Polnoe sobranie sochinenii, 3-e izd., (9 tomov, Izdanie Glazunova, St. Petersburg, 1896), Tom 7

Gurvich, I.S. and Dolgikh, B.O. (eds.) Preobrazovaniya v khozyaistve i kul'ture i etnicheskie protsessy u narodov severa (Nauka, Moscow, 1970)

Itogi Vsesoyuznoi perepisi naseleniya 1970 goda (Statistika, Moscow, 1973), Tom 4

Lorimer, F. The Population of the Soviet Union: History and Prospects (League of Nations, Geneva, 1946)

Muksunov, D.V. 'Obshchii obzor programm nerusskikh nachal'nykh shkol na 1947-1948 uchebnyi god', V pomoshch' uchitelyu, vyp. 2 (1947) pp. 3-14

Narodnoe khozyaistvo SSSR v 1969 g. Statisticheskii ezhegodnik (Statistika, Moscow, 1970)

Narodnoe khozyaistvo SSSR v 1970 g. Statisticheskii ezhegodnik (Statistika, Moscow, 1971)

Okoemov, G. 'Rodnoi yazyk v yakutskoi shkole', Sovetskaya Yakutiya, no. 1 (1936) pp 49-67

O predvaritel'nykh itogakh Vsesoyuznoi perepisi
    naseleniya 1979 goda (Statistika, Moscow, 1979)
Prokof'ev, M.A. 'Ruskii yazyk v natsional'noi shkole
    i doshkol'nykh uchrezhdeniyakh', Ruskii yazyk v
    natsional'noi shkole, no. 6 (1975)
Samsonov, P.G. 'Bilingvizm i etapy ego razvitiya v
    yakutskoi ASSR', Baskakov and others Puti
    razvitiya natsional'no-russkogo dvuyazychiya
Shadrin, P.I. Osnovnye problemy nachal'nogo
    obrazovaniya v yakutskoi ASSR (Yakutskoe knizhnoe
    izdatel'stvo, Yakutsk, 1972)
Shadrin, P.I. 'Set' obshcheobrazovatel'nykh shkol
    yakutskoi ASSR', Yakutskii Gosudarstvennyi
    Universitet, Trudy istoriko-filologicheskogo
    fakulteta, vyp. 2 (1969) pp. 302-15
Skryabin, P.S. 'Ob osnovnykh problemakh povysheniya
    effektivnosti uroka v usloviyakh perekhoda na
    novye programmy', Rabota po novym programmam v
    shkolakh Yakutii (Doklady nauchno-prakticheskoi
    konferentsii po problemam povysheniya
    effektivnosti uroka v usloviyakh perekhoda na
    novye programmy) (Yakutskoe knizhnoe
    izdatel'stvo, Yakutsk, 1974)
Superanskaya, A.V. (ed.) Spravochnik lichnykh imon
    narodov RSFSR (Russkii yazyk, Moscow, 1979)
Vestnik statistiki, no. 7 (1980)
Vinokurov, I.I. 'Nachal'noe obuchenie ustnoi russkoi
    rechi v yakutskoi shkole', V pomoshch' uchitelyu,
    vyp. 2 (1947)

INDEX

INDEX

INDEX

NOTES ON CONTRIBUTORS

GEORGE AVIS is Lecturer in Russian Studies at the
University of Bradford and was for several years
editor of the Journal of Russian Studies. His
articles on the Sociology of Soviet Higher
Education appeared in Bildungsforschung und
Bildungspolitik in Osteuropa und der DDR (edited by
O. Anweiler and published by Schroedel in 1975) and
in Education and the Mass Media in the Soviet Union
and Eastern Europe (edited by B. Harasymiw and
published by Praeger in 1976).

FRANCES COOLEY is a research student at the Scott
Polar Research Institute, University of Cambridge.
She is working on a thesis on aspects of education
in the Yakutskaya ASSR. In 1980, in conjunction
with this research, she spent four months in the
USSR, in Leningrad and Yakutsk.

JOHN DUNSTAN is Deputy Director and Lecturer in
Soviet Education at the Centre for Russian and East
European Studies, University of Birmingham. He is
an attached member of the Faculty of Education.
His Ph.D. was on problems of provision for high-
ability children in the USSR. He has published a
book, Paths to Excellence and the Soviet School
(NFER, Windsor, 1978) and several articles on
Soviet education.

NIGEL GRANT is Professor of Education at the Univer-
sity of Glasgow. His writings include Soviet
Education, Society, Schools and Progress in Eastern
Europe, The Crisis of Scottish Education and (with
R. E. Bell) A Mythology of British Education and

NOTES ON CONTRIBUTORS

<u>Patterns of Education in the British Isles</u>. Current teaching and research include studies of minority and multicultural education in Scotland and abroad.

ELISABETH KOUTAISSOFF was Lecturer (later Senior Lecturer) at the Centre for Russian and East European Studies, University of Birmingham, for over twenty years. In 1968 she became the first Professor of Russian at Victoria University, Wellington, New Zealand. She has published a book, <u>The Soviet Union</u> (Benn, London, 1971) and many articles about Soviet education and Russian literature. She is now retired and lives in Oxford.

MERVYN MATTHEWS is Reader in Russian Studies at the University of Surrey, Guildford. Most of his research has been devoted to problems of Soviet social structure. His most recent book, <u>Education in the Soviet Union, Policies and Institutions since Stalin</u> (Allen and Unwin, 1982) is concerned with educational developments up to the late 'seventies.

JOHN MORISON is Lecturer in Russian History at the University of Leeds. His publications include two articles on education and revolution in late Imperial Russia. He is at present working on a book on that theme with specific reference to the 1905 Revolution. He is also completing a shorter study on educational reforms in contemporary Czechoslovakia. He is immediate past chairman of the British National Association for Soviet and East European Studies, chairman of the Russian Language Undergraduate Study Committee and a vice-president of the International Committee for Soviet and East European Studies.

FELICITY O'DELL is a former research student at the Centre for Russian and East European Studies, University of Birmingham, now teaching English as a foreign language in Cambridge and a course on Soviet education at Cambridge University. An adapted version of her Ph.D. thesis was published as <u>Socialisation through the Children's Literature: The Soviet Example</u> (CUP, Cambridge, 1978). She has also published (with David Lane) <u>The Soviet Industrial Worker: Social Class, Education and Control</u> (Martin Robertson, London, 1978), and several articles on Soviet education.

327325

NOTES ON CONTRIBUTORS

JAMES RIORDAN is Senior Lecturer in Russian Studies
at Bradford University. He finished his Ph.D. in
1975 and an adapted version of it was published as
Sport in Soviet Society (CUP, Cambridge, 1977). He
also edited Sport under Communism (Hurst, London,
1978) and his book Soviet Sport: Background to the
Olympics was published by Blackwell in 1980. He
has also published many articles on Soviet sport and
leisure, and written several children's books. He
worked in the USSR for five years as a translator
and played for Moscow Spartak.

JANUSZ TOMIAK is Senior Hayter Lecturer in Russian
and Soviet Education and in Comparative Education at
the University of London Institute of Education and
School of Slavonic and East European Studies. He
is the author of The Soviet Union (World Education
Series), published by David and Charles, Newton
Abbot, in 1972 and of several chapters in books on
education in Eastern Europe, published in English
and German, as well as numerous articles and book
reviews in educational journals and periodicals.